Invisible Giants

The Van Sweringens' triumph in Cleveland. For almost forty years, the 52-story Terminal Tower was the tallest building outside New York City. From here, the brothers administered their huge railroad, real estate, and transit enterprises. At the right is the Vans' 1918 Hotel Cleveland, the earliest element in the Terminal complex; at the left is their Higbee Company department store. Frank A. Wrabel collection

Invisible Giants

The Empires of Cleveland's Van Sweringen Brothers

Herbert H. Harwood, Jr.

Bloomington and Indianapolis

This book is a publication of

Indiana University Press
601 North Morton Street
Bloomington, Indiana 47404-3797 USA

http://iupress.indiana.edu/

Telephone orders 800-842-6796
Fax orders 812-855-7931
Orders by e-mail iuporder@indiana.edu

© 2003 by Herbert H. Harwood, Jr.
All rights reserved

No part of this book may be reproduced or utilized in any form or by any means, electronic or mechanical, including photocopying and recording, or by any information storage and retrieval system, without permission in writing from the publisher. The Association of American University Presses' Resolution on Permissions constitutes the only exception to this prohibition.

The paper used in this publication meets the minimum requirements of American National Standard for Information Sciences—Permanence of Paper for Printed Library Materials, ANSI Z39.48-1984.

Manufactured in the
United States of America

Library of Congress Cataloging-in-Publication Data

Harwood, Herbert H.
　Invisible giants : the empires of Cleveland's Van Sweringen brothers / Herbert H. Harwood, Jr.
　　p. cm.
Includes bibliographical references and index.
　1. Van Sweringen, Oris Paxton, 1879–1936. 2. Van Sweringen, Mantis James, 1881–1935. 3. Businessmen—Ohio—Biography. 4. Real estate development—Ohio—Cleveland—History. 5. Railroads—Ohio—History. 6. Cleveland (Ohio)—History. I. Title.
　HC102.5.V36 H37 2003
　385'.092'2771—dc21
　　　　　　　　2002004355

1 2 3 4 5 08 07 06 05 04 03

CONTENTS

Introduction vii

1 • Oasis in a Gritty City 1
2 • The Ideal Suburb 11
3 • Mr. Smith Sells a Farm 27
4 • Mr. Smith Sells a Railroad 36
5 • Shaping Solid Forms 48
6 • A Difficult Birth at the Public Square 58
7 • The Beginnings of an Empire 71
8 • To the South, East, and North 85
9 • Taking Stock: 1924 100
10 • Some Shadows Fleet By 114
11 • Building, Rebuilding, and Juggling 125
12 • Consolidation Anarchy I: The Maverick and the General 141
13 • Consolidation Anarchy II: The Street Fighter 151
14 • The Summit I: An Appalachian Peak in the Rockies 161
15 • The Summit II: Filling Out the Railroad Map 174

16 • The Summit III: Consummation in Cleveland—and a Jolt	188
17 • Completions and Complications	200
18 • Taking Stock: 1930	217
19 • Sudden Darkness	234
20 • The Rails Roll Downgrade	246
21 • A New World	255
22 • The Cruelest Year	269
23 • The Last Train	281
24 • Epilogue I: New Empires from Old	292
25 • Epilogue II: The Ghosts	305
Notes	313
Sources and Acknowledgments	333
Index	337

Introduction

It was the most important single event in the city's history. Actually, it was only a dedication ceremony for a railroad passenger terminal, the sort of celebration cities constantly stage to baptize some new edifice or other civic achievement. But symbolically it commemorated much more.

On June 28, 1930, Cleveland, Ohio, dedicated the new Cleveland Union Terminal. What the event really celebrated, though, was Cleveland's visible transformation from a nondescript midwestern industrial city to a showcase of visionary urban and suburban planning and its ascension to national economic power through its control of the country's largest transportation system. All of that had happened almost at once, and all of it was done at the hands of two extraordinary men—the brothers Van Sweringen.

All the usual civic dignitaries were there, of course, along with railroad presidents and executives of Cleveland's steel and manufacturing industries—2,500 of them in all. Not present were the Van Sweringen brothers. They were home listening to the affair on the radio. Nobody who knew them was at all surprised; it was simply their way. It was said that they were afraid they would be called upon for speeches, and there was probably truth in that. The fact was, though, that they almost never appeared before large groups for any reason and, besides, wanted no part of personal glorification.

They were enigmas in their own time and are more so now—two shy, tightly bonded, almost reclusive bachelor brothers who seemingly came out of nowhere and suddenly were counted among the country's economic rulers. In 1930, they controlled 30,000 miles of railroads reaching from the Atlantic to the Rockies and from Ontario to the Gulf of Mexico, plus trucking companies, shipping companies, and warehouses—and they had planned and built two nationally admired models of innovative urban and suburban development. What was being dedicated on this day aptly demonstrated that last variation of the Van Sweringen vision.

The new Cleveland Union Terminal was no ordinary big-city railroad station. Commodious inside, it was virtually invisible outside, and there lay the essence of the vision. Here in Cleveland's historic heart was an entire new city designed as a single integrated, interconnected unit. From below the station concourse, trains took Clevelanders to most places in the East and Midwest and, through connections, to virtually any place in the United States, Canada, and Mexico. And very soon, it was anticipated, city dwellers would also board rapid transit trains here for anywhere nearby. (Immediately outside were local streetcars reaching all parts of the city. Soon these, too, would be placed underground as part of the complex.) Already, one rapid transit line delivered them directly to what already had become one of the country's best-known and most exquisitely planned upper-class suburbs, Shaker Heights —also a Van Sweringen creation. Perhaps it is superfluous to say that the brothers had built the rapid transit line exclusively to serve Shaker Heights.

Above the terminal was the tallest office building outside New York City, which housed—among many other things— the headquarters of the vast Van Sweringen transportation and real estate empires. Also over the top of the terminal were three other office buildings, a large hotel, and the city's premier department store—along with restaurants, banks, smaller stores, and indoor automobile parking—all of them interconnected and flowing into one another. The complex also included generous provision for more office buildings, the city's central post office, a theater, and more large retail businesses.

In short, the Union Terminal development pulled together intercity and urban transportation and all forms of city commerce into one huge structural unit. It was a radical and unique conception which in one stroke reestablished the city's center and made it the new focus of the city's life. Indeed, it was unlike anything elsewhere at the time and was destined to be so in the future; although imitated in part, nothing else went so far in uniting all forms of urban life and transportation on this scale. Now, with travelers taking to the air and roads, it could never again be exactly duplicated.

Sadly, the Union Terminal ceremony was symbolic in another way: It was the turning point in the Van Sweringen story. Remember the year: 1930. To put the best light on it, the times were uncertain, although most people, including the brothers, thought that the worst was pretty much over and that the expansion could quickly resume. Instead, the story ended in a shambles, with still grander visions unfulfilled.

In its essentials, it was a somewhat typical story of the time: Oris Paxton Van Sweringen and Mantis James Van Sweringen were born in rural Ohio in the late nineteenth century to a footloose father who was more adept at producing children than income. Eventually the family drifted to Cleveland, where the two boys went to work after the eighth grade to help support the family and subsequently stumbled through a succession of jobs and business ventures that went nowhere. Then something took hold. Shortly after the turn of the century they became suburban real estate promoters—obscure, but with interesting ideas and methods. On the eve of World War I, they added railroading to their ventures, taking in a cast-off regional line and breathing new life into it. Fourteen breathtaking years later they not only controlled the country's largest single rail network but were poised to put together the first truly coast-to-coast line. And at the same time, of course, they had remade Cleveland's physical face in their image and to their lofty standards.

If their rise was fast, the fall was faster. The Great Depression tore apart the underpinnings of their empire—or rather empires, since there were several. Still, they remained amazingly adept and creative and somehow managed to hold everything together—until the struggle literally killed them. They died prematurely and, as in life, close together; afterward they quickly vanished from consciousness. But they had built well, and afterward the corporate power structure they created lived on in other hands, while many of their railroads and physical works survived and prospered as strong entities on their own.

So much for the simple outline. Inside it is a bewilderingly complex maze of separate stories running in parallel: the planning and building of Shaker Heights and its rapid transit line, the vision of the Union Terminal complex and the battles to build it, the acquisition of one railroad system after another, the management and rebuilding of the railroads, the legal and regulatory problems in putting them together, the churning power politics in the railroad industry and their often colorful manipulators, the financial sleight-of-hand which was unequalled in convolution and outright daring.

And underrunning all that is the riddle of who these two people actually were. Ohio historian Harlan Hatcher summed up the judgment of many: "[They were] certainly as strange a pair as ever made a contribution to the development of the [region] in all its history." But lest that sound mysteriously alluring, one journalist remarked that he could not write anything interesting about them because "the brothers were such dull people."[1]

It was true. On the surface there seemed to be nothing there. They had no outside interests. They took almost no vacations and traveled hardly anywhere, except on business. Their tastes were refined but conservative and entirely conventional. As bachelors, they had no family lives and no love affairs—at least none that were publicly known. They were shy to the point of reclusiveness and obsessively private. They shunned all public speaking and seldom even appeared at public gatherings. They had no known vices, interesting or otherwise. They were universally judged to be quiet, polite, almost pathologically modest and self-effacing—and by implication, prim, bland, and faceless.

Yet there is the essential enigma. What they accomplished —and how they did it—was anything but bland and ordinary. They conceived imaginative, radical, grandiose schemes. They were adept at articulating their visions and effectively persuading others to share them and underwrite them. And in effecting them they moved surely, swiftly, and aggressively—using the riskiest and most treacherous of financial methods to do the job. What they created could never have been conceived by conservative minds or achieved by retiring personalities.

There were other anomalies. The Van Sweringens' peers in the railroad business mostly viewed them as speculators "in it for the money," as Pennsylvania Railroad president W. W. Atterbury bluntly put it. And admittedly they made lots of money for themselves—for a time, at least—by manipulating holding companies and securities to their benefit. Yet they were nothing if not long-term builders. In their real estate ventures they held and developed properties over what was considered absurdly long periods. It took over twenty years just to physically complete the Public Square–Union Terminal project and it was years more before it became commercially productive—and what was completed was only part of an even larger plan. Their suburban developments in Shaker Heights and beyond were planned to mature over a period of about twenty-five years. For all of these projects, there was absolutely no compromise with the highest standards. It was much the same with their railroads. The Van Sweringens bought undervalued properties, put all the money into them that could be afforded and built them up slowly; many were made into models of operational efficiency and service quality. That was hardly the method of most railroad speculators, who typically preferred to produce short-term profits by cutting maintenance and selling properties.

And those physical creations pointed up other parts of the puzzle. The architectural styles of the downtown buildings and the suburban homes were intentionally unadventurous, backward-looking, and derivative. Yet those same buildings gave form to uniquely innovative urban and suburban planning concepts. Personally, the brothers were as staid and gray as any human can be, but they constantly reached out to embrace the most advanced transportation technology. The Van Sweringen railroads sponsored and helped develop the ultimate expressions of steam-locomotive design in America. Ahead of most of their peers, they also recognized the potential of motor transportation in all its forms. They brought trucking operations into their corporate fold, they built one of the earliest automobile-oriented shopping centers, and they planned a system of limited-access urban superhighways (which they integrated with rapid transit lines) that were at least two decades ahead of their time. Dreamed of but unrealized were freight-container systems integrating rail and truck transportation—again, ideas that were far ahead of reality.

Admittedly, the means to these ends were sometimes less than lofty. There were justified accusations of lapses in corporate ethics and shadowy legal subterfuges that were questionable even by the more freewheeling business standards of the 1920s. And of course there were virulent outcries of betrayal as investors lost fortunes and banks closed when their Van Sweringen holdings collapsed. But just as the Van Sweringens never compromised on their physical standards, they also never compromised their personal integrity. Where some of their fellow failed empire-builders and financial manipulators fled the country, shielded their assets, or otherwise slithered out of their obligations, the Van Sweringens took full personal responsibility; they not only stayed put to ride their ship down but pledged all they owned on it.

Little wonder that they confounded their contemporaries and later historians. This work will not resolve all these enigmas and anomalies. None can without large doses of pure speculation and posthumous psychoanalysis. But while nobody can now probe the collective Van Sweringen psyche, at least it is possible to tell the story of an adventure like few others.

It is also an opportunity to pay homage to what these singular men accomplished. Their Union Terminal complex remade downtown Cleveland and changed its course of development; its centerpiece—the soaring Terminal Tower Building—instantly became the city's symbol and has remained so ever since. Similarly, their planning of over ninety years ago has kept the Shaker Heights suburb strong, stable, and little changed. It has been imitated but never quite duplicated—partly because of its unusually foresighted rapid transit link to the remade city center.

In 1967, Cleveland writer George Condon paid them this tribute: "Of all the men and women to walk the Cleveland scene over the past 170 years, O. P. and M. J. Van Sweringen did more to alter the face of the city than any other private citizens, individually or in combination. They left a deep imprint that shows no sign of eroding. They were the builders of modern Cleveland." Now, thirty-five years after Condon wrote that epitaph, there are still few signs of erosion, despite enormous changes in the urban and suburban landscape.[2]

In the wider world, most of the Van Sweringens' railroads vindicated both their management and their judgment by becoming some of the best performers in the business. Almost all are now key parts of larger systems. The brothers may have been silent and indistinct in life, and are much more so today, but their creations still speak and are solidly present.

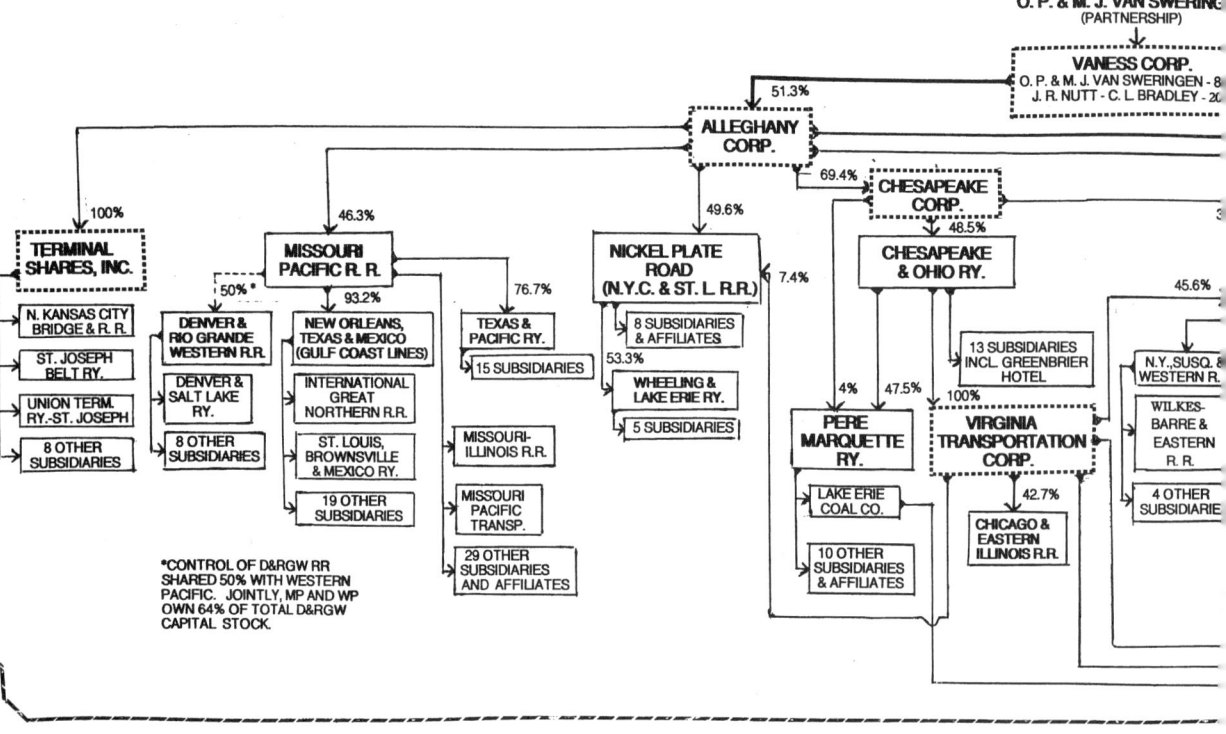

THE VAN SWERINGEN E[MPIRE]

RAILROADS

INCLUDING RAILROAD-OWNED SUBSIDIARY RAILROAD, TERMINAL, LAND, TRUCKING, AND MISCELLANEOUS COMPANIES

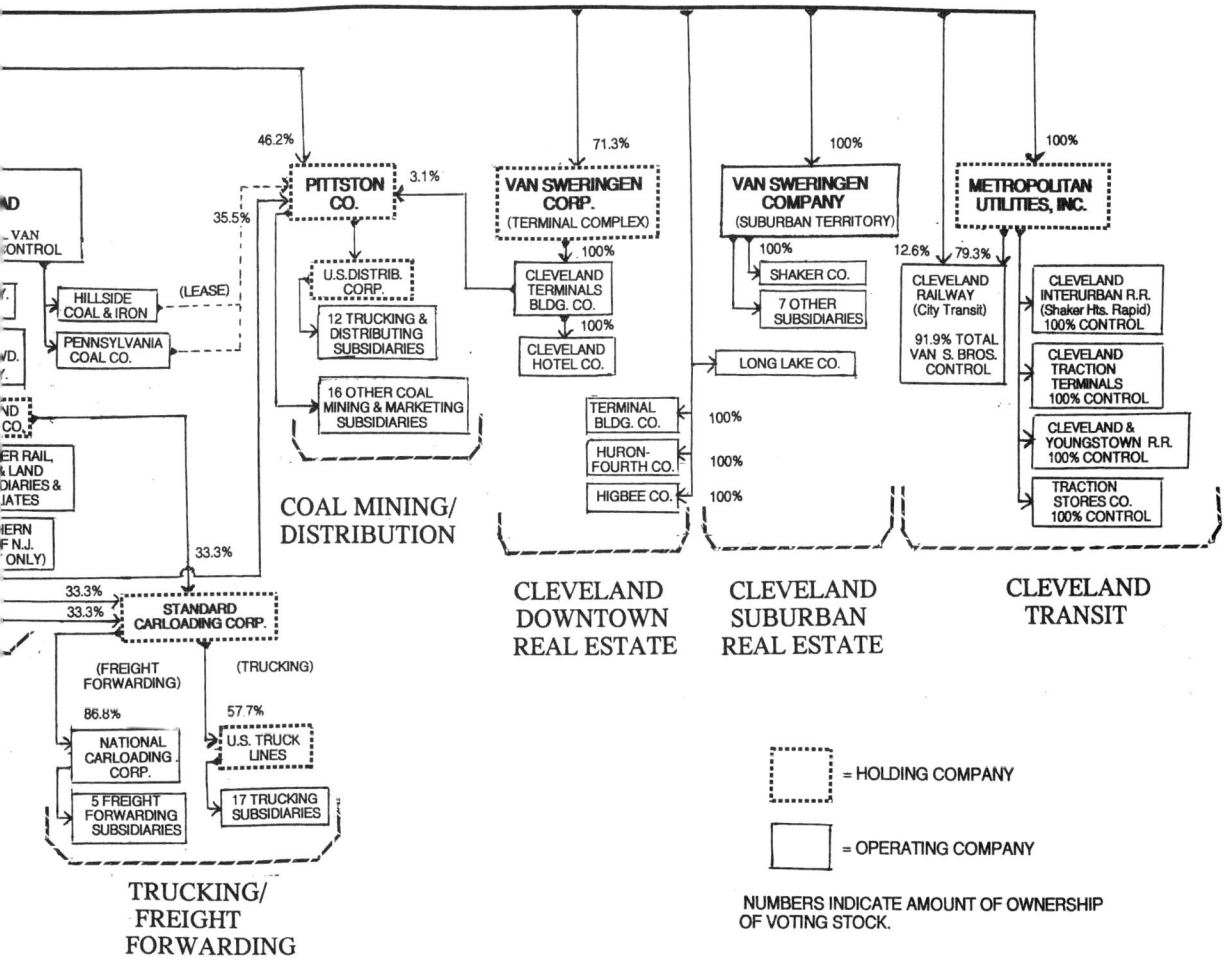

Invisible Giants

One

Oasis in a Gritty City

Cleveland, Ohio, at the turn of the twentieth century was a booming, wealthy city but not a particularly pretty one. Being pretty was not its business. True, it advertised itself as the Forest City, but that went back to the bucolic mid-nineteenth century—shortly before the invention of the Bessemer steel process, before the first boat bearing Mesabi iron ore arrived, before the city became a major railroad junction, before those railroads began hauling in trainloads of coal and crude oil from western Pennsylvania. Now steel mills, refineries, power plants, and a shipyard lined the kinky Cuyahoga River which bisected the city's center, and manufacturing industries of all types spread east along Lake Erie and along the railroad lines to the southeast and southwest. Railroad tracks lined the lake shore, covered the Cuyahoga valley, and were crammed in all quadrants of the city. On the water, the oddly elongated Great Lakes freighters carried in ore from Lake Superior and carried out coal to other industrial cities along the Great Lakes.

Also streaming into the city were European immigrants come to work in the mills and factories. In the twenty years

A serious-looking M. J. Sweringen poses in one of his early jobs as a newsboy.

after 1880, Cleveland's population had increased 138 percent and was still heading dramatically upward; it was Ohio's largest city and the seventh largest in the country. It was also now culturally a continent away from its New England settlement origins; by the turn of the century those new immigrants made up over half the city's population. Undereducated and unfamiliar with the language and customs, they clustered in tight eth-nic enclaves randomly scattered in all parts of the town—each a miniature Germany, Bohemia, Italy, Poland, Serbia, or Hungary—and together created an incohesive, polyglot working city.

It did have a center—the Public Square, pretty much all that remained from the city's early New England heritage, which sat on high ground ninety feet above the lake and river but close to both. Once a pasture in the old New England tradition, the large square was now divided into four quadrants by main streets. Around it was a downtown in flux; a few large buildings, such as the dazzlingly ornate Arcade, were beginning to replace a typically nondescript collection of late-Victorian commercial structures, one of which accommodated the city government in rented space. Visually disjointed as it was, it was also a seat of midwestern economic power, housing the headquarters of manufacturing, mining, and lake-shipping companies and the banks that serviced them.

It was, in short, a fine place to make money, if not always a fine place to live. But even that situation created opportunities.

Among the many people hunting such opportunities was a pair of unprepossessing young brothers who had ended up in Cleveland after a childhood of family poverty, tragedy, and rootlessness. The oldest, Oris Paxton Sweringen, had turned 21 in 1900; his younger brother, Mantis James, was 19. Their odd first names were always a source of mystery. One biographer claimed—without clear documentation—that they were bestowed by the brothers' footloose and sometimes drink-addled father, James Tower Sweringen, who had heard some names that appealed to him but muddled their sound or spelling. In naming the elder brother, Jim Sweringen supposedly had heard a parent calling a wandering child who might have been named Horace. By the same reasoning, Mantis allegedly was a Sweringen corruption of Mandus, a farmhand at one of the many rural spots the family once lived. On the other hand, the brothers themselves professed that they never knew the source. If they actually did, they never told anyone.[1]

In any event, neither brother seemed especially entranced by his name—especially Mantis, who as a child quickly made the obvious link to the unpleasant-looking insect. As the two became better known, almost everyone called them simply "O. P." and "M. J."—and always in that order. Their names were not all that was unusual about them. The two were tightly bonded—so much so that they were physically inseparable and, despite wide differences in intellect, abilities, and temperament, almost wholly dependent on each other.

They were also motivated and ambitious but floundering aimlessly. So far their record was not impressive. They had left school after the eighth grade, had worked in a succession of menial jobs such as selling newspapers, had done a variety of types of office work, and, in about 1898, had opened (and soon closed) a bicycle rental and repair shop. Then came more clerical jobs and, in 1901, O. P. formed a stone dealership with another brother. That lasted only a year, after which O. P. and M. J. tried their own partnership as the Prospect Storage and Cartage Company. It, too, was a dead end, and they folded the operation in even less time. At about this time, O. P. did some part-time work for lawyer Frederick L. Taft and got his first real education in negotiating project financing and handling various other business deals. O. P. then decided to pursue the real estate business, and M. J. inevitably joined him in another informal partnership. This time they made an auspicious first move by getting an option on a house near their East Side home and reselling it a day later for a $100 profit. A similar coup came a short time later.[2]

There was also some hope in their genes. They were descended from a well-bred and educated seventeenth-century Dutch settler named Gerret Van Sweringen, who arrived as a 21-year-old in what is now New Castle, Delaware, in 1657 and proceeded to make himself wealthy as a landowner and a distinguished political administrator. Along the way he adapted himself to the English culture and dropped the "Van" from the family name. Subsequent Sweringen generations also prospered as farmers and landowners.

The exception, unfortunately, was Jim Sweringen, their father, who at age 32 had received a severe leg wound in the Civil War and was unable to do demanding work afterward. Following the war he worked for several years in the western Pennsylvania oil fields, where he met and married Jennie Curtis in 1867. But after that he never seemed able to settle anywhere for long and moved his growing family from place to place in northern Ohio while eking out a marginal living at odd jobs. O. P. was born on a farm outside Wooster, south of Cleveland, on April 24, 1879; M. J. was born in a remote rural spot called Rogue's Hollow, near Doylestown, on July 8, 1881. After bearing six children (and losing one in infancy) and struggling to maintain the family, Jennie died of tuberculosis in 1886 when Oris was 6 and Mantis 4. What remained of the family—Jim Sweringen, three sons, and two daughters—then moved to the East Side of Cleveland, where the father, by now an alcoholic, essentially retired himself, leaving the five children to carry the load. The two young boys were raised by their two older sisters, while their older brother Herbert supported everyone with a steady job at the Cleveland Storage Company.[3]

According to a later Van Sweringen associate, the two sisters, Carrie and Edith, "saw to it that [the boys'] youthful enthusiasms never came to a full boil, and that they were wrapped up, like precious bric-a-brac, in cotton wadding. The ministrations of the spinster sisters, abetted by . . . Herbert, fashioned two rather lonely young fellows with leanings pronouncedly toward the serious side." They worked hard and stuck close together.[4]

Both were of medium height but were physically different, temperamentally opposite, and intellectually unequal. The blondish M. J. was active, a quick mover, and somewhat intense; his imagination was earthbound, his outlook conservative, and his talents best suited to handling day-to-day details. He was, in a word, ordinary.

His shorter, dark-haired older brother was another breed, and a unique one. The stolid-looking O. P. was dreamy and physically languid. As a child he had no interest in sports, and as an adult he had none in exercise—at least partly the result of what was diagnosed as a weak heart and low blood pressure, which led him to avoid exertion and sleep a lot. (Although almost never seriously sick, he also had an almost pathological fear of disease as well as an acute sensitivity to tobacco smoke and alcohol.) But he had a remarkably creative and incisive mind. Said one later assistant: "It was quick, capable of grasping any situation, no matter how complicated. He was capable of forecasting accurately the consequences of any set of causes. . . . He was an incredibly fast reader, could catch the salient fact of any situation and decide what to do and how to do it." More than that, he had a visionary imagination which, while not at the highest creative level, could take some innovative concept in new and greatly expanded directions. And, in contrast to M. J.'s practical conservatism, O. P. had a relentlessly optimistic outlook which constantly propelled that creativity.[5]

O. P.'s personality was a curious stew of opposites. Although extremely shy and highly uncomfortable in crowds, he was also firmly self-assured and daringly aggressive in his own way; he could articulately describe and defend his visions in sometimes rough company. One friend, lawyer Charles W. Stage, called him "timid but irresistible." Another noted that he was usually charming, friendly, good-humored, and highly diplomatic—"the perfect little gentleman"—but could be sharp-tempered when crossed.[6]

The seemingly mismatched brothers worked and lived as one unit; by all accounts, there were virtually no arguments between them. Despite his clearly superior intellect and abilities, O. P. particularly seemed to need M. J.—perhaps as the only person he could be truly comfortable with, perhaps as a pragmatic anchor, perhaps as his right hand in handling the everyday details of living and working for which he had little time or interest. Possibly it was all of that. For his part, M. J. saw it as his duty to protect his brilliant brother from physical and emotional stresses and mental distractions. Together the two shared their large ambition and penchant for hard work. They were also genuinely modest and intensely private; as they became more well known, they were embarrassed to see their names in print and were annoyed by any public interest in them. Friends and associates typically described them jointly as always courteous and tactful, sensitive, neat, and, using other words, priggish. In all, they hardly fit the image of aggressive would-be entrepreneurs in an ill-bred city.[7]

Shortly after their $100 coup with the East Side house, they apparently decided to concentrate on suburban properties, an astute choice in turn-of-the-century Cleveland. For those with the imagination and nerve to venture into this field, the opportunities were suddenly magnificent. A swelling but bottled-up market and the technology to uncork it had come together almost simultaneously, opening up an enticingly new field for enrichment.

The city's gritty environment was creating the market, visibly and dramatically so. All those steel mills and refineries along the Cuyahoga River sat next to the city's heart, spewing out dark clouds of varied colors, odors, and chemical content; beyond them on three sides were plants turning out all manner of industrial and consumer products. And moving through it all were hundreds of coal-fired steam locomotives and lake freighters, all adding their own rich mix of black bituminous smoke. Then there were the people—those immigrants and their cloistered neighborhoods, destabilizing property values. And finally there was the delicate problem of odor—put more bluntly, the stench. The industrial air and the unwashed human bodies were not the only problems. Horses still moved all the goods and many of the people around the city; there were thousands of them and their inevitable by-products were all dumped onto the streets.

Thus, the owners and managers of Cleveland's industry felt a rapidly escalating urge to put themselves at a distance from their creations—as did the bankers and lawyers who serviced them and the retailers who were growing wealthy selling to them.

But for most, escaping the city had not been so easy. Until the 1890s, getting anywhere was limited by the speed and stamina of a horse (or human feet), and the notoriously wicked Lake Erie winters sometimes made any animal-powered movement impossible. Living in the country was to be dreamed of, but the practicalities of getting to work, to stores, and to any entertainment were something else. That changed almost overnight. In 1888, electricity was first successfully applied to city transportation on a large scale. Electric streetcars moved far faster and more cleanly than horse cars; people could now move farther out and still get downtown in the same time, or less. Throughout the '90s, Cleveland joined all other cities, large and small, in electrifying its street railways and extending them. Not only that, but longer and even faster variations of streetcar lines, called interurbans, were being built outward to link cities with nearby communities and the hinterlands in between. By the turn of the century, interurbans radiated out of Cleveland to Akron, Canton, Painesville, Lorain, Elyria, Oberlin, Medina, and even the remote reaches of rural Geauga County. Within three years, they would reach as far as Toledo and Wooster.

Close by the city were miles of woods and farmlands—country living, far enough away from the city's more noxious aspects but near enough to be reached by fast, clean, dependable transportation.

The enormous potential of suburban real estate was clear enough, but still it was no sure thing. True, a huge market was there, and it was certain to grow—and the electric streetcar and interurban were also now there to open the gates. But the trolleys came with a price. Electrified railways were costly to build and equip; that cost could be justified by hauling the masses around the city, but building tracks and stringing electric wires miles through barren fields meant capital tied up for years before the hope of a payoff. And if the payoff did come, it more likely came for the real estate developer than for the car-line operator.

And for the developer, there was always that maddeningly unpredictable ingredient of social cachet. What kind of people would accept his development? Would their friends come?

Cleveland's vibrant Public Square was a sea of streetcars in this 1910 scene, which looks southeast on Superior Avenue toward the Square. The old Forest City House hotel occupies the corner in the photo's center; the tall building in the rear center is the new Williamson Building, where the young Van Sweringen brothers had their first downtown offices.
John A. Rehor collection

Would it be fashionable? And if so, to what extent? All of this ultimately dictated how the developer designed and marketed the property and, ultimately, how much he could sell it for.

Thus far, Cleveland's slow suburbanization had followed the line of least resistance along the flatter ground near the lake to communities such as Lakewood, East Cleveland, and Euclid. The most wealthy were in the process of abandoning their "Millionaire's Row" mansions on Euclid Avenue and sequestering themselves in a sylvan settlement called Bratenahl, six miles to the east on the lake's shore. Trains from the nearby Lake Shore & Michigan Southern Railway station at East 105th Street took them to town quickly, with minimal exposure to the city en route.

As their first major real estate gamble, the young Sweringen brothers picked Lakewood, a new village on the city's West Side which was being developed as a middle-class suburb. Lakewood had organized itself as a hamlet in 1889 but at first fought off the invasion of the streetcar through its gardens and vineyards. In 1893, a car line was completed along

Oasis in a Gritty City • 7

unpaved Detroit Avenue to the Rocky River; another was built through the rustic northern section in 1903, and Lakewood was incorporated as a village the same year. At about this time, O. P. and M. J. picked up a string of lots on what is now Cook Avenue; sadly, their gamble paid off with a foreclosure judgment which took two years to work off. It was then back to earning money any way they could, and in 1905, "Judge" Taft, O. P.'s former employer, arranged an interesting job for him as caretaker of the home of Cassie Chadwick, the infamous eccentric con woman who had just been convicted of bilking millions from investors while posing as the illegitimate daughter of Andrew Carnegie. Years afterward, he still relished relating his experiences while presiding over her flamboyantly furnished Euclid Avenue mansion.[8]

Unhappy as it was, the Lakewood affair did produce one notable landmark in the brothers' lives. At about this time, the Sweringen brothers were operating a butter-and-eggs delivery wagon. One day, to the family's surprise, the wagon was re-lettered "Van Sweringen." Perhaps to enhance their image in their new venture, they had reinstated the original family name, which had been long abandoned in the United States. "Van Sweringen" became more or less official when it showed up in an August 1903 city directory. (In Holland, the "Van" prefix never carried the aristocratic connotations that "Von" did in Germany, but there is no doubt that "Van Sweringen" had a distinguished roll to it.) As they became better known, Clevelanders universally referred to them as "the Vans."[9]

After their Lakewood disaster, the two brothers retreated to more familiar territory—the city's East Side, specifically the so-called Heights area in the southeast where they had sometimes played as boys. By this time they had decided to specialize in residential property for Cleveland's new industrial royalty—and with their quiet, earnest demeanor; refined tastes; and O. P.'s low-key salesmanship, they seemed to have the right touch for this kind of market.

That market and the Heights seemed made for each other, too. Theoretically, the location had all the right elements. It consisted of a woodsy plateau averaging about 400 feet above the lake level, occasionally cut up by pleasant little streams flowing down to the lake but otherwise a terrain ideal for building. (Geologically, the Heights mark the last gasp of the Alleghenies in this region; to the east, the land gradually rises and becomes hilly. West of the Cuyahoga River in Cleveland begin the flatlands which, by one name or another, stretch to the Rockies.) Situated above the city and about six miles from the Public Square, it was properly removed from all the urban ills and was also virtually untouched; part of it had once been called Turkey Ridge for its plentiful wild turkeys.

The elevation of the Heights was also the reason why it had remained largely untouched. Before the electric streetcar, climbing the hill in horse-drawn vehicles was a chore in good weather and a wretched ordeal in winter. But development began in the early 1900s, after a streetcar line was built up the hill in 1897 to open Euclid Heights, an elite garden suburb developed by a transplanted southern entrepreneur named Patrick Calhoun. Beginning in 1892, Calhoun had laid out Euclid Heights as a carefully planned upper-class "garden" suburb; it was soon followed by adjacent Ambler Heights. (In 1903, these developments became part of the new village of Cleveland Heights.)[10]

O. P. was especially interested in the area southeast of Euclid Heights, which was still a large expanse of woodlands and small farms. He was especially intrigued by a single tract of 1,366 acres which began about a mile southeast of the Euclid Heights streetcar-line terminal. Following the pattern of its near neighbors, the property was known as Shaker Heights, but that was the end of the resemblance. Shaker Heights consisted of two pretty lakes in a rather remote city-owned park surrounded by abandoned farmland and the ruins of buildings.

"I looked over the land and considered its possibilities," O. P. later wrote. "Then and there I had a vision of how the whole region could be developed, but I did not say much about it. My experience is that it is best not to reveal all of your vision at first. Make good on part of it, and then you will be in a better position to take the next step." O. P. was not one for self-aggrandizement, so his recollection of this early vision may well be true.[11]

The unusually large size of the tract and what was left of those old buildings were the visible heritage of a community of Shakers, that peculiar celibate communal sect which blended spirituality, utopian idealism, and earthy pragmatism.

The ascetic Shakers established a fully self-sufficient farming settlement they called North Union on this land beginning in 1828. Doan Brook, which flowed through their property, was dammed for power, creating the lakes. Over the next twenty-five years, a stone gristmill, a large brick woolen mill, a sawmill, a blacksmith shop, a meeting house, and communal living buildings all appeared as North Union grew and prospered. High-quality Shaker canned goods, butter, cheese, flour, and yarn were also sold locally and were always in demand.[12]

But Shaker celibacy and changing fashions in spiritual outlook ultimately doomed the enterprise, and by 1889, only twenty-nine members remained. The group decided to disband and sell the property. Since it was communally owned, the entire community was sold as a single parcel in 1892 to a group of Cleveland investors. Vaguely hoping to develop it as a suburban community, the new buyers christened it Shaker Heights and incorporated themselves as the Shaker Heights Land Company. Three years later, in the hope of making the remote property more attractive, they donated 278 acres along the lakes and stream to the city of Cleveland for its growing park system. Helped by a heavy donation from native son John D. Rockefeller and more property from the land company, the city cut two roads up the hill and around the park in picturesque curving patterns. A foot-powered swan boat paddled around on the larger lake in season.[13]

But that was as far as development went. The Shaker property owners resold the remaining acreage to a Buffalo syndicate headed by Great Lakes ship operator William Henry Gratwick, Sr. Gratwick died soon after, but his son, W. H. ("Harry") Gratwick, Jr., a tall, husky Harvard-educated lawyer, felt a responsibility to carry out his father's plans and bought out most of the other partners. The younger Gratwick appointed a Cleveland sales agent, O. C. Ringle, and hired the F. A. Pease engineering company to plat the property. But still it lay mostly vacant. Other areas with better access were being opened, the aftereffects of the 1893 financial panic lingered, and absentee ownership did not help. Shaker Heights entered the twentieth century looking increasingly overgrown and bedraggled; by 1905, its assessed value was almost 25 percent below the original purchase price.[14]

All that was fine with O. P., who always had a sharp eye for undervalued properties. Already his restless imagination was churning over his vision for it.

Two

The Ideal Suburb

As with almost everything they got into, the brothers began slowly in Shaker Heights, with little evidence of what might come. They made their first move in the spring of 1905, when they arranged a meeting with Harry Gratwick in Buffalo through O. C. Ringle, Gratwick's Cleveland sales agent.

Their proposal was simple and involved little or no outlay on their part: They asked for an option on a few lots which they would then sell, giving Gratwick's group the proceeds. If they sold them within a certain length of time, Gratwick would give them options on another block twice the size for twice the length of time. A contract was drawn up in May, and they were on their way.[1]

The brothers got to work selling their still-nebulous scheme for a planned suburban village for the well-to-do and managed to dispose of the lots in the set time. They then came back for more.

Their first serious development was along the northern border of the property on present Fairmount Boulevard east of Coventry Road. Fairmount was one of the original Shaker roadways and led west toward the Euclid Heights car line; with the proper improvements—notably transportation—it was the most readily accessible. O. P. envisioned subdivisions for large homes, much like those then appearing in Euclid Heights and other nearby developments.

Although the brothers had worked off their Lakewood debts and were respectable again, the experience did not cure them of the habit of working with thin capital, relying heavily on loans and other means of minimizing their own stake. This first major Heights venture was typical: The total price of the property was $3,000; they paid $1,000 down and borrowed most of that. "We sold lots," said O. P., "and, as fast as we got money in our contracts, we acquired options on nearby land and continued selling."[2]

To open the property for upper-income homes, the brothers had to provide transportation, and there remained the problem of enticing the street railway company to build into an expanse of unproductive trees and fields. A 1906 extension of the Euclid Heights line to Mayfield Road put the tracks somewhat closer to the area the Van Sweringens were interested in, but a lengthy branch was still needed. The original Euclid Heights line had been partially subsidized by Calhoun's Euclid Heights Realty Company, and in 1906, O. P. approached the Cleveland Electric Railway's president, Horace Andrews, with a similar offer. If Andrews built a branch out to their rebuilt Fairmount Boulevard, the brothers would give him the land and cover his interest costs on the construction for five years. Andrews begrudgingly acquiesced; a franchise was granted in August 1906, and the line was completed to Lee Road in 1907. The new line was designated the Shaker Lakes line, doubtless an attempt to enhance its traffic by also advertising the attractive city park developed around the old Shaker millponds.[3]

To the misfortune of Andrews, his predictions of meager trolley business proved accurate, but the Van Sweringens had their transportation. Their development along broad Fairmount Boulevard, with the car tracks set in a grassy median, was a solid success; a succession of impressively sumptuous homes arose which remained imposing in the year 2002. Andrews could take modest solace in telling his colleagues in the business that the line had the unusual distinction of two-way rush-hour traffic; commuters going into town were balanced by servants and gardeners for the mansions coming out to their jobs.

This piecemeal approach was successful enough but did

not fit O. P.'s larger plan, vague as it may have been at the time. Within about a year, the brothers organized their efforts by arranging to acquire all of the remaining Shaker property as a single unit. In 1907, they and the Gratwick group set up the Sedgwick Land Company, presumably as a temporary means of financing the purchase and developing the land. How this short-lived company was financed and how it functioned is unknown now. But based on the records of its successors, it appears that the Buffalo investors—most notably financier John J. Albright—put additional funds into the Shaker project while the brothers rounded up local money. Whatever it was and did, the Sedgwick Land Company had the distinction of being the first of a long and diverse line of Van Sweringen companies. It also set a pattern for virtually all Van Sweringen companies to come, in that the brothers put little of their own money into it and relied on outsiders for their capital.[4]

Essentially it was a more elaborate form of the same shoestring financing style used for the Fairmount Boulevard project. The brothers made it work, but it was still a perilous technique for the development philosophy O. P. had settled on, which was to hold property for the long run and open it in stages as his "vision" could be slowly consummated. That process could take a decade or more; the basic planning and groundwork alone might take several years before much of anything was sold.

For their local backers, the two young entrepreneurs (O. P. was 28 in 1907 and M. J. 26) slowly gathered in a coterie of mostly younger comers in what would normally be called the city's legal and financial establishment—except that at the time it was anything but a monolithic "establishment." Cleveland was passionately divided as it never had been before and never would be again. Since 1901, the city's government had been in the hands of the portly but dynamic Tom L. Johnson, a millionaire industrialist who had fallen under the spell of Henry George and turned idealistic reformer. The Democrat Johnson, a century later still regarded as Cleveland's greatest mayor, was energetically remaking the city politically, economically, socially, and visually—but as a declared enemy of privilege and a proponent of public ownership of utilities and street railways, he was the Antichrist in the eyes of the Republican business and banking elite.[5]

Yet while the warring camps were crucifying one another in public, they were both charmed by O. P. and his vision. One early backer was the young Charles W. "Billy" Stage, a former star athlete at Adelbert College and now a lawyer in Johnson's administration. Stage in turn introduced the brothers to another Johnson acolyte, the scholarly looking, soft-spoken city solicitor Newton D. Baker. (Baker would soon serve as mayor himself, then as Woodrow Wilson's secretary of war.) On the other side of the Vans' politically ecumenical group was Parmely Herrick, son of banker, entrepreneur, and Republican politician (and ex-governor) Myron T. Herrick.

Banker Joseph R. Nutt, a sometime associate of Myron Herrick and solid fellow Republican, also joined the group. The patrician-looking Nutt, O. P.'s senior by eight years, would become one of the brothers' closest and most valuable associates. A much younger recruit was Charles L. Bradley, a third-generation Cleveland industrial aristocrat then in his early 20s. He and his brother Alva had inherited a Great Lakes shipping and Cleveland real estate empire founded by their grandfather, the locally legendary Captain Alva Bradley, which had been expanded by their father, Morris Bradley. Like Nutt, the chunky, cheerful Bradley eventually became part of the brothers' innermost councils.

Whatever had charmed this diverse group was elusive but compelling. Billy Stage later recalled his first exposure to O. P.'s salesmanship: "He was so doggone timid about the matter that when he left I remarked 'That young man will never make a real estate salesman.' But a short time later [he] came back. He spent several hours outlining what he saw for the undeveloped land. . . . At first I was not interested, but when he left I joined his little syndicate."[6]

The brothers also reached into their old friendships to find property-buyers. One was Benjamin L. Jenks and his wife Louise—best known to everyone as "Daisy." Although Ben was about nine years older than O. P., he and the two brothers had been friends from their East Side boyhood days. Jenks subsequently went into the family lumber business and then became an attorney. Along the way he married Louise Davidson, about eleven years his junior. Much the opposite of her tall, mild-mannered, and accommodating husband, Daisy Jenks was stunning, bright, aggressive, and, as one writer put it, "had more than a mind of her own." The brothers and the Jenkses became an unusually close foursome—so close, in fact, that the two bachelors regularly lodged overnight in the Jenks home, which scandalized their prim sisters and generated the obvious local gossip. Ben was given a job as their office attorney and became one of their primary aides in putting O. P.'s plans for the new community into effect.[7]

At about the same time, O. P. also invited Herbert, the oldest Van Sweringen brother, to join them as a triumvirate in their new Williamson Building offices. Herbert did so, but a true partnership relationship never developed, and he found himself mostly supervising the routine office functions—in part because of his own limitations but also, it was speculated, because of M. J.'s jealousy.[8]

In planning their new suburb, the brothers followed the basic concept of the planned garden suburb, which had been around since the 1850s and gradually refined through the later nineteenth century. Patrick Calhoun's Euclid Heights, begun in 1892, followed the pattern, with large pseudo–English-style homes set on curving streets which fed into a wide central boulevard carrying a streetcar line to town. Euclid Heights was O. P.'s nearest inspiration, but his principal model probably was a landmark upper-class development in Baltimore called Roland Park, which also had gotten under way in the early 1890s and eventually evolved a far more comprehensive set of planning principles.

Like the Shaker tract, the original Roland Park project had been backed by out-of-towners—in this case from Kansas City and London—who were floundering around for a successful marketing approach. And like Shaker, it was some distance from the city's center with no easy transportation. One of the syndicate, an imaginative 32-year-old Kansas City developer named Edward H. Bouton, came east in 1891 to try to rescue it. Although Bouton arrived in Baltimore fresh from a failure in Kansas City, he slowly evolved a winning formula. He aimed to appeal to upper-class buyers by offering a completely planned, regulated, and harmonious community built around an integrated set of principles ultimately aimed at one purpose: long-term stability—stability of setting, stability of property values, stability of an aesthetic ideal, and stability of the community's congeniality.

The "package" Bouton developed had several essential elements. Fundamental was the concept of property-deed covenants with specific restrictions governing house size, cost, architectural style, placement, and resale procedures. Plans for new houses were to be reviewed and approved, and, not surprisingly, they were expected to be conservative; no two houses were to be alike and no attached or row houses were permitted. Minimum setbacks from the street were specified. The size of a lot and the cost of the house were to be correlated, with a controlled mixture of larger and smaller homes. Commercial structures were banned.

Next came a carefully planned environment which was visually pleasing and included the type of amenities needed by this level of clientele. Bouton hired professional landscape architects to create aesthetic surroundings of curving, tree-lined residential streets leading into a wide central boulevard. (Interestingly, the initial Roland Park planning was done by George E. Kessler, who had designed the Euclid Heights development in Cleveland; he was succeeded by Boston's Olmsted brothers.) First-class educational facilities were mandatory, and generous amounts of land were set aside and donated for top-quality schools (with special emphasis on private schools, or "country day schools"). Similarly, land was given for churches and for the latest upper-class essential, a country club.

Commercial structures were entirely banned, except for a small integrated shopping-center building built by the development company—reputedly the first suburban shopping center in the country.

High-quality transportation to downtown was another critical element. Roland Park was built around an electric car line laid in a park-like setting in the center of the wide boulevard which formed the spine of the development. Although the cars then had to cope with city streets on their way into town, they originally used a three-quarter-mile-long elevated section into the downtown area. It was "rapid transit" as best as could be accomplished in the early 1890s.

And finally, of course, the community's standards were maintained and controlled by its own authority; in this case, the development company.

None of these elements were especially radical, and, to one degree or another, all had been applied individually elsewhere. Restrictive deed covenants, for example, dated back to the earliest American garden suburb, Llewellyn Park, developed in 1853 in Orange, New Jersey, and were further refined for Pierre Lorillard's Tuxedo Park in New York State in 1885. Patrick Calhoun, too, used them in Euclid Heights. But Roland Park's Bouton brought it to its most extensive and sophisticated form so far. More important, Bouton's inspiration was to put all the planning elements together in a comprehensive, tightly controlled package in which everything would smoothly interrelate—landscape, home design, transportation, and the civic and recreational amenities appropriate to the upper-class homeowners.

Contemporary real estate developers greatly admired Roland Park but did not often emulate it. Their hesitancy was well grounded: For all their virtues, Bouton's high standards of planning practically guaranteed slow development, and his excessively liberal allocations of land for non–revenue-producing uses—such as schools, churches, country clubs, parks, and wide streets—seemed financially suicidal. And in fact

Roland Park developed slowly and never paid big dividends: After fourteen years of meager returns, its English backers withdrew and put their money in a much surer thing—South African diamond mines. Yet Bouton surely achieved his aim; in the year 2002, Roland Park was still one of Baltimore's most desirable neighborhoods, and its appearance and standards had not changed since the Bouton era.[9]

It was that kind of community that the Van Sweringens wanted. They adopted virtually all the elements of the Roland Park plan and, characteristically, expanded and embellished them—but the principles remained precisely the same, beginning with the concept of a fully planned and integrated community design under a single control. (It was usually left to the property-buyer to design and build his house, but he could only do so within severe restrictions.) Deed covenants (in even more elaborate form); landscaping; wide boulevards and curving back streets; land given for schools, churches, country clubs, and the like; high-speed rail transit to the city; and tight control over all became O. P.'s plan for Shaker. To one degree or another, Shaker Heights in turn became a model for subsequent developments—but the degree was mostly lesser since one key to the Van Sweringens' success was their single control of what became a substantially sizeable area and the transportation serving it.

To help put their vision into concrete form, the brothers hired Cleveland's F. A. Pease engineering firm, which in 1909 produced its plan for platting the first section of the Shaker development and the layout of its streets. For its axis, the designers laid out an extension of Coventry Road from Fairmount Boulevard through the Shaker property. Originally drawn as a wide but otherwise ordinary street, the Coventry Road extension was soon touched by the Van Sweringen wand and metamorphosed into broad Shaker Boulevard. Most of the initial platting was confined to the area around the Shaker Lakes north of present Shaker Boulevard, ending a short distance east of Lee Road—a bit over a mile and a third. To attract varying (but always upper-) income levels, lot frontages were planned to range in increments from 40 feet to 100 feet, each size carefully grouped together. (The initial plats were almost all 100 feet, however.) Ben Jenks helped develop the all-important standards for house design and subsequently became their chief enforcer.[10]

At about the same time, it was decided that the new community's basic tone would be an idealized blend of New England village and old England itself, an image then becoming fashionable for upper-class developments—which would continue nationwide through the 1920s. (Calhoun's Euclid Heights was an earlier and perhaps inspirational example.) As the streets slowly materialized, they bore such names as Attleboro, Southington, Fernway, Larchmere, Litchfield, Sedgewick, and the like.

Architectural standards followed suit. The most popular approved designs were variations of suburbanized Georgian, Tudor, Cotswold, Dutch Colonial, and French Chateau styles —preferably built in solid masonry with discreetly muted colors. Mediterranean villa styles, popular in many other suburbs, were rejected as out of place in Shaker Heights. Bungalows were banished to outer darkness—as, needless to say, were eccentricities such as the works of Frank Lloyd Wright and his followers or anything flamboyant. All houses were to be designed by registered architects who were approved by the company. There were to be no apartment houses. Somewhat surprisingly, a few attached houses were permitted in specific areas, although they could not look obviously attached. As with Roland Park, each house design would be distinctive—that is, no two exactly alike—but not ostentatious. As they evolved, the village's building standards included elaborate detail about permitted and forbidden construction materials and specified precisely what exterior trim, shutter, and roof colors were appropriate for each wall coloring. One early resident reminisced: "The roof specifications were strictly enforced. The Van Sweringen Company had its own inspector, but the city did not." Essentially, the Van Sweringen philosophy was one of conformity without uniformity.[11]

At the same time, the Vans were careful to preserve at least some vestiges of the Shaker heritage. While the remnants of the old masonry and wooden buildings were razed, some touches were kept as symbols, such as a pair of stone gateposts and a large elm tree. The head of an idealized Shaker maiden became the community's symbol. Local legend holds that Lee Road, the village's main north-south street, honors the sect's founder, "Mother Ann" Lee, although spoilsport historians maintain that a local landowner named Elias Lee is the more likely suspect. Whatever the facts, the name is an apt reminder of the vanished settlement.

As was typical of many tightly controlled upper-class developments of the time, the Van Sweringen Company enforced the concept of "compatible neighbors" when selling Shaker Heights property—which was understood to be mostly white Protestants. The key word was "mostly," however; unlike some old eastern cities such as Boston and Baltimore, with their rigid social distinctions, Shaker reflected a slightly more easygoing midwestern attitude and was never entirely exclusive. For example, the Jewish department-store owner Salmon Halle built a mansion on Parkland Drive, and Jews of lesser means and many Catholics (some of them in the upper Van Sweringen ranks) established themselves elsewhere in the community. Nonetheless, there were some absolute barriers, particularly for blacks. The original deed restrictions did not cover resales, and homeowners could sell to anyone they wanted. But after two episodes where black families moved in and were unpleasantly pressured to move back out, the covenants were rewritten in 1927 to require any home resales to be approved either by the Van Sweringen Company or by neighboring property-owners. Even that was not entirely ironclad, though; owners of property bought before 1927 had to agree to have their old deeds rewritten, and some did not.[12]

The most immediate problem was transportation. By 1908, a dozen or so pioneering houses had appeared on and near the intersection of Shaker Boulevard and Lee Road, about a third of a mile south of the terminal of the Fairmount Boulevard streetcar line. (Ben and Daisy Jenks were among the first settlers.) But further development depended on electric railway service into the heart of the Shaker property. In developing their Fairmount Boulevard properties, the brothers were able to persuade the Cleveland Electric Railway to extend out that boulevard by partly subsidizing it—giving it the right-of-way and paying the interest on its construction costs for five years. They were less successful in persuading the railway company to go any further. Around 1907, O. P. approached John J. Stanley, the railway's new president, and proposed an extension which would run through the heart of the tract. According to O. P.'s later testimony, "He flatly declined, saying that it had become evident to him since the building of the other line . . . that [such] extensions were 'bleeders instead of feeders.' . . . If we would give him the whole line built ready for operation, he would decline to accept it."[13]

Stanley was certainly right from his viewpoint, since his business was transportation and not real estate development. Furthermore, if O. P.'s 1907 date is correct (he may have been early by one or two years), Stanley was deeply immersed in Cleveland's infamous Traction War, fighting a battle with municipally sponsored three-cent-fare competitors which threatened his company's financial stability. While Stanley's attitude did not necessarily close the door to a more liberal subsidy arrangement, O. P.'s thinking went off in another direction—two directions, in fact.

One was the realization that for the Van Sweringen brand of long-term planning and development to succeed, the brothers had to control all the elements themselves. Otherwise, financial expediency would always compromise or frustrate the slowly maturing visions. If nothing else, O. P. always had confidence in his vision, however unformed it might be at the moment, and had the nerve it needed. The compulsion for undisputed personal control would extend to all his other ventures.

It also dawned on him that a conventional streetcar line would not be attractive enough for the type of community that was now forming in his mind. Fairmount Boulevard riders had a relatively fast and pretty ride through the Heights, but once onto Euclid Avenue, Cleveland's main street, their streetcar plodded along for over four and a half miles in heavy traffic. What Shaker Heights would have would be true rapid transit directly to the Public Square—fully under Van Sweringen control.

By the early 1900s, rapid transit—that is, electric cars and trains running on routes free from street traffic—was well established in Boston, New York, Philadelphia, and Chicago. Boston had opened a streetcar subway in 1897, and New York's first full-scale subway followed in 1904. Although subway schemes in Cleveland first appeared in 1909, and fairly regularly thereafter, the city was not yet in the subway league and, in fact, never would be. The Vans visualized sort of a compromise rapid transit system: Within the suburb itself, cars would run on private tracks set in the center median of Shaker Boulevard (and perhaps future boulevards) with widely spaced intersections to speed running. But once west of Shaker Heights, the route would be grade-separated—that is, streets would be carried over or under the rail line, eliminating grade crossings. That was a problem, however; the deeper one got into the city, the more numerous the street crossings became, making construction more difficult and costly.[14]

The brothers quickly spotted a potential pathway through at least a part of the built-up area between the Heights and the Square. On topographical maps of the time, a brown-and-blue–tinted corridor cut clearly between the streets and the black blocks representing buildings—the course of a stream called Kingsbury Run and one of its small tributaries. By building along it the brothers could avoid a little over one and a half miles of solidly developed territory between about East 75th and East 34th Streets. Access from the Shaker property, about three and a half miles to the east, was direct and mostly open, although some heavy excavation work was needed to provide a good grade down the hill from the Heights. Kingsbury Run left their route near East 34th Street to course down to the Cuyahoga River, leaving the brothers on their own for the remaining two urbanized miles to the Public Square. Putting that problem aside until later—possibly to be solved by a subway—they began picking up property along Kingsbury Run. Also, in 1909, they bought four acres on the southwest portion of the Public Square for a terminal; they picked up more property in 1911.

Even though it was in the geographic center of town, the Public Square property was a relative bargain. While the Square was still the center of Cleveland's extensive street railway system and the terminal of its six interurban electric lines, it had otherwise slipped into decline as commercial activity moved eastward along Euclid Avenue to East 9th Street and beyond. The Square's southwest quadrant, where the Vans had bought, was particularly problematic as a commercial site since it was close to a steep slope which dropped down to the Cuyahoga River level. In the early 1900s, it consisted mostly of aged four-story brick buildings, liberally coated with Cuyahoga Valley industrial grime and housing a rabbit warren of small businesses and rundown hotels. The most notable landmark was the Forest City House, once the grande dame of Cleveland's hostelries but now a threadbare dowager. Symptomatic of the Square's fortunes, the Higbee Company, a highly successful dry goods store, moved from this site to palatial quarters at 13th and Euclid in 1910. Two years later, the city's newest and largest hotel, the Statler—"one of the nation's finest hostelries"—opened next door to Higbee's at 12th and Euclid.[15]

As the future owners of the Kingsbury Run line, the brothers created the Cleveland & Youngstown Railroad (C&Y) in July 1911, one of a trio of new subsidiaries set up that year to carry out their transit and Public Square development plans. (Along with the Cleveland & Youngstown came the Terminal Building Company in June and the Terminal Realty and Securities Company in August.) They managed to obtain a steam railroad charter for the C&Y with the right to build from Cleveland to Youngstown, although they surely never thought of going anywhere near Youngstown. But considering that they had mostly broad general goals and few precise plans at that point, the charter allowed wide latitude. They could build as far east as they might need for their real estate development. With a liberal "steam" railroad charter, they could also handle freight for the possible future development of freight terminals and warehouses. Also, they could use any form of motive

The southwest corner of the Public Square in 1914, looking ripe for a savior. In the center behind the shaft of the Soldiers and Sailors Monument is the Forest City House, which would soon make way for the Vans' new Hotel Cleveland.
Cleveland Public Library

power, and they would have right of eminent domain. It might allow other steam railroads to use the Public Square passenger terminal. Flexible instruments like this became a Van Sweringen hallmark as they moved into new projects while still forming their ideas.[16]

Three months after its formation, the Cleveland & Youngstown was asking the Cleveland City Council for a franchise for a four-track route along Kingsbury Run. The line was then to follow the right-of-way of the Nickel Plate Road, one of Cleveland's several steam railroads, to about East 9th Street, where it would plunge into a four-track subway to reach the Public Square. There was also vague talk about several of the East Side interurban lines also using the right-of-way into the equally vague Public Square terminal. But the C&Y was destined to do nothing for several years. To build it to Van Sweringen standards would cost large amounts that they did not have—at least not yet. They had to bide their time while they waited for an opportunity to finance the project.[17]

But that was no hindrance to O. P.'s imagination. In late March 1911, a nearby newspaper reported: "An immense interurban station, hotel, and office building, to cost $4.5 million and occupy an entire block between the Public Square

Shaker Boulevard in its primeval state in 1914, looking west from Lee Road. The new Van Sweringen–financed car line is in operation and ready to serve the mansions that eventually would rise in this wilderness.
Cleveland Union Terminal collection, Cleveland State University

and West 3rd St., including the Forest City Hotel property, the old Higbee Co. site, etc., is to be erected during the coming year. It . . . will include a twelve-story hotel facing the southwest side of the Square. A twin structure to be used as an office building is planned to corner on Superior and the Square. A great arcade to carry six car tracks connecting with the city lines is planned. Former Governor Myron T. Herrick is in New York to arrange financing." The "elegant" office building was to be sixteen stories tall.[18]

Nothing happened "during the coming year" of course, nor would the building ever happen in that form. But it would happen.

More concretely, the Shaker real estate visions began to jell. In October 1911, Shaker Heights Village was incorporated as a politically independent community with a population of about 250. The new village took in most of the original Shaker community tract except for a strip along Fairmount Boulevard on its northeastern border, which remained in Cleveland Heights; other farmland was gradually added to the east and south. The single-story Van Sweringen Company field office on Shaker Boulevard at Lee Road served as the village hall as well as the school, which was populated by four teachers and thirty students. The village marshal was also the entire police force. The first church, a crude temporary building, was put up on donated land in 1916.

With the planned rapid transit still just a tenuous line on a map—the inner part of its route not even known—the brothers needed some kind of interim public transportation;

This unassuming all-purpose building at Shaker Boulevard and Lee Road variously housed a Van Sweringen Company office, the new village's government offices, its school, and the police force.
Cleveland Press collection, Cleveland State University

the nearest car line was on Fairmount Boulevard, almost half a mile away. For the sake of expediency, they went back to John J. Stanley, now president of the Cleveland Railway—the old Cleveland Electric Railway's successor and the operator of all the city's car lines. By 1913, Stanley was apparently more willing to deal, and the brothers laid out a line along Shaker Boulevard which would connect with the streetcar company's Fairmount Boulevard route via Coventry Road. Shaker Boulevard itself was the first visible example of Van Sweringen–style planning: It was designed on the pattern of Roland Avenue in Baltimore and Fairmount Boulevard in Cleveland Heights, but to a vaster scale—it was a prodigal 180 feet wide, with a grassy center median wide enough to carry the two rail tracks with ample provision for two more if ever needed.

This time the Van Sweringens built and controlled the projected new Shaker Boulevard car line themselves. Still another Van Sweringen subsidiary, the Cleveland Interurban Railroad (CIRR), was created March 19, 1913, to be the line's titular operator. But like the Cleveland & Youngstown, the CIRR started life simply as a property-owning "paper" company that contracted the construction and actual operation to the Cleveland Railway. The Cleveland Railway would operate the branch as an integral part of its system with its own crews and cars while the Vans would pay all construction costs and guarantee any operating losses. The formal contract was finally signed December 5th, but construction work in the flat, open terrain actually started early in the year. It went quickly, and on a cold, snowy December 17, 1913, yellow city streetcars began running out Shaker Boulevard to Fontenay Road, near the east end of the Shaker property. There was still that long grind down Euclid Avenue, but that was temporary, of course. The Van Sweringens assured Shaker property-buyers that the "rapid," as it was commonly known, would eventually aim straight downtown on its own right-of-way, and in their sales contracts, they even guaranteed the service with the right of a refund.[19]

Concurrently, the Vans were working to bring in the proper amenities for their upper-class homeowners. One of the first was the Shaker Heights Country Club, which was opened in May 1915 on land donated by the Vans south of Shaker Boulevard at the east end of the village. At the same time, the Shaker Boulevard car line was extended six-tenths of a mile farther east to Courtland Road, where cars turned south to reach the club. In the meantime, two more real estate companies had appeared—the Van Sweringen Company in February 1913 and the Long Lake Company that April. Also in April, the brothers organized a group of financial backers as the Shaker Heights Syndicate. Out of that collection the Van Sweringen Company became the primary developer for present and fu-

The brothers built this fortress-like mansion on South Park Boulevard in Shaker Heights about 1910, shown here in its original form. In 1924, Philip Small softened its forbidding facade with a Tudor-style remodeling; by then, however, the brothers had moved to Daisy Hill, leaving it mostly the domain of their two unmarried sisters, Edith and Carrie.
Cleveland Public Library

The Ideal Suburb • 25

ture suburban properties; to head it the Vans picked Ben Jenks, by then their closest and most trusted personal friend.[20]

These were the germs of the corporate complexity that became another Van Sweringen characteristic. But the ruling trait was the constant reaching out to something new before the last project was finished. "O. P. was never happier than when exploring new territory," Jenks's wife Daisy later reminisced, "going over dirt roads far from the main highways. He was often brought home by strangers, his machine mired in the mud or left in care of a nearby farmer."[21]

By then, too, they had gathered up a goodly amount of the Kingsbury Run property needed for their rapid transit link. But finding financing for such a project was more difficult than suburban real estate. Even in this era, urban transit was generally not considered a very lucrative business, and their high construction expense made rapid transit lines even more questionable. The brothers probably never expected to make money strictly from hauling people, but they strongly believed that such a service was essential both to the success of their suburban development and their more nebulous downtown commercial plans. So their Cleveland & Youngstown Railroad remained a phantom, still awaiting the opportunity.

That opportunity came surprisingly soon. And when it came, it turned out to be an opportunity which would yank their careers into a new and startling direction.

Three
Mr. Smith Sells a Farm

It was almost a chance meeting.

By early 1913, the Van Sweringens were beginning to make tangible progress. They had just moved across the Public Square from the Williamson Building to larger offices on the top floor of the newly completed Marshall Building, directly across the street from the spot on which they planned some day to build their traction-terminal, hotel, and office-building complex. Out in the Heights, work was well underway on the first small rapid transit segment along Shaker Boulevard. And although their original Shaker Land Company allotments were still far from filled, their land agents were busy secretively picking up large quantities of farm property to the immediate east and south to expand the community which was forming in their minds. (In a careful strategy to conceal their plans and thus keep prices low, they arranged to have the purchases made in a variety of other names, including that of Ben Jenks. Also, they often delayed recording their deeds so that their activities would not all show up at once.)[1]

They had also picked up more remote country property for their own use as a spot for weekend relaxation and business entertainment. In December 1911, they bought a 25-acre farm at the northeast corner of S. O. M. Center² and Old Kinsman Roads about six and a half miles farther east from the center of the Shaker development. The Jenkses were put in charge of the land and farmhouse; in fact, the deed was recorded in Ben Jenks's name. They first called it Orman Farm, blending their two first names, but soon settled on Daisy Hill—whether for Daisy Jenks or the floral environment, or both, was never certain. Characteristically, they never explained.

As always with O. P., twenty-five acres was only the beginning, and he was soon at work expanding the Daisy Hill property. Across Kinsman (later Old Kinsman) Road was another farm which had been owned by Harry Chapman, an ailing railroader who died soon after buying it in 1910. Chapman's widow Caroline inherited the farm but moved to Cleveland, giving O. P. his opportunity. He contacted Caroline Chapman, who told him that her brother, who now lived in New York, was handling her affairs but that he was expected in Cleveland the next week and might see O. P. then.³

Her brother turned out to be a railroad executive named Alfred H. Smith. The 50-year-old Smith was a native Clevelander and, like the Vans, he had been pushed out of the nest early. His father died when he was 14, and he was forced to find work quickly to support the family. Just before his 15th birthday, he took a job as a messenger downtown at the Lake Shore & Michigan Southern Railway's (LS&MS) big brick headquarters building on West 3rd Street and St. Clair Avenue. Railroading in those days was not particular about education, and an aggressive young man could move fast in the growing industry. Bright, supremely energetic, and charismatic, Smith moved faster than most; when O. P. met him in 1913, he was senior vice president of Vanderbilt's lordly New York Central system—which owned the LS&MS, among other things—and effectively was running the railroad for its president, William C. Brown, who was increasingly handicapped by deafness. Less than a year later, he would step into the president's job himself.⁴

Alfred H. Smith in his charming mode.
New York Central photo, H. H. Harwood, Jr., collection

O. P. usually was not a haggler and always tried to pay a fair price. "I closed the deal in less than three minutes" he later recalled. Three minutes it may have been, but for the Van Sweringens, the aftereffects were cosmic and lasting.

Smith was forceful and sometimes profane (one New York Central official later sarcastically remarked that he had gotten

28 • Invisible Giants

where he was by outshouting everyone else) but could be charming as needed. More important, he was also perceptive and fully as visionary as O. P. Van Sweringen. Some kind of chemical reaction occurred as the two intuitively took to each other. Smith did not leave right away.[5]

As an old Clevelander himself, Smith was impressed by the brothers' expansive plans and the progress they were making. He was much more directly interested in their rapid transit project and their somewhat misty ideas for a Public Square terminal, which he already knew something about. He also may have spotted something in the bright, ambitious, but reserved and circumspect O. P. That last quality was something he needed.

At the time, Smith had much on his mind. Freight and passenger traffic on his New York Central system was burgeoning, and the railroad was struggling to handle it all with obsolete facilities. Cleveland was a special sore point; its passenger station and its freight terminal facilities desperately needed to be replaced with modern, high-capacity structures at better locations. By Smith's calculations, Cleveland's population had grown almost 300 percent since 1890, and as of 1913, its freight business was increasing at a rate of 7 percent a year—and as the dominant railroad in town, the New York Central was absorbing most of the new business. Cleveland was also one of the system's most critical bottlenecks. Four main-line routes converged here, reaching New York, Chicago, Cincinnati, Indianapolis, and St. Louis, plus a newly opened route to Youngstown and Pittsburgh. Of the seven railroad companies reaching the city, the Central operated the two oldest and best located—the Lake Shore & Michigan Southern and the Cleveland, Chicago, Cincinnati & St. Louis (which, mercifully, everyone called simply the "Big Four"). In addition, it controlled a third company, a secondary main-line railroad most familiarly known as the Nickel Plate Road. But its facilities for handling what looked like an ever-expanding load were antiquated, one of them spectacularly so.

Worst was the passenger station situation. Cleveland's principal passenger station, known as the Union Depot, stood close to the lakefront at West 9th Street, about six blocks northwest of the Public Square. Used by the Central's LS&MS and Big Four lines and the Pennsylvania Railroad, it was a dingy, vastly overcrowded stone hulk that had been completed in 1866. Shortly after its completion, the Union Depot was comfortably handling twenty-nine trains a day under its eight-track fortress-like train shed. By 1916, the two New York Central subsidiaries were pushing about sixty trains a

The bane of Alfred H. Smith and all Clevelanders was the moth-eaten, overcrowded 1866 Union Depot. At one point, a city businessman erected a huge billboard near its entrance that proclaimed to new arrivals "DON'T JUDGE THIS TOWN BY THIS DEPOT." Cleveland Union Terminals Co., John A. Rehor collection

day through it, and the Pennsylvania was contributing thirty-five—at least ninety-five trains in all, not counting the almost constant switching movements needed to shuffle cars from train to train and move empty equipment in and out. All that was somehow accomplished on those same eight tracks, a tribute to tight management and much manpower.[6]

Externally, the Union Depot was an aesthetic insult; not only was its post–Civil War architecture unfashionable and darkly forbidding, but by then the train shed had been removed to improve clearances and ventilation, giving it a half-demolished look. For passengers, access was awkward, since the building sat at the lake level and faced a hill leading up to the city's center on high ground. Not surprisingly, Clevelanders passionately hated the Union Depot, and for both image and operating reasons the railroads themselves were anxious to do something about it. Exactly what to do was another question.

While the Union Depot generated the most civic invective and the most railroad-operating headaches, the Central's freight-handling facilities were almost equally bothersome—perhaps more so, since freight was more profitable. The Central's two principal Cleveland freight houses were both old, overcrowded, and badly located. The principal one sat on the lakefront at Front Street, just west of the reviled Union Depot; the other was some distance south in the Cuyahoga River "Flats" area. Besides their capacity problems, the two shared a serious commercial handicap: They sat on low river ground and lake-level ground, while most of the freight customers were located near the city's commercial center on the plateau above. In the days when local freight drayage was still heavily horse-powered, hauling heavily loaded wagons up and down the hills was costly. Eight years before, the Pennsylvania Railroad—the Central's archrival—built a new freight house on high ground at Davenport Street and, according to Smith's figures, had already increased its local business by 600 percent.[7]

These were not the end of Smith's Cleveland problems; among other things, the lakefront itself was generally a congested operating nightmare for both the Central and the Pennsylvania, which had a tangle of tracks crisscrossing one another to reach lakefront docks (including the Pennsylvania's busy coal and ore transshipping docks) and local industries and to carry some through-freight movements. But creatively resolving the passenger and freight-station situation would relieve much of the pressure.

At the time, the Union Depot replacement finally seemed to be on its way, albeit slowly. Its location plan had its genesis in the "City Beautiful" vision of the 1893 Columbian Exposition, Coincidentally, Cleveland was then also facing the need for large new public buildings of all types—federal, county, and city offices; courts; and a public library. Agitation began soon afterward to develop a unified plan to group these buildings around a wide mall near the Public Square and design them along harmonious neoclassical lines.

The "City Beautiful" concept and Cleveland's legendary reformer Tom L. Johnson were made for one another. Almost immediately after he was elected mayor in 1901, the zealous Johnson got the idea moving, commissioning the Columbian Exposition's chief architect, Daniel H. Burnham, to repeat his Chicago triumphs for Cleveland. Burnham's group went to work and within a year produced a grandiose plan to condemn 101 acres of rundown property northeast of the Public Square and transform the area into a City Beautiful on Lake

Erie, with an ordered grouping of new Beaux Arts–style government and civic buildings arrayed along a broad mall which would stretch north toward the lake. Anchoring the mall at its north end was to be the new railroad station, which would be located only about four blocks east of the old Union Depot on the same lakefront railroad lines. Like its predecessor, it would primarily serve the two New York Central subsidiaries and the Pennsylvania, but it was hoped that at least some of Cleveland's four lesser railroads would also use it.

Although a tired and burned-out Johnson lost a bitter election in 1909 and died two years later, his plan continued to hold Cleveland's imagination and energy. The federal building was completed in 1911, followed by the Cuyahoga County Court House in 1912 and the Cleveland City Hall in 1916. (The public library followed in 1925, and two sections of the Public Auditorium were built in 1922 and 1929.) But the New York Central's participation in the mall-lakefront station plan was delayed by a complex and long-running property dispute with the city dating back to 1893. By the time Smith and the Vans met in 1913, this was finally being resolved and Smith had begun negotiations with Mayor Newton D. Baker (a Johnson protégé) and the Pennsylvania to set the financial terms for the long-awaited new station. Smith probably had his private doubts about the location, which posed some nasty operating problems for him, but for the moment he kept his peace.[8]

In the meantime, however, Smith was determined to resolve his freight-terminal problem quickly. This seemed simpler to accomplish than the lakefront passenger station, since it did not involve financial negotiations with the city or dealing with other railroads. But some creativity was needed to locate and build the facility, which would also require a completely new access route and a support yard. To Smith, the Van Sweringens' planned rapid transit route along Kingsbury Run looked like an ideal answer. A year earlier, in 1912, the Central had completed a freight-only bypass line which swung in an arc around the southern part of the city. Built under the name of the Cleveland Short Line Railroad (but best known as the Belt Line), it crossed the Van Sweringens' projected line near East 91st Street and Buckeye Road. By building a three-mile branch partly alongside the rapid transit route from the Cleveland Short Line crossing, Smith could reach the city's commercial heart from its backside and build the largest and best-located freight terminal of any Cleveland railroad. (Ultimately the site selected was at East 15th Street and Orange Avenue.)

Obviously, a joint project between the New York Central and the Van Sweringens would be less costly for both parties. But sharing the costs of land acquisition and construction was only one of Smith's motives, and probably the lesser one. For one thing, he was fearful of political roadblocks that would stand in the way of anything done in the Central's name. As Cleveland's dominant railroad, it was not universally loved in the city, and the legal tangle delaying the new lakefront passenger station project further generated political irritation. A large freight house and its adjacent expanse of open public delivery tracks and driveways inevitably required street closings and neighborhood disruption, ensuring more political opposition. Also, whether it was true or not, the Central name implied great wealth, which inevitably translated into inflated land prices—especially since Smith envisioned a high-capacity facility that would require a goodly amount of in-town property.

On the other hand, a project promoted by a pair of independent local real estate operators as a by-product of their rapid transit line provided a passable cover. And since the Vans' Cleveland & Youngstown had a broad railroad charter rather than simply a street railway franchise, it could reasonably build railroad freight facilities on its own, conceivably as a real estate promotion.

Smith may or may not have had all this in mind when he met with O. P. to sell his sister's farm, but if he did not, the idea formed quickly. Their meeting promptly led to looking at maps of the Van Sweringens' projected rapid transit route, which then led into an auto trip to look over part of the terrain. Before leaving to catch his train, Smith asked O. P. to put together data and drawings for rights-of-way and new land acquisition. "I soon learned Mr. Smith was a fast mover," O. P. later noted; Smith expected the material by the time he came back through Cleveland a few days later.[9]

Indeed, Smith wasted no time; he seldom did. After his local managers and engineers reviewed and refined the Vans' plans, a contract was put together in August 1913. In essence, the Vans' Cleveland & Youngstown Railroad (C&Y) would build a four-track line between the Cleveland Short Line connection and East 34th Street, with two tracks for the rapid transit and two for freight. The Central, however, would provide all the needed funds with advances to the C&Y, which would later be repaid after expenses were allocated between the two projects. Once the final accounting was complete, the C&Y would then turn over the freight line to the Central. To further reinforce the project's "independent" image, a group of about thirty-five local entrepreneurs and investors formed themselves into the Glenville Syndicate to acquire land in the area of the planned freight terminal. This group agreed to be bought out at a specified profit when the project was finished; ultimately, the Central would own it outright. Neither Van Sweringen was directly involved in the syndicate, but several of their close associates were among the heaviest investors, including Joseph Nutt, the Hayden-Miller partnership, Charles Bradley, and Parmely Herrick. Nutt and Warren Hayden managed the operation.[10]

As anticipated, the joint project got off to a contentious start. The city council had to approve the street closings and other aspects of the freight terminal portion, and, correctly suspecting a New York Central subterfuge, a minority of councilmen led by Alex Bernstein attempted to stop it. Failing in that, the opponents managed to put the issue on the ballot for the November 2, 1915, general elections. In the process, O. P. quite innocently explained to Mayor Newton Baker and the city council that the new freight terminal would be used by "various railroads," the New York Central among them; he neglected to mention his agreement with Smith. In the end, the electorate approved the project by almost a 3-to-1 majority. The new lakefront passenger station was also overwhelmingly approved in the same election.[11]

Although O. P. later stated that "I always felt Mr. Smith traded too fast for us," the net effect of the joint project was that the Central initially underwrote the financing of the Vans' rapid transit line between East 91st Street and East 34th Street and, as it turned out, their debt to the Central was never fully repaid.[12]

Perhaps encouraged that the rapid transit project was off dead center, the brothers also started work on their planned Public Square hotel. In September 1915, the hoary Forest City House at the southwest corner of the Square closed its doors after serving for sixty-three years as a center of Cleveland business and social life. Ten months later, the Vans' Terminal Hotels Company subsidiary bought the property, cleared it, and began building the first element of their hoped-for terminal complex, the fourteen-story, 1,000-room Hotel Cleveland. In keeping with their penchant for producing a first-class product, they went outside Cleveland and hired Chicago architects Graham, Burnham & Company to design it. Coincidentally or not, the Graham, Burnham firm was the direct successor of Daniel H. Burnham, designer of Cleveland's civic Group Plan, who had died in 1912. (The company, which shortly thereafter changed its name to Graham, Anderson, Probst & White, would continue to work with the Vans as their Public Square project gradually unfolded.) The granite and terra cotta structure would be the city's newest and, along with the 1912 Hotel Statler, the largest—and would remain so for many years.[13]

Thanks to the joint project and the Central's sub rosa underwriting, Smith got his fine new freight terminal, which finally opened in 1918. The Vans got almost three miles of heavily built, fully grade-separated rapid transit line which now reached as far west as East 34th Street and put them within a mile and a half of the Public Square. The project could be called physically finished when the rapid transit line began operating between Shaker Heights and the Public Square via East 30th Street in April 1920.

But they had hardly seen the last of Alfred H. Smith. By then, in fact, he had opened an entire new world to them.

Four

Mr. Smith Sells a Railroad

The Vans' 1913 deal with A. H. Smith promised to finance their rapid transit route as far west as East 34th Street, and work began the next year. They were still uncertain about how to cover the remaining mile and a half of railway to their planned Public Square terminal, but at 34th Street they were next to the tracks of the Nickel Plate Road, a Buffalo-Cleveland-Chicago railroad controlled by the New York Central but not directly operated by it. In passing through Cleveland from the east, the Nickel Plate swung slightly south of the city's center, then headed northwest in the direction of the Square before turning west again at about East 14th Street to cross the Cuyahoga valley. Its ornate brick-and-stone Cleveland station sat in a smoky gulch west of Broadway near East 14th Street, at the point where the line turned to cross the river.

Between East 34th Street and the Broadway station, the Nickel Plate's line was hung partway down the hillside between the city itself and the Cuyahoga River and was away from streets and other urban obstructions. If they built alongside the railroad through this area, the brothers could gain another three-quarters of a mile of grade-separated right-of-way in their march toward the Square—about half the remaining distance. It was not much in mileage, but it offered a relatively cheap way to get through an area that otherwise would require very expensive property acquisition and construction.

While they were pondering their next moves and approaching the Nickel Plate's management, their new friend Mr. Smith was wrestling with a far more serious problem than his Cleveland freight house. Coincidentally, he was also concerned about the Nickel Plate.

The railroad's formal corporate title actually was the New York, Chicago & St. Louis Railroad Company, but from its opening in 1882 to its merger eighty-two years later, nobody ever called it anything but the Nickel Plate Road. The curious nickname dated back to the railroad's earliest days; being more memorable and forthright than the full corporate name, it instantly caught on and stuck. It is just as well, for the Nickel Plate went nowhere near New York or St. Louis. It actually consisted of a single 523-mile line between Buffalo and Chicago via Cleveland and Fort Wayne, Indiana.[1]

The Nickel Plate was created in early 1881 and was completed in the spectacularly short time of twenty months by a group of financial speculators during the golden era of railroad expansion, when every town wanted at least one railroad. It was also the time when the dominant companies in the East and Midwest—Vanderbilt's New York Central system, the Pennsylvania Railroad, and the weaker Baltimore & Ohio—were consolidating their power while trying to fend off powerful poachers such as Jay Gould. A dubious by-product of this heated competitive environment was the creation of speculative railroads, some of which blatantly paralleled a large established road with the hope that either the victim or one of the victim's competitors would then buy it. The Nickel Plate was widely thought to be the result of one such scheme; it duplicated the route of Vanderbilt's Lake Shore & Michigan Southern Railway between its two terminals and hung right alongside it between Buffalo and Cleveland.

William H. Vanderbilt capitulated quickly; three days after the Nickel Plate opened for business, he surreptitiously bought a 53 percent controlling interest for $7.2 million, giving the original promoters what they calculated was a profit of 75 percent. While he doubtless wished he could immediately dismantle it, that was impossible from almost every viewpoint. It was not even politically prudent to put his

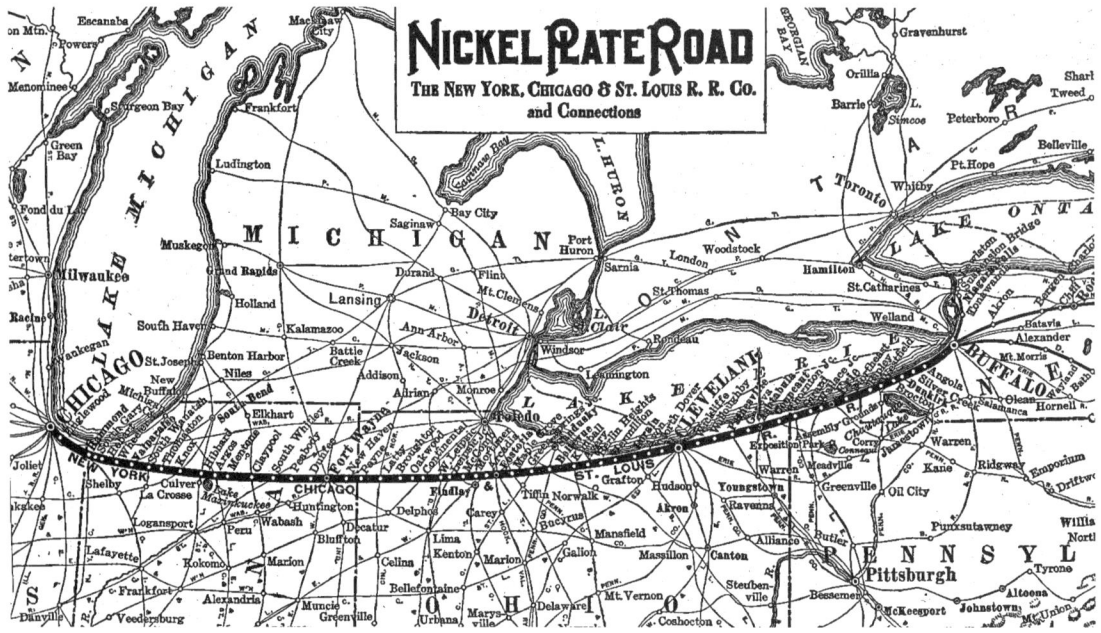

new purchase directly under Vanderbilt system management, much less to merge it with the Lake Shore & Michigan Southern or some other New York Central subsidiary. So the Nickel Plate remained more or less autonomous, with its own management and its locomotives and cars resolutely lettered "Nickel Plate Road." Since 1898, it had been headed by William H. "Paddy" Caniff, a former LS&MS general manager who had fostered a high level of employee pride and harmony but was careful to do nothing that would nettle his bosses in New York.[2]

Although Vanderbilt sneered that it was a shoddy property, the Nickel Plate actually was well located and well built; its route was generally straight and its grades were easy. But as a relative latecomer in its territory, it had to struggle to develop on-line freight business; most large freight shippers and receivers were already located on the well-entrenched LS&MS, and although industry was expanding dramatically along the route, the Vanderbilts were hardly motivated to steer new plants to the Nickel Plate. Nor were they much interested in upgrading their unwanted orphan; the Nickel Plate remained mostly a single-track railroad with small yards and obsolete facilities as the LS&MS blossomed into a four-track main line with constantly expanding yards and new shops.[3]

Making the best of what it had, the Nickel Plate quickly carved out a niche for itself as a fast freight line, specializing in expediting fresh meat shipments from Chicago to eastward connections at Buffalo. It made little attempt to compete with the New York Central–LS&MS route for volume passenger business and satisfied itself with two comfortable but rather leisurely "expresses" and one all-stops local each way between Buffalo and Chicago.

Vanderbilt had bought his Nickel Plate control in the carefree days before federal regulation and antitrust legislation. In fact he and his father, the old Commodore, had managed to gather in all three direct-rail routes between the important Buffalo gateway and Chicago. In addition to the Lake Shore & Michigan Southern and the Nickel Plate along Lake Erie's south shore, the New York Central also controlled the Michigan Central–Canada Southern route through southern Ontario, Detroit, and central Michigan. Of the three, the LS&MS was the primary main line, and by 1914 had been rebuilt to the point where it was one of the finest railroads

The Nickel Plate was basically a flatlands railroad, but east of Cleveland it was forced to hurdle several deep river valleys on spectacular trestles. In this 1915 view, which is typical of the early Van Sweringen days, a Ten-Wheeler pilots an eastbound passenger train over Ashtabula Creek in eastern Ohio.
John B. Corns collection

anywhere, operating a straight, fast, mostly four-track line that was constantly busy. (And in fact, in 1914 Smith completed a difficult and expensive full merger of the LS&MS into the New York Central.) The Michigan Central was an important secondary route, particularly for reaching Detroit and the rapidly industrializing central and southern Michigan area. The Nickel Plate was clearly the most redundant route; it was useful primarily for overflow traffic in times when business was heavy and the other lines congested.

But by 1914, the political environment was emphatically different. Somehow the Central's effective monopoly of the Buffalo-Chicago corridor had survived the 1890 Sherman Antitrust Act, but Woodrow Wilson's Clayton Act promised to end that happy state of affairs. In that year, Smith received the inevitable notice from the Department of Justice questioning the legality of controlling so many more or less parallel routes. He was not specifically told to divest himself of the Nickel Plate, but he knew that something had to go and that the Nickel Plate would be the one.[4]

Smith's dilemma was an especially nasty one. Although he dutifully went through the motions of defending the Central's control, he knew it was probably futile and that he would be forced to sell the railroad. But to whom? Despite the Nickel Plate's dubious origins and the Central's benign neglect, it was a highly strategic route linking the Midwest with eastern markets through its Buffalo gateway, and, of course, it closely paralleled the Central over its entire length. In the hands of any competitor it could be extremely dangerous—and virtually all the likely buyers were competitors.

Worst was the powerful Pennsylvania, which had no main lines in this territory, was ever eager to best the Central wherever it could, and was certainly wealthy enough to pay whatever the price might be. While its president of the moment, Samuel Rea, was not an expansionist in the A. H. Smith mold, the company had an inbred passion for dominance and a peerless record of achieving it. Only slightly less worrisome was the Delaware, Lackawanna & Western, whose main line linked Buffalo with New York Harbor. The Lackawanna was also one of the New York Central's major connections at Buffalo, and a Lackawanna–Nickel Plate combination would take that business off the Central and at the same time create a strong new east-west trunk line which could do even more damage. And, thanks to its booming anthracite coal business, the Lackawanna's treasury was also ample enough. Investors outside the railroad business were no less suspect, since they could easily turn out to be speculators who would eventually sell out to some empire-builder or otherwise destabilize the situation.

In short, the options were all bad. Yet he had to do something quickly; as it turned out, he had only about a year's breathing time. In mid-December of 1915, Wilson's attorney general, Thomas Gregory, sent him the official notice that the Central's control of three paralleling routes violated the Clayton Act. But by then Smith was working with his potential buyer. It was typical of Smith's imagination that he had found a reasonably tolerable solution—his friends, the Cleveland real estate operators.

So far, he had been happy with O. P. Van Sweringen's deft and competent handling of the delicate freight-station project —and with his ability to hold confidences and say as little as possible. More than that, a personal bond had somehow developed between the driving up-from-the-ranks railroader and the quietly creative—but also quietly aggressive—young O. P.; both of them thought large in their own ways, and both got things done. The brothers were solid builders who invested for the long range rather than speculators. They were also ambitious and might want to stretch beyond their Cleveland real estate world. And, although it was perhaps a stretch, they did have a reason for being interested in the railroad: They needed a short piece of Nickel Plate right-of-way for their rapid transit. Given the right incentives, the two brothers could take the Nickel Plate off his hands and, most important, keep it independent. True, it would need to be a more effective competitor than before, but there was also that personal relationship—and with it trust that the new owners would do nothing to seriously harm the Central.

It must be stressed at this point that although Smith played an increasingly important role in the Van Sweringens' careers over the next nine years, and although he was doubtless the dominant personality and senior mentor (significantly, to Smith, O. P. was always "Van"; to O. P., Smith was always "Mr. Smith"), it is nonetheless difficult to answer the critical questions of which of them first broached an idea or who persuaded whom to take some action. Many of these actions involved great political sensitivities or business relationships that were best left undisclosed. Much was handled privately, and the Van Sweringens were nothing if not private. Telephone calls and personal meetings often preceded any formal correspondence. So while the written record is usually not untruthful, too often it does not tell the full story.

In this case, the surviving written record implies that O. P. Van Sweringen made the first move. In February 1915, he formally wrote Smith asking for information about the Nickel Plate, including a possible sale price. O. P. himself later testified, with the same innocence he displayed in the freight-terminal case, "We heard rumors to the effect that the Nickel Plate holdings of the New York Central would probably be sold due to the act relating to parallel and competing lines. This led to the thought that if we could buy the railroad, we could provide excellent high-level freight facilities for it, [and] later give it access to a large [new] warehousing and commercial district . . . which was then much needed. The ownership also would enable us to put some added revenue on the Nickel Plate for extra use of its right-of-way [for] interurban and rapid transit." The public read a simpler version; the story took hold that the brothers casually stumbled into buying the railroad simply because they needed that short stretch of right-of-way for their Shaker Rapid line.[5]

There was some truth in all that, but it was hardly the whole story. Everything O. P. mentioned could have been easily accomplished without the huge expense and risk of buying an entire railroad and entering a business they knew nothing about. The evidence is strong that Smith initiated the idea and that he was very persuasive, offering extremely liberal terms and the promise of a good professional manager to run it. And the railroad's potential was a selling point in itself; under competent independent management, the brothers would have little to lose and much to gain.

A year of thought, calculations, and negotiations followed the first formal correspondence between O.P. and Smith. Finally, in February 1916, Smith set a price of $8.5 million for the Central's Nickel Plate holdings, which amounted to 51 percent of the railroad's stock—enough for unquestioned control. The terms were as liberal as he could make them: $2 million in cash and the remaining $6.5 million in $650,000 (plus interest) installments spread out over fifteen years. The first installment would not be due for five years. The Central officially accepted the Vans' offer on April 13th and set a consummation date in July.[6]

While the brothers were now beginning to prosper, they lacked the $2 million down payment. Tapping their real estate assets for credit was sticky, since other investors were involved in these; the Gratwick group in Buffalo was especially reluctant. Smith obliged by introducing them to Thomas W. Lamont of J. P. Morgan, the Central's banker. In the end, though, O. P. sensed that the New York bankers might take control themselves, and he went home to work through local sources. The brothers then negotiated a short-term loan from Cleveland's Guardian Savings & Trust Company, which gave them the needed immediate cash and allowed time to set up more permanent financing structure. The Nickel Plate—or at least 51 percent of it—became theirs on July 5, 1916.[7]

Whatever their original motives, the Van Sweringens were now in the railroad business and obligated to make a good showing. Yet they had neither the experience nor the desire to manage the Nickel Plate directly themselves. Unfortunately, however, the railroad was coming to them with no ready-made top management. Its president, William H. Caniff, was 69 and ready for retirement; its other executives were New York Central officers in New York. As part of his package, Smith offered them one of his own promising executives, a 48-year-old vice president in Chicago named John J. Bernet.

It was an interesting choice. Like Smith, Bernet began humbly with a limited education and quickly worked his way up through the ranks of operating management. The son of a Swiss immigrant blacksmith, he grew up mostly in Farnham, New York, a small town on Lake Erie midway between Buffalo and Dunkirk, and spent his teen years working with his father at the smithy. Railroading was a rapidly growing industry and offered good opportunities for bright, hard-working young men, and Bernet was bright, capable, and certainly hard-working. Fortuitously, Farnham was located on the Lake Shore & Michigan Southern's (and Nickel Plate's) main line, and in his off-hours he haunted the LS&MS station and learned telegraphy. When he was 21, a full-time telegrapher job opened, and he was off. Six years later, he was a train dispatcher, and then he moved meteorically; by 1906, the 38-year-old Bernet was general superintendent at Cleveland. From there he moved to Chicago, where he was named vice president in 1913. Short and myopic, Bernet was not a commanding figure to look at, but he had a fine analytical mind and vast energy.[8]

It was later claimed that Bernet had been Smith's hand-picked candidate to succeed him; on the other hand, rumors within the Central ranks at the time said that Smith was anxious to rid himself of an irritant. Bernet had an independent streak and was sometimes impulsive; he seldom wasted words, but when he spoke he tended to be direct, if not blunt. Whatever the facts, in 1916 Bernet seemed to be on a shelf. Smith was a very vigorous 53 at the time and obviously nowhere near any pasture. Bernet's title of vice president was prestigious, but the job was actually merely a high-level staff position with no direct authority over operations; its principal function was to represent the Central in its dealings with the multitude of connecting lines in Chicago, many of which were

John J. Bernet was 47 when he gave up his secure New York Central executive position for the uncertainties of the presidency of the Nickel Plate. Frank A. Wrabel collection

headquartered there. To the truly ambitious railroad operating manager, such a position could be a frustrating sidestep out of the stream of command.

While Smith may or may not have liked Bernet, he was perceptive about how his talents could be used and did him an enormous favor. He arranged for Bernet to visit the Vans. Recognizing the uncertainties of the situation, no contract was offered and, in fact, no salary was discussed. But for Bernet it was a chance to run his own railroad with a free hand; even more appealing was the chance to create an outstanding property from a nonentity. He readily took the job.

The sale and Bernet's appointment generated tepid interest within the industry. The principal trade magazine, *Railway Age,* did not even mention the Van Sweringens by name, noting only that the railroad had been sold "to a syndicate of Cleveland bankers." Their names would have meant nothing to *Railway Age* readers anyway. Bernet himself was damned with faint praise: "Mr. Bernet belongs to the class of men whose progress is not spectacular, but who achieves success by great thoroughness and efficiency in every task." A dedicated plodder, in other words. As for the railroad itself, the magazine noted—with some truth—that "at the present time the company is making a fine showing, but the volume of traffic cannot be expected to continue. The road lacks terminals, both at Buffalo and Chicago." Altogether, though, *Railway Age* thought the sale was a good thing.[9]

Bernet moved into the Nickel Plate's Cleveland headquarters on July 17th and set to work with his characteristic energy. With the railroad's management off their minds, Bernet's young bosses now had to scramble to set up the permanent financing of their new acquisition. Their $2 million Guardian Trust loan was strictly an expediency measure to provide the immediate cash to close the deal; it was to be repaid in six months.

For their new venture, the Vans came up with a device which would let them keep their full extent of control with a minimum outlay for themselves—the holding company. The basic concept of a corporation which existed strictly to "hold" the controlling stock of other companies had been around for over forty-five years; one of the first was the Pennsylvania Railroad's Pennsylvania Company in 1870. It was more broadly legalized beginning in 1888 and already had gained national ill fame with J. P Morgan's Northern Securities Company.[10] As with their design of Shaker Heights, the brothers were less original innovators than gifted adaptors and embellishers.

In their hands, the technique later took elaborate forms, but the principle was simple: Outside investors would supply most of the money needed to buy control of companies, they would receive either bonds or preferred stock that assured them an attractive fixed return on their investment, but they would have no voting rights and thus no control of anything. The holding company's common stock—which voted—went primarily to its promoters, who put up relatively little for their shares. The dividends or interest paid to those outside investors would come out of the dividends that the operating company—in this case the railroad—paid into the holding company; what was left from the railroad's dividends after that would go to the holding company's common stockholders. It was a classic early form of what later financial writers would call a leveraged buyout. The downside, of course, was that the holding company had to pay the outside investors their assured return—which meant in turn that operating companies had to feed enough dividends into it to cover that return. If they did not, then the investors usually had the right to take over themselves.[11]

But in a growing and prospering economy, seemingly everyone won. The outside investors who basically supported the system got a safe, fixed return—and as the dividends of the operating companies increased, those who controlled the holding company kept a greater proportion of them.

Thus appeared the Nickel Plate Securities Corporation on December 4, 1916. As designed by the Vans and their close associates, this holding company would take over all their Nickel Plate stock, the obligation to pay off the $2 million Guardian Loan, and the future installments and interest owed the Central. To do so, it issued two classes of stock: preferred and voting common. The preferred stock, which went primarily to the Vans' friends and their friends, would return up to 7 percent, depending on the Securities Company's profitability. Seventy percent of the common stock, which carried all the control, went to the Van Sweringens at no cash cost. The Vans were obligated, however, to buy $520,000 of the preferred issue as their investment in the enterprise.[12]

Said another way, their full control of the Nickel Plate and their $8.5 million purchase obligation theoretically cost them only $520,000. (And as it eventually worked out, the brothers actually paid just $355,509 of their own funds.) Characteristically, they chose to borrow their $520,000 from the Guardian bank—and, also characteristically, part of that loan was still on the bank's books twenty years later. By then the bank itself was closed, a victim of its overenthusiastic loans.[13]

The Nickel Plate adventure not only put the brothers in a new business but it brought together all the essentials of the Van Sweringen method—a combination of sometimes frighteningly risky means to achieve solid, long-lasting ends.

Minimizing the brothers' personal financial stake while keeping full control of the various projects and operations was central to their method. The means were loans, the underwriting of projects by others (as with the New York Central freight terminal), and the latest and most promising method, the leveraged holding company. All took creativity and skill to execute properly—plus a liberal amount of nerve, since the projects promised to take years to reach a full payoff and required quantities of nurturing capital beforehand. O. P. was the skilled creator—outwardly quiet, confident, and nerveless. M. J., upon whom many of the more mundane execution chores fell, more clearly betrayed the strains of the constant but ever-changing tightrope act.

That act was made chancier by another Van Sweringen trait. Typically the brothers first entered a business or project with only a vague goal and no specific ultimate plan. The Shaker development had started almost willy-nilly; it took about eight years before the intricately thought-out elements of the planned community coalesced. They had picked up the first Public Square property for their terminal in 1909, but at the time they bought the Nickel Plate seven years later, the form of the terminal was still uncertain and changing regularly. And there seemed to be no immediate sense of how the Nickel Plate itself would be developed beyond possibly providing some freight and warehousing facilities in Cleveland and using that three-quarter-mile stretch of its right-of-way for their Shaker Heights rapid transit line. Their savior again was O. P.'s creativity, supported by some first-class management and guidance.

And that was the critical Van Sweringen characteristic: They were able to pick the best people for a given job and then let them do the job without interference. John Bernet was the best example; not only was he given a free hand, but wherever possible he was given the resources to remake the Nickel Plate into the efficient carrier he envisioned. Granted, he had to accommodate the Vans' financial needs—most notably by paying regular dividends and, on occasion, helping to finance new acquisitions—but Bernet and the brothers both believed in spending liberally to build up a property.

During the Nickel Plate deal still another trait also solidified. The Van Sweringens had now edged into the national transportation scene, but they remained Clevelanders and always would. Over the past several years they had gradually formed a small, tight circle of local associates which endured as the heart of their organization for the rest of their careers. Soon enough Wall Street would enter their world and become an ever-growing presence, but the two shy bachelor brothers and their inner Cleveland circle firmly controlled things.

By then that inner council had coalesced into a tight handful, consisting primarily of Joseph Nutt, Charles Bradley, investment bankers Warren Hayden and Otto Miller, banker John Sherwin, Sr., and lawyer Frank Ginn. Nutt, described as a "handsome man with finely chiseled features"—every inch the distinguished, confidence-inspiring financier—was 42 at the time of the Nickel Plate purchase and president of the Citizens Savings and Loan Company. Four years later, he would merge Citizens into the newly created Union Trust Company, reputedly the country's fifth largest trust company at the time, and became Union Trust's president under chairman John Sherwin. Through his rather dubious dual role of bank executive and Van Sweringen stockholder, Nutt became the brothers' primary pipeline to local financing. The energetic, capable young Charles Bradley (he was 31 in 1916) was also a vice president and a large stockholder in the Union Commerce National Bank, one of the city's largest. It too would merge into Union Trust, and Bradley then moved over as a vice president of that institution.[14]

A young and handsome Joseph R. Nutt, a leading Cleveland banker and the closest of Van Sweringen partners.
Cleveland Press Collection, Cleveland State University

On April 6, 1917, the United States finally was formally forced into the European war. In Cleveland, O. P. and M. J. were contemplating an intimidating array of expensive projects in progress, most of which were nowhere near maturity. From their offices on the 12th floor of the Marshall Building they could look across Superior Avenue at the construction progress of their new Hotel Cleveland, but the adjacent rail and rapid transit terminal and office building was still in an unshaped limbo, its prospective tenants uncertain. Out in the Heights, their Shaker development was beginning to evolve, but the critical rapid transit link to downtown was uncompleted. And now they had a mediocre, medium-sized railroad which had promise but needed work.

Five
Shaping Solid Forms

Ownership of the Nickel Plate immediately brought the Vans and Bernet financial, physical, and commercial challenges. In order to make the financing of the leveraged holding company work, the railroad had to produce at least enough dividends to cover the interest payments to the Nickel Plate Securities Corporation's preferred stockholders, and it had to do so quickly. Not surprisingly, the Nickel Plate resumed paying full dividends in January 1917 after two years of somewhat erratic payouts; it now needed to stay on solid financial ground and grow.

Doing so was not so easy. The Nickel Plate had been born with some congenital weaknesses, and the Central had done little to overcome them. Its physical facilities were limited; it was a single-track railroad with short passing sidings and small yards. And although most of its locomotives were fairly new, they were of obsolescent designs unsuited for heavy main-line hauling. So while the railroad was busy enough, its short trains made it inefficient and expensive to run.

More worrisome over the longer range was its ability to generate new business. The Nickel Plate of 1916 consisted of only a single Chicago–Buffalo line that had no traffic-gathering branches and few industries located directly on its own tracks. For the past three decades, it had slogged along mostly by moving business between connections at Chicago and other connections at Buffalo. With its main line relatively uncluttered by yards and industrial switching, it offered a fast service and thus got a share of premium shipments, such as meat, that might have gone over the New York Central. But this was a fickle kind of traffic; without plants on its line, freight customers had no direct ties to the Nickel Plate and could easily be wooed away by someone else. And without much traffic that it could control, it had little bargaining power with its connections, who could feed it or not depending on their own self-interest.

Bernet proved to be anything but a plodder. His previous employer was an industry leader in collecting operating talent and developing locomotives, and he moved quickly to bring the New York Central style to the Nickel Plate in the form of young, talented Central men. In October 1916, he brought in an old Central associate, 37-year-old A. R. "Gus" Ayres, as his motive power superintendent; a month later, he persuaded a fellow Lake Shore & Michigan Southern alumnus, Charles E. Denney (also 37), to serve as his top engineering assistant. He picked well in both cases. Ayres became the Nickel Plate's general manager in 1927 and specialized in moving fast freights with cutting-edge locomotive technology; by 1920, Denney was its operating vice president. He soon moved into the select circle of senior Van Sweringen railroad operating managers, ending his career as president of the Vans' Erie Railroad.[1]

A quick and fairly easy way to boost the railroad's profitability was to move longer freight trains faster. Ayres immediately went to work to upgrade the Nickel Plate's teakettle motive power. Shamelessly borrowing the Central's latest locomotive designs, he bought thirty-five high-capacity Mikado freight engines and a fleet of modern switchers. At the same time, passing sidings were lengthened, an intensive rail replacement program was started, and some bridges were upgraded.[2]

A bit of the Van Sweringen personal touch quickly showed up on the railroad as well. A project to eliminate two-and-one-half-miles of street grade crossings through Cleveland's built-up West Side had been waiting in the wings since 1910 and was finally started in 1915—paid for mostly through a city bond issue. As it got underway, the Vans made sure that the

Two clean-cut young aspirers: O. P. (left) and M. J. (right) somewhere in their 30s.
Cleveland Public Library

right-of-way and street overpasses along the route were designed to accommodate two additional tracks for a future rapid transit line through that populous part of town.³

The war brought the Nickel Plate a healthy new rush of business but also led to some severe wobbling of the Vans' financial tightrope—and some frustrating delays on their various building projects.

Unfortunately, the country's railroad system—which was made up of hundreds of private companies with widely varying financial strength and physical resources—was not prepared to handle the sudden and huge influx of troops and war materiel heading east for overseas shipping. Many railroads had been starved for new capital and lacked sufficient equipment and yard capacity. Nor could the railroads be managed as a unified, coordinated network. Intensely aggravating their problems was a chaotic governmental shipment priority system in which virtually everything was supposed to be given special handling over everything else. Freight-car shortages became acute, terminal yards on the east coast became paralyzed, and the entire system verged on collapse.

A harsh early winter was the last straw, and on December 28, 1917, President Woodrow Wilson issued an emergency executive proclamation temporarily nationalizing every railroad. On that date, the United States Railroad Administration materialized out of thin air with the mandate to lease virtually all of the country's major railroads and manage the clotted tangle as a single system. To head the agency, Wilson picked his treasury secretary, political backer and son-in-law William Gibbs McAdoo, a former business entrepreneur and builder of the Hudson & Manhattan rapid transit lines in New York. McAdoo set up three operating regions and, knowing A. H. Smith and his abilities, put him in charge of the East, where most of the problems were. Smith became the government overseer of all the railroads east of Chicago and the Mississippi and north of the Potomac and Ohio Rivers—including his own New York Central, his major rivals the Pennsylvania and the Baltimore & Ohio Railroads, and a mass of medium-sized and smaller lines such as the Nickel Plate.[4]

Temporary though it was to be, government operation suddenly created a crisis for the brothers. Their Nickel Plate Securities Corporation depended on its regular injections of railroad dividends to pay its preferred stockholders and the interest owed to the New York Central on its installment notes. But now the Railroad Administration controlled dividend payments and held them up, and there was a real danger of losing the railroad through a default. O. P. pleaded with William K. Vanderbilt, Jr., the Central's acting president during Smith's absence, for forbearance on a $130,000 payment due July 1, 1918, and managed to get a postponement. The problem dragged on through the rest of the year, however, and in desperation, the Vans finally arranged a temporary $210,000 loan through their Cleveland associates, primarily Joseph Nutt's Citizens Savings Bank. By 1920, all had stabilized and the loan was repaid.[5]

While his bosses were sweating through their financial crisis, John Bernet had to put up with some operating and motive-power frustrations the wartime Railroad Administration imposed on him. Yet the Nickel Plate was one of the few railroads to make a profit for the government during the war and was a heavy troop carrier. With peacetime and the return of the railroads to private hands on March 1, 1920, Bernet returned to full form; at the end of the year he could report a $3.7 million net income and note that operating revenues had increased two and a half times over 1915 even though there had been no significant increase in freight tonnage. Thanks to Bernet and his cadre, "Van Sweringen management" soon carried the same connotation of quality in the railroad industry that Van Sweringen planning and construction implied for their real estate creations.[6]

At the same time, one small corner of the Nickel Plate's line through Cleveland was seeing another kind of activity. While the Van Sweringens' expanding world was now split two ways—between railroading and real estate—their real estate roots were hardly neglected. So as Bernet started rebuilding the Nickel Plate, their rapid transit, downtown, and Shaker Heights projects slowly began taking form. As the railroad's unpretentious passenger trains passed the area around East 37th Street, its riders could catch a glimpse of construction work alongside the tracks for the rapid transit route to Shaker Heights, much of which was being built through the auspices of the New York Central.

To the observant, the little bit they could see was impressive—a substantial girder bridge over the Nickel Plate built to carry not two but four electric railway tracks. It was another typical Van Sweringen touch; although the Shaker line scarcely needed that kind of capacity, the brothers were careful to provide for the future. That future was, as usual, indistinct, but it might include interurban cars from places such as Akron, Painesville, Chardon, and Chagrin Falls; it might also include rapid transit trains from East Cleveland, following alongside the Nickel Plate right-of-way.

What those Nickel Plate passengers could not see farther to the east was even more impressive: a heavily built line spanning streets and railroads, including a massive multiple-arch concrete viaduct at East 90th Street and Holton Avenue—followed by a deep, mile-long cut through shale and sandstone as the route ascended the hill up to the Heights. At the top of the hill and for three miles beyond, the pioneering Shaker Village homeowners could watch a fury of construction crews cutting through new roads, grading land, laying sewers, setting up electric poles, and laying tracks for electric railway extensions that would soon form a real rapid transit system.

The original 1,366-acre Shaker tract had been almost tripled to 4,000 acres; it now extended east to Warrensville Road and south to Kinsman Road. In this vast former farmland, the Pease Company engineers laid out a revised and expanded boulevard system oriented to the new rapid transit route downtown. As the Rapid line emerged from its cut at the top of the hill heading eastward, it split into two branches. One continued east in a straight line in the center of Shaker Boulevard (which now began at Buckeye and Woodhill Roads) at the west end of the long cut and extended east to meet the original section (and original temporary streetcar line) at Coventry Road.

The other rapid transit branch swung southeast on a wide new boulevard, which paralleled Shaker Boulevard a mile and a half to its south. Christened South Moreland Boulevard, it was to be 190 feet wide—ten feet more than Shaker Boulevard and wider than the widest avenues L'Enfant had laid out for Washington, D.C. Van Sweringen liberality allowed space for four rapid transit tracks in South Moreland Boulevard's grassy center median, flanked by roadways on each side.[7]

The new residential streets in the area between the two boulevards were brought together in curving intersections which flowed into Moreland every third of a mile. This design kept the boulevard uncluttered with numerous side-street intersections and allowed better rapid transit speeds by limiting stops to only three per mile. Even so, the entire layout was designed so that no home would be more than three-quarters of a mile from a stop, and most would be a quarter of a mile or less. At each stop a small, picturesquely designed masonry station would house a news and refreshment stand or some other community-service business.

The construction of all of this went on as best it could through the war, but there were the inevitable material and labor shortages, which particularly hampered work on the rapid transit line. The graded roadbed west of Shaker Heights was finished by the end of 1916, but track and overhead wire had to wait until the war's end. In fact, the brothers released rail stockpiled for Moreland Boulevard so that it could be sent overseas. A postwar steel strike added more delay, and serious work did not resume until mid-1919. (A. H. Smith had made sure that the New York Central's Orange Avenue freight branch—which was part of the same project—was given a wartime priority; it was opened in January 1918.)

With the line nearing completion, the Vans were still not yet ready to go into the business of running trains themselves. Their Cleveland Interurban Railroad—the subsidiary set up in 1913 to operate their rapid transit—negotiated an elaborate agreement with the Cleveland Railway to supply them with cars, crews, electric power, and operating supervision. Unlike the original 1913 Shaker Boulevard line, which was essentially a fully subsidized city streetcar line, the Cleveland Interurban was a wholly separate operation with its own dedicated fleet of cars. Until the Cleveland Interurban acquired its own custom-built equipment, it was agreed that the company would rebuild a group of city streetcars to rapid transit standards and lease them to the new line.

The operating contract was signed in September 1919, and the first genuine Shaker Heights rapid transit service

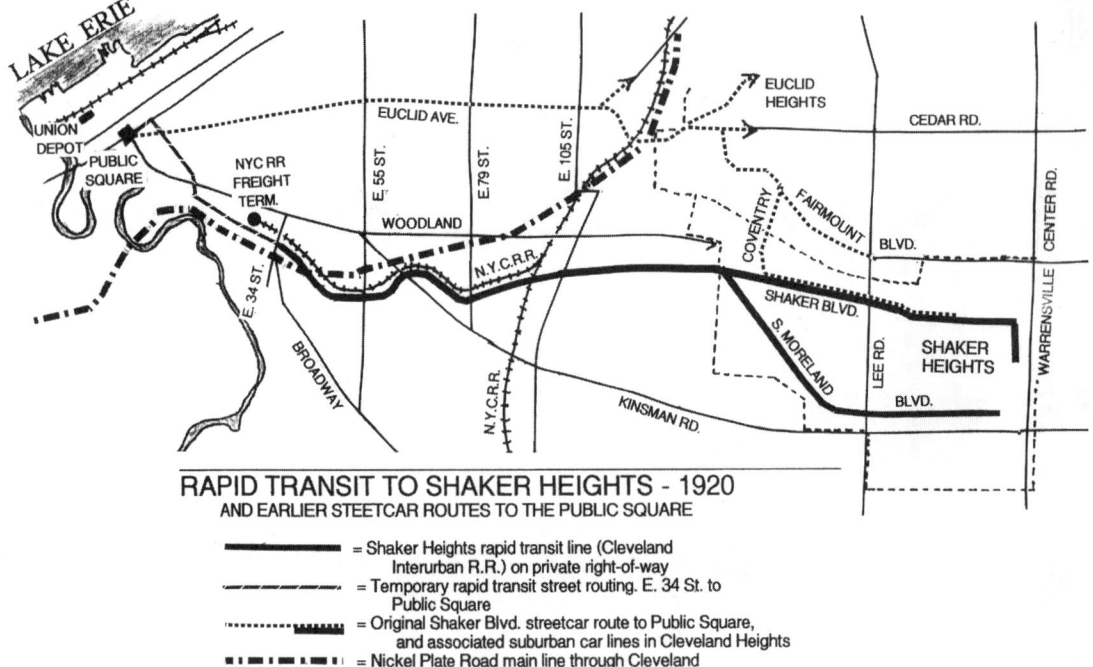

RAPID TRANSIT TO SHAKER HEIGHTS - 1920
AND EARLIER STREETCAR ROUTES TO THE PUBLIC SQUARE

▬▬▬ = Shaker Heights rapid transit line (Cleveland Interurban R.R.) on private right-of-way
━ ━ ━ = Temporary rapid transit street routing. E. 34 St. to Public Square
⋯⋯⋯ = Original Shaker Blvd. streetcar route to Public Square, and associated suburban car lines in Cleveland Heights
■ ▬ ■ ▬ ■ = Nickel Plate Road main line through Cleveland

In its original form, the Shaker Heights "Rapid" used city streetcar tracks between Public Square and E. 34th Street. The Shaker Boulevard line terminated at the Shaker Country Club on Courtland; the South Moreland branch ended at Lynnfield Road. Note the New York Central freight branch alongside the western portion of the rapid transit line, built jointly with the Vans. Also note the Nickel Plate main line, which was to form the eastern access route to the new Union Terminal (including the Shaker rapid transit) and the planned East Cleveland rapid transit route.

started in mid-April the next year. By then the suburb had grown from its 1911 population of 250 to 1,600, a spectacular percentage increase but still a modest total number. The initial rapid transit operation was scaled accordingly; to get things started quickly, four 1914-era city streetcars handled the initial schedules. These were soon replaced by more cars of the same type, which had been refurbished and equipped to run in trains at 50 miles per hour. Out in Shaker Heights, three of the planned permanent station buildings were finished: one at the Moreland branch's Lynnfield Road terminal, one at the Courtland Road terminal on Shaker Boulevard, and one at Coventry Road where the original line to Fairmount Boulevard joined.

The final cost of the finished rapid transit, including interest on construction loans, came to $8.16 million, a substantial sum in 1920 dollars. For that the brothers got an unusual combination of a fast but otherwise conventional surface-level suburban trolley system within Shaker Heights itself and a heavily built, fully grade-separated rapid transit line between Shaker Heights and East 34th Street. (Much of the latter section was part of the New York Central–funded joint project and was built to steam-railroad standards.) At East 34th, the route left its own right-of-way to finish out the last mile and a half to the Public Square over a city streetcar line.

That last stretch, of course, was another temporary expediency pending resolution of the still-unsettled question of design of and access to the terminal. The transit line was still growing one step at a time, but nonetheless it was now the best transportation in Cleveland. Even though the cars ran on downtown streets, they took only twenty-seven minutes for the entire length of their runs, compared to the forty-five or more needed for the original operation.[8]

At the city end of the Rapid, things were also beginning to move along. A month after the armistice, on December 16, 1918, a great civic reception celebrated the opening of the Hotel Cleveland. It was an immediate success that began the slow process of pulling commerce back toward the Public Square—in this case, specifically from the rival "uptown" Hotel Statler at 12th and Euclid.[9]

Next to the new hotel were the same grimy four-story brick buildings where O. P.'s rail terminal-office-store complex was to be, but his ideas had metamorphosed into a new plan and then metamorphosed again. In the earliest days, O. P. had conceived a terminal strictly for electric railways—his Shaker Heights rapid, plus possibly some or all of the six interurban lines entering town. (Four of these came in from the east over long stretches of city streets and perhaps could use part of the rapid transit right-of-way.) But not long after that—probably in the 1911–1913 period—the brothers began picking up additional property in the area and found that the

The original terminal of the Moreland branch of the Shaker Heights "Rapid" was this handsome stone building at Lynnfield Road, shown with one of the original rebuilt 1914 Cleveland Railway cars. Stations like this were to adorn all the car stops in the suburb.
Anthony Krisak photo,
Richard Krisak collection

Baltimore & Ohio Railroad owned a small piece they needed. This led to a trip to Baltimore, where B&O officials expressed an interest in the Vans' terminal plans and suggested that the B&O and two of Cleveland's other lesser railroads—the Wheeling & Lake Erie and the Erie—might also be interested in using the site as a steam-railroad terminal. The brothers studied the idea and developed a proposal. (At this time, their Nickel Plate acquisition was at least three years in the future, and initially they did not include it.)[10]

Why the B&O initiated this idea is a minor mystery. Of Cleveland's six major steam railroads, it seemed to have the least reason to relocate to a new terminal. Its own Canal Road station was only about three blocks from the Public Square, albeit at the bottom of a hill. Completed in 1898, the large stone and brick building was no more than fifteen years old at the time and was one of the newest and best of Cleveland's sorry assortment of rail passenger facilities. (When it opened, the railroad advertised it as the city's "most artistic, commodious, and up to date.") Furthermore, the B&O would need to build a new line up a steep grade to reach the level of the Public Square; its own line was located on the Cuyahoga valley's floor with no easy direct connection to what would be a station on high ground close by.[11]

In any event, a new terminal plan evolved, albeit slowly. It was not until the brothers bought the Nickel Plate that there was substantive action. Finally, on March 1, 1917, a joint committee of engineers from the Nickel Plate, the Wheeling & Lake Erie, and the Erie—plus the Vans' own Terminal Properties Company—produced its proposal. (Once it started the whole process, the B&O apparently dropped out.) The new Public Square terminal would consist of a twelve-track stub-end steam-railroad terminal to serve those three railroads plus a pair of elevated loops above it for rapid transit and interurban cars. Office buildings and stores would be built above the tracks, which would also adjoin the Vans' Hotel Cleveland. It was assumed that the New York Central and Pennsylvania would use the proposed new lakefront station.[12]

The final agreements with the railroads were being put together when the war came and the government took over the railroads. The plan then needed an additional new step of approval from the wartime Railroad Administration. A routine request was submitted, but as it went through the agency's high command a surprising change took place—or at least it seemed surprising. Suddenly it was proposed that all Cleveland railroads, including the New York Central, use the Vans'

Public Square station, transforming it from a minor facility into the center of all Cleveland's intercity transportation. The person doing the proposing was the regional director for the United States Railroad Administration's eastern region—Alfred H. Smith.

Six

A Difficult Birth at the Public Square

When Smith made his suggestion in early 1918, he was speaking as the chief operating officer for the United States Railroad Administration's eastern region; as such, he was ostensibly concerned with coordinating railroad facilities in the most effective and efficient way. But he had also been the New York Central's president and would return to that job once the war was over. And since the Central dominated Cleveland's passenger business, it was plain that any "union" station would be mostly a Central station.

What motivated him to make this bold decision? Did he come to this epiphany on his own? Did O. P. talk him into it? Or was it some kind of quid pro quo wrapped up with the Nickel Plate sale? The answer is forever lost in the unrecorded private understandings between Smith and O. P. But whatever his thinking, he had assured that the Vans' Public Square terminal not only would go forward but would be heavily underwritten by the New York Central.

It is possible that Smith had something in the back of his

mind from the time he first approached O. P. about the freight-terminal project back in 1913. Being the experienced operating man that he was, he had good reasons for being dubious about the lakefront site proposed in Daniel Burnham's 1902 "City Beautiful" mall plan (locally known also as the Group Plan). On the surface, it looked like a logical place to put the station. The lakefront land was flat, open, and reasonably wide; the station site itself was on vacant land; rail access routes were already in place; and little new line construction would be needed. At the same time, though, it was hideously congested. Between them, the Central and the Pennsylvania pushed roughly 100 passenger trains a day through the old station. These had to maneuver through coal and iron-ore train movements, freight-house switching, and much miscellaneous freight activity—with everything crossing in front of everything else as it went. And at the west end of the site, most of the Central's traffic and all of the Pennsylvania Railroad's ore trains had to squeeze onto the single-track swing bridge over the mouth of the Cuyahoga River. The Cuyahoga was no placid stream, either. During much of the year it carried a constant succession of long Great Lakes freighters to and from the upriver steel mills and bulk terminals, and the bridge had to creak open for each one.

Those problems could be overcome to a degree. With proper engineering, for example, the troublesome swing bridge could be replaced by a higher-level structure, and the unnecessarily convoluted track layout could be simplified. But Cleveland was one of the East's worst bottlenecks during the war; assuming that rail traffic would only increase over the coming years, the lakefront would always be a clotted choke point.

But underlying these physical concerns was something less quantifiable but even more critical—the growing personal relationship between Smith and O. P. If nothing else, Smith trusted O. P. and admired his imagination and capabilities. He also saw the obvious market advantages of being located on the Public Square and being part of a complex which brought together rapid transit lines, a hotel, offices, stores, and city transit. Having been intimately involved with the Central's pioneering and lucrative air-rights development project in New York—which utilized the "air" over the tracks behind Grand Central Terminal to build luxury apartments, hotels, and office buildings—then underway along Park Avenue over the tracks, he knew how well such an idea worked. He may even have encouraged O. P. to translate it to Cleveland.

On the other hand, Smith the practical railroader must have known that he was asking for trouble at this particular site. The Public Square was on high ground, but it was backed up closely against the Cuyahoga River valley, producing a constricted site on sloping terrain. This posed no problem for the Vans' original conception of a stub-end terminal. In that plan, the three or four railroads which might use it—the Nickel Plate; the Erie; the Wheeling & Lake Erie; and the B&O—would approach it in a direct line from the east, partly using the Nickel Plate's main line. Their trains would then simply dead-end on the hillside south of the Square.

But for the location to work for the New York Central's heavy east-west business, the layout would need to be completely revised and expensively expanded. Cleveland was only an intermediate point for the Central; most of its passenger trains ran through the city on their way to someplace else. Thus a stub-end station would be impractical, if not impossible, to operate. To serve the Square site, the line reaching the terminal had to be continued directly west across the river and its wide valley so that trains could pass through the station without reversing direction. At this tight location, that in turn demanded some engineering contortions: Through trains from the east, for example, would need to negotiate a curve right on the station site, then immediately swing west across the river valley on a high viaduct. It would take difficult engineering design and high construction costs to achieve that feat, and operating problems were almost inevitable.

Nor would the expenses end there. Costly access lines and connections had to be built, including clearing out and digging through almost a mile of built-up downtown property for the eastern approach as well as a shorter but equally densely developed stretch at the west side of the viaduct. In addition, the Van Sweringens' planned "air rights" office and store development over the station's top would require deep foundations in uncertain terrain under the terminal tracks and supporting pillars throughout the rail facilities. And since the planned station would be below street level with buildings overhead, the terminal railroad had to be electrified to eliminate steam-locomotive smoke and gases. That meant locomotive changes at each end of the terminal line, with separate crews and power.

In sum, the Central would pay a fearsome cost for a facility which would give it a more curving, roundabout, and time-consuming route through Cleveland—and which would be more expensive to operate. For the Van Sweringens, the railroad's partnership promised to be a boon, but for railroaders it was a terrible spot for a large terminal. To them, the project could only be justified by the assumption that rail passenger business would continue growing to cover the huge overhead.

Whatever his motives and reasoning, Smith's suggestion set the planning for the terminal off in a new direction. Not only did it mean a vastly different and much more elaborate design, but it would require a selling job on Cleveland's six major railroads, all of which were wary to one degree or another. At the same time, it set many other minds in the city to thinking. Having the principal—perhaps only—railroad station at the Square would conveniently focus all transportation there, but there were other implications. What little formal urban planning had been done would be shortstopped; Burnham's mall plan, now well underway, would lose its anchor at the mall's north end, and with it a major magnet for people. Businesses would be affected even more. In a less planned way, the city's commercial center was heading eastward along Euclid Avenue away from the Square, and a powerful new concentration of transportation, hotel, stores, and office buildings at the Square threatened to disrupt that.

None of that stopped the Van Sweringens. In May 1918, they enthusiastically (and prematurely) contacted the Chicago architectural firm of Graham, Anderson, Probst & White, the architects who had designed their Hotel Cleveland. Probably by no coincidence, this company had done a preliminary proposal for the planned new lakefront station and was the successor of Daniel Burnham. Through the balance of the year an ad hoc railroad engineering committee worked with the architects and Van Sweringen planners to develop a preliminary plan. Then, on August 28, 1918, the Vans made the first formal corporate move and created the Cleveland Union Terminals Company (CUT), which would be fully responsible for financing, building, and operating all the necessary railroad facilities. (The odd plural "Terminals" was repeated in the names of several related Van Sweringen companies; presumably it implied that the facility would serve several modes of transportation—railroads, rapid transit, interurbans, perhaps even street railways.) Initially CUT was simply a "paper" company owned by the Van Sweringens, but once the project got underway, the railroads would take over full ownership. For the Van Sweringens this accomplished two things: It relieved them of the expenses of building the rail terminal itself and the headaches of operating it, while at the same time it provided the foundation for their commercial developments to be built over it.[1]

From his first tentative plan in 1911, O. P. had wanted to integrate commercial buildings with a railway terminal. In its

The anchor for Tom Johnson and Daniel Burnham's grand new civic mall—and the replacement for the sorry structure shown in Chapter 3 —was to be this monumental union railroad station.
Frank A. Wrabel collection

earliest form, it was to be strictly an electric railway terminal—"traction," in the parlance of the time. By 1917, the terminal plans had expanded to include both steam railroads and traction lines, still including some kind of office building plus the adjacent Hotel Cleveland, then underway.

Now the latest twist in the terminal's planning led O. P. into a more sophisticated variation of the idea which would create a wholly integrated urban center built on air rights over the railroad and traction terminals. The space needed for the railroad facilities—which, thanks to the sloping site, could be easily located under street level—was large enough to provide for at least eight sizeable buildings over them. That would accommodate several office buildings, a large department store, a central post office, and stores and restaurants within the terminal area itself. All of those could be interconnected by underground passageways which also would link the complex with the hotel. In effect, every element of city life would be concentrated there—and all of it in the same facility as both city and intercity transportation. It was a concept unique in its time and never exactly duplicated elsewhere.

Once again the Vans had a model—two, in fact. Most important was the New York Central's own Grand Central Terminal in New York. Opened in 1913 after ten years of difficult construction, Grand Central was built on the basic designs of another brilliant visionary, the Central's chief engineer, William J. Wilgus. Among Wilgus's innovations were the concepts of an underground electrified terminal, reached by long ramps rather than stairways, with the property overhead developed for commercial and residential use under air-rights arrangements. To O. P., the air-rights idea was especially appealing. In Grand Central's case it was already leading to the creation of the legendary Park Avenue "Gold Coast" north of 45th Street as well as three hotels clustered around the terminal; soon it became a financial mother lode for the railroad. Also in New York, William Gibbs McAdoo's Hudson & Manhattan Railroad, a rapid transit line between New York City and Newark, New Jersey, had built its Hudson Terminal office complex over the line's lower Manhattan loop terminal.

The terminal project would be the most expensive and complex enterprise the Van Sweringens had attempted so far, and it promised a thicket of political, legal, engineering, and financial problems. Most immediately, they had to build up public and political enthusiasm to overcome the project's negative aspects. The political situation was especially uncertain, since the already approved lakefront mall station would be abandoned. Furthermore, many downtown and West Side blocks would be razed and people relocated, and city ordinances would be needed to close or realign numerous streets. They also had to overcome some political distrust lingering from the fairly transparent Cleveland & Youngstown–New York Central freight-terminal subterfuge of 1913.

At the same time, they had to persuade Cleveland's seven railroads to be part of the project. (Actually it was only six railroads, since one, the so-called Big Four, was a New York Central subsidiary.) Then would come regulatory approvals and financing, and although the total cost was uncertain at this point, it was clear that it would be beyond the resources of the Vans' traditional Cleveland sources. As always, O. P. was the negotiator and public spokesman; M. J., in fact, remained in the background and was never quoted on anything.

So while the engineers struggled with their plans, the public debated—sometimes heatedly. By far the most vehement antagonist was Peter Witt, who at that moment was merely a private transportation consultant. Witt was one of Cleveland's most colorful and impassioned public figures and always put on a spectacular show. The antithesis of Van Sweringen diffidence, he was a fiery, caustic-tongued, evangelical socialist—a self-proclaimed "skunk skinner" who missed few chances to excoriate the business establishment and the politicians supporting it. Witt had quit school at 13 to make baskets, then became an iron-molder's apprentice and later a union activist. He was bright and capable, too; he caught Tom Johnson's eye, and when Johnson was elected mayor he made Witt his city clerk. When Newton D. Baker became mayor in 1912, he appointed his old Johnson-era colleague as street railway commissioner, the official who oversaw the city's interest in the Cleveland Railway's operations. Witt then made himself into a transit expert; he designed a more efficient streetcar floor plan that was widely adopted in the industry and developed methods of speeding up services. With Baker's backing, he ran for mayor in 1915 and lost, but he was always popular with working Clevelanders.[2]

Tom Johnson was Peter Witt's idol, and his antipathy for the Van Sweringens was partly rooted in what he viewed as their betrayal of Johnson's mall dream. He had also pegged the brothers as underhanded schemers who had hoodwinked the city during the Cleveland & Youngstown–New York Central freight-terminal project. In August 1918, Billy Stage, then a Van Sweringen lawyer, invited Witt to his office in an attempt to disarm him. Stage straightforwardly reported their dialogue in a memorandum which must have pained the prim and sensitive O. P. Typical bits of the Witt style that he passed on were: "The Cleveland & Youngstown Railroad has screwed the Public . . . and City by misrepresentation. . . . Inner officials of the New York Central have screwed their own people for the benefit of the inner-ring and the Cleveland & Youngstown. . . . and the [terminal] proposition is a damn fake."[3]

Despite Witt's objections, the City Council approved the Union Terminal ordinances in October. The issue was then put to a special referendum vote on January 6, 1919, which was preceded by an intense public-relations campaign by the Van Sweringens. Leaflets flooded the city; colorful folders appeared along with newspaper ads and specially organized citizens' committees. It worked, and the voters approved the referendum by a two-thirds majority. The city's electorate may seem fickle, having overwhelmingly voted for the lakefront plan only three years earlier, but it is more likely that Clevelanders cared less about civic perfection than they did in getting something done after so many years of talk.[4]

The next problem was getting commitments from the railroads. Smith returned to the New York Central on June 1, 1919, and set to work exercising his strong charms to get his company behind the project. Naturally, the Vans' Nickel Plate also had to be involved. Beyond those two participants, however, it was still uncertain how much of a true "union station" the new facility would turn out to be. The Pennsylvania Railroad was the Central's partner at the old Union Depot; with the new lakefront station now dead, presumably it would join the Public Square project—although with the Pennsylvania one could never be sure. The three remaining lesser lines—the Erie, the Wheeling & Lake Erie, and the B&O—were noncommittal; later, they made very tentative promises to use it as tenants but not as joint owners.

Soon enough the Pennsylvania made up its mind and announced that it wanted no part of the project. The Pennsylvania was a proud, powerful, and often arrogant company which usually avoided union station arrangements which it did not control. By this time too, it had concluded that its relatively new station at East 55th Street and Euclid Avenue was in a potentially strategic spot to serve as its main station now that the more affluent parts of the city were moving eastward. Its downtown and West Side customers could continue to use the Union Depot which, if no less squalid, would at least be less crowded. So, citing the anticipated expense and operating difficulties of the Public Square terminal (which were all too real), the Pennsylvania withdrew in December 1919, leaving the Central and the Nickel Plate as the only firm users.[5]

The rail terminal part of the project was estimated to cost $60 million, which would be covered by Cleveland Union Terminals Company bonds; their interest and principal would be guaranteed by the railroads. About $10 million was needed as start-up capital. O. P. took on the responsibility of finding sources to handle the bond issue and uncharacteristically made a bumbling start. Working through his close banking friends in Cleveland—John Sherwin, Joseph Nutt, Warren Hayden, and Otto Miller—he was sent to New York in May 1920 to deal with potential underwriters headed by the Chase Bank. The experience turned out to be frustrating. Unfamiliar with New York banker protocol, O. P. made some tactical errors, and the bankers themselves unaccountably took too hard a line, demanding a high effective interest rate and a share in the Vans' own air-rights development. (The brothers' own personal credit was a bit shaky at that time, which may have contributed to the unsettling demands.)

Since in the end O. P. was really acting for the New York Central, Smith and his financial vice president, Albert H. Harris, stepped in to put the process on a more satisfactory track. In July, O. P. was introduced to the Central's primary banker, J. P. Morgan & Company, and better terms were eventually arranged. It had been a somewhat rocky beginning, but O. P. ended with a solid contact that would soon carry him into a far wider world.[6]

As the terminal plans took more concrete form and O. P. was negotiating for financing, a new hurdle appeared. The Esch-Cummins Act was passed in 1920 as a comprehensive federal measure which officially returned the railroads to private ownership and tried to resolve some of the problems which had created the wartime transportation crisis. The act (later commonly called the Transportation Act of 1920) took effect July 11th, and among other things it required any new rail line construction to be approved by the Interstate Commerce Commission (ICC). (The same legislation set up a program to consolidate the multitudinous railroad companies into stronger large systems.) That meant that the Union Terminal project had to be submitted to the ICC, and over the next several months the key agreements between the railroads and the Van Sweringen companies were put in final form for the application.

As they were finally developed, the financial and corporate arrangements blatantly favored the brothers. The Cleveland Union Terminals Company, thus far only a set of corporate papers, would finance, build, and operate the railroad terminal part of the project, which formed the foundation for everything else. It would technically be an independent union terminal company, a device common in the railroad industry by which several separate railroad companies share a common facility. Cleveland Union Terminals was to be wholly owned by the participating railroads, with ownership shares based on traffic volume. In this case, only the New York Central, its Big Four subsidiary, and the Nickel Plate ended up as owners, so the Central held a 93 percent share and the Nickel Plate a 7 percent share. Without a doubt, it was a New York Central project.

But there was a quirk. Although the railroads would become its immediate owners, the Van Sweringens were to control the Union Terminals Company management until the station was ready for operation. While it was stipulated that the railroads would be consulted on any major expenditures and would directly participate in the terminal design, the Vans technically had ultimate control over design and construction. While that provision seemed to blatantly favor the Vans while subordinating the railroads which were paying for it, it at least had one highly necessary virtue: It established a single authority and responsibility for a complex but interrelated group of projects which would have several ownerships and serve a variety of different economic or commercial functions. Needless to say, O. P. and the Terminals Company staff would have an extremely delicate and demanding job; they would need to placate all of the parties and meet their needs while keeping the project moving.

Financing the project followed a similar pattern. As already noted, CUT would issue and sell its own bonds, but payment of the interest and principal was guaranteed by the railroads. For all practical purposes, that made the Central almost fully responsible financially.

One odd and troublesome feature was the traction part of the terminal. At about the same time that the brothers set up the Cleveland Union Terminals Company, they created a traction twin—the Cleveland Traction Terminals Company. The focus of this company was far more misty than its railroad counterpart. It was to build and operate a network of rapid transit lines radiating from the terminal to Cleveland's East and West Sides, which would also provide access to the terminal for the six interurban lines entering town. Although its routes were only sketches on paper, its role in the terminal was all too real. The facility's design would include a large amount of separate space to be leased to the Traction Terminals Company for these lines—and the cost of the traction facilities was estimated to be almost one-quarter of the terminal's total construction cost. But to cover a large part of its rental payments, the company (which presumably would remain in Van Sweringen hands) was to be given all the income from the restaurants, stores, and other concessions within the terminal.

That plan had two shadowy aspects. First, the Van Sweringen–owned Traction Terminals would be heavily subsidized with money that might otherwise go toward reducing the railroads' costs. More to the point was the question of who would use the elaborate traction facilities. Aside from the Vans' Shaker Heights operation—which was the only sure thing—the plan to include the rapid transit system and interurban feeders was entirely speculative and perhaps fatally misguided. The interurban lines were especially uncertain. Even by 1920, automobiles and newly paved roads were pushing the midwestern interurban industry into serious financial trouble, and the trend would clearly accelerate. Of the six interurban companies radiating from Cleveland, only the Lake Shore Electric seemed financially stable at the time, and that was only by comparison. None had the resources to build access lines or pay rentals for the terminal. O. P.'s basic idea of a high-speed electric railway system for the city was visionary, but perhaps in this case he had more vision than foresight.

Finally there was the all-important question of air rights.

There was to be no visible railroad station as such; the entire plan was based on developing the extensive space over the underground terminal—and that was where the money was to be made. At both Grand Central and Hudson Terminal in New York, the railroads owned the air rights and reaped the benefits. Here, however, it would be the Van Sweringens' Cleveland Terminal Building Company, a new entity created in January 1921 to absorb some of their earlier Public Square enterprises. Again, the arrangements were liberal: In effect, the Vans got their rights to the best portion at only a nominal cost. They would sell the Public Square property they owned to the terminal company at their original cost plus carrying charges and give it easement rights through property they owned along the eastern approach. Their public rationale was that they had held all this property for ten years and had handled all the intervening legal and political issues; they also would bear the brunt of selling the Cleveland Union Terminals Company bonds and overseeing the project.[7]

Formal applications were finally made to the ICC in February 1921. The case turned out to be not so easy. Peter Witt reappeared with a vengeance. Witt went to Washington at his own expense (his assets at the time were reported to be $3,000 and his trip expenses $600) and was allowed to testify as a private individual. He made the best of it. Witt may have been a soapbox orator, as some called him, but he knew his facts and arrived well prepared. Ironically, he found himself fighting his old political ally and fellow idealist Newton D. Baker, who was now the Van Sweringens' chief counsel. And on the

Peter Witt in a pensive mood.
Cleveland Press Collection,
Cleveland State University

The Vans' original Union Terminal concept, before O. P. decreed that the squat central tower would soar upward to fifty-two stories. At right is the completed Hotel Cleveland and at left the projected department store which later materialized as Higbee's. Note the plan for a sloping lower-level access to the terminal from the Public Square.
H. H. Harwood, Jr., collection

Commission was another enemy who, in the long run, would be more dangerous than Witt. Joseph B. Eastman had been appointed as a commissioner by Woodrow Wilson two years earlier and was making himself into the group's conscience. Like the brothers, Eastman was a lifelong bachelor, a loner who was devoted to work; unfortunately for the Van Sweringens, though, that devotion went in a different direction. A protégé of Justice Louis D. Brandeis, he had much the same brand of idealism as Peter Witt, albeit considerably more tempered.

Dominated by Witt, opponents of the project brought out all its weaknesses—particularly the costs and the questionable financial agreements between the railroads and the Van Sweringens. The commission rendered its verdict on August 12th and gave the Van Sweringens an unpleasant surprise by turning it down.

They quickly regrouped and asked for a rehearing, citing fourteen issues the Commission should have considered more carefully. The request was granted and new hearings were scheduled to begin August 20th, this time in Cleveland.

The Vans and the railroads were unrepentant about their financial agreements, which were not essentially changed. Their basic strategy was merely to clarify and augment the original facts and justifications and to overwhelm the Commission with a show of public support. This time it worked. Witt produced even more than his usual pyrotechnical display, which seemed to succeed mostly in irritating Commissioner J. B. Campbell, who presided. On December 6th, the Commission ruled in favor, and the matter was ended. The lone dissent came from an equally unyielding Eastman, who wrote a long, well-reasoned restatement of all the original weaknesses.[8]

With all legal hurdles now cleared, the agreements between the railroads, the Cleveland Union Terminals Company, and the Vans were quickly consummated. The Central and the Nickel Plate took all of the CUT's stock—93 percent for the Central and the Big Four and 7 percent for the Nickel Plate—and the Vans turned over their Public Square property to it. The air-rights agreement was also signed, as was the reviled rental contract with the Traction Terminals Company. The beginnings of a full-time working organization came in January 1922, when Henry D. Jouett arrived from the New York Central's engineering department to become the Cleveland Union Terminals Company chief engineer. O. P. hastened back to the Morgan bank to work out the details of the initial $12 million CUT bond issue, which was put on the market in June 1922. He saw to it that his Cleveland friends got as much of the business as Morgan would allow, but it was clearly now a New York show.[9]

The dynamic Jouett rapidly became known as "the busiest man in Cleveland"—and for good reason, since all of the design and construction difficulties ultimately fell on him. As architects for the project, the Vans again hired Graham, Anderson, Probst & White, the Chicago firm which had designed their Hotel Cleveland. The architects had their own challenges, since the planned new complex of commercial buildings had to blend visually with one another as well as with the earlier hotel—and maintain Van Sweringen standards of quality and conservative tastes.

Demolition on the site began soon after, and formal groundbreaking followed in September 1923. It had been a long and sometimes nerve-wracking path from that first venture into the Public Square in 1909, but O. P.'s entire integrated terminal complex was on its way. But by then O. P. was on his way too, in new directions—now accompanied by his new New York friends.

Seven

The Beginnings of an Empire

The Van Sweringens had entered the railroad business in 1916. Unknown to them or anyone else, that year also marked a milestone which would lead them into a world wider than they could ever have imagined at the time. To understand why, a brief lesson in railroad history and economics must follow.

The milestone was a single statistic: 254,251 miles—the total route mileage of all American railroads. That number would never be greater. The nation's rail system had reached its peak and would grow no further. The years after would see a slow but relentless decline; while a few significant new lines would be built, they would always be outweighed by those that were abandoned. For all practical purposes, the era of railroad building was over. The industry was now officially "mature."

Not only was it mature, but it was showing creaks of age. Financial performance, especially, was becoming sluggish. In 1911, return on investment for all railroads in total dropped below 5 percent; by 1915, it was below 4 percent. To be sure, most of the traditional blue chips—the New York Central and the Pennsylvania Railroad among them—were blue enough, but too many companies were indifferent earners or worse, and their owners were beginning to wonder what to do.

The problem surely was not lack of demand for rail services. Intercity trucking was almost unknown and commercial air travel simply did not exist. Virtually all of the nation's intercity freight and most passengers still rolled behind smoking steam locomotives. But the excesses of the last century had caught up with the industry. Between the Civil War and the McKinley years, railroads had been built everywhere, too often with little sense of economic reality. Some railroad builders, in fact, had motives which had little to do with earning a profit from carrying goods and people. Now, too many independent lines connected the same cities, and there were too many branches to unproductive places. Aggravating the profitability problems in the first decades of the twentieth century was ever-tightening government regulation, which especially inhibited pricing flexibility. But the law of the jungle never fully applied to railroads. A marginal factory or a played-out mine can be closed; businesses in overcrowded markets can sometimes relocate or go into another line. But once built, a railroad had to stay put, regardless of solvency. It could not be picked up and moved elsewhere to a better market, nor could it be adapted for some other use. Besides, industries and communities now depended on it, and not much else could be done with the physical plant anyway. It represented a sunk investment which was of no use for anything but running trains. And since railroads are notorious capital consumers, the sunk investment was too great simply to walk away from—so great, in fact, that any large-scale financial instability in the industry would seriously jeopardize the financial markets.

As a result, the weak and redundant railroads did not die; they kept competing as best they could, splitting the available traffic too many ways and draining business from the stronger lines. In the more freewheeling days of the late nineteenth century, they engaged in rate-cutting wars, which made matters worse by further weakening everyone. In such an environment, pumping in more money seemed foolish; even the strong railroads had problems justifying new investments. Led by the formidable J. P. Morgan, the large New York investment banks began trying to stabilize the situation in the 1890s; by the early 1900s, they had injected themselves heavily into policymaking on many railroads. (In 1915, the Morgan interests alone controlled almost 12 percent of the country's railroad mileage.) At about the same time, the Pennsylvania Railroad and the New York Central joined in a short-lived "community of interest" plan to take control of some of the more troublesome weaklings. That helped stop new building and created more corporate stability, but by then the damage had been done and could not be undone. It was becoming clear that some more unified method and radical type of rationalization was needed.

By 1916, the problem had become worrisome enough to warrant government interest. Early that year, efforts were made to form a joint congressional committee to study the financial problems of the railroads and recommend changes in regulatory policy. The committee materialized before the year's end under Senator Francis G. Newlands, but it had hardly begun its work before the oncoming war made the issue temporarily academic. It did not remain academic long; the collapse of the railroads during the war was blamed partly on lack of capacity, which in turn was a direct result of underinvestment. The country emerged from the war with a strong sense that the federal government needed to do something to help strengthen the railroad industry by resolving the problems of overcompetition, overregulation, and underinvestment.

Significantly, though, the politicians and economists did not view it as a question of too many redundant rail lines running to the same places. After all, they logically reasoned, the economy would keep growing and the railroads were certain to carry most of that ever-expanding business. There would be plenty of traffic for all. Rather, solving the railroad industry's woes was perceived to be a matter of resolving the economic disequilibrium caused by so many different companies with such unequal earning power.

The solution which evolved was to consolidate the various strong and weak railroads into a limited number of balanced competitive systems which would have roughly equal earning power. This, it was hoped, would produce the best of all possible worlds: It would preserve and protect past investments and thereby also assure that rail service was maintained on the maximum number of lines and to the most number of communities. It would encourage the new investment needed to modernize and build capacity to handle the expanded business. And, perhaps just incidentally, it would provide an escape hatch for any railroad owners who wanted to sell out.

By extension, this new philosophy also implied a softening of the political antipathy to large-scale railroad mergers handed down from President Theodore Roosevelt. Competition was still an essential policy cornerstone, but it was to be made more even and manageable.

The Van Sweringens' entry into the railroad business at this point was happenstance, but like that first meeting with Alfred H. Smith, the happenstance came at precisely the right time. The environment was about to change, and the brothers' ambitions and methods were well suited to exploitation of the new business climate. More perceptive and aggressive than most of his peers, Alfred Smith saw what was coming and its implications; he knew it would affect him, too, but in a less positive way, and he began preparing for it in his own style.

What many hoped would be the new era was ushered in with the Transportation Act of 1920 (or the Esch-Cummins Act), which formally returned the railroads to private operation after the war and made some major changes in national transportation policy. On the one hand, it gave the Interstate Commerce Commission even greater powers, especially in regulating railroad finances and approving corporate consolidation or control. But at the same time, it formally set up the machinery to plan and support the large-scale railroad consolidations which were to bring strength and stability to the industry. The ICC was charged with developing and implementing the plan; its job was to maintain competition and create balance in traffic and financial strength. An unwritten rule also governed the design: Traditionally, the railroad companies were fairly cleanly divided into territories—eastern, southern, and western—and their boundaries were not to be transgressed. Along with the New York Central and the Pennsylvania Railroad, the Vans were part of the eastern territory, and their immediate horizons were limited to such major western interchange gateways as Chicago and St. Louis. Their territory, however, was considered the most important, since it contained most of the country's industry and coal resources.

In 1920, there were no less than 186 so-called Class I railroads—major companies with revenues of over $1 million—and a grand total of 1,085 railroads of all sizes. The prospect of redesigning this complex multibillion-dollar industry with all its intricate traffic relationships and conflicting private interests—not to mention all of the industries, communities, financial institutions, and labor interests affected—was daunting, if not terrifying. Nobody was more daunted than the ICC; the agency had no competence to do it and it knew it. By design it was geared to react to piecemeal proposals and problems which were presented to it, not to initiate anything—and it certainly was not structured to create grand economic designs. In practice it functioned mostly as a specialized court that primarily handled rate cases; it received requests, listened to arguments, and rendered some kind of judgment. Its eleven commissioners were a diverse group of largely undistinguished political appointees (Joseph Eastman usually was a lone exception). They shied from major controversy, and the new rail consolidation program promised plenty of that.

Furthermore, the new law had a fatal weakness: The resulting consolidation plan would be voluntary. Whatever its wisdom and competence might be, the ICC had no power to force consolidations. It could only try to put together a blueprint and then approve or disapprove any specific mergers which might be presented to it. The law did give it power over new railroad securities issues and, in a separate section, over any proposed consolidations—but as will soon be seen, the ICC was uncertain how to exercise that power.

Unenthusiastic and ill-equipped, the Commission began its perilous mission. To design the consolidation plan, it hired William Z. Ripley, a distinguished Harvard economics professor and transportation specialist. Ripley was an excellent choice, but he had been thrown into a shark tank. Almost anything he proposed would alter the existing balances of power and disrupt long-standing traffic relationships among railroads. In addition, the financially healthy railroads obviously wanted no part of the more anemic ones. Perceptive railroad managers were well aware of this, and the more aggressive ones immediately began moving to protect or enhance their own interests.[1]

A. H. Smith had no peers in either perceptivity or aggressiveness, but in his position he could not take any overt action. In their own way, the Van Sweringens were equally aggressive and saw an enormous opportunity to go beyond the limited confines of their Nickel Plate. They could act and had the ambition to do so. The two parties had different goals, but they matched beautifully.

Essentially, Smith faced a larger and much more complex version of his old Nickel Plate quandary. He recognized that consolidations were inevitable but also was pragmatic enough to know that they would do him little good and could cause serious harm. Next to the Pennsylvania Railroad, his New York Central system was already the largest and most powerful in the eastern territory; it was unlikely to gain much from the consolidation program except probably to be saddled with some weaklings. On the other hand, many of the smaller lines were now heavy feeders for the Central: Combining them into large, strong systems of their own or giving them to some other major competitor would cut this business off and add new threats at the same time.

From his wartime experience, Smith probably knew the eastern railroad system better than anyone, and he had his own ideas about how things might best fit together. If he could not directly take these lines for the Central, he could at least take them off the market—and thus out of potentially dangerous hands—and piece them together into a new, self-sustaining system that would be in reasonably friendly hands. Those friendly hands were the same ones he had helped with their rapid transit, with the Nickel Plate, with their terminal project, and with an introduction to the Morgan bank.

Superficially, Smith's strategy seemed self-destructive. After all, not only would he help create stronger competition for the Central, but he stood to reduce its interchange business with these smaller lines. But it was a case of making the best of an unpredictable and potentially more dangerous situation. If successfully executed, the Central would have sort of a satellite system without either the antitrust problems or the financial investment and obligations. Although Smith could not control his satellite, he could at least influence it through his personal friendship, his strategic guidance, and his help in getting the brothers financing and political support. And behind both the Central and the Vans would be the Morgan bank, which would assure some commonality of interests. So started a partnership that produced spectacular results in an amazingly short time. No less important to the brothers was John J. Bernet, who supplied the detailed practical advice that helped translate general strategy into specific application.

In 1921, Professor Ripley had just begun his work, and nobody was certain where it would lead. The ICC itself was unsure about what it could do or how to do it. Already Ripley had polled the Vans and many others and had put together a very tentative plan which, among other things, built up a system around the Nickel Plate. But the brothers and Smith saw an opportunity to shape the process more concretely by moving ahead of it. That demanded quick decisions and action before the ICC's planning went too far and before others woke up and took their own actions. Here too the Van Sweringens were ideal. They were fast, effective movers themselves; they had the required ambition and nerve; and their tightly held holding company technique facilitated speedy action—it was unencumbered by the decision-making procedures of large corporations and required minimal capital.

It also had an enormous new advantage. Under the 1920 Transportation Act, any railroad wanting to control another railroad now needed the Interstate Commerce Commission's permission. The ICC also had been given control over new railroad stock and bond issues, including any used to finance acquisitions. All of that severely inhibited any expansionist railroad owner or president: At best, any ICC proceeding would take time and probably would generate opposition; at worst, the Commission simply might refuse to consider any proposal until it worked out its own consolidation plan. But holding companies were not legally carriers and were thus beyond the Commission's jurisdiction. Theoretically they could freely buy or sell railroads and otherwise influence their policies and actions. Eventually, of course, the holding company would need permission from the ICC to merge its railroads, but for the moment, the essential first step was to tie down those railroads before somebody else did, and the holding company could do that without interference.

Even had the brothers been less ambitious, it was plain that they would have to augment their Nickel Plate somehow. As of 1921, it still operated only its single 523-mile line between Buffalo and Chicago. Thanks to its strategic location as a bridge between certain eastern and western railroads, it was doing a healthy business, and Bernet had already built it into a strong earner. Although 1921 was a recession year, he managed to show a 73 percent increase in net income over 1916, the year the Vans took over. But its limitations showed in other statistics. For one, its freight tonnage trend had been essentially static; Bernet achieved his results primarily through operating efficiencies bolstered by higher rates and more selective solicitation of traffic. To grow, the railroad needed more western traffic gateways and more on-line industry.[2]

One of the enduring Van Sweringen legends is that someone once asked O. P. who his favorite authors were. "Rand and McNally," he supposedly replied. True or not, the Van Sweringens were certainly major customers throughout the 1920s as they learned railroad geography and planned acquisitions and alliances. The "Rand McNally era" started early with their initial order for 1,500 eight-by-ten-foot maps showing the national railroad system. Said Joseph Doherty, their public relations representative, "The brothers were in too much of a hurry to order the maps by mail. They dispatched young Billy Wenneman, their office boy, to the Chicago office of Rand McNally via the Nickel Plate, with instructions to emphasize speedy delivery. . . . They were bulky and hard to handle. They cluttered up not only the Van Sweringen suite of offices, but also the nooks, crannies, and closets on several floors. . . . Virtually the whole staff, with the exception of the men of the real estate office, was assigned to the task of inking, in greens, blues, and yellows and whatnot, the tracings of the systems the brothers devised."[3]

They moved fast, but in steps as the opportunities presented themselves. There were two immediate opportunities ripe for picking: The Toledo, St. Louis & Western and the Lake Erie & Western (LE&W) were available and, for different reasons, were undervalued by the financial markets. Together they would put the Nickel Plate into two new western gateways—the very important southwestern and western railroad interchange point of St. Louis and a secondary gateway at Peoria, Illinois. (Peoria was mostly valuable as a bypass for ever-congested Chicago and its slow transfers between railroads.) The two railroads also gave the Nickel Plate access to Detroit, Toledo, Indianapolis, Muncie, and several lesser midwestern industrial centers. Both railroads were mediocrities with checkered histories and erratic financial records, but, like the Nickel Plate, they were strategically well placed.

The 454-mile-long Toledo, St. Louis & Western—best known as the Clover Leaf Route—cut a diagonal swath across the Midwest from Toledo to St. Louis, crossing the Nickel Plate at Continental, Ohio, about midway between Fostoria, Ohio, and Fort Wayne, Indiana. Like the Nickel Plate, it consisted of a single line with no branches and modest on-line industry; en route between its two terminals it passed through only a few medium-sized cities, some of the largest being Bluffton, Marion, Kokomo, and Frankfort, Indiana. Together with the Grand Trunk Western, it jointly owned the Detroit & Toledo Shore Line, which connected Toledo and Detroit.

The Clover Leaf was born in 1877 as a short Ohio narrow-gauge line and blossomed rapidly to become a part of one of the late nineteenth century's most misbegotten railroad projects—a 1,628-mile-long narrow-gauge "grand trunk line" stretching from Toledo to the Mexican border at Laredo, Texas. Needless to say, that idea vaporized quickly, but the railroad did manage to complete its three-foot-gauge route between Toledo and St. Louis in 1882. Afterward it suffered through two bankruptcies, a difficult changeover to standard gauge (which was finally completed in 1889), and a disastrous investment in the Chicago & Alton Railroad. That produced still another receivership, but by 1921 it had resolved its financial obligations and was physically run down but otherwise fairly healthy.[4]

At 719 miles, the Lake Erie & Western was considerably larger than the Nickel Plate itself, but that was about its only distinction. Its unlikely route connected Sandusky, Ohio, with

In a typical scene from the pre–Van Sweringen days of the Lake Erie & Western, a 2-8-0 hauls a string of refrigerator cars and boxcars westward from its New York Central connection at Sandusky, Ohio. Roy W. Carlson collection

Peoria, Illinois, running southwest and west and crossing the Nickel Plate near Fostoria, Ohio. Two north-south branches reached terminals at Indianapolis, Michigan City, and Fort Wayne, Indiana (where it connected again with the Nickel Plate). The LE&W's genesis dated to 1853 as a locally promoted line running west from Fremont, Ohio, but it owed its full form to many of the same people who subsequently built the Nickel Plate. (Ironically, the original intent of the Nickel Plate was to give the LE&W an eastern outlet.) Its fortunes gyrated up and down, mostly down, while its chief promoter, the manipulator Calvin Brice, tried to put together a route east.

But when Brice suddenly died in 1898, the elder J. P. Morgan moved in and bought control for the New York Central as part of the "community of interest" plan to stabilize rates by taking control of troublemaking weaklings. The Lake Erie & Western went nowhere important that the Central and its Big Four subsidiary did not, and the railroad lapsed into the status of a feeder for the stronger Central lines. To A. H. Smith, it was not only superfluous but a financial drain on its parent; it made more sense as part of the Van Sweringens' system, and he was happy to unload it on his friends.[5]

Probably with Smith's encouragement, if not initiative, the Vans began moving late in 1921 to acquire both railroads. Beforehand (following Smith's advice), they also persuaded Ripley to put them with the Nickel Plate in his tentative plan so that there would be no conflicts.

It took less than three months to negotiate a price for the Lake Erie & Western with Albert H. Harris, the Central's financial vice president. The Central finally agreed to give up its 50.13 percent controlling interest in its orphan for $3 million and swallowed almost a $3 million loss on its original investment. As with the Nickel Plate, it also made the terms as easy as possible—$500,000 down in cash and the balance in promissory notes in yearly installments spread out over five years.

The Clover Leaf was only slightly more complicated and went almost as quickly. The estates of a pair of deceased investor partners—Edward F. Searles and Thomas Hubbard—held the largest interest in the company; they in turn had given their negotiating proxies to Walter L. Ross, the railroad's receiver and president. The estates were anxious to sell—so anxious that they agreed to give Ross a commission amounting to half of the sale proceeds. After some all-night negotiating sessions in Toledo, Ross agreed to a total price of $2.7 million ($1.4 million of which went to him) with no cash down and installment payments spread over twenty years; he also got a five-year executive employment contract for himself totaling $250,000. In this case, however, the Vans had to buy more stock on the market to give themselves a clear majority stake, so their total cost came to $3.5 million.

The Lake Erie & Western sale was signed in January 1922, and the Clover Leaf followed on February 7th. Within eleven days, the brothers had bought enough additional Clover Leaf stock to give them a 50.2 percent ownership. Their total immediate cash outlay was slightly less than $1.3 million—$500,000 for the Central's down payment and $777,625 for the extra Clover Leaf stock.[6]

Financing the purchases required some sophisticated maneuvering, since, as usual, the Vans did not have the ready cash. In preparation for it—and anticipating more and larger acquisitions to come—they decided to reorganize the holding company structure set up for their 1916 Nickel Plate acquisition. In January 1922, they formed the Vaness Company to replace the Nickel Plate Securities Corporation. Vaness was designed to be the peak of what eventually would become a complex pyramid, what O. P. later called "our own personal basket."

In dismantling the old Nickel Plate Securities and reassembling it as Vaness, the Vans also tightened the inner circle which owned and governed it. Aside from the two brothers, the principals were narrowed down to their longtime standbys Joseph Nutt and Charles Bradley—now respectively president and vice president of Union Trust—and investment bankers Warren Hayden and Otto Miller. (Hayden and Miller dropped out in 1924, probably to avoid a conflict-of-interest problem, since Hayden was a New York Central director.) The six (later to be four) then set up a cleverly crafted management trust agreement which in effect perpetuated their control over the company—even after the brothers' deaths and even if they sold their Vaness stock. It was the ultimate expression of their obsession for full control of whatever they were involved in.[7]

Vaness began its long and perilous life by financing the $1.3 million cash immediately needed for the Lake Erie & Western and Clover Leaf purchases. As a typical Van Sweringen expediency, two new holding companies materialized under Vaness to acquire the railroads' stock—the Western Company (born March 11, 1922) for the Lake Erie & Western and the Clover Leaf Company (born February 25th). Vaness then borrowed $500,000 from Nutt and Bradley's Union Trust, which it turned over to the Western Company to cover the New York Central's down payment. (As a New Deal–era Senate investigating committee report wryly remarked, "Mr. Nutt, as president of the Union Trust Co. and Mr. Nutt as a director and shareholder of Vaness, were in agreement that the Lake Erie & Western deal was a good one and Vaness a company with proper credit for carrying it through.") Similarly, the Clover Leaf Company took in the stock bought through Ross (which required no immediate cash outlay) and received a loan from Vaness to cover the $777,625 for the extra shares bought. Union Trust provided this to Vaness, too. Presumably Mr. Nutt had the same amiable conversation with himself.[8]

With financing completed, however temporarily and precariously, the brothers could take control of their two prizes. The Western Company took title to the Lake Erie & Western stock on April 26, 1922, and the Nickel Plate began managing the railroad on July 1st. The Clover Leaf situation was more complicated, since the management contract with Walter Ross allowed him to remain head of the company for five years, or until it was corporately merged. A merger was mandatory anyway, since by now the Van Sweringens had immediate and future debts totaling about $15 million for their various railroad acquisitions and needed a mechanism to reduce them while still maintaining their control.

The Nickel Plate, the Clover Leaf, the Lake Erie & Western, and two LE&W subsidiaries put together a merger agreement in December 1922 in which the Nickel Plate would be the surviving company. Details of capitalization and stock exchange were worked out early the next year, and in the process the Van Sweringens accomplished another bit of financial finesse. The stock of all three of the old companies was split roughly fifty-fifty between common and preferred, and all classes of stock had voting rights. In the new Nickel Plate's capital structure, 57 percent of the stock was common and 43 percent was preferred—but under normal circumstances the preferred stockholders could not vote. It was another variation of the same leveraging technique used by their holding companies. Not only was less direct investment needed to control the company, but the Vans could sell off the preferred stock they received through the merger, since they did not need it.

Despite their partial disenfranchisement, the minority stockholders of the three companies voted approval for the merger during March and April 1923. Under the new Transportation Act, the Interstate Commerce Commission had to approve the new securities to be issued, and there was no escape from this. But its authority over corporate consolidations was contained in a separate section of the law, and the

The "new" Nickel Plate after its 1923 merger with the Clover Leaf and the Lake Erie & Western. The former Clover Leaf route ran from Toledo to St. Louis; the former LE&W route stretched from Sandusky, Ohio, to Peoria, Illinois, with branches to Indianapolis, Rushville, Fort Wayne, and Michigan City, Indiana.
H. H. Harwood, Jr., collection

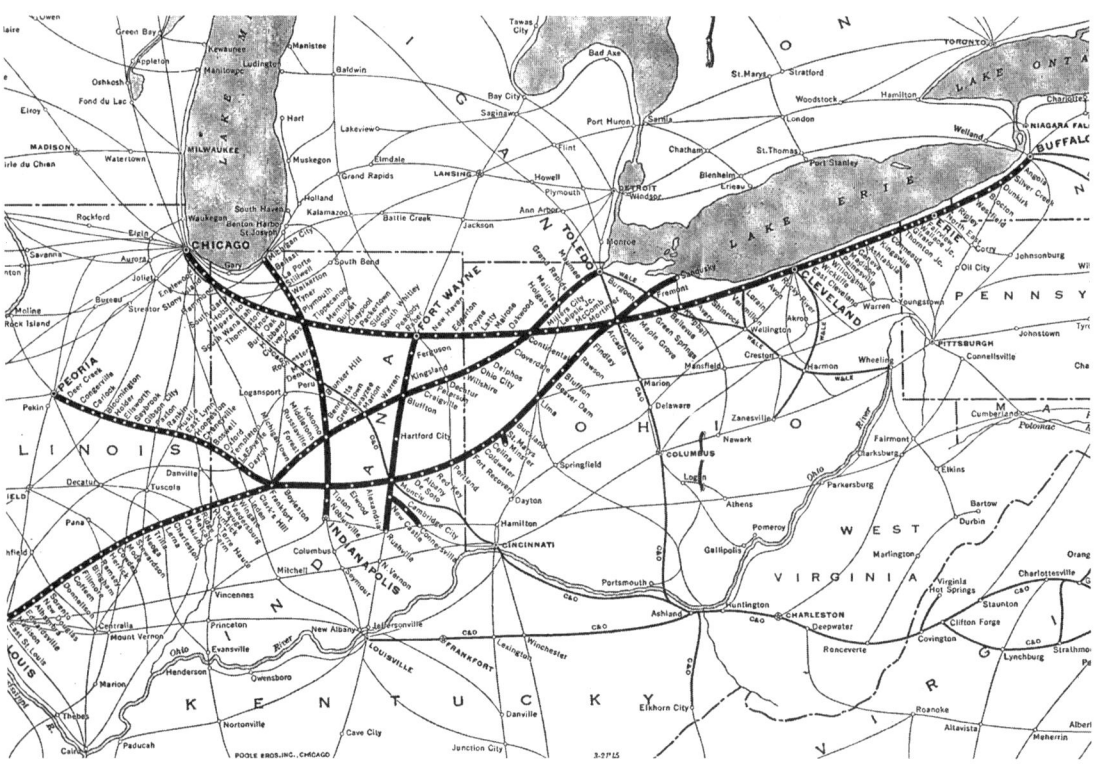

commissioners were not certain how they were supposed to judge any proposals. The Transportation Act said that the ICC was to approve or disapprove consolidations based on how they fit into its final plan, but in 1923 there was no final plan. In fact, the Commission did not intend to have one for several years at least. Nor were there any clear interim guidelines. Was the agency to hold up all consolidation cases until it finished its plan? If not, what standards was it to use? And if so, then what would become of its plan? All too aware of the perils of confronting that issue head on, the Van Sweringen lawyers decided to try a legal end run. Before submitting their ICC case, they had all of the states in which the railroads operated approve the merger. They then simply asked the ICC's blessing for the new securities, citing state authorities for the merger itself—and praying that nobody would raise any deeper questions.

Considering its precedent-setting implications, the case moved through at an amazing speed. The application was filed April 28th, hearings were held, and on June 18th the Commission voted its approval. The stratagem of getting state approvals and Ripley's tentative blessing apparently allowed the more uncertain commissioners a dignified escape from this troubling new mission that had been thrust on them. Furthermore, nobody had showed up with serious objections; there was no Peter Witt there to fight his loathsome dragons.

There was a Joseph Eastman, however. Almost predictably, Eastman strongly dissented. This time he found two allies—one of whom was former congressman John J. Esch, the Transportation Act's co-sponsor. Eastman stated the obvious—that the merger preempted whatever might come out of the ICC's consolidation planning process. "I am wholly unable to accept a construction of the law which reduces the plan of consolidation to helpless futility," he wrote. He berated his irresolute colleagues for not asserting the authority that he felt Congress had given them, and he decried the ploy of going to states for authority whenever it was convenient to do so as an invitation to chaos.⁹

Once again Eastman was in the minority, although he was not quite so lonely as he had been in the Cleveland Union Terminal case. Voice in the wilderness or not, Eastman was dedicated and respected; regardless of what political party or president was in power, he was regularly reappointed to his commission seat. He would be around for a while.

For the present, however, the Van Sweringens were triumphant again. Thanks to the canny design of the new capital structure, they now controlled 59 percent of the "new" Nickel

As part of the Clover Leaf deal, the Vans also inherited Walter L. Ross, the railroad's former receiver and president. The job turned out to be no sinecure for the able Ross, who later took John Bernet's place as the Nickel Plate's president.
Frank L. Wrabel collection

Plate's common stock (whose owners voted) and had ended up with slightly over 161,000 shares of nonvoting preferred stock which they could sell to liquidate their debts. Selling it turned out to be another complex and frustrating ordeal that involved buying more to try to keep up the price of what they held. When everything had settled down, their total current debt for acquiring the three railroads (including what was still owed the Central for the original Nickel Plate purchase) amounted to $21 million. They were able to liquidate 150,000 shares of their preferred through New York's Guaranty Trust Company for $12.2 million and received an additional $7.9 million loan from Guaranty, giving them a total of $20.1 million. They then partially liquidated the $7.9 million loan by selling more preferred stock and some unneeded common stock to Guaranty for $4.9 million.[10]

In the final accounting, the Vans had to pay a total of $21 million for the three railroads. They were then able to liquidate $17.1 million by selling the unneeded stock which came to them from the merger. That left a net cost to them of $3.9 million. But in the intervening years, they had received $6.7 million in railroad dividends. To oversimplify a bit, that meant they had paid nothing for their railroads and, in fact, had netted close to $3 million. And when all was said and done, they still owned 54 percent of the new Nickel Plate's voting stock.[11]

More important was what all that financial legerdemain produced. John Bernet now had a 1,696-mile railroad system instead of a single 523-mile line. It was financially solid, reached three key western gateways, and covered large parts of the industrial and agricultural Midwest. It was physically lean—mostly single track with small yards—but Bernet could turn even that into an advantage. Its costs were low, and with few places to store cars and trains, it had to keep them moving. With Bernet's high-performance motive power, the Nickel Plate quickly developed into an efficient, fast freight carrier that could usually outperform its more sluggish large rivals. There were some physical problems—some of the Clover Leaf's original narrow-gauge heritage remained and would never be entirely wiped out, for example—and the system still had some traffic weaknesses. Lacking much heavy on-line industry, it was overly dependent on "bridge" traffic carried from connection to connection, and its eastern end remained at Buffalo, far from the large eastern markets.

Already O. P. and M. J.—with A. H. Smith lurking in the shadows—were at work to rectify those weaknesses and create something far larger and more powerful.

Eight
To the South, East, and North

Back in late 1920, when Professor Ripley began his intimidating consolidation-planning job, his first logical (and diplomatic) move was to canvass various railroad executives for their ideas. O. P. was on his list, and Ripley wrote him on November 10th suggesting a conference as soon as possible. Significantly, O. P.'s first reaction was to pass the letter on to A. H. Smith and ask him for a suggested answer. Smith responded the same day but was careful to couch his advice in generalities. "You might merely say to him," Smith suggested, that "you have opinions [about] reaching into the coal districts . . . and that you also believe there are other possibilities for the Nickel Plate extending into Michigan."[1]

Smith purposely gave broad outlines without being specific, but in this case the specifics could be easily deduced. The most promising coal districts were in the so-called Pocahontas region of West Virginia, where there were two major carriers—the Norfolk & Western and the Chesapeake & Ohio (C&O). The Norfolk & Western was already under the Pennsylvania Railroad's large wing, so that left the C&O. Likewise, in Michigan, only three railroads comprehensively covered the state's major population centers and industrial areas. One was the New York Central's Michigan Central subsidiary, and Smith had no desire to give that up; the second was an extension of Canada's Grand Trunk Railway, which was off limits for several reasons. The third was a regional company called the Pere Marquette.[2]

By early 1921, the Van Sweringens were actively exploring both the C&O and the Pere Marquette. In March, O. P. met with Frederick H. Prince, a Boston capitalist who, with some friends, had a large block of Pere Marquette stock. Prince was a friend of Smith's and three months earlier had helped O. P. launch his Clover Leaf conquest by investigating the railroad's ownership situation. Although powerful and mostly respected, Prince was a pariah to the Interstate Commerce Commission, which condemned his blatant plundering of the Pere Marquette seventeen years earlier. Negotiations between Smith and O. P. soon hit a dead end, however, in part because O. P. insisted on a complex variation of his holding company method which would give him maximum control for a minimum investment. That and some other control proposals went nowhere, and the Vans gave up on the Pere Marquette for the time being.[3]

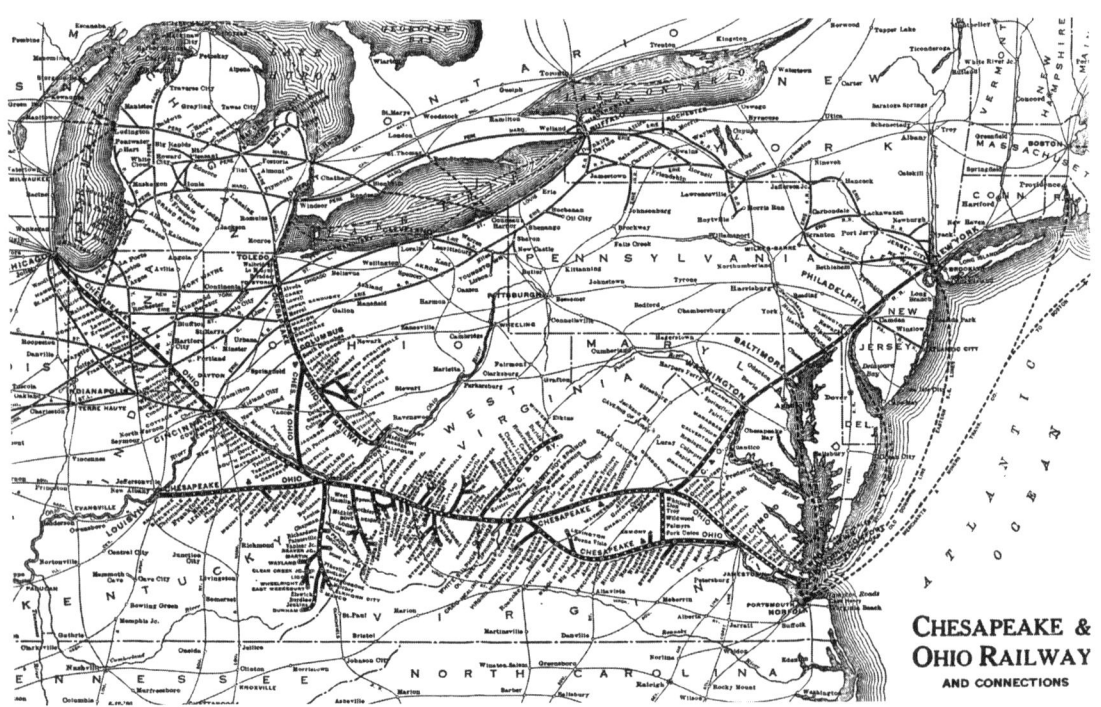

But they kept moving on the Chesapeake & Ohio. In May, they hired two agents to investigate how to get control of the company's stock and handle the negotiations—Judge David W. Fairleigh and Matthew L. Akers. Both were from Louisville, Kentucky; Fairleigh was a lawyer and Akers had close business contacts with the C&O's operating management. Aside from travel expenses, Akers and his partner were to work on a commission tied to the price they negotiated. C&O stock had a $100 par value; if they could get it at $70, they would get 1.5 percent of the sale price. Their commission percentage was scaled down as the negotiated price rose; at $100 they would get nothing.[4]

To those in a certain social stratum, the C&O was known mostly as the way for the First Families of Virginia and affluent easterners to reach the resorts at White Sulphur Springs, West Virginia; Virginia Hot Springs, Virginia; and the host of lesser springs tucked away in the Alleghenies near the Virginia–West Virginia border—or to deposit them on the beaches and steamboat piers at Old Point Comfort at Hampton Roads. To most others, the railroad was an off-the-beaten-path nonentity running west from Newport News, Richmond, and Washington to Cincinnati and Chicago, with a branch to Louisville, Kentucky; together with its Hocking Valley Railway subsidiary, it also reached coal-shipping docks on Lake Erie at Toledo.

En route it wound through the West Virginia mountains, a region legendary for its isolation and clannishness. While the springs in this territory may have given the C&O some social cachet, the railroad's roots were a thick collection of tendrils reaching deep in the West Virginia and eastern Kentucky hollows, touching spots with names like Marrowbone, Slab Fork, Peach Creek, Glen Jean, and Elkhorn City. This was rich bituminous coal country, and it was C&O's life; by 1923, 79 percent of the railroad's total freight tonnage consisted of coal, most of it moving east to docks at Newport News or west to the Great Lakes and midwestern industrial centers. The business had begun to grow rapidly, too, as the older western Pennsylvania fields became more costly to work. Long black coal trains coiled through the creek valleys pulled by plodding, ponderous articulated steam locomotives, past the spot where the Hatfields and McCoys shot each other up and through Big Bend tunnel, where John Henry reputedly beat the steam drill.

Smith's role in initiating the C&O quest is the usual mystery. The New York Central had a historic interest in the C&O and would have been concerned about its future status. Not

The heart of the Chesapeake & Ohio's traffic was in West Virginia's hills and hollows; circulation was provided by powerful, low-speed Mallets like this, outside St. Albans, West Virginia. The photo dates to 1954 but could easily be in the early 1920s. Little changed in this territory.
Gene Huddleston photo,
H. H. Harwood, Jr., collection

too many years earlier, the two railroads had a close affiliation, and the Central's bitterest rival, the Pennsylvania, now controlled the Pocahontas region's other major hauler, the Norfolk & Western (N&W). Along with J. P. Morgan, the Vanderbilts had taken over C&O's management in 1888; beginning in 1900, the Central and Pennsylvania jointly controlled the C&O during the short-lived "community of interest" era—the same time that the Pennsylvania bought control of the Norfolk & Western.

But antitrust pressures persuaded both railroads to back away from the C&O, and in 1908, the Central sold its interest. This left it at a strategic disadvantage against the Pennsylvania in what was slowly becoming the country's dominant coal-producing region. Although the Central partly tapped the C&O's territory through a subsidiary line reaching from Columbus to the Gauley, West Virginia, coal fields via Charleston, it was a lesser factor in the traffic than either the C&O or N&W. So while the Central knew it could not be directly involved in the C&O, it nonetheless needed it as a counterbalance for what it viewed as the Pennsylvania's malign influences in the territory.[5]

Be that as it may, the C&O and the Nickel Plate fitted well together. The C&O needed better midwestern outlets for its coal, and the Nickel Plate needed on-line traffic-generating sources—and the C&O certainly qualified for that. The C&O's route to its coal docks at Toledo crossed the Nickel Plate main line at Fostoria, Ohio; from there the Nickel Plate had a straight, heavy-duty route to Chicago, Cleveland, Buffalo, and numerous other coal-consuming points. (The C&O did have its own line to Chicago via Cincinnati, but it was lightly built and had capacity problems.)

In taking over the Nickel Plate, the Clover Leaf, and the Lake Erie & Western, the Vans were able to pick up a clear majority control through a few simple block purchases. The C&O was different; its stock was widely scattered, and for the first time the brothers faced a situation where no single person, group, or bank had the 50-plus percent stock ownership needed for undisputed control. In this case the "control" came by virtue of a much smaller share coupled with an accepted tradition.

The railroad had been built in the 1870s by Collis P. Huntington, a Connecticut-born entrepreneur who by then was famous as the biggest of California's "Big Four" who built the Central Pacific Railroad, the western half of the first transcontinental. Collis P. died in 1900 and passed on his C&O holdings to his widow Arabella and nephew Henry, who was amassing his own fortune from Los Angeles real estate, public utilities, and electric railways. Henry and Arabella married in 1913, uniting the Huntington fortunes. In the past, portions of Huntington's C&O stock had passed to and from the New York Central, but everything was now back in the family fold. Together Henry and Arabella owned 12 percent of the company's stock, the largest single block, but that obviously did not amount to undisputed control. The Huntington domination rested on a combination of family tradition and a widespread stock ownership with no other focus.

Happily, they were ready to sell, or so it seemed. Both Henry's and Arabella's health had been steadily declining, and in 1921 Henry was 71 and in semi-retirement. With his generous white mustache and balding head, he was the picture of an aging mogul; his most intense interest now seemed to be embellishing his palace in San Marino with art and rare books and manuscripts. (That summer, in fact, Lord Duveen had bought him Gainesborough's *Blue Boy*.)

Dealing with owners in Southern California presented logistical problems at a time when a trip between Cleveland and Los Angeles took four days each way. Rather than handle things himself, O. P. dispatched one of his two agents, Matthew Akers, to Los Angeles in May 1921 to broach the subject with the Huntingtons.

There followed a cat-and-mouse game, partly in California and partly in Huntington's New York office, with nobody sure who was the cat and who the mouse. The Huntingtons proved to be wily negotiators and held out for $105 a share; O. P. had hoped for $90, or $100 at worst. Things dragged on into 1922, but by then the brothers were tying down the Clover Leaf and the Lake Erie & Western and taking on more debt to do it. In the meantime, Professor Ripley's tentative consolidation plan had put the C&O in its own separate system, complicating the federal diplomacy.[6]

O. P. let the C&O ride for the moment while he got the Clover Leaf–LE&W situation under control, but Akers revived negotiations in September. In mid-October, Huntington finally agreed to sell for $100 a share—$7.3 million in total. But unlike the Vans' previous sellers, he wanted full cash, with a deadline of February 1, 1923.

Cheerfully disregarding Dr. Ripley and the ICC's plans, the Van Sweringens hastened to find the cash and consummate the deal. Pressed for time and with Vaness temporarily juggling the Clover Leaf and the Lake Erie & Western purchase debt, they had to find some other safe source. Whether by intent or not, shortly before Akers resumed serious negotiations with Huntington, the Nickel Plate received permission from the ICC to sell a new bond issue totaling $8.66 million. Supposedly the money was to fund earlier "additions and betterments"—presumably locomotives, cars, or plant improvements. Suddenly, though, the Nickel Plate's board decided that the C&O would be a better "addition."

There was still a problem. The Vans were committed to $100 a share for stock that was selling in the $72–$75 range in the open market. The Nickel Plate could scarcely pay this premium price without incurring a stockholder rebellion and possible action by the ICC. The solution was to have the Nickel Plate buy about 96 percent of the Huntington stock at $80, which could be reasonably defended. That contributed a total of $5.6 million toward Huntington's $7.3 million. To make up the remaining $1.7 million owed, the balance of the stock had to be bought by someone at $566.67 a share. The Vans' Nickel Plate Securities Corporation graciously volunteered to do that and paid for it through a loan from the Vaness Company—which in turn got it as part of a loan from the Guaranty Trust Company in New York, which handled the sale of the Nickel Plate bond issue. Nickel Plate Securities also paid a premium to Guaranty Trust to compensate for a price differential in the Nickel Plate bonds.[7]

In January 1923, Huntington transferred his stock and relinquished his control of the C&O, which had been exercised through seven of the nine C&O directors' seats. ICC approval was needed for seven Nickel Plate directors (including the two Van Sweringens, Miller, Nutt, and Bradley) to take their place. At that date, the Nickel Plate's application to merge the Clover Leaf and the LE&W was several months away, and the Commission rather routinely approved the request on January 27th. Its philosophical conflicts with the 1920 Transportation Act were theoretically minimal anyway, since this was not presented as a merger or consolidation. There was, of course, one lone dissent.[8]

The Vans' "control" of the C&O was a tenuous thing, since in reality they inherited the Huntington tradition but actually had a relatively small proportion of its stock. Over the next year and a half, the Nickel Plate spent another $6.5 million to buy enough additional C&O stock on the open market to give it a more comfortable 19.9 percent ownership. (The figure was intentionally held to less than 20 percent to forestall possible problems with the ICC.) The average cost per share for all this was $76—$24 less than the Huntington price. At the same time, the Vaness Company—the brothers' "personal basket"—spent $16.2 million for another 23 percent of the stock, for which it paid $93 a share. Those purchases, financed by loans from the Morgan bank and brokers Hayden, Stone and Paine, Webber, were made secretly and were not even recorded on Vaness's books for two and a half years. In all, the brothers got firm control of the C&O—about 43 percent of its stock—while keeping out of the ICC's reach for the time being.[9]

By the market standards of the time, O. P. did not get his usual bargain, and the C&O would soon cause him immense grief. Still, he had just bought his crown jewel.

While gathering up the Clover Leaf, the Lake Erie & Western, and the C&O, the brothers were also wrestling with a vital but difficult strategic situation to the east. Their Nickel Plate ended at Buffalo, where it interchanged its eastern business with the New York Central and three independent lines—the Delaware, Lackawanna & Western; the Lehigh Valley; and the Erie. All three of these independents connected Buffalo with New York and in turn had other connections into New England and the Delaware Valley of Pennsylvania. (Actually, they all terminated on the New Jersey side of the Hudson River, either in Hoboken or Jersey City, but they could reach anything in the harbor by car float.) Without its own route to New York, the evolving Van Sweringen system had a serious weakness which might even be fatal if its connections turned unfriendly for any reason.

Unfortunately, the pickings were not as easy as they had been so far. In all three cases, the stock was broadly scattered, so the brothers would need to buy their control largely on the open market—always an expensive proposition. And, whichever they might choose for their New York link, the brothers were entering the home territory of two of the country's most powerful financial institutions. For while there was no single controlling interest in any of the three lines, to one degree or another their financial policies were influenced either by J. P. Morgan & Company or George F. Baker's First National Bank of New York—or both. (Baker had long been a close friend of Pierpont Morgan, and the two often worked in concert.) This meant acquiescence and support on the bankers' terms, and the shrewd New Yorkers well knew what to give up and what not to. It helped somewhat that this group also had the strongest voice in the New York Central and knew the Vans through A. H. Smith.

Either the Lackawanna or the Lehigh Valley would make an excellent end-to-end fit. Both were limited to the New York–Buffalo territory, so they made ideal continuations of the Nickel Plate without overlaps or line duplications. Neither had a particularly productive intermediate territory except for one area—and that was the problem. Both were born in the eastern Pennsylvania anthracite country and were heavy hard-coal haulers. In the early twentieth century, anthracite was a hugely lucrative business; it was virtually the only home-heating fuel in large parts of the country and was also used by many manufacturers. As a result, both railroads were wealthy, and buying control—especially on the open market—would come very dear.

The Lackawanna was ruled out almost instantly; it was financially impossible. The railroad had virtually no funded debt, was regularly paying 12 percent on its stock, and in 1922 paid a 17 percent return. The brothers pinned their hopes on the Lehigh Valley, as they told Professor Ripley when he asked in late 1920. Ripley gave them the Lackawanna instead, but the ICC's 1921 tentative plan duly substituted the Lehigh Valley. That was little help; like the Lackawanna, the Lehigh Valley was too prosperous, and its board, dominated by the Baker–First National group, was not interested in giving it up. A. H. Smith made an effort to act as an ambassador to George Baker, but nothing came of it. Buying a clear ma-

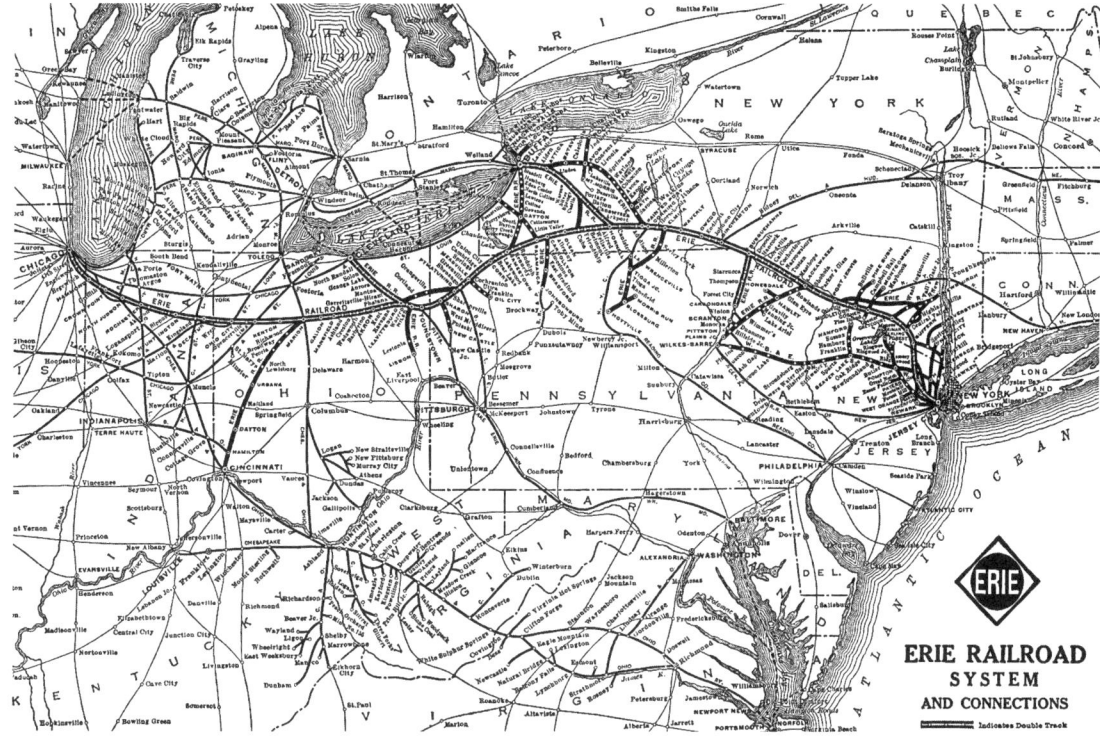
ERIE RAILROAD SYSTEM AND CONNECTIONS

jority of stock on the market would cost at least $42 million, over four times as much as the Van Sweringens had paid for any railroad so far.[10]

That left the Erie, which was a different story. The Erie was Wall Street's perennial problem child. The railroad looked impressive on a map—a 2,325-mile system with a trunk line between New York and Chicago and branches to Buffalo, Rochester, Cleveland, and Dayton, Ohio—but it also had an impressive legacy of poverty and disaster. Its nineteenth-century history was variously characterized by management miscalculations, misfortune, and mistreatment—the most notorious being its spectacular plundering by Daniel Drew, Jim Fisk, and Jay Gould in the 1860s. After enduring three bankruptcies, it was reorganized and stabilized by Pierpont Morgan in 1895. Despite Morgan's touch, it continued to live precariously into the twentieth century, partly because the bankers had not significantly reduced its heavy funded debt. But as the 1920s dawned it was, by Erie standards, doing fairly well. Except for a $3 million deficit in 1922, partly because of the national railroad shopmen's strike, it had netted between $3 and $5 million annually since the war's end.

Nonetheless, it remained financially hobbled and physi-

The perennially poverty-stricken Erie did its best to move freight faster than its powerful competitors. Here an antique "Mother Hubbard" Ten-Wheeler and a newer Consolidation start a westbound merchandiser out of Secaucus yard west of Jersey City, New Jersey
Charles Chaney photo, Smithsonian Institution collection

cally weak. Its funded debt was over $230 million, and its capitalization per mile was higher than the Pennsylvania Railroad or New York Central, although an Erie mile earned much less. It had the longest through-route between New York and Chicago, and much of that trackage avoided major traffic-producing centers. Its eastern section wound picturesquely through New York's Southern Tier, traditionally one of the state's least developed regions; on its way west to Chicago it passed through miles of flat, mostly unproductive agricultural country in western Ohio and Indiana. Other than the steel mills along the Mahoning valley in the Youngstown, Ohio, area and some plants in Akron and Cleveland, it had little heavy on-line industry. It made much of its modest living moving two sizeable commodity flows—coal and perishables. The coal was predominantly Pennsylvania anthracite, dragged uphill out of the Wilkes-Barre–Scranton–Carbondale area by two, three, and sometimes four steam engines. Perishables—mostly California fruits and vegetables—came through Chicago destined for New York and New England markets. Like the Nickel Plate, the Erie had compensated for its lack of on-line industry by running fast freight schedules geared to this demanding business.

And there lay a special problem for the Van Sweringens. The Erie's line to Chicago more or less paralleled the Nickel

94 • Invisible Giants

Plate's and the two competed for much the same kind of traffic, raising serious questions about whether acquiring the Erie would violate antitrust regulations. Then there was the ICC consolidation plan, to the extent that anyone took it seriously. Assuming that one of the new eastern systems would be built on the Nickel Plate, Ripley and the ICC had pieced together still another balanced system founded on the Erie. Without the Erie, this combination would fall apart, since there was no other railroad, or assemblage of railroads, which could practically take its place. Ironically, the Vans had little use for the Erie's west end, which was the source of all these problems; they would be paying for a redundancy.

Altogether it was not a cheering outlook, but the brothers had little choice. Their chief consolation was that the Erie was relatively cheap; estimates of what it would take for them to gain clear control ranged between $13 million and $16 million, a bargain compared to what it would cost to buy the Lehigh Valley.

The Erie was also in the domain of Morgan, Baker, and First National, and in contrast to their jealous guarding of the Lackawanna and Lehigh Valley lines, the bankers were happy to find a home for it. The man to see was octogenarian George F. Baker, the head of First National and the patriarch of New York finance. Baker not only had investments in the railroad, he had personal contact; he was a regular rider in the private club car between New York and his Tuxedo Park, New York, estate. Smith helped again by contacting Baker himself, and in January 1923, the Vans began working with others in the Morgan-Baker circle.[11]

It was to be another lengthy, frustrating exercise. Devising a Van Sweringen–style method of obtaining control, given the Erie's complex and bloated capital structure and its low earning power, taxed everyone. While the New York bankers wanted to solve their own problems with the Erie, they and the Vans had different goals; essentially the bankers wanted to preserve the capital structure as it was. O. P. at first insisted on a voluntary reorganization, which was coolly received; various proposals and counterproposals flowed back and forth through the rest of 1923 with little forward progress. In the meantime, national prosperity was returning, railroad traffic was rising, and the Erie began doing better. Its stock started to rise, forcing the brothers to take some action before it, too, became too expensive.

Somehow the Vans not only finally got through directly to George Baker but also managed to inspire his full confidence and active cooperation. It was quickly decided that both par-

In the early 1920s, the Pere Marquette still operated a tangle of branches left over from Michigan's lumbering era. Freights to and from the Buffalo–Niagara Falls gateways used trackage rights over the New York Central's Canada Southern subsidiary east of St. Thomas, Ontario. Note the Lake Michigan car ferry routes to Milwaukee and Manitowoc, Wisconsin, which bypassed the always-congested Chicago gateway.
H. H. Harwood, Jr., collection

ties would begin buying Erie stock on the open market, with Baker's First National Bank loaning the funds needed. (The specific understandings were never brought to light, but it was assumed that Baker expected the Vans to buy him out later, presumably at a profit to him.) Buying the Erie had devolved into a simple case of getting control first, then figuring out the mechanics of a new financial structure and integrating the corporate structure with the other Van Sweringen railroads. The buying campaign began in November 1923 and continued for close to two years, at which point the Vans, through the Vaness Company, had spent $10.1 million; together with the Baker group, they then had about half the Erie's stock. In the process, said a Senate report later, "The Van Sweringens had definitely been admitted to the best financial society."[12]

One more step remained—to get back to the Pere Marquette, which had been deferred but not forgotten. The strat-

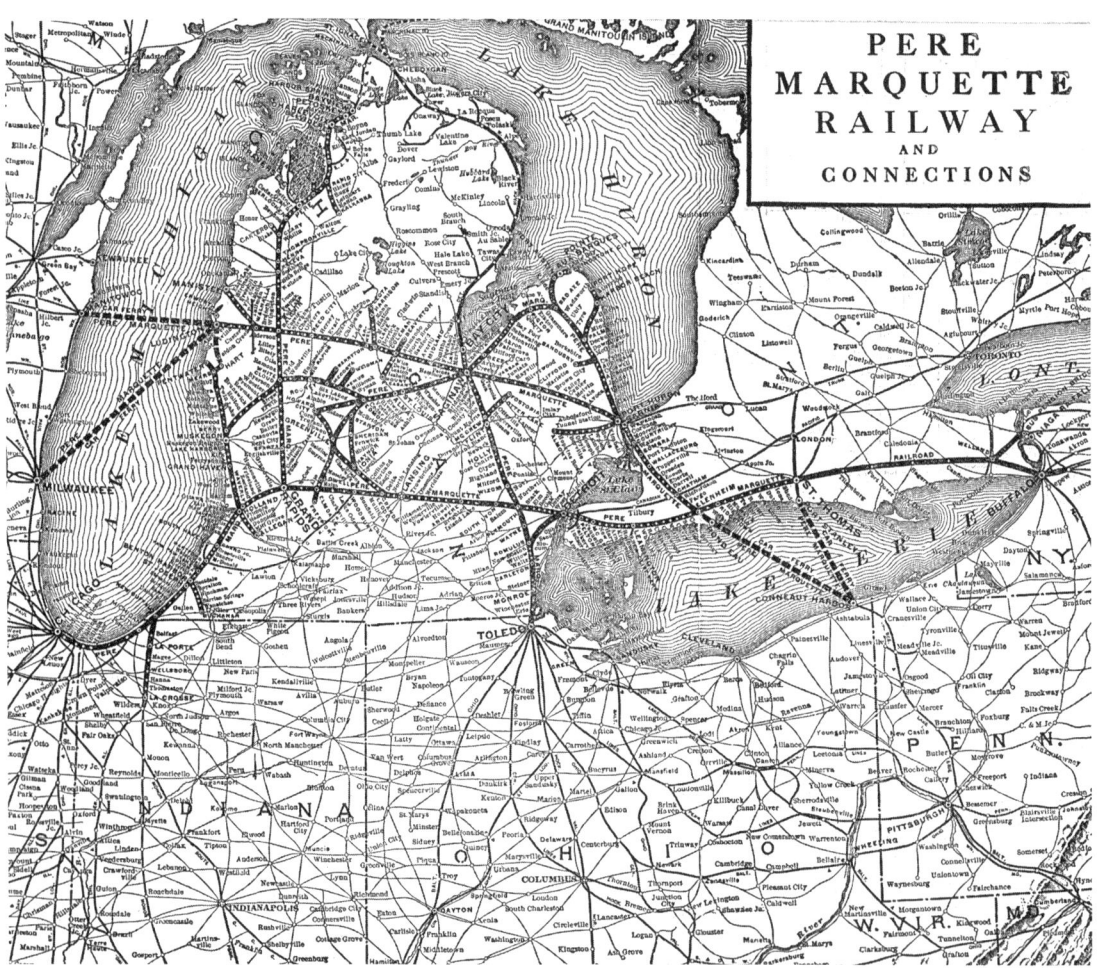

egy was to add some substantial on-line industry which the growing Van Sweringen system still lacked. Even with the Clover Leaf and the LE&W, the "new" Nickel Plate still heavily depended on moving freight between connections; aside from its coal business, the Erie had the same problem. The C&O gave the Vans a strong base of raw material, but it had even less manufacturing industry on its tracks. Thanks mostly to Michigan's fast-growing automobile industry, the Pere Marquette could fill in the gap.

Measured by mileage, the Pere Marquette (PM) was a respectable size—2,265 route miles—but it was a different kind of creature from the other Van Sweringen lines. Instead of a single long trunk line, the PM consisted of a dense thicket of lines crisscrossing Michigan, radiating from roots at Detroit, Toledo, and Chicago. This compact system reached almost every manufacturing and population center in the state, including Detroit, Grand Rapids, Lansing, Flint, Saginaw, and Bay City. Many summer vacationers got their first whiff of cool northern Michigan air as they stepped off Pere Marquette Pullmans at Petosky, Traverse City, or Charlevoix. A long eastern tendril took PM freights across southern Ontario to Buffalo, where they connected with the Erie and the other eastern lines. At the Lake Michigan port of Ludington, PM cars were shoved onto large steel car ferries and carried across to Milwaukee and Manitowoc, Wisconsin, which together with Chicago formed the railway's three western gateways. At Toledo, it connected with both the C&O and the Nickel Plate.

Like most of the other orphans the brothers were gathering in, the Pere Marquette had an unhappy past and an ambiguous future. It had been born in 1900 as an amalgam of three medium-sized Michigan railroads originally built by New Englanders in the 1870s and 1880s to haul out the state's vast timber resources. But by the '90s, reckless deforestation had stripped the lower peninsula bare, leaving the railroads to fend for themselves in the denuded landscape. Consolidation offered some hope for survival and the Pere Marquette was born, but it got off to a ragged start as Michigan itself struggled through its own awkward period between the end of the lumbering boom and the beginnings of industrial strength. At the same time, the infant company was brutally manhandled by a succession of financial groups which used it to float profitable bond issues and unload properties they wanted to get rid of. (Frederick Prince, their initial contact in early 1921, was the leader of one such group.) Between 1902 and 1917, the hapless PM underwent six management changes and two bankruptcies.[13]

Bay View, Michigan, near Petosky, was the Pere Marquette's farthest northern extremity and a world away from its bread-and-butter auto plants. The polished PM Pacific 714 has just deposited its load of summer vacationers in 1930. William C. Moore photo

By 1920, when the Vans first began unrolling their Rand-McNally maps, it seemed to be at last on an even keel with a trimmed financial structure and a rapidly growing business in autos, auto parts, and chemicals. Its weakness was the opposite of the Nickel Plate's and the Erie's—it generated high-rated industrial traffic but had nowhere to take it. Despite its link to Buffalo and its reach into Chicago and Wisconsin, it was really a one-state short-haul railroad. In most cases, the outgoing business had to be given to some connecting railroad at a nearby junction to get to market; at the same time, it had little control over incoming traffic, since other lines—some of them competitors—served the origins.

Plainly the PM fitted well into the Van Sweringen scheme. Not only could it produce business for the Nickel Plate and Erie to carry to market, but the industrial plants which dotted its right-of-way clearly could be consumers of C&O coal.

The Van Sweringens' active new alliance with George Baker gave them their opportunity to take in the Pere Marquette along with the Erie. Again their method was an assault in the open market. Beginning in April 1924, the brothers and their New York friends quickly bought up about 30 percent of the PM's stock at a total cost of $10.3 million. The Vans took most, and to pay for their share they once again used the Nickel Plate, which was just in the process of selling another bond issue. The Pere Marquette stock was then turned over to the Nickel Plate, although it would be five years before the railroad was put under direct Van Sweringen management.[14]

Swiftly and mostly silently, the Van Sweringens had put together the makings of a major eastern railroad system in less than four years—and had effectively accomplished the goal of preempting the ICC's consolidation plan and shaping it their way. It was an astonishing performance, facilitated in part by the now-enthusiastic backing of the Morgan and Baker banks. A. H. Smith could be proud of his protégés.

Nine

Taking Stock: 1924

By 1924, the brothers O. P. and M. J. Van Sweringen were generally regarded as a dazzling, albeit baffling, national business phenomenon. They had materialized out of a netherworld of local suburban real estate, picked up one obscure 523-mile railroad, and within a breathtaking eight years were major powers in the country's transportation system. Traditionally, the East had been dominated by three trunk-line railroad systems—the Pennsylvania, the New York Central, and the somewhat weaker Baltimore & Ohio. The brothers were now suddenly in the same league; they had created a fourth system totaling over 10,700 miles, consisting of four major companies plus various subsidiaries such as the C&O's Hocking Valley Railway and the Erie's New York, Susquehanna & Western. The Van Sweringen system ranked third in size, behind the Pennsylvania and the Central and ahead of the B&O.

Their railroads stretched from the Hudson River and Hampton Roads to the Mississippi and the west shore of Lake

Michigan; they blanketed many industrial centers in northern Ohio, Michigan, and Indiana and penetrated eastern Illinois; they hauled trainloads of bituminous coal out of West Virginia, eastern Kentucky, and southern Ohio, as well as anthracite from eastern Pennsylvania. They operated ferryboats, tugs, and car floats in New York Harbor and train ferries across Lake Michigan. They carried commuters in New Jersey and took the wealthy in considerably greater style to the C&O's own Greenbrier Hotel at White Sulphur Springs, West Virginia.

Essentially the Van Sweringen system had two east-west main lines—the Nickel Plate between Chicago and Buffalo (with close working connections to New York) and the Erie between Chicago, Buffalo, and New York, with a link into New England. The Pere Marquette added a blanket of lines in Michigan and a secondary east-west route between Lake Michigan gateways and Buffalo. The system's southern anchor, the Chesapeake & Ohio, not only fed coal east to Hampton Roads and west to the Midwest and Great Lakes, but its Hocking Valley subsidiary formed the Van Sweringen system's spine, linking the C&O, the Erie, the Nickel Plate, and the Pere Marquette.

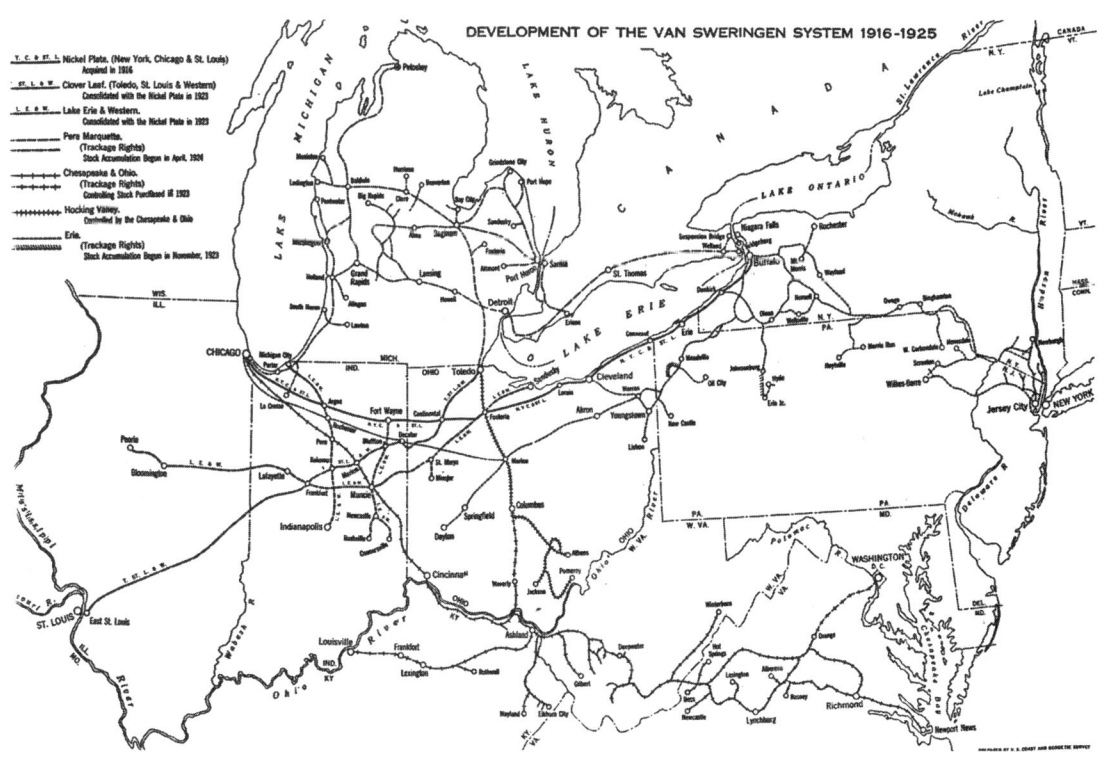

Perhaps not coincidentally, their system in many ways was a shadow of the New York Central, reaching much of its same territory—especially west of Buffalo. But it was leaner and better balanced than its three peers, with simpler traffic patterns, fewer overlapping lines and marginal branches, and—except for the Erie's vexatious New Jersey commuter operations—relatively minimalistic passenger services.

So far it was merely a work in progress, however. In fact, it could not be called a system, only a potential system. Only the Clover Leaf and the Lake Erie & Western had been merged and put under a single management with the Nickel Plate. The C&O's board of directors was overwhelmingly weighted by the two Van Sweringens and their friends, and in 1923 its corporate secretary moved to Cleveland. But otherwise it was very much a southern company, safely sheltered from midwestern hustle in its headquarters building at 9th and Main Streets in Richmond, just down the hill from Thomas Jefferson's statehouse. There it was run by the capable William J. Harahan, who had come from the presidency of the Seaboard Air Line Railway four years earlier. (Harahan had also spent five years on the Erie, which seemed to have served as battlefield training for many early-twentieth-century railroad executives.)

The Erie and the Pere Marquette were even less integrated; neither was yet even under direct Van Sweringen management control, and in 1924 the brothers were still in the process of buying up Erie stock. The respected but now aging Frederick Underwood occupied the Erie president's office in the Hudson Terminal Building at 50 Church Street in lower Manhattan, where he had been for twenty-three years. As yet there was no Van Sweringen presence on the Erie's board, although their new friend George Baker was its acknowledged patriarch. Frank H. Alfred, a former railway civil engineer, presided over the Pere Marquette from the Romanesque brick Fort Street Union Depot in Detroit. As with the Erie, the PM's board was unchanged and independent.

Railroads might now be taking most of their time, but the brothers had not forgotten their real estate roots. There too everything was a work in progress, and much more visibly so than the railroads—perhaps more rewardingly so, since Shaker Heights and the slowly materializing Union Terminal complex were being admired as landmarks of urban and suburban planning. As they stepped outside their offices in the Marshall Building, they could look across Superior Avenue at their six-year-old Hotel Cleveland and behind it the land now cleared for the Union Terminal development, which O. P. hoped would reorient and remake downtown Cleveland. His vision of a large, unified office-retail-hotel-transportation complex was still mostly in his head and in the constantly changing architectural plans, but the ideas were solidifying and the basic work was underway. He had already determined that the central office building would rise over fifty-two stories, taller than anything west of New York City and clearly dominating the city. As yet, though, Clevelanders did not know they were about to get their city's most enduring symbol and one of the Midwest's most memorable landmarks; he would not unveil it until February 1925.

The brothers could walk east up Euclid Avenue for a firsthand look at their challenges. By then all of the new construction was "uptown," and it was extensive and impressive. Just completed at 9th and Euclid was the twenty-story Union Trust Building, advertised as the second largest office building in the world measured by internal space—and built, incidentally, by their close friends Joseph Nutt and Charles Bradley. The "best" retailers were clustered around 13th Street—the Halle Brothers and Higbee Company department stores, dating to 1910–1914, along with Cowell & Hubbard jewelers, who arrived in 1920. Next to this cluster was the Hotel Cleveland's chief rival, the 1912 Hotel Statler at 12th and Euclid. In 1921, the 14th and Euclid intersection had been transformed into Playhouse Square with three grand theaters—Loews State, the Ohio Theater, and the Allen—plus the Hanna and Buckley office buildings and Hanna Theater. The following year, the 21-story B. F. Keith Building was completed a block to the east, rising over the 3,680-seat Keith's Palace Theater—"the finest in the world," it claimed. Their Union Terminal complex would have to stop that trend and reverse it.[1]

Also outside their offices they could see the cars of their Shaker Heights rapid transit line looping around the Square. Heights residents could now get home in twenty-seven minutes or less (even though two miles of the line still operated temporarily on downtown streets), and in the four years since the line had opened, the suburb of Shaker Heights had boomed. In 1900, the Shaker land had been appraised at $240,000; the 1923 figure was $29.3 million. As another indication of Shaker's spectacular growth, rapid transit riding shot up from 439,539 in 1920 to 1,520,608 in 1924, a 246 percent increase. (By the next year it would be 2,325,000—58 percent more in one year.) The original four-car fleet of city streetcars which opened the line in 1920 had now grown to twenty, all of them rebuilt to operate at 50 miles per hour, often running in multi-car trains.[2]

And just as the brothers were in the process of rearranging eastern railroad geography in 1924, they were looking at their engineers' maps to see how they could redesign Cleveland's rail-transit system. With the Shaker line proving what rapid transit could do to real estate development and the Union Terminal underway, the Vans also ordered a plan for high-speed electric lines radiating from the terminal to other parts of the city—presumably to be operated by their Traction Terminals Company. For the most part, these would pragmatically use existing railroad rights-of-way. Their thinking included an east-west main line that followed the Nickel Plate from Euclid and East Cleveland to Lakewood and Rocky River; the part of this route between the Terminal and East Cleveland would be done as a by-product of the terminal railroad project itself, and on the city's West Side, provision already had been made for it as part of the Nickel Plate's project to eliminate street grade crossings. Two other routes would branch off the combined East Cleveland–Shaker lines east of East 55th Street, one following the Erie Railroad east to North Randall and the other following the Wheeling & Lake Erie southeast to East 93rd and Broadway.[3]

Out on the Public Square, mingled with their Shaker Heights trains, the brothers saw a constant stream of other electric cars making their terminal loops around various parts of the Square's four quadrants. Most were the yellow streetcars of the Cleveland Railway, but among them were the more lordly electric interurbans which connected Cleveland with virtually every town of note in northern Ohio, plus many of little or no note. In 1924, five such lines radiated from the city. The queen of Cleveland's interurbans, the Lake Shore Electric, ran trains of orange cars to Toledo and Detroit and was almost single-handedly developing the western lakeshore suburbs of Rocky River, Bay Village, and Avon. The extensive Cleveland Southwestern system—most called it the "Green Line"—reached Medina, Wooster, Mansfield, Bucyrus, Elyria, and Oberlin. Clevelanders going to Akron rode the dark red interurbans of the Northern Ohio Traction & Light Company. From Akron, Northern Ohio cars and their connections reached Canton, Massillon, New Philadelphia, and Urichsville as well as Ravenna, Warren, and Alliance. Cars of the more humble Cleveland & Eastern rolled through the hilly rural country to Gates Mills, Chardon, and Middlefield. Finally, the Cleveland, Painesville & Eastern offered two routes which paralleled the Lake Erie shore through Willoughby and Mentor to Painesville. (A sixth line, the Cleveland & Chagrin Falls, no longer entered town; it met the Shaker Heights rapid transit trains at their Moreland Boulevard and Lynnfield Road terminal.)

All five interurban lines were forced to reach the Square by grinding slowly over many miles of city streetcar tracks. This handicap the Van Sweringens intended to cure; their planned rapid transit system would connect with most of them at the city's fringes and bring the cars directly into the Union Terminal over high-speed rights-of-way. This, they were certain, would help everyone. The interurbans, now beleaguered by private autos, could offer faster, more attractive services and perhaps regain financial strength, and the Vans would have several more Union Terminal tenants who (they hoped) not only paid rent themselves but brought customers to the Terminal's stores. But by 1924 this was beginning to look like a long shot; all of the companies were financially shaky and the important Cleveland Southwestern was already in receivership.

This swiftly expanding empire of railroads, real estate, and rapid transit was all conceived and controlled from four or five floors of the Marshall Building on the northwest quadrant of the Public Square, where the Vans had moved when the building opened in 1913. O. P.'s and M. J.'s offices adjoined each other on the twelfth floor, the building's top. At age 43 in 1924, M. J. still looked trim, blond, and athletic; thanks to his indifference to exercise and "predilection for creamed codfish," as one associate put it, the 45-year-old O. P. had begun putting on weight which was complemented by his naturally large, round head.

Their railroads may have blanketed the East and Midwest and their money now came mostly through New York, but their inner circle remained resolutely hometown Cleveland. Most of their working associates seemed to be bankers and lawyers of one type or another. John Sherwin, Joseph R. Nutt, and Charles L. Bradley, now chairman, president, and vice president respectively of Cleveland's Union Trust, were the closest; Frank Ginn and Newton D. Baker served sometimes as personal lawyers; Baker had represented them in the politically sensitive unification cases before the Interstate Commerce Commission. Their Union Terminal and some holding company work was handled by "Billy" Stage, a Western Reserve track star during his college days in the early '90s, a Tom Johnson and Newton D. Baker associate, and one of the Vans' early Shaker backers. Notre Dame law graduate John P. Murphy, 37, was another railroad litigation specialist who acted as the brothers' personal attorney.

A few "outsiders" did filter in: Two years before, the brothers had hired Colonel William A. Colston away from the ICC, where he was director of finance; as vice president and general counsel of the Nickel Plate, he carried much of the tangled load for the ICC hearings. And concurrently with moving into the C&O they picked up Herbert Fitzpatrick, a political lawyer from Huntington, West Virginia, who was then the C&O's law vice president. Fitzpatrick—actually born a Virginian—shared several of the brothers' traits; he was modest, smooth, worked subtly and quietly, and he was also a bachelor. Raised to revere classical literature and fond of quoting Shakespeare, the tall, somewhat frosty Fitzpatrick was probably the most intellectual of the brothers' associates. The brothers increasingly depended on him to handle their ever-growing railroad acquisition and consolidation work, and he soon became the closest non-Clevelander within the Van Sweringen clique.[4]

When he was not on the road somewhere, John J. Bernet—"Boss," as the brothers called him—would regularly drop in late in the afternoon to go over railroad acquisition strategy. One Van Sweringen associate recalled Bernet as "gruff in manner, stern in appearance, in reality a man of kindly instinct and generous nature which he kept well hidden."[5]

All Van Sweringen companies were controlled primarily through a single private holding company, the Vaness Company, which was essentially the brothers' personal property; Joseph Nutt and Charles Bradley, their two closest associates, held a minority stake in Vaness and were part of its secret management control trust. Vaness held the Nickel Plate's controlling stock, it had much stock in the other railroads (the Nickel Plate also owned some railroad stocks), and in most cases it had full ownership of the various real estate operations.

Always close by the brothers' offices was a small, tightly knit personal staff made up mostly of bright young Cleveland men chosen for their discretion, rectitude, and special aptitudes for numbers. Consistent with the brothers' own modest style, nobody had a formal title. The brothers' chief personal assistant was 33-year-old Darwin S. Barrett, Jr., a thin, glum-looking man with engineering training whom O. P. had first spotted on a surveying crew for the Cleveland & Youngstown project. Since 1913, he had served as O. P.'s secretary, emissary, and general confidential assistant; among other things, he acted as a principal go-between with the Vans' bankers and as sort of a chief of staff, screening their mail and visitors. Barrett was the definition of discretion; office jokesters claimed that "whenever he opened his mouth a moth flew out." Another trusted aide was William H. Wenneman, 21 at the time, who had started as an office boy at age 16 and had a notably precise mind and an outstanding memory for numbers.[6]

The eldest brother, Herbert Van Sweringen, was also there, still technically the office manager but regularly bypassed and unhappy in what had become a meaningless role. Within the year, he would leave and try his own hand at real estate development, plunging into the Florida boom by promoting a new community near Bradenton. It soon turned out to be the wrong place and time; and he was caught short when the Florida bubble burst in 1926. Fearing his failure would pollute their name and reputation, O. P. and M. J. covered his losses and persuaded him to retire from business.[7]

To their assistants, the brothers were "Mister O. P." and "Mister M. J."; to one another they were always "Oris" and "Mantis." "The Van Sweringen staff regarded O. P. as a veritable genius," one employee later reminisced. "Many a time they had seen him take over a problem that had overtaxed the best subsidiary brains of the organization, penetrate the core of it and come up with the answer quickly. . . . His brain was faster than a present-day electronic calculator. . . . He [also] had a faculty for reconciling any seeming incoherence of ideas and of rearranging them into a pattern that made sense. Never one to waste words on minor matters, he would highlight the salient points of a plan and leave to his assistants the task of taking care of the details."[8]

But O. P. was not always easy to work for. His incessant and rapid flow of ideas (which often were not expressed precisely enough for lesser minds to grasp quickly), the heavy workloads he carried and imposed, and his demands for accuracy could fray tempers on both sides. M. J., with his more common touch and intuitive understanding of his brother, was the essential facilitator. Said William Wenneman: "O. P. could delegate wonderfully well, but when others failed to carry out his ideas of how things should be done, M. J. could show them without O. P. being bothered. Nothing is more annoying to a planner than to find his delegates lack the ability to carry out his ideas. M. J. was invaluable in saving O. P. the irritation of having to show them step by step." But whatever the problems, most Van Sweringen workers revered him. Remarked another writer, "If [O. P.] sometimes swore at office employees, they always swore by him."[9]

By 1924, O. P. obviously had a lot on his mind, but he seemed to handle it with flexibility and equanimity. "When wearied by over-concentration on railroads, O. P. would shift his attention to another activity—his real estate development, or his rapid transit line, or Cleveland Union Terminal, or his plans for commercial structures that were to occupy air rights above and around the proposed union station proper. These shifts of attention from one enterprise to another refreshed and relaxed him."[10]

At the same time, O. P. was deceptively slow, quiet, and understated. "[He] regularly slept the clock around, from nine p.m. to nine a.m. . . . Regularly he would appear at the office at eleven in the morning. M. J. would be at his desk, often as early as eight o'clock and never later than nine, and . . . would brief his brother on the more important matters that came in the morning's mail. . . . [O. P.] performed his work easily and quietly, without fuss . . . [but] would get so engrossed in his labors that he would lose all track of time. Mantis would inform him that it was time for lunch or that the chauffeur was outside and it was time to be on their way." Indeed, the practical M. J. literally functioned as his brother's keeper, making certain that his bags were packed, that he had pocket money, and that any other mundane details of life were taken care of.[11]

He was understated in almost everything else, too. In Van Sweringen real estate advertising, O. P. ordered, "the superlative was to be used never; the comparative rarely. Advertising, to be effective, must reflect restraint." Naturally that extended to appearance. "[The brothers'] tastes in apparel ran to suits of subdued greys and oxfords, and to such accessories as black ties, black shoes, and hats of neutral shades," one former employee recalled. This more worldly writer wrote, "These habiliments comported with personalities of soft-spoken, shy, self-effacing men, minus conceits of any kind. They were men who advanced on the world on tiptoe to avoid occasioning any commotion. It could be taken for granted that they would never savor life in red, raw chunks."[12]

One thing was firm, however. "See nothing, know nothing, tell nothing was the abiding rule of the men who worked for the Van Sweringens. It was not a formal prescription, it was something you surmised from the atmosphere of the office. Your senses warned you that here were two men who wanted no affairs of theirs hawked about or talked about in the market places. You sensed on the instant that an incautious word could cause the head that uttered it to roll." Those words, by the way, were written by the brothers' public relations representative, who sometimes wondered what he was there for. Prospective new clerks were carefully screened and chosen. O. P. personally made sure to interview each one, and occasionally some were even quietly investigated.[13]

There was also a primness which emphatically frowned on alcohol and tobacco and disdained many forms of amusement. (Actually, in earlier years M. J. was not adverse to drinking and occasionally smoked cigars, but he gave them up because of O. P.'s sensitivities.) Joseph Doherty concluded: "It could be readily surmised that the brothers had never been unwrapped from the cotton wadding their spinster sisters had put them in. They had never played at cards, had no interest in literature, and were completely out of touch with the hoi polloi." Even so, they were kind and sensitive bosses who paid well, were generous with travel expenses, and often helped out underlings who were sick or otherwise in some kind of trouble.[14]

The brothers' living quarters pointed up another peculiarity of the Van Sweringen psyche. Although they were genuinely and emphatically understated, unpretentious, and self-effacing, they housed themselves in a tasteful but opulent style. O. P. especially enjoyed his luxury. In the early Shaker Heights years, they built a large home on South Park Boulevard, which they shared with their two unmarried sisters. Soon, though, they fell in love with the Daisy Hill property as a weekend retreat and began spending more and more time on the pleasant rolling, wooded Hunting Valley farmland. During the World War period, the Jenkses fixed up the farmhouse and moved in with the brothers. Inevitably, the Vans gradually acquired adjoining property so that Daisy Hill's original twenty-five acres grew to 477. There they kept horses (ridden by M. J. and their friends, but not by O. P.) and, originally, pigs and a herd of Holsteins, housed in a large new concrete barn.[15]

By the early 1920s, O. P. had finally concluded that Daisy Hill would be their ideal secluded haven in which to live and entertain business associates. At about this time they met architect Philip L. Small, an MIT graduate then in his early thirties who impressed the brothers with his ability to work in their favorite conservative architectural styles. The cows and pigs having already been evicted, Small was charged with remodeling and expanding the huge barn into a huger Georgian-style mansion, retaining the original silos as a decorative touch. It was still in progress when the brothers moved in late in 1924, but when fully completed the next year it came to include twenty-four bedrooms and attached dressing rooms, two dining rooms (one of which could seat thirty to forty people), a library, various sitting rooms, a gymnasium (shunned by O. P.), and a swimming pool. M. J. used the pool, as did neighbors and their children, but of course no one ever saw O. P. in it. The mansion's showpiece was the Ship Room, a 40-by-80-

ABOVE: *Roundwood Manor at Daisy Hill Farm, the Van Sweringens' cozy country retreat. Behind the new neo-Georgian building was the enormous concrete former cow barn (roughly marked by the water tower), which had been converted to living, lounging, and exercise quarters.*
Cleveland Public Library

RIGHT: *Daisy Hill Farm from the air; the mansion's rear side is at the center, and its cow-barn origin clearly shows.*
Gerald Adams Collection, Cleveland State University

foot downstairs sitting room adapted from the barn hayloft and heavily timbered and paneled; adjacent was a gallery with an organ, which was sometimes played by one of the sisters. (It got its name from a model sailing ship that Philip Small had found on one of his buying trips and that happened to fit the area over the fireplace.)

There were fifty-four rooms in all, but despite the opulent

Where cows once contentedly slept, architect Philip Small created the vast Ship Room, Daisy Hill's showpiece within a showpiece. The namesake ship-model's prow can be dimly seen in the center rear. Note also the metal rings in the ceiling, reputedly kept as picturesque relics of the bovine days.
Cleveland Public Library

Amid Daisy Hill's sprawling splendor, the two brothers shared this single bedroom.
Cleveland Public Library

space, the brothers shared a simply furnished single bedroom on the second floor. In keeping with the low-key personalities of his clients, Small managed to achieve the impossible by making this enormous complex seem almost unobtrusive, both outside and in. Large or small, the interior spaces were carefully designed and furnished to give them an intimate feeling and to reflect a variety of English historical periods.

Taking Stock: 1924 • 111

Roundwood Manor, as they called it, was stocked with English and eighteenth-century American craftsman antiques—Chippendale, Hepplewhite, Sheraton, and Windsor furniture and Wedgwood and Staffordshire china. Most were brought in from numerous eastern trips by architect Small and an interior decorator—sometimes in the company of the Vans themselves. The brothers were neither collectors nor avid readers, but one small room was made into what they called the Dickens Room, built around a collection which Small had picked up. The Dickens Room was furnished with first and limited editions of the English author's works, the chair he used while editor of the *London Daily News*, a portrait, and some other Dickens artifacts.

Their artworks were of respectably high quality, but they were chosen more to fit the general decor than for pure artistic virtue. Besides the Dickens portrait there were several Thomas Rowlandson watercolors; a Charles Willson Peale portrait; an Asher B. Durand painting; several other early American portraits (including a pair of George and Martha Washington attributed to Gilbert Stuart), and the inevitable Currier and Ives and English equestrian prints. Books were acquired and given by friends to fill shelf space but were seldom taken down by the mansion's masters. It was said that if O. P. read anything besides business documents and maps it was Westerns.

The house itself was run by a staff of fifteen to eighteen servants overseen by a butler; about 150 people in total worked on the estate, which continued to be expanded and eventually included a fourteen-room superintendent's home, stables, multiple garages, a blacksmith shop, and a woodworking shop that employed a full-time cabinetmaker, and greenhouses (which provided flowers not only for the estate but for the dining rooms of the Hotel Cleveland). It naturally fell to M. J. to oversee all of this, which was just as well with the employees, who found him more friendly and accommodating and usually more willing to spend a little time chatting.

The grounds were determinedly informal, with the air of a country club, and they were used much like a club by the families of neighboring estates as well as the brothers' business friends. Bridle paths wound up and down the hills, a lake was created, and a field was leveled for polo and, later, airplanes. It was used once by Charles A. Lindbergh, who gave M. J. a ride while O. P. nervously fretted.[16]

The Jenks house—which was also rebuilt at the same time—was opposite Roundwood Manor, and there was much casual visiting back and forth. When the brothers entertained their business friends, the worldly and charismatic Daisy Jenks often acted as the hostess. She was, in fact, as close as anyone came to a regular female presence in their lives, helping them socially and with household aesthetics such as flower arranging (which she did personally) and dining menus. She also occasionally accompanied them and their architects and decorators on antique-buying trips. In all, she seemed to substitute for both the mother they barely had a chance to know and their two rigidly prim sisters whom they may have known more than they wanted to.

All that fueled the old local speculation about this too-close foursome. Charles Bacon ("Carl") Rowley, Philip Small's architectural partner, recalled: "Mrs. Jenks was quite some gal. She had a power." Rowley recollected the regular Saturday breakfast meetings at Daisy Hill to discuss building projects. Often one or both Jenkses would be there—the laconic Ben Jenks as president of the Van Swaringen Company—and before Roundwood Manor was finished, the meetings would usually be at the Jenks's house. Said Rowley: "You can't prove anything by me, but at those breakfasts Mrs. Jenks wore a kimono."[17]

Nobody could prove anything by anyone, in fact, and while the gossip was sometimes spicy, it was never specific. More likely it was a case of two lonely, self-cloistered men who needed familiar and unchallenging company, and possibly a bit of flair in their lives did not hurt. Although she was a year younger than he was, O. P. called Daisy "Mother."

Beyond their offices and their business travel, Daisy Hill was the Van Sweringens' world. Once a year—if they could get away from work—they would try to take a brief chauffeur-driven trip in one of their five Cleveland-built Stearns-Knights (or later Lincoln) limousines, often to the Kentucky bluegrass country or perhaps New England. But there were no exotic destinations; travel for its own sake—or any extended relaxation, for that matter—was simply not in the Van Swaringen makeup.[18]

Almost incidentally, in 1924, Philip Small remodeled the large but rather ordinary South Park Boulevard town house into a larger and more fashionable Tudor mansion. Although the two sisters remained there, it was only a token residence for the brothers. As for Small himself, he increasingly became the Vans' house architect for most of their personal and corporate projects in Cleveland—of which there were many more to come.[19]

There was much to look on with pride in 1924 and much more to look forward to. But a shocking event early that same year signaled that the future would be different.

Ten

Some Shadows Fleet By

Saturday, March 8, 1924, was a normal half-day in the New York Central's new headquarters office building at 466 Lexington Avenue in New York. At about one o'clock, President Alfred Smith ended a meeting with one of his executives, George Harwood, put on his hat and coat, and left "full of his usual high spirits and joy of living," as Harwood noted. Active and virile at age 60, Smith later joined a friend, Edward Hoopes, to go horseback riding in Central Park. He was cantering in the dark at about 6:30 P.M. when a woman horseback rider suddenly appeared in front of him on a cross path. Smith reined up sharply; his horse reared, and he was thrown off. His head and shoulders hit the ground first, his neck snapped, and he was dead. "One of the greatest railway executives of his day," *Railway Age* magazine said in tribute, although, sadly, he was largely forgotten soon after.[1]

Given Smith's age and physical vigor, the Central unsurprisingly was not prepared for the loss and had to quickly scramble for a successor. The leading candidate was finance

A. H. Smith faced the cold in style as he inspected progress on a new cutoff line south of Castleton, New York, in December 1923—two and a half months before his fateful horseback ride. At left is George A. Harwood, his chief engineering assistant.
H. H. Harwood, Jr., collection

vice president Albert H. Harris, who had had his eyes on the job when Smith was chosen. In the interim, however, he had lost that ambition and demurred; instead, he recommended Patrick E. Crowley, the 59-year-old operating vice president. The choice of Crowley also followed the traditional railroad industry pattern of picking an operating man—as Smith had been—to run the company.

Crowley was close to Smith's age and shared a similar background; his own railroad career began at age 14 as a telegrapher for the Erie Railroad, and he had quickly worked his way up the New York Central's operating ranks. But otherwise, Pat Crowley was everything Smith was not. A short, dapper, somewhat dour man, he was polite, kind, reticent, and low key. Not only did he lack Smith's drive and vision ("a Milquetoast" said one railroad executive), but his experience and talents were limited to the narrower field of operating management. (Harris continued to handle the major corporate and financial matters.) Crowley was committed to continuing Smith's projects but reluctant to reach out beyond them; he also continued the Central's friendly relationship with the Vans, but at arm's length. The personal rapport and enthusiastic support were gone.[2]

On the surface, losing Smith was more a personal blow than it was any serious future impediment. The Vans had grown up quickly under his tutelage and had benefited from

Some Shadows Fleet By • 115

the doors he had opened for them at the Morgan and Baker banks; his crucial aid in Cleveland also would not be undone. O. P. was certainly resourceful enough on his own anyway. But if nothing else, the end of the Smith era was symbolic. It may well have been simply coincidence, but Smith's death signaled a subtle change in their fortunes. While their domains and power would continue to expand, their most lasting achievements were in the past; underlying their subsequent triumphs would be a succession of frustrations and misjudgments which would ultimately prove fatal.

Be that as it may, the brothers were now powers in eastern railroading and peers of the traditional "big three" trunk systems. In addition, their acquisition spree had achieved its goals all too well. Their system was generally accepted as a fait accompli which effectively dismembered the Interstate Commerce Commission's 1921 tentative plan. Their swift conquests had left many troublesome untied strings, however.

First on the brothers' minds was a consolidation of their four separate railroad companies. Their hastily acquired "system" had to be physically unified and, not incidentally, the brothers had to be relieved of the weighty debt incurred in acquiring it. They had been able to load only so much onto the Nickel Plate directly, and altogether Vaness owed $33.8 million to the Morgan bank, their brokers, and others. Consolidation, in whatever form, required another confrontation with the ICC, and that promised to be chancier than the merger of the Clover Leaf and the LE&W into the Nickel Plate. Before attempting it, they wanted to be sure they had the support of their three powerful peers.[3]

Beyond that, everyone was concerned about the future course of the government's consolidation program. With Smith's guidance, the brothers had deftly managed to assemble their system without disrupting major traffic relationships or antagonizing anyone. But there remained numerous other lines which had to be allocated to someone; some were quite strategic, and giving them to one party would be detrimental to someone else. There was also the lingering question of how many full trunk systems there should be in the East. The ICC originally contemplated five; the Vans' acquisition of the Erie effectively stymied that idea, although it was possible to patch something together from other lines. Finally, everyone—including the ICC—was wary about the "voluntary" nature of the consolidation program under the Transportation Act and how it could be done without bloodshed.

After releasing its tentative consolidation plan in August 1921, the Commission had dawdled for two years, holding hearings to gather more information and opinions. It well knew the temperature of the hot potato Congress had handed it and still hesitated to push the process; at the same time it feared that if visible progress were not made, Congress might get impatient and pass a new law requiring the ICC to force consolidations. The thought of that frightened the railroads even more.

By early 1924, the Commission had finished its hearings and some next step had to be taken. Since their need was the most immediate, the Vans took the initiative and arranged a series of summit conferences at which, everyone hoped, the four ruling powers of eastern railroading could peacefully divide up all of the uncommitted railroads in a way that would achieve the Transportation Act's goals. Relieved, the ICC welcomed the idea and waited.

The heads of the New York Central, the Pennsylvania Railroad, the Baltimore & Ohio, and the Van Sweringen lines first faced one another in New York early in May. O. P., M. J., and John Bernet came from Cleveland to negotiate for their interests; at the table with them were Pat Crowley from the Central, President Samuel Rea of the Pennsylvania, and the B&O's Daniel Willard. Rea was a 69-year-old self-taught civil engineer who had made a name for himself as the chief overseer of the massive Pennsylvania Station project in New York. Since he was close to his company's mandatory retirement age, he had at his side his heir apparent, operating vice president W. W. Atterbury. Willard, then 63, was widely respected as an industry statesman; he had headed the B&O since 1911 and had done a remarkable job of rebuilding prestige and morale in a proud company that had been through a relentless succession of humiliations and hard times.[4]

Up to this point the "big three" eastern lines had warily waited out the ICC's planning procedures, hesitating to do anything overtly aggressive until they had a better idea of what shape the program would take. Smith had been the only activist, but most of that was behind the scenes through the Van Sweringens; his only direct move was to pick up two Chicago switching lines for the Central in 1922 over the objections of the Pennsylvania and the B&O. But with the market now apparently thrown open, human and corporate personalities quickly emerged. As the conferences continued erratically into the fall, these proved difficult to reconcile and ultimately doomed hopes for any "final" plan in the near future. In retrospect, it was the end of hope for the entire consolidation planning process.

Part of the blame may rest with O. P., who led off with his

own ideas of how everything should be allocated. Happily, nobody had problems with his own system as it then stood. But he grievously miscalculated the mood of the Pennsylvania Railroad, which viewed itself as a company not to be trifled with.

It did not take long for power alignments to form. While the Central and the B&O were certainly competitors, they competed less with each other than both did with the Pennsylvania. Because they owed so much to A. H. Smith, the Van Sweringens naturally tended to align themselves with the New York Central. All three railroad systems viewed the Pennsylvania as the largest and most powerful in their territory as well as the most dominant single company in the industry; to their way of thinking, it needed nothing beyond what it already had. For its part, the Pennsylvania—which had begun advertising itself as "The Standard Railroad of the World"— was determined to keep that status and protect itself against any incursions. It further felt that it could use some strengthening in a few areas where it was admittedly weak. Thus, an informal "triple alliance" among the New York Central, the B&O, and the Van Sweringens emerged, and the Pennsylvania was increasingly isolated.

In presenting his plan, O. P. may have been misled by Samuel Rea's behavior over the past several years. Rea himself was a builder of physical things rather than a territorial expansionist; his primary aim was to protect and perfect the Pennsylvania Railroad as it was, and he had been generally passive toward the Vans. Most on his mind was the part of the ICC's tentative plan which took the Norfolk & Western (N&W) out from under control of the Pennsylvania and made it the nexus of a separate coal-oriented system. Like the Chesapeake & Ohio for the Van Sweringens, the N&W gave the Pennsylvania a powerful presence in the Pocahontas coal region and was a moneymaker besides. (The ICC's plan had built a similar system around the Chesapeake & Ohio. That, of course, was already made academic.)

Everyone agreed that the Pennsylvania should keep the Norfolk & Western. There also seemed to be general agreement that the consolidation program should produce only four major trunk-line systems in the East—which, of course, would be based on the Pennsylvania, New York Central, B&O, and Van Sweringen lines. It was theoretically possible to patch together a fifth system from the smaller regional lines which were now up for grabs, but it would be relatively weaker, would add to their competitive problems, and would take away valuable feeders.

But beyond that, dissension quickly surfaced about the allocation of several key smaller railroads. First were the two remaining direct New York–Buffalo routes—the Lackawanna and the Lehigh Valley. The Van Sweringens gave themselves the Lackawanna, and the Lehigh Valley was to go to the New York Central. But since the Pennsylvania had no direct line in this territory, Rea and Atterbury felt that the Lehigh Valley should be theirs.

Then came the Reading Company, which was outside the Van Sweringen orbit but greatly important to both the Central and the B&O. The Reading was the Pennsylvania's chief irritant in its eastern territory; it was strong in its sacred citadel of Philadelphia and formed the eastern end of several competitive routes to both the Delaware valley and the New York–New Jersey area. The B&O depended on it and its subsidiary, the Central Railroad of New Jersey, to reach New York Harbor as well as much of the industry in eastern Pennsylvania and New Jersey. The Reading also served as the New York Central's entree to some of the same territory via a route through Williamsport, Pennsylvania. To Rea and Atterbury, giving the Reading to either of its rivals amounted to an invasion of its territory; they wanted it to remain independent and technically neutral, but the other conferees gave it to the B&O.

Finally, the Van Sweringens gave themselves the Virginian Railway, the third of the three Pocahontas region lines. Smaller than either the C&O or the Norfolk & Western, it nonetheless was the most efficient of the three, had the best engineered route to tidewater at Hampton Roads, and would give the Vans' C&O the direct rail entrance to Norfolk that it lacked. This upset the Norfolk & Western, which in turn upset the Pennsylvania.

As the conferences went on, the Vans, Crowley, and Willard found themselves agreeing with one another, with the Pennsylvania the odd party out. What the press had come to call "the triple alliance" presented its own plan to the ICC in October, which the Pennsylvania promptly attacked. At that point the Commission threw up its hands; it could not accept what was not a unanimous agreement, but at the same time it was powerless to force any resolutions. It tried to take the easy way out and in February 1925 asked Congress to be relieved of responsibility for carrying out any consolidation program. The attempt failed, and the Commission continued to struggle onward, but as one scholar later noted, this point "signalized the breakdown of law and order in trunk line territory." Furious activity would follow for the rest of the decade, but for all practical purposes the great hopes of 1920 were already dead.[5]

While the Vans were getting their first heavy dose of major railroad power politics, they were also busy preparing their system unification case for the ICC. Bernet headed one line of attack, developing a carefully formulated operating plan which would meld traffic flows and use the most efficient routings and facilities of the four Van Sweringen railroad companies. The Vans themselves had the challenge of devising another financial arrangement which would be acceptable to the ICC but still allow them to liquidate their $35 million debts while maintaining clear control.

Bernet's plan was impressive: The Erie would carry the C&O's coal for the Chicago area west from the Erie–C&O crossing at Marion, Ohio, over its straight, heavily built but underutilized double-track main line. This routing was shorter and less congested than using the Nickel Plate via Fostoria, with its long single-track stretches; it was also considerably superior to the C&O's own low-capacity Cincinnati–Chicago line, which was plagued with grades and wooden trestles. In turn, both the Erie's and the Nickel Plate's heavy eastbound perishable business out of Chicago would move over the Nickel Plate main line. A new 60-mile double-track cutoff line would be built between the Nickel Plate at Dunkirk, New York, and the Erie at Hornell, Pennsylvania, creating a shorter Chicago–New York route than either the Nickel Plate or Erie had on their own. New autos and chemicals from the Pere Marquette in Michigan would flow through Toledo to the C&O, which would take them to the Nickel Plate at Fostoria or the Erie at Marion to continue east. Fostoria and Marion also would see C&O coal shipments moving onto the Nickel Plate for Cleveland and Lorain and the Erie would do so for the Youngstown district mills.[6]

In addition to the cutoff line between the Nickel Plate and Erie, the Vans intended to build a 63-mile double-track main line for the C&O in southern Ohio, which would complete its own route from the coalfields to Columbus, where it connected with its Hocking Valley Railway subsidiary's line to Toledo. At that time, the C&O reached Columbus partly over Norfolk & Western trackage rights, which the N&W had threatened to cancel when the contract expired in 1927. The new construction would give the C&O its own high-capacity railroad free of the N&W's restrictions and delays.[7]

The financial structure turned out to be a more complex variation of the device used for the merger of the Nickel Plate, the Clover Leaf, and the Lake Erie & Western. Once again the basic idea was to reduce the amount of voting common stock and convert much of the equity to nonvoting preferred stock. The aim was to give the Van Sweringens tighter control at a lower investment and allow them to sell their new preferred stock to settle their debts. In this case, though, the four railroad companies would not be corporately merged; the Vans' lawyers were reluctant to tempt fate by presenting the ICC with another full merger proposal, particularly such an extensive one. Instead, they came up with the concept of a holding company built around the Nickel Plate, which would both own and lease the railroads. This accomplished essentially the same thing but avoided the more irrevocable implications of welding all four railroads into one corporate unit.

The financial details of the unification were worked out in mid-1924 and presented to the stockholders of the four railroads in August. In essence, the new company would acquire all the stock of the four railroads in exchange for its own stock and would then lease the railroads for ninety-nine years. None of the railroads would be reorganized, and all of their funded debt was to be carried over in the same form. But the new company's common and preferred stock structure and the various exchange ratios were artfully designed to increase the extent of the Van Sweringens' control. At the time, the brothers held less than 50 percent of the C&O, the Pere Marquette, and the Erie, and their clever gerrymandering would give them an absolute majority in the new company at no additional cost. The preferred stock and some of the common stock of the railroads would be exchanged for nonvoting preferred stock, and the Vans would inherit a goodly amount of that, which they could later liquidate.[8]

Through the balance of the year the Vans worked hard to convince the various railroad boards and their stockholders to accept the plan. The Nickel Plate was no problem, and all of the C&O's board but one were Van Sweringen people; it naturally voted in favor for the proposal as presented, although the minority stockholders themselves were more divided. The Erie and the Pere Marquette still had no Van Sweringen representatives on their boards, and they were able to negotiate somewhat better terms before consenting.[9]

The new company was legally launched in February 1925 and was given a variation of the Nickel Plate's corporate name —the New York, Chicago & St. Louis Railway. (The Nickel Plate itself was the New York, Chicago & St. Louis Railroad.) The Vans' plan was presented at the various railroad stockholders meetings early that year and was approved—but with some disquieting rumblings at the C&O. Despite its exotic

California Huntington heritage, the C&O was steeped in Virginia tradition. Partly from native pride and partly from a legitimate sense of being shortchanged, a dissident Richmond stockholder group led by businessman George Cole Scott protested the terms. Scott even went to court in an unsuccessful attempt to block the special C&O stockholders' meeting scheduled for March 30, 1925. In another diplomatic lapse, the Vans misread the opposition and mishandled it; rather than negotiating, they chose to flatten the dissidents with what Nickel Plate historian John Rehor described as "the rawest of steamroller tactics." They should not have.[10]

With stockholder approvals a foregone conclusion, the Vans applied to the ICC in February 1925. Along with the ownership-lease plan, they also included a request for permission to build the C&O's 63-mile connecting line to Columbus, but asked it in the name of the new NYC&StL Railway. The hearings began in April, and O. P. took the initiative by defending his penchant for majority control which he had carried down from the early Shaker Heights and rapid transit days. "We have had a feeling, and still have," he said, "that one of the most unfortunate conditions in the railroad world is the absence of parental interest, guidance and encouragement—someone responsible for the policies and pursuits of a company through having the major stock interest. . . . We have had a natural pride in feeling that we were constructive. We have tried to look into the future and be progressive, and we wanted a free hand in doing so." His claim was probably sincere and, based on the Van Sweringens' results so far, justified.[11]

On the operating side, Bernet presented an excellent case. Most of the railroad industry agreed, as did many transportation economists. Few people seriously questioned the viability of the system, which not only promised efficiencies and superior "single-line" services but also held hope for rescuing the chronically anemic Erie.

But by then the affair had turned brutal as the Richmond rebellion flared up again. The dissident Scott group had hired Colonel Henry W. Anderson to represent them, and Anderson dug diligently into the job, attacking every conceivable phase of the Van Sweringens' past career; the brothers were cast as no more than financial manipulators who would profit enormously from the deal. There were also accusations (largely true) of self-dealing by shifting large sums of C&O money to the banks within the Van Sweringen clique. Naturally too, Anderson protested the stock-exchange ratios because they undervalued the C&O's earning power and assets.

As the hearings heated up and began to drag on, several outside supporters started to worry, and in September Professor Ripley arranged a meeting in New York between O. P. and Frederick Scott, George Scott's brother. (Although his name was not mentioned, it was assumed that the B&O's Daniel Willard had instigated the idea of a peace conference.) Scott suggested a separate buyout of the dissidents, but O. P. did not take him up on it and nothing more happened. The war went on.[12]

Then the tide turned, and, for the Vans, receded. Some time earlier, Colonel Anderson had found out about the Vaness management voting trust—the agreement originally created in 1922 when Vaness was organized and revised in July 1925 after Warren Hayden and Otto Miller withdrew. As it existed then, the trust agreement perpetuated the management of Vaness by the two Van Sweringens, Joseph Nutt, and Charles Bradley, even if they sold their Vaness interests; furthermore, it was to continue for twenty-one years after the last of them died. Anderson bored in on O. P. about the Vaness trust; O. P. gave vague answers. Anderson then attempted to have Nutt called in to testify, but Nutt turned out to be traveling in the west in a Nickel Plate business car. After some delay he appeared and also was unhelpful. Finally, Union Trust Company chairman John Sherwin produced a copy of the agreement.[13]

The disarray of the Van Sweringens' defense was hurtful, but the disclosure of the agreement itself was devastating. The commissioners realized that control of what would be a major railroad system ultimately and irrevocably rested with four people who might not even have a financial stake in it—and that this control would continue through a trust even after they all died.

The ICC released its decision on March 2, 1926; it rejected the proposal by a decisive 7 to 1 vote. Disunited as always, the commissioners had varying opinions on the physical aspects of the plan, but most (always excepting Joseph Eastman) had no fundamental problems with it. Some even left a door open for a revised version that would accomplish a unification. But they were almost unanimously uneasy with the financial arrangements and especially with the Vaness voting trust. Helping to unite them was Professor Ripley, who recently had been inveighing against Van Sweringen–style structures of nonvoting preferred stock in the *Atlantic Monthly,* and who would incorporate his criticisms in the influential book *Main Street and Wall Street* the following year.[14]

Since the C&O's new Columbus line was to be built by the

new Nickel Plate holding company, it too was denied, although the project itself was uncontroversial and clearly beneficial to the C&O. The commission suggested that the C&O simply apply to build the line in its own name—which it promptly did.

It was an unexpected defeat after years of unbroken success, and the Richmonders' attacks were undoubtedly humiliating to the proud and always-sensitive brothers. But O. P. was nothing if not resilient; he could always find some way out, and he went to work immediately. His longtime associate William Wenneman noted: "O. P. was not able to give up anything until it was successful his way.... There was not only ingenuity but defiance in the methods he used." The setback was deeply disappointing, but fortunately it was only temporary. Or so it certainly seemed.[15]

Eleven

Building, Rebuilding, and Juggling

"When wearied by overconcentration on railroads," it was noted earlier, "O. P. would shift his attention to another activity. . . . These shifts of attention from one enterprise to another refreshed and relaxed him." If so, O. P. had abundant refreshment and relaxation during the late 1920s. By mid-decade his life had subdivided into at least four parallel paths, each one demanding in its own way.

Most pressing was the need to somehow get his railroad system's house in order. Having hurriedly picked up the ingredients of a viable system, he had to unify it in order to make it work both physically and financially. The Interstate Commerce Commission's dismissal of his Nickel Plate unification plan now created several challenges at once: He had to make peace with the C&O minority stockholders and devise a unification plan which would be more palatable both to them and the ICC. In the meantime, he also had to solidify his control of the railroads by obtaining more than 50 percent of each railroad's stock. At the time, he held a clear majority only of the Nickel Plate; his "control" of the C&O, the Erie, and the Pere Marquette was based on varying lesser percentages. The only apparent way to do that now was by open-market buying, since the ICC had rejected his clever method of accomplishing it at no additional cost to him. Finally, he faced a $35 million short-term debt from his headlong railroad stock acquisition spree which had to be liquidated quickly—and at the same time he had to find funds to finance the additional stock needed for clear majority control.

All of that needed to be done in a hurry, too—and without ICC interference until a coherent new plan could be designed, presented, and approved. Any delay was dangerous. Juggling short-term loans could go on only so long, carrying costs were high, and by 1926 the stock market was beginning its steady rise, making new purchases ever more costly. The Vans also needed to keep their initiative in what was becoming a very muddled national railroad consolidation program; until they got their properties firmly together, they were vulnerable to dismemberment under some new (and perhaps congressionally forced) ICC plan.

Indeed, the state of that national program was a subject unto itself and the second of O. P.'s concerns. By 1925, the government's lofty goal of creating a cleanly designed consolidated railroad network was rapidly degenerating into a free-for-all. Correctly perceiving the ICC as hesitant and divided, railroad presidents and owners were starting to scuffle among themselves to tie down strategic lines or keep them away from rivals; at the same time, some opportunists and egotists were jumping in and attempting to fashion their own systems. The Vans needed not only to protect what they had but also to maneuver through turbulent power politics to lay claim on anything else desirable.

The third item on O. P.'s list was right outside his office. By 1926, work was well underway on the Union Terminal complex, which would initially include the combined railroad and traction terminal and the central office building, with a department store and other office buildings soon to follow. In 1926, O. P. was still the titular president of the railroad-owned Cleveland Union Terminals Company along with his own building company.

Fourth, and finally, there was flourishing Shaker Heights, which the Van Sweringens had decided to double in size by adding a vast new "estates" area to its east, and which was to have its own startlingly innovative features.

For the moment, though, their own railroad situation came close to being all consuming. To liquidate the immediate

$35 million debt, the brothers simply traded one financial tightrope for another. On March 16, 1926, only two weeks after the ICC turned down the Nickel Plate unification scheme, J. P. Morgan & Company loaned them $31.7 million—a large amount by the standards of the time. An $8.2 million Morgan loan followed in August, but after a partial repayment, the net of the two loans came down to $35 million. To help ease the pressure, they also sold some Erie stock. All of that let them pay off the various brokers and banks, but they were only buying a little more time; the Morgan loans were for only six months, and they would also need to buy more Erie stock to plug that hole.[1]

The Vans swallowed their humiliations and invited the two leaders of the C&O Richmond opposition to sit on the railroad's board of directors. In April 1926, George Scott and John Stewart Bryan joined the board and were also appointed to a special board committee to develop a unification plan acceptable to the minority stockholders. Based partly on a suggestion in the ICC's ruling, the brothers now intended to base their new consolidated system plan on the C&O rather than the Nickel Plate. This made practical sense anyway, since the C&O was clearly becoming the strongest component of the brothers' empire. For the time being, the Nickel Plate would be kept separate and, by some means, the C&O, the Erie, and the Pere Marquette would be united. Everyone agreed to that in principle but reached an impasse on stock-exchange ratios. In the end, the C&O board committee decided that the C&O would simply buy a majority of the Erie's stock without attempting a corporate merger.[2]

While shunting off the older debt, the Vans took on much more in their effort to boost their control of the railroads. Since they already owned marginally more than 50 percent of the Nickel Plate, they went after the Erie, the Pere Marquette, and the C&O; through various means, they had their clear majorities of C&O and Erie stock by the spring of 1927, plus about 35 percent of the Pere Marquette's stock. The holdings of George Baker and some friends, bought in concert with the Van Sweringens, brought the Vans' theoretical totals up to 60.7 percent of the Erie and 40.5 percent of the Pere Marquette.[3]

The brothers had always been entranced by arcane corporate devices that produced a maximum output from a minimal input. The ICC's decision now forced them into a new flurry of creative complexity in order to finance the new stock acquisitions while staying away from the gaze of the Commission's baleful eye. In slightly more than a year's time—between April

1926 and May 1927—they set up five separate holding companies, each of which had a different specific purpose and a different spot in the Van Sweringen hierarchy. All, however, had a common aim—to serve as repositories for railroad stocks which would remain under railroad control but technically outside the ICC's jurisdiction. Another purpose was to pave the way for a new try at the Commission by recognizing its opinion that the C&O made more sense as the financial heart of the Van Sweringen system than the Nickel Plate. Thus, a major part of the strategy was to move the Nickel Plate's C&O stock to some other entity, which would then form this new financial heart. Ultimately that would be one of the five new holding companies, the Chesapeake Corporation. Chesapeake was also designed as a public holding company so that it could generate outside funds to help pay for the various railroad stock acquisitions.

The first of the five was the Special Investment Corporation, born in April 1926. This was a wholly owned subsidiary of the Nickel Plate, meant as a temporary home for the Nickel Plate's C&O and Pere Marquette stock; it also then proceeded to buy more C&O on its own. Next was a sort of twin, the Virginia Transportation Corporation, which appeared in October as a wholly owned subsidiary of the C&O; it held the C&O's investments in other railroads. By then the C&O was prospering and the brothers were using its ample treasury to buy more Erie stock, which went into Virginia Transportation's pot.

Then came the Chesapeake Corporation, formed early in May 1927. The most important of the Vans' five new special creations, the Chesapeake Corporation was essentially controlled by Vaness and took over all C&O stock owned by the various Van Sweringen entities, specifically Vaness and the Nickel Plate's Special Investment Corporation. A roughly estimated $40.5 million debt came along with the C&O stock, and this was discharged in usual Van Sweringen fashion by having Chesapeake Corporation issue $48 million in bonds to the public—which the public instantly and enthusiastically bought up. The great securities boom of the late '20s had begun, and investors were now lapping up everything. (After Morgan and the other banks took their cuts, Chesapeake netted $43.4 million.)[4]

Born along with the Chesapeake Corporation were the final two members of the quintet, the Pere Marquette Corporation (owned by the Nickel Plate to hold its Pere Marquette stock for the moment) and the General Securities Corporation, a subsidiary of Vaness that acted as a temporary pot for

Vaness's C&O stock. Both served their purposes as transient securities hotels and disappeared, as had the Nickel Plate's Special Investment Corporation before them. The same fate was also probably eventually intended for the Chesapeake Corporation and the C&O's Virginia Transportation Corporation once all the Van Sweringen railroads were merged, but that now had to wait on some intermediate steps. (All this sleight-of-hand gave critics of the Vans' "shoestring financing" a wonderful new store of ammunition. Ironically, however, most of it would have been unnecessary had the ICC approved the original unification plan.)[5]

The first such intermediate step was made in the midst of all the stock-buying and spawning of holding companies. On February 11, 1927, the Chesapeake & Ohio applied to the ICC for permission to control the Erie and the Pere Marquette and to issue $59.5 million in common stock to help pay for their stock. This, the Vans hoped, would be relatively simple and less controversial. There was no financial sleight-of-hand; the C&O would merely take the controlling stock in its name, manage all three railroads, and coordinate their operations. By omitting the Nickel Plate, there would be no route duplication or overlapping of territories and thus nothing blatantly anticompetitive. The reviled Vaness management trust agreement, which had helped sink the Nickel Plate unification proposal, was reluctantly eliminated during the proceedings. The leaders of the C&O minority stockholder insurrection seemingly had been pacified. Many of the same benefits in operation and flow of traffic could be carried over from the earlier Nickel Plate case.

Sadly, it was another struggle. To begin with, the Richmond opposition reappeared, but with new faces. "The brothers must have felt that they were dealing with a hydra," said a later report, and indeed there were strong elements of a double-cross. Back at his old stand was Colonel Henry Anderson, now representing George S. Kemp and Frederick W. Scott, George Scott's brother. It turned out that the two brothers had now fallen out with one another. The new minority group was somewhat divided in its opinions about the benefits of affiliation with the Erie and the Pere Marquette, but it was united in attacking the profits they thought the Vans and their friends were making from trading the stock of the two railroads.

Herbert Fitzpatrick, the C&O's law vice president and a Van Sweringen intimate, and Frank Ginn, an old associate, headed the railroad's legal effort; as before, Newton D. Baker added his elder-statesman prestige as O. P.'s personal counsel.

They based their case heavily on the role of the other two railroads in distributing C&O's growing coal traffic throughout the industrial Midwest, particularly Michigan, Chicago, the Ohio's Mahoning valley, and—through a Youngstown connection—the Pittsburgh area. The argument was valid enough but somewhat weak, since management control was not really necessary to achieve the same goals. Also, the C&O was overwhelmingly a single-commodity carrier and had little in common with the other two railroads' heavy-merchandise traffic flows.

The hearings concluded in late June, and despite Fitzpatrick's efforts to hasten a decision, the Commission spent a suspenseful ten and a half months pondering—not a good sign. Obviously it was wrestling with itself, and the final decision showed it. Through all of this, the brothers were doing positive things for their railroads. In June 1927, the C&O completed its 63-mile double-track line through southern Ohio to Columbus and for the first time had its own direct, high-capacity route between the coalfields and the Great Lakes.

More significantly and dramatically, they resolved to overhaul the underperforming Erie. Its president, Frederick Underwood, turned 77 in 1926 and had been in the job for twenty-five years; he had done well enough under often trying circumstances, but the railroad had become sclerotic and clearly needed aggressive new management. Just as clearly, John Bernet was the one needed. On January 1, 1927, Underwood was given the honorary title of President-Retired and allowed to keep his old office in the Erie's New York headquarters. Bernet brought along the cream of his Nickel Plate team, including Charles Denney as his second-in-command and Robert J. Bowman as his personal assistant. (Bowman eventually would become a C&O president.) Walter Ross, the durable onetime head of the Clover Leaf, moved up to run the Nickel Plate.

The Bernet reign over the Erie was brief—he moved on to the C&O two and a half years later—but spectacularly cathartic. Once he got the measure of the organization, he completely reorganized all major departments, pushing decision-making responsibility down to lower levels and raising morale. With Van Sweringen and Morgan backing, he moved quickly to raise money to retire short-term debt and pay for obviously needed physical improvements; in May 1927, the financial world was astounded when the perennially credit-poor railroad floated a new $50 million bond issue. Bernet also began the process of closing eight obsolete shops and centralizing major repairs in a single modern facility at Hornell, New York.[6]

John Bernet at the time he ran the Erie, looking considerably more presidential than he did in his portrait in Chapter 4.
John J. Bernet, II, collection

To rejuvenate the Erie's motley collection of locomotives, Bernet bought 105 of these hefty, high-speed, high-horsepower Berkshires—the first in a long line of "Van Sweringen superpower" engines. One of the last of the group, No. 3403, rushes refrigerator empties west at Hornell, New York
Robert R. Malinoski photo

But Bernet's most immediate and visible move was a wholesale purge and modernization of the Erie's equipment, especially its motive power. Thanks to decades of frugality, the railroad rostered a wide and highly picturesque assortment of locomotives of varying ages and designs, many of which were now obsolescent. There were over 1,500 of them, ranging from a mass of ancient center-cab "camelbacks" (called "Mother Hubbards" on the Erie) to three enormous six-cylinder Triplex articulateds—the world's largest locomotives, but never very successful. Following a "fewer but better" dictum, he scrapped 427 of them, including the ponderous Triplexes, and used the money to help buy the most advanced steam power available.

From his earliest Nickel Plate days, Bernet was an emphatic believer in running heavier trains faster. In 1925, the Lima Locomotive Works (fortuitously located on the Nickel Plate) had developed a new high-horsepower design, the 2-8-4 "Berkshire" type, a milestone in steam-locomotive development. Bernet immediately saw its possibilities and ordered fifty for the Erie in 1927 and fifty-five more in the following two years; they were promptly put to work hauling new, expedited freight schedules between Chicago and New York and Buffalo and New York. Their effect on Erie operations was astonishing; according to one early report, compared to their predecessors, the new Berkshires hauled 17 percent heavier trainloads using 32 percent less fuel—and improved running times by 34 percent. Their Erie record helped kick off the "super-power" steam revolution, and the basic design remained unsurpassed into the postwar diesel era. They also became the prototypes for new power on all the Van Sweringen railroads and to railroad historians and enthusiasts were the most enduring symbol of the two brothers.[7]

While Bernet was shaping the lackadaisical Erie into a fast, efficient competitor, the ICC was still pondering. The verdict finally came on May 8, 1928, and this time it was a half-victory, but nonetheless mostly a disappointment. The C&O was allowed to control the Pere Marquette but not the Erie, and the original request for $59 million in new stock was accordingly cut to $30 million.

One reason given was that an affiliation between the C&O and the Erie made less sense geographically. But the real problem was the Commission's discomfort with the unresolved and increasingly unmanageable state of the entire consolidation planning process; it was desperately trying to keep a shaky status quo until some final national network design could be produced and agreed upon. The Pere Marquette apparently was considered less important in that grand scheme, but the Erie was something else. As the only "independent" east-west trunk line, the Erie was essential to any new system which might be proposed, and the ICC was not ready to see it snatched away, even though it knew that, for all practical purposes, the Erie was already part of the Van Sweringen's fourth eastern system. In the end, it seemed to come down to a somewhat inconsistent "let sleeping dogs lie" approach. One commissioner was consistent: Joseph Eastman was adamantly against the entire proposal, maintaining his perfect record of absolute opposition to anything Van Sweringen. To him, the brothers were vaguely unsavory speculators and manipulators who had no place in a sound national transportation system.[8]

Again the setback seemed temporary, but more momentum was lost, more financial conjuring would be needed, and the brothers still could not integrate the operations and management of their system. And all the while they had to do some nimble dodging and snatching through the chaotic but invisible battlefield of eastern railroad power politics.

At such a time, O. P. must have refreshed himself by shutting out the railroad world for a while and turning to his Cleveland projects. These were no less risky and unsettled, but he could at least have the satisfaction of looking at tangible physical creations in the making.

The most dramatic of them was rising right across the

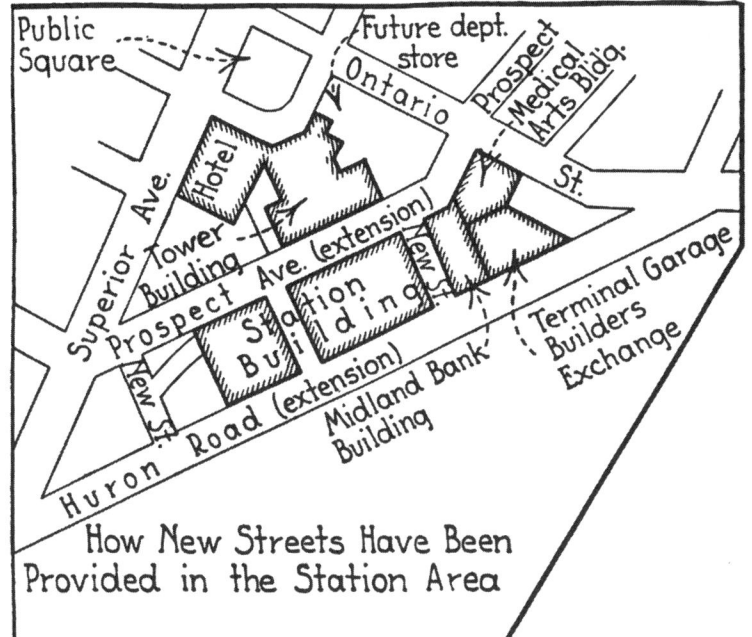

The evolving Van Sweringen "city within a city." Both the diagram and drawing look approximately north toward the Public Square and show the integrated layout of the Terminal Tower (at center), the underground railroad terminal, and the group of three satellite office buildings at the right. Note the garage, shown as a cutaway in the Builders Exchange (later Guildhall) Building.
Diagram from *Railway Age*; drawing from Cleveland Union Terminal Collection, Cleveland State University

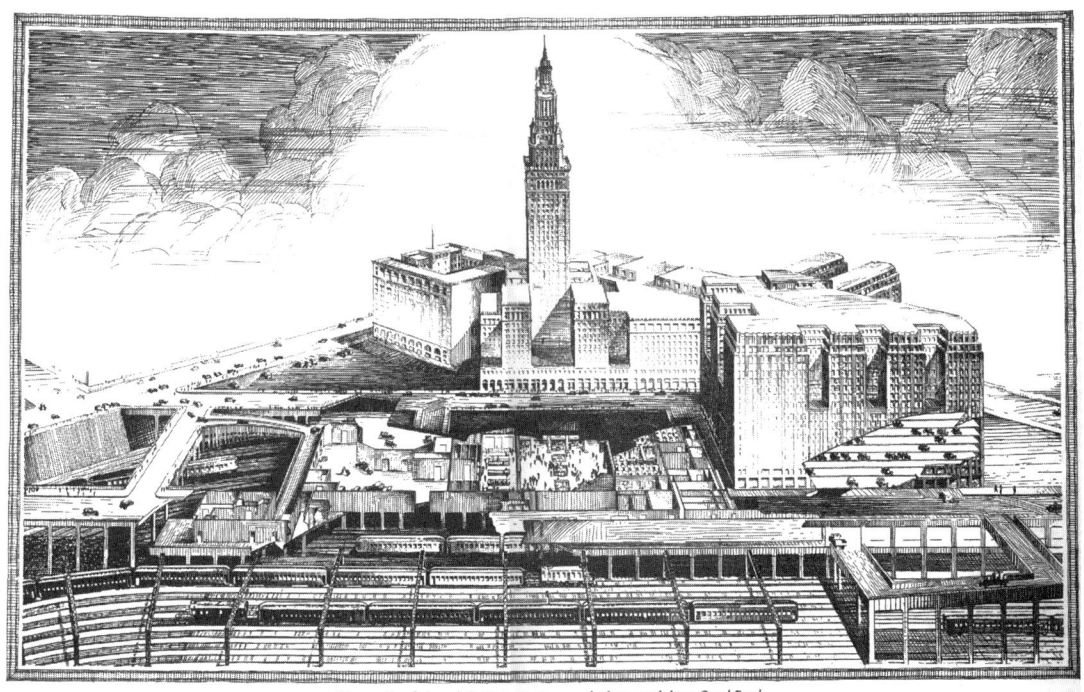

Cross-sectional view of the Union Station area, looking north from Canal Road.

Building, Rebuilding, and Juggling • 133

street from his office. In early 1925, he had finally unveiled a plaster model of his vision of the central office building in the Union Terminal complex. In place of the squat original fourteen-story conception, it was now to be a slim, tall tower rising 708 feet above the Square—52 stories in all, making it the second tallest in the United States and the tallest anywhere west of Manhattan. O. P. was inspired by New York's 1913 Woolworth Building, which at 792 feet was the country's reigning skyscraper by a wide margin; his own would not be quite the Woolworth's equal, but it would be a close rival. Toward its top, it tapered into an ever-narrowing pinnacle adorned with an exuberant profusion of classical and medieval motifs, including small turrets, columns, and balustrades and miscellaneous detailing. The effect was an emphatic exclamation point in Cleveland's otherwise undistinguished low-rise skyline.

But unlike the Woolworth Building and many others, O. P.'s landmark would not carry the name of its builder. There would never be a Van Sweringen Building; to the brothers, that sort of self-advertisement was simply unthinkable. After listing suggestions for names from their office staff along with their own thoughts, the brothers picked the last one on the list—Terminal Tower. Nobody knew who had suggested it.[9]

As with all the buildings in the Terminal complex, Graham, Anderson, Probst & White designed the Terminal Tower, basically following the Hotel Cleveland's style so that the buildings would blend with one another and with the others to come. The mixed decorative elements in its upper stories and pinnacle came almost directly from McKim, Meade & White's 1911 New York Municipal Building. O. P.'s new creation was thus an architectural throwback to the pre–World War era, which was necessary to keep the complex visually coherent but was doubtless his taste anyway.[10]

But translating the impressive plaster model into steel-and-stone reality at this bedeviled site was yet another challenge for the architects and chief engineer Henry Jouett. The Terminal Tower's concrete and steel foundation piers had to be sunk 250 feet to bedrock through varying consistencies of clay and set a contemporary record for depth. The work went on around the clock, employing 250 men on alternating eight-hour shifts.

Although plans for the railroad and rapid transit terminal underneath the Terminal Tower were still undergoing changes, the building's deep foundations were completed in July 1926, and steelwork began to go up two months later. On August 18, 1927, workers hoisted the last steel in place along with the traditional American flag. In the meantime, the limestone skin was climbing to meet it.[11]

At the same time, the entire area southwest of the Square was being dug out to accommodate the underground railroad station and the new street layout that was to be built over it on bridgework. Flanking the Terminal Tower at its rear on the other side of the realigned Prospect Avenue, the Vans and their Chicago architects laid out a complex of smaller office buildings that also would be connected with the Union Terminal, Terminal Tower, and Public Square through underground passageways. The first of these to rise was a unified cluster of three eighteen-story structures—the Medical Arts Building and Builders Exchange Building (both begun in 1928) and the Midland Bank Building (1929). As its name implied, the first was to house primarily medical and dental offices. The Cleveland Builders Exchange was to occupy its namesake, which would be a center for construction businesses; it also incorporated a capacious nine-story 1,700-car indoor parking garage to serve workers and shoppers in the Terminal complex.[12]

The third of the three would house the headquarters and main banking room of the Midland Bank and the Midland Corporation. This was a newcomer in the city; reorganized from a slightly earlier institution by the John Sherwins, Sr. and Jr.; Charles and Alva Bradley; and others in 1928. While the Vans took no direct part in the bank's organization or management (which was headed by John Sherwin, Jr.), it seemed almost custom-created both as a tenant for their development and another source of funds; they took a one-sixth interest in the company for $1.5 million.[13]

Besides the buildings now rising or about to rise, the Van Sweringens intended that the area immediately adjacent to the Terminal Tower be occupied by a large department store, giving the complex its full balance. Finding a store for the space was proving difficult, however; the city's traditional "finer" retailers such as Halle Brothers and the Higbee Company were happily dug in around 13th Street and Euclid Avenue and were reluctant to move.

Whatever the immediate problems, the Terminal building complex, the railroad and rapid transit terminals, and their approaches were an urban redevelopment project of enormous size. For the entire project, it was estimated that 2,200 buildings were demolished—mostly on the approaches—and 1,500 people relocated. Among the old landmarks sacrificed were the 1836 American House on West Superior, the city's oldest continuously operated hotel; two breweries; the Central Police Station; and Ohio Bell Telephone's main building.

The entire street pattern southwest of the Public Square was removed and realigned.[14]

In 1927, O. P. could watch all this activity with paternal pride, give advice, and make ready to move his own offices over to the Terminal Tower, but his railroad tangles were becoming far too demanding for personal supervision. That year, he gave up his presidency of the Cleveland Union Terminals Company—the railroad-owned company building the rail terminal itself and its new approach lines—and turned it over to close friend Charles L. Bradley. Bradley concurrently headed the Cleveland Terminals Building Company, which was building the Terminal Tower and other air-rights structures, thus continuing O. P.'s tight, single control over the two projects. Besides being at O. P.'s right hand for many years, he had successfully overseen construction of the Union Trust Building three years before. (He had since joined the Vans as a financial adviser after his ambitions at Union Trust had been stymied.) Age 42 at the time, Bradley was "a stocky man with ruddy features and twinkling blue eyes, a cheerful disposition and imperturbable character, [and] a reputation for getting things done efficiently." As his second-in-command at CUT, Bradley brought along George McGwinn, a Union Trust vice president and its building manager; together they had the unenviable job of riding herd on architects, engineers, and contractors; dealing with the railroad executives; and, incidentally, finding tenants for the buildings. By early 1928, the Terminal Tower's lower floors were ready, and on January 1st, the Nickel Plate moved its general offices from the seedy old Columbia Building at Prospect and East 2nd Street.[15]

O. P.'s expansive imagination stayed at work, though. Shaker Heights got similar doses of it at the same time—a dose at each end, in fact. To the east of Green Road, the Van Sweringens accumulated 4,000 additional acres in the villages of Beachwood and Pepper Pike that stretched almost to the Chagrin River valley and doubled the size of the Shaker Heights development. This was to become the Shaker Country Estates, exclusively designed for those who were prospering most in the heady Coolidge era. As first platted in 1926, the Estates would consist of home sites ranging in size from four to ten acres located on gracefully curving residential streets with nearby country clubs. Prices were to range from $2,250 to $4,250 an acre, quite lofty for the time. "All you want of the country can be yours," gushed a later advertisement, "trees, sunlit hills, rolling fields, shadowed valleys, long open vistas, peace, and calm, and restful quiet." It was to be a halcyon land of Packards, Pierce Arrows, and plus-fours.

Six-hundred-feet-wide Shaker Boulevard, as it is planned east of Center Road

More than ten years before General Motors' famous Futurama exhibit at the 1939 New York World's Fair, the Van Sweringens created this vision for outer Shaker Boulevard in their Shaker Country Estates development. Express highways and rapid transit tracks are flanked by local roadways, with plenty of room for both beautification and expansion between them all. By 1930, most of the basic work, including bridges and local roadways, had been finished.
Cleveland Public Library

An eastward extension of Shaker Boulevard would form the Country Estates' primary thoroughfare, but it was a far cry from the original Shaker Boulevard. Where the earlier Shaker Boulevard was a generous 180 feet in width and South Moreland a prodigal 190 feet, the extension was an astounding 590 feet wide, with provision for a fully grade-separated four-track rapid transit line and dual express roadways plus a pair of surface "local" roadways. At Brainard Road would be a complex separated junction where Shaker Boulevard divided in a Y pattern, with a 220-feet-wide boulevard heading northeast and a similar road running southeast. The two branch boulevards, Gates Mills Boulevard and Chagrin Falls

Building, Rebuilding, and Juggling • 137

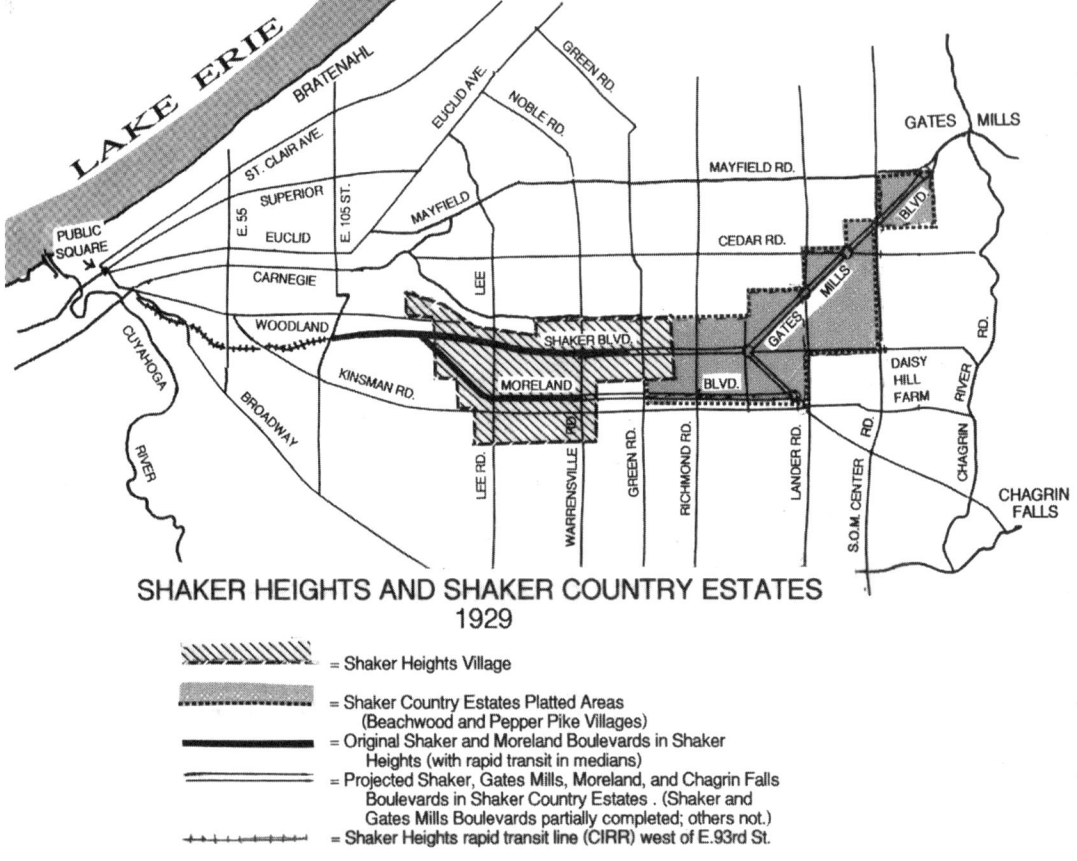

SHAKER HEIGHTS AND SHAKER COUNTRY ESTATES
1929

≋≋≋ = Shaker Heights Village

▦ = Shaker Country Estates Platted Areas
(Beachwood and Pepper Pike Villages)

▬ = Original Shaker and Moreland Boulevards in Shaker Heights (with rapid transit in medians)

═ = Projected Shaker, Gates Mills, Moreland, and Chagrin Falls Boulevards in Shaker Country Estates. (Shaker and Gates Mills Boulevards partially completed; others not.)

+++ = Shaker Heights rapid transit line (CIRR) west of E.93rd St.

Boulevard, would not be grade-separated but had provision for up to four rapid transit tracks and roadway expansion. Traffic circles were designed at several boulevard intersections, where small neighborhood shopping centers also would be built.

Also, South Moreland Boulevard was projected eastward from its terminal point at Warrensville Road, paralleling the old Kinsman Road along the south edge of the Country Estates tract. It too was designed to carry an extension of the rapid transit line. At about the same time, the brothers bought the abandoned private right-of-way of the Cleveland & Chagrin Falls interurban line into Chagrin Falls as a future extension of either their projected Chagrin Falls Boulevard or their Moreland Boulevard rapid transit route. Elsewhere in the area, other main roads were to be extended, realigned, or built new to fit the overall development plan, and existing county roads were to be widened and paved. At the same time, the brothers promoted a plan for a true urban expressway, which would reach out from the city's center to connect with the suburban network.[16]

Construction of the new Shaker and Gates Mills boulevards started two or three years later, along with some new secondary roads and the realigning, widening, and paving of the existing roads. But the new Chagrin Falls Boulevard and the Moreland Boulevard extension were deferred—for the moment.

The brothers' concept of Shaker Boulevard with its grade-separated roadways and rapid transit line in its median was amazingly visionary for 1926. Not only did it anticipate superhighway designs of a quarter-century later, but it was not until 1958 that the notion of integrating rapid transit lines in expressways first found form in Chicago. Yet their plan also had a surrealistic tinge. Considering that this area was to consist of "country estates" and golf clubs, one wonders where the volume of traffic for such an elaborate system was to come from.

Development in the "old" Shaker Heights was proceeding well too. In keeping with the Van Sweringen tradition of providing the best in education, property was given for three private schools; during 1926 and 1927 the Laurel and Hathaway Brown schools (both for girls) and University School for boys were completed or underway. By then too, eight public schools were in use or underway and had developed a national reputation for quality.

O. P. was especially fond of his new project at the west end of Shaker Heights. Thus far, the community had no real shopping area; in fact, both commerce and apartments were specifically banned in most areas of the village itself. The Vans solved the problem by ceding to the city of Cleveland the area west of the point where the Shaker Boulevard and South Moreland branches of the rapid transit divided. Since 1920, the junction had been marked by a rather bleak traffic circle, but the central location on the Rapid made it an ideal spot for a shopping center.

What evolved was another planning landmark. The idea of a fully planned suburban shopping center was something new in the late 1920s; there were only two in existence, and neither was quite comparable to the Vans' conception. (The acknowledged pioneer was the 1922 Country Club Plaza in Kansas City, which was more like a Main Street block transplanted and translated to the suburbs.) The genesis of the brothers' new project went back to 1922, when, with their blessing, local entrepreneur Josiah Kirby planned a grandiose

In addition to his longtime role as partner and advisor to the Van Sweringens, Charles L. Bradley took over the formidable job of managing the entire Terminal project in 1927. Cleveland Press Collection, Cleveland State University

complex of landscaped luxury apartments, stores, and offices extending in three directions from the circle. Kirby hired architect Alfred Harris to design his dream development, to be called Moreland Courts, which would have an appropriately Old English theme. Kirby got as far as building the first apartment unit on Shaker Boulevard west of Coventry Road, an eclectic but effective combination of English Gothic, Tudor, and Georgian styles. He then went bankrupt, and the rest of the plan died.[17]

For five years, Moreland Circle and the rapid transit junction remained a mostly barren area, broken only by the single completed Moreland Courts building. But in 1927, the Van Sweringens decided to carry out the development with their own conception of an architecturally integrated suburban shopping center. Inevitably, they hired Philip Small and Carl Rowley to lay out a grouping of low-rise chaste pseudo-Georgian commercial buildings around an idealized New England square, which would replace the old Moreland Circle. Work on Shaker Square, as it was called, began that year, and O. P. apparently found time to add his own ideas as it took shape. The $2 million complex, which fully surrounded the Square and the rapid transit tracks, included shops, a future theater, restaurant, and professional offices—and was enhanced by forty-one replanted elm trees, At the same time, Small and Rowley designed an extension of the luxurious Moreland Court apartments, which would continue the original building westward to the new Square with fifty-six apartment suites of five to seven rooms each plus a garage.[18]

Like the Union Terminal complex, elements of the Vans' Shaker Square plan were imitated and embellished to various degrees elsewhere, but the full concept was never duplicated. Shaker Square remains unique among suburban centers of this type, thanks primarily to the high-speed rail system which links it not only to the nearby residential community but to the city's center as well.

On their daily drives between Daisy Hill and their downtown office, O. P. and M. J. could regularly watch their imaginative creations at Shaker Square and the Country Estates taking form. Doubtless it was a satisfying diversion from the frustrations and turbulence of their railroad world and the abstractions of their corporate conjurings. Still, it was those invisible battlefields that now took their time, energy, and inventiveness. And now there was a new and colorful cast of characters taking them on.

Twelve

Consolidation Anarchy I: The Maverick and the General

While the brothers were enduring their ICC ordeal, the larger railroad world was beginning to churn on its own. By 1925, the Commission's lack of assertiveness and general foot-dragging on the consolidation program had encouraged everyone to make their own moves before someone else beat them to it. Some perceptive owners of strategic smaller lines were delighted to see eager bidders for their properties and did what they could to stir the cauldron.

The Van Sweringens, the New York Central, and the Baltimore & Ohio continued their three-way strategic alliance against the Pennsylvania, albeit with occasional bouts of mistrust. To complicate their lives, three new hostile faces appeared on the scene plus a pair of ghosts. The faces belonged to Leonor Loree, William Wallace Atterbury, and Frank Taplin; the ghosts were both named Gould—father Jay and son George. It was the two ghosts that set the stage for most of the trouble.

The fundamental unresolved question for the ICC and the large eastern railroads was how many trunk-line systems made sense in this territory. There were now four—in rough order of dominance, the Pennsylvania, the New York Central, the Baltimore & Ohio, and the Van Sweringen lines. In the opinion of all four, that was enough. But there were just enough leftover smaller railroads to encourage others to try to patch together a fifth.

With the Erie now Van Sweringen property, anyone's fifth eastern rail system had to be at least partially built around the aborted dreams of Jay and George Gould. During the 1880s, Jay had projected a route to the east coast based on his Wabash Railroad, which extended eastward from St. Louis, Kansas City, and Chicago to Toledo and Buffalo. Gould then acquired the Wheeling & Lake Erie (W&LE), a line originally built to tap the southeastern Ohio coal fields. Under his control, the W&LE expanded to extend diagonally southeast across northern Ohio from Toledo (where it joined Gould's Wabash) to Wheeling.

In another step on his march east, Gould intended to link the W&LE with the Buffalo, Rochester & Pittsburgh Railway (BR&P). The BR&P was another coal-hauler which ran south from Rochester and Buffalo through western Pennsylvania mining country to Butler, Pennsylvania; at Butler, it connected with the Baltimore & Ohio and had B&O trackage rights into Pittsburgh. Its primary appeal to Gould and later empire-builders was its southern end, which formed part of a potential low-grade route eastward through the Alleghenies. Gould's W&LE and the independent BR&P were not connected, but that could be resolved by some new construction, hardly an impediment in the freewheeling late nineteenth century. As it turned out, nothing further was done, and the BR&P remained independent.

Following Jay's death in 1892, his eldest son George inherited his rail empire and proceeded to careen off with his own grandiose dream of a coast-to-coast system. In the West, he built the Western Pacific from Salt Lake City to San Francisco; in the East, he initially aimed at Baltimore on Chesapeake Bay. Egged on by Andrew Carnegie, the younger Gould took his first step eastward by invading Pittsburgh from the west, using as his springboard his father's Wabash and the Wheeling & Lake Erie. Beginning in 1901, he built an entirely new 60-mile railroad, which branched away from the W&LE in sparsely settled country east of Jewett, Ohio. Called the Wabash Pittsburgh Terminal, the bold new line was beautifully engineered and impressively expensive, a succession of trestles and tunnels through the western Pennsylvania hills with spectacular bridges over the Ohio and Monongahela Rivers. At the same time, Gould bought control of the Western Maryland Railroad, a regional line based in Baltimore, and extended it west to Cumberland, Maryland. He hoped to link all these lines together into a new route to the Atlantic.

The Wabash Pittsburgh Terminal opened in 1904, but Gould's dream was quickly thwarted by J. P. Morgan, the Pennsylvania Railroad, and his own managerial ineptitude. Beginning in 1908, the new Gould empire disintegrated as his railroads went bankrupt one by one. John D. Rockefeller bought control of the Wheeling & Lake Erie and the Western Maryland; the Wabash Pittsburgh Terminal went its own independent way as the Pittsburgh & West Virginia Railway and in 1923 was bought by a Cleveland syndicate headed by coal-mining millionaire Frank Taplin. In 1912, the Western Maryland was extended as far west as Connellsville, Pennsylvania, still about forty miles shy of the Pittsburgh & West Virginia, but the gap remained open.[1] George Gould's eastern lines may have been chopped up, but if someone could put them back together, close the 40-mile gap, and add some other railroads, he might have a viable new system.

The first new face to appear in the mid-1920s was the grizzled visage of Leonor F. Loree, president of the small, staid, but rich Delaware & Hudson Company (D&H). In 1925, Loree announced that he would put together a fifth eastern trunk-line system. Loree's D&H was another eastern Pennsylvania anthracite carrier with lines extending into upstate New York and along Lake Champlain's western shore to the Canadian border. It mostly operated in a regional niche and seemed an unlikely base for a new railroad empire; undoubtedly the "big four" eastern railroad leaders were surprised by this unanticipated interloper.

They should not have been. The awesome Loree was in the process of making himself one of the legends of twentieth-century railroading. A hulking, bearlike, but brilliant six-footer who had played football at Rutgers (where he eventually earned three degrees), he had rapidly climbed the Pennsylvania Railroad's operating management ladder to a vice presidency by age 42. That same year, 1901, Pennsylvania president A. J. Cassatt picked him to be president of the Baltimore & Ohio, which the Pennsylvania then controlled under the Cassatt–J. P. Morgan–New York Central "community of interest" program intended to stabilize eastern railroading. Both an individualist and a dynamic builder, Loree plunged into a breathtaking three-year rebuilding and revitalization of the battered

B&O, a performance which reportedly was a bit too outstanding for Cassatt's taste. Antitrust pressures forced the Pennsylvania to back away from its control of the B&O, and Loree left in 1904 but apparently was not invited back to Philadelphia. Through E. H. Harriman's influence, he eventually ended up with the dual jobs of chairman of the midwestern Kansas City Southern Railway and president of the Delaware & Hudson.[2]

Leonor F. Loree at his most forbidding.
Delaware & Hudson Co. photo, Jim Shaughnessy collection

Loree's ego and ambitions far exceeded the confines of the Delaware & Hudson, which he doubtless viewed as only a temporary haven; it was no secret that he had hoped that the mantle of either Cassatt or Harriman would fall on him. But neither did, and at age 67 in 1925, he saw what might be his last opportunity in the consolidation program. Working with his mathematically gifted onetime protégé William H. Williams, now chairman of the Missouri Pacific and the Wabash (both former Gould companies), Loree fashioned a new east-west trunk line out of several unattached railroads remaining in the area—some of which were coveted by the Pennsylvania, the New York Central, the B&O, and the Van Sweringens.

Its eastern end would consist of the D&H and the Lehigh Valley (LV), giving it routes from New York and New England to Buffalo. From Buffalo, Williams's Wabash took it west to Chicago, St. Louis, and Kansas City—although not easily. (The Wabash reached Buffalo over trackage rights through southern Ontario, which also required a car float transfer across the Detroit River at Detroit.) Also in Loree's sights was the Buffalo, Rochester & Pittsburgh, a onetime Jay Gould quarry that he had never acquired. The BR&P would provide bituminous coal traffic, a link to Pittsburgh, and strategic connections in western Pennsylvania.

That was not all. In addition to the existing railroads which he planned to patch together, Loree dumbfounded the railroad world—and especially the Pennsylvania Railroad—by proposing to build an entirely new $260 million low-grade main line across Pennsylvania from a Lehigh Valley connection at Easton, Pennsylvania to Pittsburgh. Linked with two other lines that Loree planned to take—the Pittsburgh & West Virginia (George Gould's former Wabash Pittsburgh Terminal) and the Wheeling & Lake Erie—it would form the shortest rail route between New York and Chicago.[3]

Needless to say, Loree's proposal upset everyone to varying degrees. The New York Central and Pennsylvania both wanted the Lehigh Valley for themselves; the Central and the Baltimore & Ohio each had designs on the BR&P and had finally agreed to split it between them, with the B&O taking the southern portion and the Central the rest. The Vans had deferred to their friends and backed away from both, but in lieu of the Lehigh Valley they and their two allies agreed that they would get the Lackawanna for themselves. For once everyone found common ground with the Pennsylvania in fighting Loree's new trans-Pennsylvania line.

But while the Van Sweringens, the New York Central, and the Pennsylvania were debating about who should get the Lehigh Valley, Loree simply moved in. Using the Delaware & Hudson's ample resources, he bought 25 percent of the Lehigh's stock. Afterward, his friend William H. Williams of the Wabash also bought LV stock, giving the pair 44 percent by 1927 and frustrating both the Central and the Pennsylvania. (The Central had begun buying Lehigh Valley stock but soon realized it had been outrun and gave up.)

In the spring of 1925, Loree presented the outlines of his "fifth system" plan to the ICC and applied for permission to build his new railroad across Pennsylvania, citing his belief that it would be necessary since national rail-freight business would double within twelve to fourteen years. He also negotiated a long-term lease of the Buffalo, Rochester & Pittsburgh, and in July of 1926 he went back to ask the Commission to legitimize that.

He faced immediate opposition on both proposals. Everyone united to fight his new Pennsylvania route, and the Commission turned it down in 1926. The Central–B&O–Van Sweringen alliance protested Loree's lease of the BR&P, pointing out the obvious fact that the D&H had no direct connection with the BR&P and that, in fact, the two railroads were about 180 miles apart at their closest. (Oddly, Loree's use of the Lehigh Valley to bridge the gap was not considered, possibly because the Lehigh's status was uncertain and not part of the case.)[4]

While this was going on, the spirit of A. H. Smith had also reappeared—but, unfortunately, on the wrong side. On October 1, 1925, the Pennsylvania's Samuel Rea reached 70 and retired, one of the few Pennsylvania presidents actually to survive the job and live a few more years in relative good health. His successor was operating vice president William Wallace Atterbury—"General Atterbury," as he preferred to be addressed, in deference to his World War rank as brigadier general in charge of American Expeditionary Force transportation in Europe. (In Atterbury's case it was not empty pomposity. His skill in organizing the chaotic rail-supply lines earned him citations from six countries and the U.S. Distinguished Service Medal.)

A properly prejudiced viewer might well see an arrogant sneer in General W. W. Atterbury's official company portrait, and O. P. Van Sweringen could easily have been one who did. Little love was lost between the two.
Pennsylvania Railroad, H. H. Harwood, Jr., collection

Where his predecessor had been cautious and unaggressive, Atterbury was a colorful, rude, and determined activist. One writer noted that "he found his role as a listener difficult. When confronted by hostile interests, he rose to his full height and discharged statements like machine gun bullets." Needless to say, General Atterbury was far less hesitant to take countermeasures against anyone encroaching on Pennsylvania Railroad territory.[5]

Before leaving office, Rea did push through a new $100 million bond issue to help finance any new acquisitions thought necessary. He and Atterbury also had some desultory meetings with Loree with the thought that Loree's fifth system would help disrupt the plans of the so-called triple alliance. The New York investment banking house of Kuhn, Loeb & Company encouraged the talks, since it was in the embarrassing position of serving as the banker for the Pennsylvania, Loree's Delaware & Hudson, and Williams's Wabash. But the Pennsylvania executives knew Loree's maverick nature and distrusted him; for the moment, everyone went their own way.[6]

In the meantime, Atterbury made an attempt to have the incipient warfare between the Pennsylvania and the New York Central–B&O–Van Sweringen alliance resolved peacefully. Sometime in 1927, he paid a private visit to the Morgan bank and urged it to take control of the situation before everyone began spending money trying to snatch up other railroads. Morgan refused to take advice from the Pennsylvania (and a Kuhn, Loeb—not Morgan—client), and Atterbury angrily left to pursue his own aggressive strategy.[7]

He then quickly adopted the old A. H. Smith technique of secretly working through others to achieve his ends. Despite his differences with Loree, he saw the D&H president's plans as useful in helping to frustrate his three major opponents. Loree's fifth system was less of a threat to the Pennsylvania than it was to Atterbury's three rivals, and some of his planned acquisitions—notably the Lehigh Valley—would make excellent Pennsylvania additions. So there was also the possibility of shaping Loree's system into a Pennsylvania Railroad satellite, if not eventually absorbing it entirely or in part.

Thus, in February 1927, Atterbury and Loree met privately in the office of Otto Kahn, Kuhn, Loeb & Company's principal partner. At this point Loree had already lost his case for the trans-Pennsylvania line. His Buffalo, Rochester & Pittsburgh lease was still a live issue at the ICC, but it was being attacked because of the lack of a connection with the D&H. The two worked out a secret agreement whereby the

Pennsylvania would give Loree 246 miles of trackage rights to connect the D&H and the BR&P and support the lease request; it would also financially back Loree's acquisition of Wabash stock to help cement his fifth system. In exchange, Atterbury would get what amounted to a lien on Loree's Lehigh Valley and Wabash interests if the fifth system plan fell apart or if the ICC denied permission.[8]

The shrewd Atterbury had little to lose and much to gain. Probably knowing that Loree's chances of consummating all his plans were slim, he let him play out his hand. For its part, the Pennsylvania put $25 million into Wabash stock, which Loree matched. Despite Atterbury's behind-the-scenes aid, Loree's troubles continued. In December 1927, the ICC—still desperately trying to maintain a status quo—turned down the BR&P lease request. Blocked elsewhere, too, Loree's success now depended on his exercise of the 44 percent Lehigh Valley control which he and Williams's Wabash jointly held. But backed by the Morgan and Baker banks, the Lehigh's management fought the takeover and narrowly won a bitter proxy fight in January 1928—largely by disqualifying a block of Wabash-owned stock which had been transferred within sixty days of the meeting. A defeated and angry Loree blamed Williams, and their close friendship abruptly ended.[9]

It was then left to Otto Kahn to ease the proud Loree out of the game, with General Atterbury—now revealed as Mephistopheles—demanding his due. On Saturday, April 28, 1928, Atterbury and Loree met in Kuhn, Loeb's conference rooms and worked out the final settlement: For $62.5 million, Loree turned over his Lehigh Valley and Wabash holdings to the Pennsylvania, his pain eased by a $20 million profit for his Delaware & Hudson. Atterbury then quickly proceeded to buy more LV and Wabash stock to give him full control of both railroads. (How did he sidestep the ICC's authority? Atterbury had his own holding company to do the deed, too—in fact, he had the ur–holding company, the Pennsylvania Company of 1870.)[10]

(This meeting turned out to be merely the main event in a legendary Otto Kahn performance. The smooth and dapper Kahn sequestered the two railroad presidents in separate conference rooms, shuttling between them and nudging them toward agreement. At the same time, in a third conference room—and as board chairman of the Metropolitan Opera Company—he juggled a meeting to placate the Met's volatile, perennially aggrieved general manager, Giulio Gatti-Casazza, who was once again complaining about the opera house's many inadequacies. And finally, in yet a fourth room, he auditioned an aspiring young singer. All, it was said, worked out well.)[11]

Now in a position of power, Atterbury re-entered the off-and-on four-party conferences with the Central, the B&O, and the Van Sweringens. Having short-circuited the plans of the other three by taking away the Lehigh Valley (which the Central was to get) and the Wabash (which was to go to the B&O), he upset everyone with his own proposal: The Pennsylvania would fully control the Lehigh Valley, giving trackage rights to the Van Sweringens. In exchange, the Pennsylvania would have trackage rights over the Nickel Plate along Lake Erie, giving it entry to the Central's territory. The net result was continued disagreement and another complete breakdown in any unified approach to the ICC's consolidation planning. By mid-1928 a frustrated O. P. Van Sweringen declared himself "through" with any four-party conferences.[12]

The Van Sweringens and their "triple alliance" partners had been active enough on their own during the Loree drama. Although Loree had concentrated on the Lehigh Valley, the Buffalo, Rochester & Pittsburgh, and the Wabash, he also intended to take in other pieces of George Gould's dream—the Wheeling & Lake Erie, the Pittsburgh & West Virginia (P&WV), and the Western Maryland. Together the W&LE and P&WV formed a route between Pittsburgh and the Wabash at Toledo, and—if that 40-mile gap could be closed—a new route east via the Western Maryland. The Central, the B&O, and the Vans decided to nip that in the bud by taking the Wheeling & Lake Erie and the Western Maryland off the market.

The Wheeling & Lake Erie had a somewhat rocky history, but by the mid-1920s, it was stable and profitable. Aside from its sudden strategic allure, the compact 512-mile system had a healthy coal- and steel-hauling business. Southeastern Ohio bituminous flowed out of mines in the hills around such backroad towns as Dillonvale and Adena; W&LE branches tapped the northern Ohio industrial centers of Cleveland, Canton, Massillon, and Lorain; and through the Gould-promoted Pittsburgh & West Virginia Railway, it had a direct route to Pittsburgh. Piers on Lake Erie at Huron shipped out coal and unloaded iron ore from the long Great Lakes freighters. The Wheeling's principal problem was an $8 million dividend arrearage on its prior-lien preferred stock, which depressed the prices of its other classes of stock. Until it was paid off, the prior-lien stock controlled the railroad, and the Rockefellers owned that.[13]

OPPOSITE PAGE BOTTOM:
Whatever its potential allure for the 1920s railroad-empire builders, the Wheeling & Lake Erie primarily plodded along as an Ohio coal and steel hauler. Here a very typical steel-laden W&LE freight train drags through typical Wheeling countryside at Yorkville, Ohio.
J. J. Young photo

148 • Invisible Giants

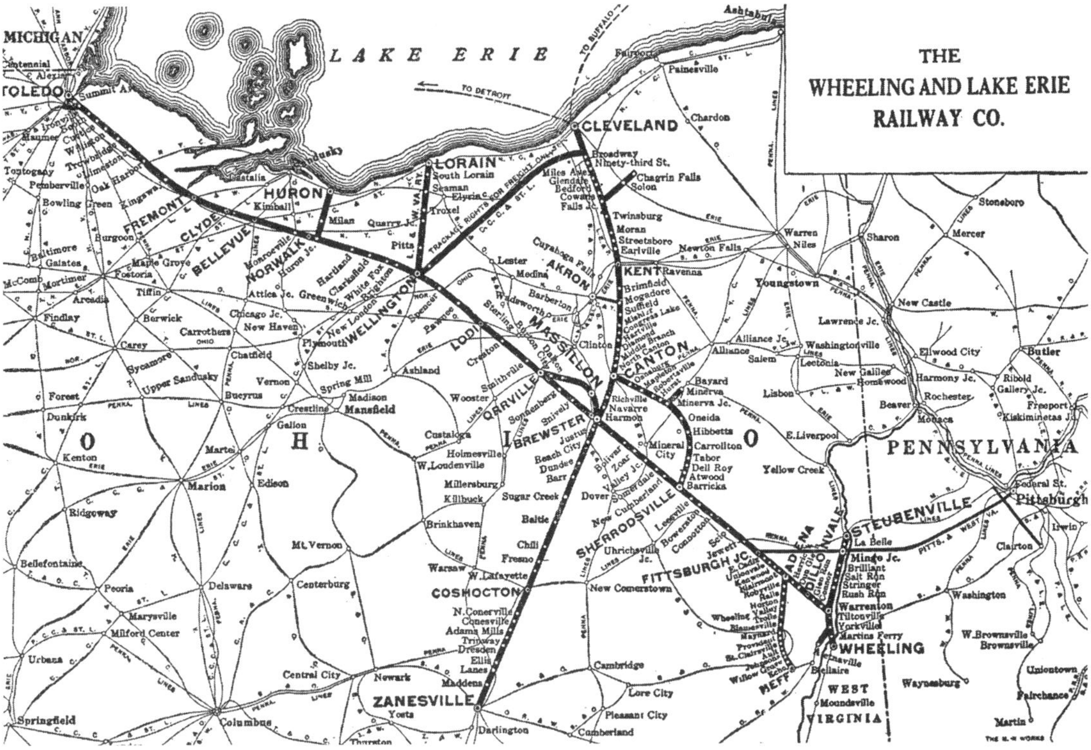

The Maverick and the General • 149

The three allies were not certain how to handle the W&LE purchase, since it would be a valuable adjunct for each one of them. They finally agreed to buy control as a joint effort and worry about what to do with it later. The Western Maryland caused less conflict. Since it closely paralleled the B&O's main line between Baltimore and Connellsville and was out of traditional New York Central and Van Sweringen territory, the B&O was allowed to take it by itself. For the Wheeling and the Western Maryland, however, the allies had to deal with the Rockefellers, who had perceptively picked up the controlling stock after the Gould collapse and now seemed ready to sell both as a package.

Serious negotiations started in late 1926 and stretched into January of the next year. The primary emissaries were Albert H. Harris and George M. Shriver, financial vice presidents of the Central and the B&O respectively; Bertram Cutler and John D. Rockefeller, Jr., represented the old man. Dealing with the Rockefellers was never easy for anyone, but because it was a seller's market, the negotiations were even tougher than usual. Cutler helped things along by darkly mentioning that "others were negotiating for the property [and] seemed prepared to pay" the Rockefellers' price. There really was little to negotiate, and the three railroads finally got their Wheeling stock in February 1927 for $21.3 million—equally split $7.1 million apiece among the Central, the B&O, and the Nickel Plate—while the B&O alone paid $12.7 million for Rockefeller's Western Maryland stock.[14]

To tie the Wheeling down more firmly, the Vans were delegated to buy more stock in the open market, which they quickly and efficiently accomplished during January; by the time they concluded the Rockefeller deal, the allies had thus spent about $9.7 million apiece for full Wheeling control. But as they were buying, the Vans made an unpleasant discovery: Someone else was also buying heavily.[15]

Unfortunately, the Rockefellers' Cutler was not bluffing when he said "others were negotiating," and the three partners well knew it. But their competitor was not Loree; it was a new, more dedicated, and much less gentlemanly nemesis. Before the Van Sweringens knew it, they were embroiled in something they had never quite experienced—nothing less than a nostalgic throwback to the bare-knuckled days of Vanderbilt versus Gould, Harriman versus Hill, and other blood feuds. All the classic ingredients soon emerged: stock corners, rump boards of directors, legal injunctions, economic blackmail. And the source of it all sat only ten blocks away from the Vans, up Euclid Avenue in the Union Trust Building.

Thirteen

Consolidation Anarchy II: The Street Fighter

Frank E. Taplin, the rugged, sandy-haired son of a Rockefeller lieutenant, grew up in Cleveland and first served time as an office boy for Standard Oil. At age 21, he moved over to the coal business and eventually owned coal properties in Ohio, West Virginia, and western Pennsylvania—including an extensive operation on the Pittsburgh & West Virginia (P&WV).

Taplin seemed to have a talent for getting into things at the right time. Just as he was expanding his coal-producing business, the world went to war and Taplin emerged with a fortune. He also had a talent for fighting rough. Aided by his attorney brother Charles, he developed a taste for aggressive litigation, successfully suing the Pittsburgh & West Virginia for discrimination in favoring its own coal mines over his in allocating cars for loading. That experience apparently got him interested in the railroad, which had been drifting unattached since its bankruptcy in 1917. In 1923 he, his brother, and some Cleveland friends bought control, largely as an adjunct to their coal interests but possibly also with an eye to its potential value in the railroad consolidation scramble.

Frank Taplin's cherubic smile usually reflected some triumph over an adversary, not beneficence.
Cleveland Press Collection, Cleveland State University

In relation to the railroads around it, Taplin's P&WV was a pea-sized property, only eighty-nine miles in total, and was weak on several counts. As one of George Gould's last major projects before his march east was stopped, it never had the chance to develop as Gould intended. As it existed in the mid-1920s, it was essentially a dead-end branch of the Wheeling & Lake Erie and was dependent on that railroad for its western outlet. On its east end, it had no friendly connection whatever; instead, it stared at that 40-mile missing link in Gould's planned route to the eastern seaboard via the Western Maryland at Connellsville. Furthermore, it was excluded from much of Pittsburgh's industry and depended on on-line coal mines, such as Taplin's, for most of its sustenance.

As Loree and Williams began stirring in 1926, Taplin saw opportunity. Thinking that he might be able to unload his Gould orphan at a goodly profit, he first approached the New York Central's Pat Crowley in March of that year. His price turned out to be $200 a share for stock then valued at about $70–$90 (and which the Taplin group had bought for about $52). Crowley hardly needed the P&WV as a Central adjunct—it already controlled the infinitely superior Pittsburgh & Lake Erie—and the price seemed far above its strategic value. He quickly declined, and later in the year Taplin went to General Atterbury. The reaction was essentially the same, but the door was left ajar and the two reportedly parted on friendly terms. (There is no evidence, however, that Atterbury later aided Taplin, as he did Loree.)[1]

So spurned, Taplin then decided to move on his own. By then it was clear that a combination of the Pittsburgh & West Virginia and the Wheeling & Lake Erie would be an important pawn in the escalating consolidation warfare—and in any event, the P&WV's future was inseparably tied to the Wheeling. At the same time that the Central, the B&O, and the Van Sweringens went after the Wheeling, he decided to do so too. Held at bay by the Rockefellers, who preferred to deal with the "triple alliance," Taplin went boldly into the open market and by the end of January 1927 had spent over $5 million for W&LE stock.

At the same time, the "triple alliance" had made its commitment to the Rockefellers, and the Van Sweringens were buying additional Wheeling stock in the market. The Vans achieved their purpose, managing to pick up the stock at between $50 and $53 a share before the end of January. But the combination of the sudden purchases by Van Sweringen and Taplin produced a spectacular aftereffect. Speculators who had sold short, expecting the price to drop, suddenly found there was no stock to be had. In the space of three days, the price shot from $83 to $130 a share. Working with the Morgan bank, the three allies relieved the pressure by releasing a limited amount of stock, and the crisis passed.[2]

By then, of course, the Vans and their two partners were firmly in control of the Wheeling, and Taplin was left as a most unhappy minority stockholder. The feud then erupted. A street-fighter at heart, Taplin almost instantly attacked from three directions: In March, he began lobbying the Interstate Commerce Commission to begin Clayton Anti-Trust Act proceedings against the three partners, beginning with a sympathetic Joseph Eastman. (Actually the ICC was already thinking along the same lines.) The next month, he surprised everyone by applying to the ICC for authority to build a new line to close the 40-mile gap between the Pittsburgh & West Virginia and the Western Maryland—a move that would transform the P&WV from a railroad cul-de-sac to an important link in the flow of freight traffic between east and west. And finally, in May, he staged a stormy raid on the Wheeling's management, with the result that two different boards of directors—the existing board and a Taplin-chosen board—competed for legitimacy. Lawsuits inevitably followed, and the "legitimate" board was finally upheld. Early in his onslaught, he offered the three allies a bit of blackmail: He was willing to drop his Connellsville connection threat and his fight for the Wheeling for the $200 a share he had offered Pat Crowley the year before. Once again he was spurned.[3]

The "triple alliance" actually was in a precarious legal position. The Central, B&O, and Nickel Plate all overlapped Wheeling & Lake Erie territory in varying degrees, the first two quite extensively, the Nickel Plate less so. While they had bought their Wheeling control simply to checkmate the Loree-Williams scheme (as well as whatever Taplin might have had in mind), any direct management of the Wheeling would be interpreted as anticompetitive. (The B&O's Western Maryland control was even more vulnerable.) Thus far, they had their stock control but could not exercise it; the Wheeling's board remained as it had been, headed by William McKinley Duncan and composed mostly of Cleveland businessmen. (Duncan, a Cleveland lawyer, had brought the railroad out of its Gould-created receivership and would remain its ruler until his death in 1945.) To put their directors on the Wheeling board, the three railroads would need ICC permission, and they so applied in April 1927.[4]

The Taplin forces turned up to object, joined by William H. Williams of the Wabash, who was still working with Loree.

The Commission took its usual leisurely time to decide the issue, and in the meantime Taplin got in another blow: In August 1927, he asked the ICC for authority to control the Wheeling. (Hearings on this request were delayed until mid-1930.) In May 1928, the ICC finally rendered its judgment and turned down the joint directorship. The anticompetitive issue was a major factor, but once again the Commission seemed even more concerned with keeping a status quo until it could resolve its own consolidation quandary.[5]

That left the three railroads still technically controlling the Wheeling but unable to effect their control—and with the Clayton Act sword still hanging over them. Then the sword started to descend. Goaded by Taplin, and with its own strong doubts, the Commission issued a formal complaint only nine days after its negative decision. A week later, it began Clayton Act action against the Baltimore & Ohio's control of the Western Maryland. The "triple alliance" now faced the possibility of a divestiture order which would nullify their two coups and give Taplin his chance to inherit the entire eastern end of the old Gould system. And with Loree and Williams still in the game at that point, he might well sell out to them and thus create an even more hideous monster.

To add more insult, a month after instituting its Clayton Act proceedings, the ICC allowed Taplin to build his new line east to Connellsville. It was not an easy decision; the Pennsylvania, the B&O, and the Wheeling & Lake Erie opposed the project, and the ICC's own examiner recommended against it. But on June 21, 1928, the full commission very narrowly approved, and Taplin was on his way. (In fighting the project, the W&LE was fighting itself, since it stood to gain substantially from the new connection. Undoubtedly its management was trying to cooperate with its new quasi-owners.) Taplin wasted no time, and he completed the line in February 1931. As he intended, the P&WV's Connellsville extension opened a strong new competitive route between the Midwest and the east coast, although by then circumstances had changed considerably.[6]

While he was at it, Taplin took the war right to the Vans' own front yard. The Wheeling & Lake Erie's Cleveland passenger station was located at a spot called Vinegar Hill, a steep bluff adjacent to Ontario Street near Huron Road. The site was directly in the path of the Union Terminal's eastern approach tracks, and by early 1928, construction of the terminal was well under way. As a railroad facility, the Wheeling station and its approach right-of-way were immune to condemnation, meaning that the Wheeling had to be willing to give it up and sell the property. It was not a great sacrifice; W&LE passenger service was always minimal, and at that time the station handled only three short local trains in and three out. In July 1928, the Wheeling's executive committee dutifully approved selling the property for $1.6 million, but Taplin insisted that the railroad ask at least $5 million. Ultimately, the Wheeling board approved the original $1.6 million, but Taplin succeeded in delaying the project for five months and giving the Vans the maximum possible discomfort.[7]

Through most of the Wheeling imbroglio the Van Sweringens were simply team players; the Central and the B&O carried much of the negotiating and legal load. The brothers were then focused on their more important C&O unification case, which was simultaneously plodding through the ICC. (As noted earlier, the Commission finally decided that one in May 1928, giving the Vans a frustratingly partial victory.) And at this point, the W&LE itself was held in sort of a joint captivity but was still functioning wholly on its own. Most likely the brothers considered the railroad a secondary concern whose direct usefulness was uncertain.

But their next move mystified everyone and thoroughly irritated their Baltimore & Ohio ally: On October 8, 1928, they bought control of the Buffalo, Rochester & Pittsburgh (BR&P). It was a bafflement. The B&O and the New York Central were both anxious to get the BR&P, and in their past relationships with their two allies the brothers had agreed to keep their hands off.

Nor did the BR&P seem to make much sense as part of the existing Van Sweringen system. The railroad's 590 miles of main line and branches ran roughly north-south through western Pennsylvania coal country, which was its principal reason for being. Its north end formed a large Y whose eastern branch extended to Rochester, New York, and a coal pier on Lake Ontario and whose western leg ended at Buffalo. At its south end, BR&P tracks ended at Butler, Pennsylvania, but it reached both Pittsburgh and New Castle, Pennsylvania, over B&O trackage rights. En route it did connect with the Vans' Erie at Salamanca, New York, and conceivably it could give the Erie an entry to Pittsburgh, but this was an awkward stretch. Otherwise the BR&P did not easily fit the traffic patterns of any Van Sweringen railroad, and now that they owned the C&O, the brothers hardly needed another bituminous coal railroad. (And, in fact, coal production in BR&P territory was beginning to decline.)[8]

On the other hand, the B&O and the Central considered it quite valuable to them. The BR&P's heaviest single-inter-

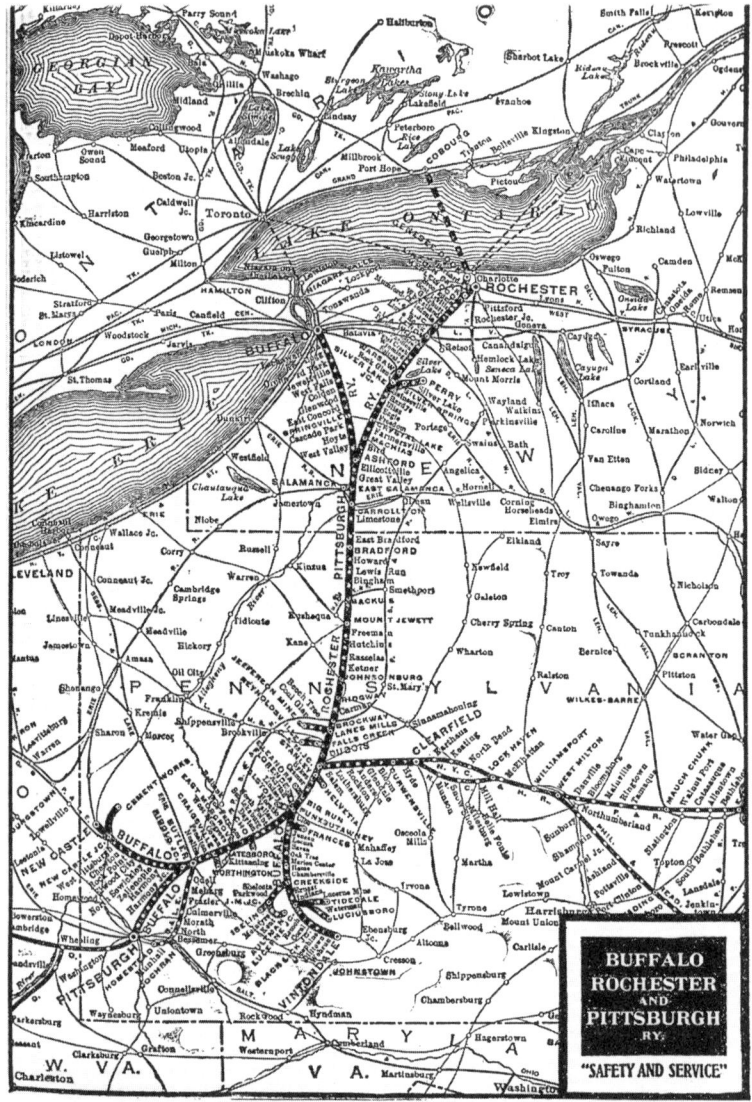

change connection was the Central; it did less business with the B&O, but that railroad served as its major southern outlet. The B&O was interested for more exotic reasons, however. Its own east-west main line was cursed with severe grades in the Pittsburgh area as well as a relatively difficult climb across the Alleghenies. Moreover, it tied with the Erie as the longest route between the Midwest and New York.

Oddly, the BR&P promised to help solve both problems. By using the BR&P's well-built and beautifully maintained main tracks from Butler to DuBois, Pennsylvania, and continuing eastward over another short rail line, the Buffalo & Susquehanna, it could eliminate its Pittsburgh grades and cross the Allegheny divide at the lowest elevation south of the New York Central's famed Water Level Route. The B&O then planned to proceed farther eastward over trackage rights—or its own new construction—to reach the Reading Company, which would give it access to both Philadelphia and New York Harbor. The resulting route would be the second shortest between Chicago and New York. The idea was certainly not new; indeed, it was sort of a nineteenth-century railroad version of the Northwest Passage. Such great railroad adventurers as J. Edgar Thomson, Jay Gould, Calvin Brice, George Gould, and Leonor Loree had all hoped to exploit it. None did. Undeterred, the B&O's Daniel Willard was determined to succeed.[9]

Knowing all this, it seems even stranger that the Vans never bothered to tell either the Central's Pat Crowley or the B&O's Dan Willard and George Shriver what they were up to. Apparently the idea came shortly after the ICC turned down Loree's BR&P lease proposal in December 1927. In April 1928, they dispatched John Bernet (then president of the Erie) to broach the subject of a sale to the BR&P's president, William T. Noonan. The railroad was controlled by the New York investment house of Adrian Iselin & Company, with most of its stock held by the Iselin and Emlen Roosevelt families. Like the Rockefellers, the BR&P's owners were delighted at the competition for their railroad, which had never been a spectacular moneymaker and was now facing hard times in the western Pennsylvania coal industry.

The negotiations lasted less than six months, and a deal was formally signed on October 8th. The brothers bought the BR&P for a total of $11.3 million—$3.6 million in cash with the balance due in nine months. (As a measure of the BR&P owners' happiness, President Noonan received a commission of $190,053.) But unlike any of their previous acquisitions, the purchase was made by the brothers personally rather than by any of their holding companies or railroads. By then their unhappy experiences with the ICC had made them particularly careful to keep out of the Commission's jurisdiction. Their $3.6 million down payment came from a loan which followed a tortured path from their brokers, Paine, Webber & Company, through the Vaness Corporation to the brothers as individuals.[10]

Neither of the Vans' two railroad allies knew anything about the negotiations or pending sale until O. P. casually mentioned it to the B&O's George Shriver as the two were walking to the ICC Building in Washington for a conference on October 6th. Considering their team efforts on the Wheeling & Lake Erie coup, it was not only a shock to Shriver but

Daniel Willard headed the Baltimore & Ohio for thirty-one years, from 1910 to 1941. He was already 65 when he posed here in 1927. Unbeknownst to "Uncle Dan" (as some B&O employees called him), the Van Sweringens fleetingly considered his B&O as a target for takeover. B&O Railroad Museum

looked like blatant betrayal. Dumbfounded, Shriver tried to convince O. P. to discuss it in a joint meeting with Central and B&O executives. O. P. would have none of it and especially did not want to talk to Pat Crowley. At the time, O. P. was feeling severe frustration over the state of the joint conferences with the three allies and Atterbury—and the still-unsettled status of his own railroad system. He had suggested that the Commission act as umpire in their disputes, which nobody—including Crowley—had supported, leaving him even more frustrated. Shriver also reminded him of the agreements of the B&O and the Central on the BR&P and delicately hinted that the Vans were being perfidious. In a rare fit of temper, O. P. replied (according to Shriver): "If that's your attitude you can go to hell."[11]

And indeed the brothers' behavior in the BR&P affair is a mystery today. When tempers cooled, O. P. explained to his partners that he bought the BR&P strictly because he was afraid Frank Taplin would snatch it up; he always intended, so he said, to then make it available to the B&O, the Central, or both. Willard was especially dubious, since he could not get O. P. to make any commitments about timing or price.[12]

He may well have had cause to be doubtful. The perceptive William Wenneman, who was in the center of the action on the Van Sweringen side, strongly suspected that one of O. P.'s major motivations was to hold the BR&P hostage to assure the support of the B&O and the Central for his own strategies—or, if the alliance broke up, to make use of it himself in some way. Wenneman also noted something never known outside the Cleveland office walls: O. P. was at least casually studying acquiring control of the B&O itself. It was not a wholly unreasonable idea. Financially the weakest of the traditional "big three" eastern systems and heavily leveraged, it would have been a relative bargain. And despite some overlaps and duplication of routes, the B&O complemented the Van Sweringen lines quite well in many areas and would have considerably broadened the brothers' markets in both the East and the Midwest. O. P.'s interest in buying the B&O never had a chance to develop further, but interestingly, thirty-five years later, the merged Chesapeake & Ohio–Pere Marquette did exactly that.[13]

When 1929 arrived, the brothers still held the Buffalo, Rochester & Pittsburgh as their personal property, much to the B&O's chagrin. The ICC was still pondering the Wheeling & Lake Erie's status, but the three allies knew they might face a divestiture order. (Anticipating that, Taplin was set to pounce, and in February he reapplied for ICC authority to

Work is well along on the Terminal office buildings, and clearing has begun for the railroad terminal itself and its eastern access line. But stubbornly in its path sits the Wheeling & Lake Erie's modestly used "Vinegar Hill" passenger station—now suddenly extremely valuable as another pawn in the Frank Taplin–Van Sweringen warfare. Frank A. Wrabel collection

control the railroad.) And finally, the Vans' debts for the railroad acquisitions now totaled about $53 million, while their railroads were not much nearer unification than they had been five years earlier.[14]

Then, with more of their trademark swift, deft maneuvering, they managed to resolve all the problems practically at once. Afterward, the Vans and the B&O were friends again, although their relationship with Crowley remained strained. The BR&P was amicably disposed of, and this in turn helped solve the Wheeling & Lake Erie Clayton Act dilemma while keeping the dreaded Mr. Taplin at bay. Their debts were taken care of and their system was united as best it could be under the circumstances.

The first step was the creation of a new super–holding company, the Alleghany Corporation, in late January 1929. Much more will be said about that soon; suffice it to say here that Alleghany served as a convenient medium for handling the BR&P and Wheeling & Lake Erie situations. A multiple handoff quickly followed. The brothers turned over their BR&P stock to Alleghany, which still kept it away from ICC jurisdiction. Then, almost simultaneously, the New York Central sold Alleghany its Wheeling interest for $10.7 million. The B&O in effect then swapped its own Wheeling stock to Alleghany for the BR&P interest, owing Alleghany a difference of $3.6 million. The entire shuffle was completed by

The Street Fighter • 159

March 1st; the net result was that the Vans—in the form of Alleghany—now had a clear 51 percent control of the Wheeling & Lake Erie, and the B&O had its prized Buffalo, Rochester & Pittsburgh.[15]

(With the BR&P in hand and the New York Central apparently out of the contention, the B&O's Dan Willard promptly moved to consummate his dream of the new low-grade line east. Soon afterward, he paid $6.3 million for the more threadbare Buffalo & Susquehanna, which connected with the BR&P at DuBois and continued the new route fifty-two miles eastward through the low-level Allegheny crossing at Sabula, Pennsylvania. Later in 1929, he applied for ICC permission to control both lines and received it by mid-1930. He was then well on his way—or so he thought.)

Belatedly, the ICC delivered its decision on the Wheeling case on March 11th. As Taplin hoped, the Commission ruled that the three railroads had violated the Clayton Act and ordered them to sell their stock. But by then it was academic; the three-way handoff had been completed less than two weeks earlier, and the Vans' new Alleghany Corporation now controlled the Wheeling; Alleghany in turn was beyond the ICC's reach. Cautious about pushing their luck further, the brothers then decided to put their Wheeling stock under an independent trusteeship, and the ICC subsequently approved the arrangement. This left them with ownership but only limited direct control; William McKinley Duncan continued his reign as W&LE chairman (it had no president) and kept his charge independent, although he cooperated closely with the Van Sweringen railroads.[16]

The Wheeling–BR&P scramble was a confusing sidestep from the carefully planned system-building of the A. H. Smith era; it was done more as a hurried defensive maneuver than anything else. Yet in the long run, the Wheeling turned out to be a fine fit with the other Van Sweringen lines, especially the Nickel Plate. Their two main lines crossed at Bellevue, Ohio, and over the years new joint east-west merchandise movements were developed—particularly after Frank Taplin completed the Pittsburgh & West Virginia's connection to the Western Maryland in 1931. Afterward, the Nickel Plate–Wheeling & Lake Erie–P&WV route could offer a new and lucrative fast freight service between its western terminals at Chicago and St. Louis and the East Coast which for many years consistently outperformed the B&O and the Pennsylvania.

In 1929, however, the Wheeling was merely a minor matter to be taken care of quickly. Much larger matters and a big surprise were in the offing.

Fourteen

The Summit I: An Appalachian Peak in the Rockies

Alleghany, Virginia is just barely on the road maps, a classic off-the-beaten-path spot nestled high in a mountain notch across the ridge from the West Virginia border. In 1929, it was less a town than a small collection of gray railroad buildings, sidings, and signals. But the name showed up in large print on the working timetables of Chesapeake & Ohio train crews; when they passed the austere frame station, they knew their hardest work was over. For Alleghany marks the summit of the C&O's main line between the West Virginia coal fields and the tidewater docks at Newport News. Sitting 2,072 feet above sea level, it is the end of the grueling grind eastward up the Allegheny slope out of the New River valley at Hinton, West Virginia. The heavy coal trains would pause there to uncouple their ponderous pusher locomotives and set their brakes before dropping down the eastern slope to the yards at Clifton Forge. The mountain air at Alleghany was perennially filled with the sound of slogging steam engines and tinged with the sharp smell of coal smoke and hot oil.

Alleghany's gritty atmosphere was far from O. P. Van Sweringen's always-neat desk in Cleveland, both physically and spiritually. In fact, if he ever saw the place himself, it is doubtful that he took any notice. But as the highest point on the Van Sweringen railroad system, it was an apt symbol for his new super–holding company which was to gather together all the present Van Sweringen railroads and any more to come. Alleghany—the corporation—was truly the summit of the Van Sweringen empire. Apparently overlooked, though, was another aspect of the symbol: Every summit also has a downgrade, and at Alleghany, Virginia, the eastern downgrade is almost twice as steep as the western.

The Alleghany Corporation's genesis went back to May 1928, when the Interstate Commerce Commission finally issued its mixed decision in the C&O unification case. It was then clear that the Commission intended to stay cautious and drag its feet until it could resolve the national railroad consolidation muddle—and that still seemed some years away. In the meantime, the brothers were out on a financial limb; they had about $53 million in short-term debts and, as O. P. put it, "five broken up propositions [his separate railroads] which I am trying to unify and coordinate."[1]

The solution was a publicly financed holding company which, in one form or another, would control all of the Van Sweringen railroads. The money would come primarily from outside investors and, as before, the holding company would avoid the pesky ICC—and the particularly pesky Commissioner Eastman, who fought them at every turn, convinced that they were simply financial manipulators who did not belong in a strong national transportation system.

In the fall of 1928, serious planning got underway with the Morgan bank, which would underwrite what promised to be a massive new creation. The Alleghany Corporation came into formal being on January 26, 1929, in the happiest and eagerest of financial markets.

Alleghany's basic purpose was simple enough: It would be the single repository for all railroad interests then being held by the brothers personally and by Vaness and the various existing special-purpose railroad holding companies, such as the Pere Marquette Corporation. That said, the details could be bewildering. For example, Alleghany would control the Chesapeake Corporation, which controlled the C&O, which controlled the Pere Marquette and owned the Virginia Transportation Corporation—which in turn controlled the Erie.

Huge as it was—and it was labyrinthine when charted— Alleghany was nothing more than a vastly pumped-up version of the 1916 Nickel Plate Securities Corporation, built on precisely the same simple principle of leverage: The Vans would hold voting control while most of the money came from elsewhere; in this case, the eager public. Of the $85 million to be initially raised from outside investors, over 70 percent was in the form of nonvoting securities—$25 million from preferred stocks and $35 million from bonds. The remaining $25 million would come from selling $20 par-value common stock, which did vote—but about 64 percent of the total of this stock issue went to the Van Sweringens and their group in exchange for the railroad investments they were turning over. In the process, their immediate debts could be liquidated through the influx of outside money—although some perceptive observers later noted that the debts did not really disappear but simply changed form. The new creditors would be the Alleghany bondholders. But they were only potential creditors; as long as Alleghany paid the interest, things would be fine, and that prospect looked excellent.[2]

Everything was auspicious for Alleghany's debut. The stock market was now beyond euphoric and seemed ready to take almost anything offered. But even discounting that, Alleghany was an attractive investment. The public rarely read anything said by a Van Sweringen and it scarcely saw them at all, but it certainly recognized the names and knew their record.

And the record was solid. The ICC and Joseph Eastman aside, the brothers' accomplishments were now nationally known and admired. While all railroads were sharing in the Coolidge boom times, the Van Sweringen lines were doing especially well. By then, the Pocahontas fields dominated national coal production, and the C&O was hauling ever-greater volumes of this most profitable commodity. A record 4.5 million automobiles would be sold in the year (plus 623,000 trucks and buses), the highest figure for twenty years to come; the Pere Marquette sat in the center of motor-production territory, moving trainloads of parts to assembly plants and the finished vehicles out. (True, those autos were also having a baneful effect on railroad passenger traffic, but none of the Van Sweringen lines were heavy passenger carriers. Nobody thought much about intercity trucking, which was hardly a threat at all.) The Nickel Plate, too, was sharing in the industrial boom, and even the once-woebegone Erie was perking up under John Bernet's therapy. The statistics were impressive: Between 1925 and 1929, the C&O's net income rose over 60 percent, the Nickel Plate's rose 15.6 percent, the Pere Marquette's rose 17 percent, and the Erie's rose a spectacular 82 percent. (That last figure admittedly still represented a relatively narrow margin on total revenues but nonetheless was a fine testimony to Bernet.) Between 1925 and 1929, the price of C&O common stock soared from a low of 89 to a high of 279, the Pere Marquette common climbed from its low of 62 to 260, the Erie common rose from 26 to 93, and the Nickel Plate common went from 118 to 192.[3]

Once the Alleghany Corporation was formed, no time was wasted putting it into business. Indeed, it went public in what must have been a record speed. Even before Alleghany was formally incorporated, Morgan was pushing the New York Stock Exchange to expedite listing the securities, and the entire process was completed in eight days—with virtually no careful review. By January 30th, everything was ready for public sale.[4]

The public took to it instantly. In initial trading, the Alleghany bonds sold at a 10 percent premium, the preferred stock at 5 percent over par, and the $20 par common stock was quoted at 37. (Later in the year it hit 56.) Much of the common stock, however, went to market by a different and more controversial route. While the Morgan bank normally did not directly handle common stock, it made an exception with Alleghany. The bank, which was allocated 1,250,000 shares, decided to distribute them at what was suddenly a bargain price of $20 a share to what was delicately called a "preferred list" of buyers—its own partners; its banking, brokerage, and political friends; and key clients. Interestingly, large blocks were taken by General Motors executives Alfred P. Sloan, Lawrence Fisher, and John J. Raskob. A select group of Van Sweringen associates that included Charles Bradley, Newton D. Baker, John Bernet, Joseph Nutt, and Darwin Barrett were also so rewarded. Morgan also favored a few national notables, such as Charles A. Lindbergh and General John J. Pershing, the American commander-in-chief during the World War. Truly, Alleghany was a crown jewel of New York finance, and some of the fortunate "preferred list" members made out exceptionally well by selling at the right time. Morgan partner George Whitney, for example, was able to sell a large portion of his allotment at an average of over $48 a share—a 114 percent profit.[5]

There were also gratifying profits within the Van Sweringen corporate circle. As the various railroad and holding company stocks were moved from Vaness and other internal entities into Alleghany, the accounting reflected the heady rise in share prices over the original purchase costs. It was estimated that the brothers and their immediate associates took an on-paper profit of $35 million and a cash profit of $6 million.[6]

Alleghany's first assignment was to help clear up the Wheeling & Lake Erie–Buffalo, Rochester & Pittsburgh tangle, which it did quickly. As noted in the last chapter, the brothers, along with the New York Central's Pat Crowley and the Baltimore & Ohio's Daniel Willard and George Shriver, resolved among themselves that the Vans would take the Wheeling and the B&O would get the BR&P. Alleghany became the holding and sorting mechanism. The brothers had been holding the BR&P stock in their own personal account; in early February, Alleghany relieved them of that burden and promptly resold the stock to the B&O. In return, it received the B&O's interest in the Wheeling & Lake Erie. At the end of the same month, it committed itself to buying the New York Central's portion of the Wheeling control. The net result for the Alleghany was that it now fully controlled the Wheeling in addition to the Vans' "traditional" four rail systems.[7]

Having accomplished that, the brothers might reasonably have been expected to pause to catch their breaths and let Alleghany concentrate on overseeing the existing Van Sweringen railroad system. After all, they now controlled five major eastern railroads plus several subsidiaries; these needed to be pulled together and eventually fitted into the still-roiling eastern consolidation scheme. All that would surely come, but O. P.'s imagination already was reaching beyond those boundaries. After paying off $36 million of the brothers' most pressing debts, Alleghany still had $46 million left over in its treasury, which was no accident. O. P. intended to use it, and more, for a new venture which stunned almost everyone.

Alleghany had hardly settled down when the stock of the Missouri Pacific Railroad began behaving peculiarly. Rumors began winging through Wall Street that the Van Sweringens were hurdling the Mississippi and heading west. From Cleveland came only the accustomed silence.

But it was true. Actually the brothers had begun serious buying in the open market in early January, before Alleghany legally existed. Once it did exist, the corporation began a steady but discreet campaign; by mid-1929 it already owned more than a quarter of the Missouri Pacific's stock—unbeknownst, of course, to the public investors who had just bought Alleghany's securities.[8]

The Missouri Pacific connected with the Vans' Nickel Plate at St. Louis, its headquarters city. The "MoPac" or "Mop," as railroaders nicknamed it, was much more than just a single railroad company; it was a vast, if ungainly, 12,000-

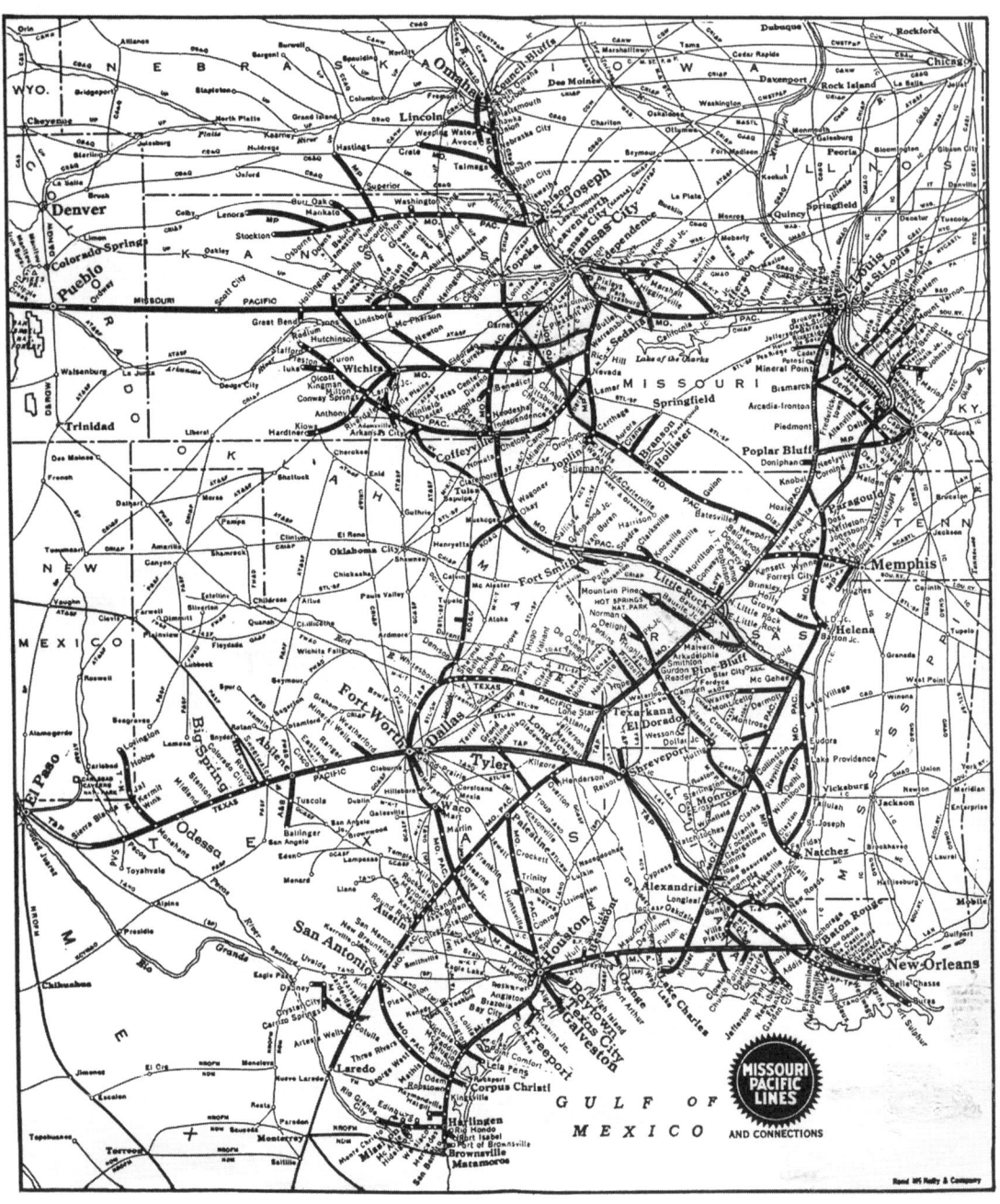

mile system which included the Texas & Pacific Railway, several other large but only partly digested subsidiaries, and a half-interest in the Denver & Rio Grande Western Railroad (D&RGW). Altogether, it blanketed the Southwest and much of the West. Missouri Pacific lines radiating from St. Louis and

Kansas City reached southwest to the Rio Grande River at Brownsville, Laredo, and El Paso; south to Memphis and New Orleans; west to the base of the Rockies at Pueblo, Colorado; and northwest to Omaha. In addition, it had a tenuous finger pointing toward the Pacific. The half-owned Denver & Rio Grande Western's main line continued west from Denver and Pueblo, snaking into the mountains through the Royal Gorge and over Tennessee Pass to reach Salt Lake City. From there, the D&RGW's other half-owner, the Western Pacific, completed a route to San Francisco Bay.

The Missouri Pacific, the D&RGW, and the Western Pacific had all been parts of George Gould's short-lived empire; Gould, in fact, had built the Western Pacific. As the Gould system slowly crumbled, the Missouri Pacific collapsed into receivership in 1915. The New York investment banking firm of Kuhn, Loeb & Company moved in and quickly reorganized it; afterward it kept control of the railroad's management. Kuhn, Loeb installed William H. Williams as board chairman in 1923—the Loree protégé and ally who also headed the Wabash, another onetime Gould line. Williams in turn brought in the capable 48-year-old Lewis W. Baldwin from the Illinois Central as president to put the somewhat wobbly property in shape.

It needed Baldwin's ministrations. Although its territory had begun to blossom, the Missouri Pacific was weaker than its large competitors. It had some formidable competition, too, from the likes of the Union Pacific, the Santa Fe, and the Southern Pacific—as well as regional lines such as the St. Louis–San Francisco, the Missouri-Kansas-Texas, and the St. Louis–Southwestern (which the Southern Pacific picked up in 1932). To hold its own, it kept close traffic interchange relationships with the other refugees from the Gould empire—the Wabash, the D&RGW, and the Western Pacific—none of which were especially strong, either. Efficiency was one problem: The Missouri Pacific's operating ratio (the ratio of direct operating expenses to revenues) in 1927 was ten points higher than the Union Pacific's, nine points above Santa Fe's, and five more than the Southern Pacific's. In addition, it had a heavy ratio of debt to equity, making it a highly leveraged property.[9]

That aspect alone may have intrigued the Van Sweringens, who were now acknowledged masters in exploiting leveraged corporate structures. But it was hardly enough to justify this hugely expensive foray into an entirely new territory. So why the Missouri Pacific? And what started them in that direction? O. P. offered some post-facto explanations which boiled down to a desire for diversification, but nobody knows if that was

A typical Missouri Pacific freight headed by chunky Mikado 1521 heads a northbound mixed-freight train out of one of the railroad's major operating centers at North Little Rock, Arkansas, in 1930, at about the time the Clevelanders were taking it over. Joe G. Collias collection

the primary incentive. It did make some sense: The West and Southwest were beginning to grow dramatically, spurred by Texas and Oklahoma oil and large-scale agriculture. The existing Van Sweringen system had been built on traffic balance and diversity, and adding the Missouri Pacific system simply extended that principle. It offered a different mix of industry and raw materials to help balance and augment the more traditional "maturing" territory covered by the Vans' eastern lines. Most notably, they would tap the up-and-coming fuel—petroleum—as a hedge against their dependence on coal and thus dominate all energy markets. (This, remember, was before the era of long-distance pipelines.)

As for the company itself, Baldwin was taking it in hand and producing promising results. Although revenues had increased only 7 percent between 1925 and 1929, MoPac's net income had improved by 60 percent.

The Van Sweringens' interest in MoPac went back at least to mid-1928, when they assigned their chief economic advisor, Colonel Leonard P. Ayres, to study the railroad and its territory. Another old Clevelander, the tall, soft-spoken Ayres was a nationally noted economist and statistician who had made a name for himself during the World War by applying statistical methods to logistics management. While working for the Van Sweringens—typically, without a formal title—he also served as a vice president for the Cleveland Trust Company. (In order to keep the valuable Ayres in Cleveland, the Vans and Cleveland Trust had agreed in 1927 to split him fifty-fifty. Generally he spent mornings at the bank and afternoons with the Vans.)

In essence, Ayres reported that the railroad had both operating and financial weaknesses—notably its huge bonded debt—but also considerable potential. Some think that the brothers saw in the report a railroad which was a large-scale reflection of the Nickel Plate and the C&O. Both of those properties were deemed unpromising when the Vans took them over, and under their management both were now strong and profitable. The Missouri Pacific "offered an almost unique chance of [such] a miracle on a heroic scale." And despite the brothers' genuine modesty, pure ego also may have crept in: By taking the Missouri Pacific, they would control the largest railroad system in the country. In a way, too, it was merely a much vaster variation of O. P.'s thinking two years earlier when he doubled the size of the Shaker Heights development by launching his projected Shaker Country Estates.[10]

Some less lofty motives also have been suggested. One historian saw it at least partly as a bold strategic ploy to put pressure on the Wabash, which was still making trouble in the railroad consolidation arena. By this time, the Pennsylvania's General Atterbury had scooped up Leonor Loree's interests in the Wabash, which further disrupted the strategy of the New York Central–B&O–Van Sweringen alliance. Still headed by William H. Williams, the railroad was continuing the push for a fifth eastern system; it had designs on the Vans' Wheeling & Lake Erie, among other things. But the Wabash and the Missouri Pacific had a close traffic relationship, and the Wabash depended heavily on their interchange business. By controlling the Missouri Pacific, so this reasoning runs, the Vans could divert Wabash traffic to the Nickel Plate, undercutting Williams and putting Atterbury off balance.[11]

Whatever their reasons, the brothers moved steadily but still silently ahead, buying in the ever-rising open market. Kuhn, Loeb, the Missouri Pacific's titular masters, quickly caught wind of what was happening and who was behind it. They assigned one of their brighter young analysts, John W. Barriger, to watch the situation and study Alleghany's structure and operations but otherwise made no move to fight the invasion. As Barriger later noted, their sentiment and sense of possession seemed tempered by the opportunity to make a good profit. That they did, as did numerous other MoPac shareholders. The stock, which sold at a low of 30 in 1925, hit a peak of 101 in 1929.[12]

The choleric Williams, though, was determined not to be a pushover. He tried two financial dirty tricks, both aimed at increasing the amount of MoPac common stock which any buyer would need to get control. His first move, executed on May 1, 1929, was to refund a maturing MoPac bond issue with $46.4 million in new bonds which were convertible to stock, thus forcing the Vans to spend more money to buy the new bond issue. Then, on November 1st, Williams applied to the ICC to fund $35.7 million in accumulated unpaid preferred-stock dividends by a new $38.6 million common-stock issue. O. P. was stung by the first stratagem but managed to encourage enough stockholder opposition for the second to delay the ICC case.[13]

As always, the brothers were pushing for absolute majority control, which promised to take time and generous amounts of money—made more generous by Williams's maneuverings. During the balance of 1929, the Alleghany spent a total of $88 million on Missouri Pacific and almost $12 million more in early 1930—close to $100 million for clear control. To help pay the cost, in mid-1929 it sold additional bonds and preferred stock totaling $50 million and common stock valued at $15 million; in April 1930, it created another $25 million bond issue plus $12.5 million in new preferred stock—a grand total of $102.5 million. Essentially, one highly leveraged company was buying another leveraged company, and Alleghany was now far out on a financial limb.[14]

But be that as it may, by March 1930, the Vans had their majority control, although it was all still theoretically a secret. As his first public move, O. P. phoned board chairman Williams at his New York office to announce his coup and invite him to Cleveland to discuss the transition. Williams duly complied, but when he arrived in the Terminal Tower, he proceeded to produce his own surprise. Missouri law, he pointed out, prohibited any company from controlling a railroad incorporated in the state without the permission of the Missouri Public Service Commission. It was nothing personal, he implied, but purely to preserve the integrity of public policy, he simply could not allow Alleghany to exercise its control.[15]

Actually, Colonel Ayres had stumbled onto the law earlier and had warned O. P. several days before Williams's visit, but lawyer John Murphy was inclined to brush it aside—not only was it obscure but apparently it had never been enforced. Nevertheless, the Vans now had to face the Public Service Commission and somehow get a quick, favorable decision. As a later writer wryly reported, "An effectively confused and confusing application was drafted and presented . . . asking for permission to buy Missouri Pacific shares, and, at the same time, announcing that they had been bought." This was coupled with an intense public-relations campaign which, in fact, Missouri Pacific's management supported and aided.[16]

The crisis was overcome, and on May 6th, the Missouri Public Service Commission rendered a favorable verdict, although there were some hints of sophisticated political bribery along the way. Williams then resigned his chairmanship and O. P. Van Sweringen took his place, although Lewis Baldwin remained in charge of the railroad. Aside from Baldwin, the MoPac's executive committee was replaced by an array of familiar Cleveland faces: O. P., Leonard Ayres, Darwin Barrett, John Sherwin, Charles Bradley's brother Alva Bradley, and Great Lakes shipping operator George Tomlinson. The Missouri Pacific was now officially a Van Sweringen railroad, and at one stroke they had more than doubled the size of their empire. To keep their management legally clear, the brothers nominally divided themselves into an "eastern empire" and "western empire," with O. P. assuming chairmanship of the western lines and M. J. replacing him as titular head of the eastern system. (From start to finish, O. P. had never seen the Missouri Pacific; he took his first ride over the railroad in February 1931, nine months after he assumed control.)[17]

Once the coup was made public, the press instantly began speculating about a coast-to-coast Van Sweringen railroad system. This was the holy grail of railroading; several empire-builders, including Collis P. Huntington and George Gould, had tried to achieve this goal, but none had yet succeeded. Now it certainly looked as if the brothers were poised to pull it off by resuscitating the western part of the old Gould system to link with their lines to the Atlantic. Counting the half-owned Denver & Rio Grande Western, they were only 928 rail miles from the Pacific. Completing that last stretch was the Gould-created Western Pacific (WP), the Rio Grande's other half-owner and the natural traffic partner of both the Rio Grande and the Missouri Pacific. Was the WP—and San Francisco Bay—the next logical Van Sweringen step? Maybe so. It may have been coincidental, but shortly before the Vans officially took control, the Missouri Pacific's management announced its desire to absorb the Western Pacific as part of the general railroad-consolidation program.

But despite the evidence, O. P. blandly disclaimed any such ambitions or, in fact, any plan to integrate the Missouri Pacific itself with his eastern system. He insisted that his prime motivation was diversification of traffic and territories—southwestern oil to balance eastern coal, for example—and years later, his onetime personal assistant William Wenneman backed that up. But since O. P. rarely shared his innermost thoughts with the world, no one but perhaps M. J. really knew where he was heading or what he planned to do when he got there.[18]

Whatever O. P. may have been planning, there were some immediate hindrances to a coast-to-coast system. For one, the Western Pacific had recently come under the control of Arthur Curtiss James, the bewhiskered son of an associate of the Great Northern Railway's Jim Hill, the legendary "Empire Builder" of the Pacific Northwest. James was in the process of rebuilding the WP and extending it toward the Pacific Northwest and, although he was not hostile, he had no interest in any overtures from Cleveland.[19]

Some ingrained institutional problems also had to be overcome. To traditionalists in the business, the Vans had committed the cardinal sin of breaching the boundary between railroad territories. Through historical accident rather than any particular plan, the American railroad system had developed along regional lines, with one of the most sacred divides separating the eastern and western railroad systems. Chicago, St. Louis, and New Orleans, along with lesser cities such as Peoria and Memphis, marked the gateways between East and West. At these points, the eastern trunk lines such as the New York Central, the Pennsylvania, the B&O, the Erie, and the Nickel Plate interchanged traffic with their western and southwestern counterparts—the Santa Fe, the Chicago & North Western, the Milwaukee Road, the Burlington, the Missouri Pacific, the Illinois Central, and the like. (True, some railroads such as the Wabash and the St. Louis–San Francisco somewhat overlapped territories, but the effect was minor.) Railroads on each side of the divide freely exchanged freight business as they and their customers chose.

Control of the Missouri Pacific by one eastern system promised to upset some of those balances and relationships. Privately, MoPac president Lewis Baldwin and his equally able counterpart on the Texas & Pacific, John L. Lancaster, were unhappy at the prospect of being pushed into favoring the Nickel Plate connection at St. Louis over their strong relationships with the Central, the Pennsylvania, and the B&O. The other eastern roads were even less pleased.[20]

But all those were problems for the future; for the moment, the purchase of MoPac was an enormous new coup to savor. And by this time, they had also celebrated a physical summit of their own. On May 26, 1928, they had moved out

At the peak of their careers in the late 1920s, M. J. (left) and O. P. (right) posed for these rare formal portraits. O. P. was then about 50 and M. J. in his late 40s.
Shaker Historical Society, Shaker Heights, Ohio

of their old quarters atop the Marshall Building and into a sumptuous executive suite on the thirty-sixth floor of the Terminal Tower, which at last was virtually complete and already well occupied. At that height, the building began to taper into a slim tower, making the office areas compact, intimate, and very private. Their 36th-floor sanctum provided for only four spacious oak-paneled offices—one each for the two brothers and the other two for their closest associates, Charles Bradley and Darwin Barrett. They were literally at the top of their city, figuratively on top of the transportation world, and, characteristically, as alone as possible.[21]

An Appalachian Peak in the Rockies • 173

Fifteen

The Summit II: Filling Out the Railroad Map

O. P. and M. J. may have been walled off from the world, but there was constant motion within those walls. Alleghany and the Missouri Pacific were merely the major ventures of 1929; there were plenty of "elsewheres" and "in-the-meantimes" to manage and maneuver through at the same time. In this best of all possible times, almost all of their various parallel streams —the suburban real estate projects, the Union Terminal complex, railroad acquisitions, railroad consolidation politics— seemed to be heading toward completion or resolution at once. And in typical Van Sweringen style, a few new directions were appearing.

On the railroad front, their new western incursion inspired two side forays. One seemed almost casual: While marching into the Missouri Pacific, the brothers spent $10.1 million for a one-fifth interest in the Kansas City Southern Railway (KCS). The 854-mile KCS made almost a direct north-south shot from Kansas City to the Gulf of Mexico at Port Arthur, Texas, touching parts of Oklahoma, Arkansas, and Louisiana on the way. En route, it also intersected with numerous Missouri Pacific lines and, like the Missouri Pacific, it tapped into petroleum-producing and agricultural country.[1]

The KCS's chairman was none other than Leonor Loree, who had been given the job years earlier by his old friend E. H. Harriman; Loree handled it along with his presidential duties on the Delaware & Hudson, and he did so quite effectively. (At the same time that he was trying to string together his eastern system, Loree attempted to promote something similar in the Southwest. The Loree Southwestern Lines, as they were informally labeled, consisted of the KCS, the Missouri-Kansas-Texas, and the St. Louis–Southwestern. But he was no more successful in this territory and was forced to give up in 1927.) The Vans' interest, however, probably had less to do with their relationships with Loree and more with the railroad's potential as an adjunct to the Missouri Pacific. For the moment, they made no move to increase their one-fifth ownership or to stir up Loree, who remained secure in his chairmanship most of the rest of his career.

They were also moving more decisively in another direction. In April 1929, they began negotiating for full control of the Chicago & Eastern Illinois (C&EI). Descended from an assemblage of small Indiana and Illinois coal-hauling lines, the C&EI extended south from Chicago through eastern Illinois and western Indiana. At Danville, Illinois, it divided into two branches, one continuing south to the Ohio River at Evansville, Indiana, and the other veering southwest to St. Louis (which it reached through New York Central trackage rights). A third branch dropped south through the southern Illinois soft coal fields, ending on the Mississippi at Thebes, Illinois, near the far tip of the state.

The C&EI's wishbone shape on the map was matched by a split personality. It was a regional eastern railroad heavily dependent on on-line coal. But it also functioned as two separate connecting links for other territories. At its Evansville terminal, it met the Louisville & Nashville, forming a route between the Deep South and Chicago. Its St. Louis branch served the same function for the various southwestern lines that ended at St. Louis—including the Missouri Pacific.[2]

And therein lay the C&EI's allure to the Van Sweringens. It certainly was not financial promise. Unlike the stable and relatively prosperous Kansas City Southern, the C&EI had been a historic loser. Its major livelihood, Illinois coal, found itself priced out of the market after a 1922 strike, and even in the booming late 1920s, traffic was slowly shrinking. By 1929, the railroad was barely in the black, showing a net in-

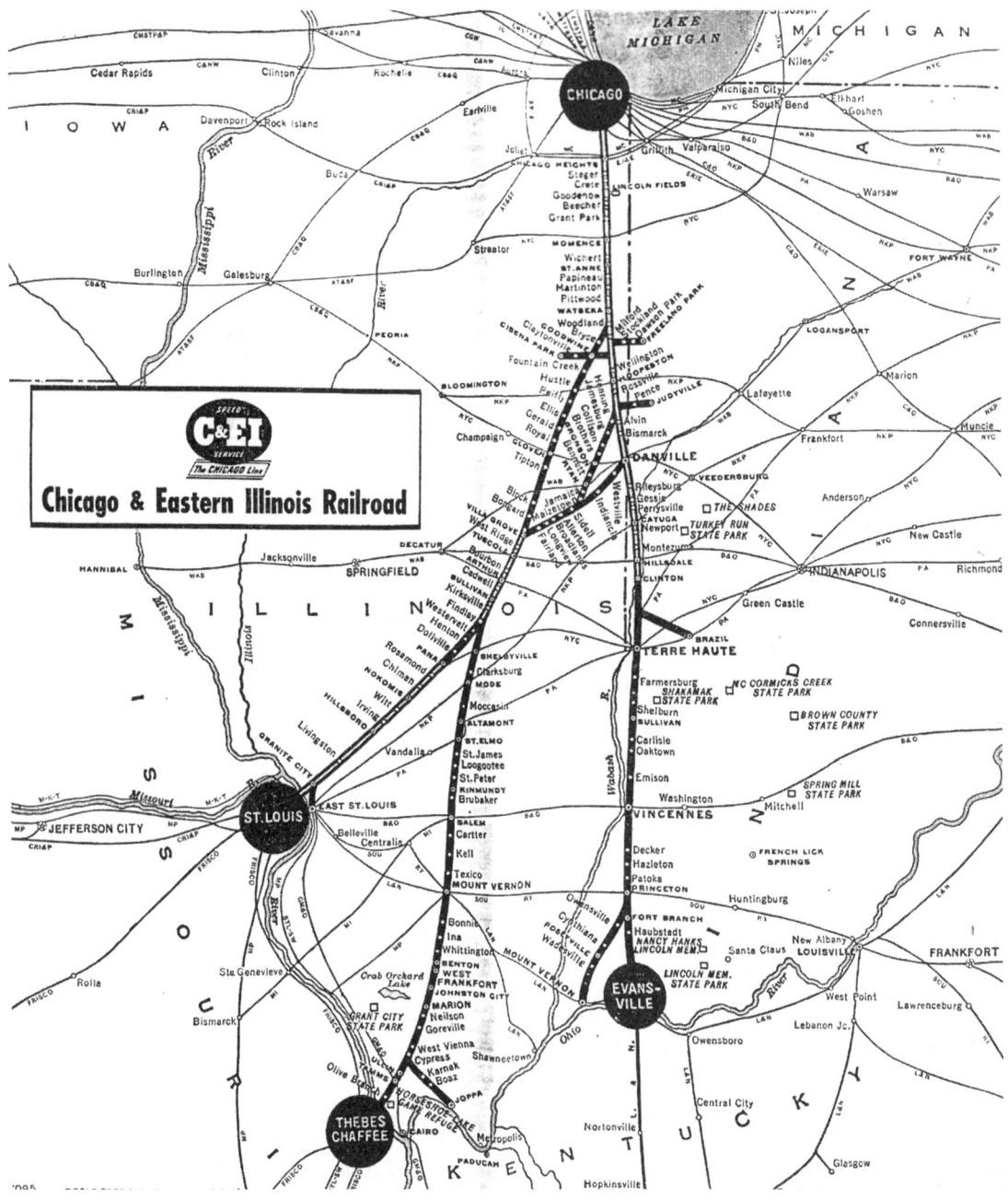

come of only $200,824 on total revenues of $25.4 million—and it was suspected that even that was achieved by creative accounting. But its strategic value offset the liabilities, or so it seemed. The Missouri Pacific would have a direct route to Chicago, giving it a competitive edge over its other southwestern rivals that terminated in St. Louis. A second MoPac connection at Thebes, Illinois, provided a bypass route that avoided the tangled St. Louis gateway. And while the C&EI had only nominal traffic relationships with the Vans' Nickel Plate and C&O, it could provide a southwestern channel for Michigan plants on the Pere Marquette.[3]

Fortunately for the Vans, they did not need to go into the stock market. The C&EI was another example of closely held control, in this case the estate of financier Thomas Fortune Ryan, who had died the year before. Fortunately too, the estate trustee was New York's Guaranty Trust Company, a Morgan ally and a close Van Sweringen financial supporter for several years. Unfortunately though, Guaranty was working for the Ryan family in this instance and apparently had no pangs of conscience about extracting the best price—an exorbitant price, in fact. It persuaded the brothers to settle for $8 million for a 51 percent interest, $2 million over the stock's market value at the time.

To consummate the deal—which was finally made in early January 1930—the brothers edged into some dark realms. For reasons known only to themselves, they chose a particularly devious and legally dubious device to shroud their ownership. No Van Sweringen holding company or railroad was recorded as having any interest in the C&EI. In actual fact, the C&O —the Vans' wealthiest railroad—bought it, but at the same time it did not buy it. It worked thus: Guaranty sold the stock to Paine, Webber & Company, the Vans' primary brokers, who became the ostensible owner. At the same time, the C&O signed a contract with Paine, Webber for an "option" on the stock, paying the broker $5 million and guaranteeing payment of the remaining $3 million. Paine, Webber was to "own" the stock and vote it until the C&O received ICC permission to control it directly. In a blatantly misleading accounting maneuver, the C&O then charged the $5 million as an unexplained "special deposit" on its books and neglected to record the $3 million debt anywhere.[4]

As always, the prime motive was to keep clear of ICC jurisdiction, although why the brothers picked this means is a mystery. The same end could have been accomplished more cleanly and with less legal risk by having Alleghany, the Chesapeake Corporation, or some other holding company buy the stock. Early 1930 was not a happy time for holding-company finances, of course, although the stock market looked briefly encouraging and Alleghany was still raising some funds. Probably the C&O's robustly healthy cash flow was the deciding factor.

In any event, the C&EI acquisition was meant to be secret,

Modest in size, equipment, and aspirations, the Chicago & Eastern Illinois was nonetheless an important link in several traffic flows that focused on Chicago. Included was a north-south passenger route—a route and business which interested the Vans far less than the railroad's links to their Missouri Pacific. One such C&EI passenger flyer poses at Danville, Illinois, in the mid-1930s.
Richard P. Wallis photo, H. H. Harwood, Jr., collection

but like the Missouri Pacific venture that was simultaneously concluding, the secret was open to anyone with even a dim interest in business affairs. But the "option" arrangement continued for seven years afterward. Paine, Webber dutifully voted the stock on Van Sweringen orders, and in January 1931, the C&EI's board chairman was replaced by Kenneth D. Steere, a onetime Van Sweringen associate who was then the Paine, Webber partner handling the Van Sweringen account. At the same time—and on O. P.'s recommendation—Charles O'Neal, a former Buffalo, Rochester & Pittsburgh vice president, was named president. By then the railroad had other concerns, however.

Sadly, the C&EI affair seemed to signal other ventures into even darker territory. In this case, the goal was unquestionably laudable—to keep and build traffic on their railroads—but some of the means were, to be charitable, less than exalted. The problem was that several of the Van Sweringen railroads depended heavily on the goodwill of various industrial traffic managers—the corporate officers who bought and managed their companies' freight transportation. Unlike their older and stronger competitors such as the New York Central and the Pennsylvania, both the Nickel Plate and the Erie lacked large concentrations of on-line industry. With less traffic locked in to their lines, they were forced to scramble for business, which the traffic managers could route at their discretion. Bernet accomplished this with first-class fast freight services and intense sales efforts, but unfortunately some less virtuous techniques also crept in.

In what later became a notorious example, the Vans picked up a group of industrial switching railroads and associated land companies in North Kansas City and St. Joseph, Missouri, while they were in the process of buying the Missouri Pacific. This little collection, which was put into a new holding company called Terminal Shares, Inc., happened to be owned by the meatpackers Swift & Company and Armour. It also happened that in 1927 the meatpackers were facing a forced sale; they had been ordered to divest themselves of their terminal properties under the antitrust laws with a deadline of January 31, 1932. Although it was a buyer's market, the Vans paid Swift and Armour an exorbitant $20.3 million—about one-fifth what they had paid for control of the entire Missouri Pacific system. They justified the purchases as valuable traffic sources for the MoPac, which they undoubtedly were, and admittedly the rival Chicago, Burlington & Quincy was also interested in them. But later evidence indicated that the sale was attached to a tacit agreement that the meatpackers would route their traffic over the Van Sweringen railroads—principally the Missouri Pacific and Nickel Plate. (The Nickel Plate particularly made a specialty of moving trainloads of meat from Chicago and St. Louis to Buffalo for eastern markets.) Put more bluntly, it appeared to be a case of buying business using a concealed illegal rebate.

Alleghany consummated the Terminal Shares purchase in October 1929, keeping it away from the jurisdictions of ICC and state regulatory agencies until the Van Sweringens formalized their control over the Missouri Pacific in 1930. Then they transferred the properties to the Missouri Pacific at the same inflated cost, piling new straws on the debt-ridden railroad's back. The following year, the Missouri Pacific was inspired to acquire another Swift railroad, the Fort Worth Belt Railway, at a similarly lofty price.[5]

Concurrently the Van Sweringens involved themselves in an even more dubious traffic-buying relationship. In 1928, a group of midwestern industrial traffic managers and other investors formed a holding company called the Bremo Corporation. Headed by Patrick H. Joyce, a wealthy and flamboyant railroad-car manufacturer, and Richard O'Hara, Swift & Company's transportation manager, the group took control of the Chicago Great Western Railroad in late 1929. By buying the hard-luck Great Western—described by railroad expert John W. Barriger as "a mountain railroad in a prairie country serving a traffic vacuum"—the traffic managers–investors planned to use their positions to route business over the railroad, thereby enriching both it and themselves.

The Vans had no interest in the Great Western itself but were apparently eager to garner favor with O'Hara and the other influential railroad shippers who made up Bremo. Their organization actively aided the Bremo group, and some officials even invested in it. John Bernet regularly advised Pat Joyce; and the Vans' stockbrokers, Paine, Webber & Company, also helped by financing the purchase of the stock. In fact, Bremo's first president and treasurer was none other than Paine, Webber's Kenneth D. Steere, the former Van Sweringen agent who was in charge of the brothers' brokerage account. (Bremo's name purportedly came from a small Virginia town on the C&O west of Richmond. It was an odd choice for a group of midwesterners, and—purposely or not—thus carried a subtle Van Sweringen connection.)[6]

Unfortunately, Bremo's timing was imperfect; it achieved control of the Great Western in October 1929. Almost instantly the group was in financial trouble, and the Vans came to the rescue by extending cash and credit. A more sordid story then unfolded, but that will be told in its time.

The brothers' railroad ventures may have had their lapses in virtue, but they were also accomplishing much that was positive. At the same time that they moved into the West, they were also patching together their "old" eastern system. Taking advantage of the half-loaf the ICC gave them in the C&O unification case a year earlier, they began the process of putting together the C&O and the Pere Marquette. On June 1, 1929, John Bernet moved out of the Erie presidency to head a joint C&O–Pere Marquette management. This meant technical demotions for the C&O's William Harahan and the PM's Frank Alfred, who both had been running their respective railroads before the Vans first appeared. Harahan was given the title of senior vice president and remained at the C&O's traditional Richmond headquarters handling day-to-day operations for both railroads. Alfred, the PM's president since 1912, now became its operating vice president. Harahan managed to swallow his pride and stick it out (and was later rewarded for his patience), but the 63-year-old Alfred almost immediately took an early retirement. Bernet replaced him with Robert J. Bowman, a protégé who had followed him from the Nickel Plate to the Erie. Walter Ross, the durable

Clover Leaf veteran, remained in charge of the Nickel Plate but doubtless took frequent advice from Bernet.[7]

The Erie was still kept in sort of a colonial status, but for the first time a Van Sweringen presence appeared in its board of directors in the form of their longtime intimate, Charles L. Bradley. Bradley became board chairman and Charles Denney, Bernet's old associate and second-in-command from the early Nickel Plate days, moved into the presidency.

Operating from his Terminal Tower office one floor below the brothers, Bernet quickly pulled together as many management functions as he could. One of his first moves was to combine C&O and Pere Marquette sales offices at various locations. He also brought together some headquarters functions such as law, corporate secretary, and purchasing in Cleveland. At the same time, he set up what was called the Advisory Mechanical Committee (AMC) to coordinate and standardize locomotive and car designs for the C&O, the Erie, the Nickel Plate, and the Pere Marquette—and to develop new designs where needed. Headed by 52-year-old W. G. Black, who had followed Bernet through the Nickel Plate and the Erie, the AMC was based in the Terminal Tower, where it was under Bernet's watchful eye.

One of Bernet's particular passions was modern motive power. He immediately charged Black with creating a new locomotive for the C&O to replace the powerful but ponderous and inefficient articulated cars that hauled coal to the Lake Erie docks at Toledo. The AMC went quickly to work and produced one of the most powerful two-cylinder steam locomotives ever built, a huge 2-10-4 type based on Bernet's heavy Erie Berkshires of a year earlier.[8] The first of the innovative and handsome C&O T-1 class, as they were called, rolled out of the Lima Locomotive Works in August 1930 and immediately began turning in sensational performances on 15,000-ton coal trains. They also established the Van Sweringen railroads as leaders in locomotive development, and their basic design spawned a fleet of fast, powerful 2-8-4s on the Nickel Plate, the Pere Marquette, and the Wheeling & Lake Erie during the 1930s and 1940s. Many lasted well into the diesel era and were hailed by one railroad writer as "steam's finest hour." (The Pennsylvania Railroad, which traditionally touched nothing but its own home-grown designs, was forced by the exigencies of World War II to copy the C&O T-1; the result was deemed one of the Pennsylvania's best classes of steam locomotive.)[9]

The Van Sweringens were also pouring money into other physical improvements for their railroads. In June 1929, for

Van Sweringen superpower at its mightiest: a brutish but still handsome Chesapeake & Ohio T-1 class 2-10-4 pounds through Columbus, Ohio, six years after it was delivered.
Glenn Grabill, Jr., photo,
H. H. Harwood, Jr., collection

example, the Nickel Plate opened a showpiece of freight-traffic development in Cleveland—the Northern Ohio Food Terminal. A $10 million joint project of the Nickel Plate and the Cleveland produce trade, the ultramodern fresh fruit and vegetable terminal replaced the hodgepodge wholesale district displaced by the Cleveland Union Terminal's eastern approach line and helped ensure that the Nickel Plate would handle a substantial part of Cleveland's perishable traffic. The new terminal sat on thirty-four acres and included four buildings to house food wholesalers, a private cold storage plant, an auction building, and track capacity for 460 railroad refrigerator cars. For many years afterward, it was considered the finest facility of its kind in the United States. The Nickel Plate and the Erie built a similar joint facility in Buffalo in 1930 and 1931.[10]

The government's railroad-consolidation program was now in its ninth year and still not making much progress. In fact, the process had taken on the image of a helpless schoolteacher trying to line up a mass of back-alley kids preoccupied with ganging up on one another and stealing lunch money.

The Pennsylvania's General Atterbury had become the

leading rowdy, brazenly picking up the Wabash and the Lehigh Valley without the Commission's leave and possibly even in violation of the Clayton Act. At the same time, he encouraged the Wabash's Williams (and perhaps Frank Taplin, too) to be as disruptive as they wished. Neither needed much encouragement.

He then flattered the Van Sweringens by imitating them, creating a new super–holding company to do the same kinds of things the Vans were doing—and with the same insulation from ICC supervision. His purpose was different, however. Although naturally aggressive, what Atterbury wanted was an effective defensive weapon—a method of keeping strategic railroads out of hostile hands rather than working to directly enhance the Pennsylvania system. Mindful of this and the political and regulatory perils, he varied the Van Sweringen technique. In April 1929, the Pennroad Corporation appeared, empowered to buy and hold railroad securities. The Pennsylvania had no financial interest, however. Pennroad's stock (in the form of voting trust certificates) would be publicly sold but offered first to Pennsylvania Railroad stockholders, who presumably had the company's best interests at heart. To assure that, Pennroad was governed through a voting trust agreement administered by General Atterbury and two Pennsylvania directors; its board consisted of seven other Pennsylvania directors. The result was something even better than a Van Sweringen could conceive: The Pennsylvania effectively managed Pennroad but had no financial obligations whatsoever. And since there was no bonded debt, there was no risk of outsiders taking over the management in case of a default.[11]

At the same time, the ICC was finally bestirring itself to bring order out of the anarchy. Having failed several times to escape the responsibility, it finally gathered up new resolve in 1929 to complete a "final" plan by the year's end. Nobody knew what was supposed to happen after that, but at least there was hope—particularly on the Vans' part—that the Commission could then begin approving mergers such as theirs.

Needless to say, the ICC did not lack for advice or pleas for recognition—and also needless to say, the Vans were among the earliest to appear with their pleas. In mid-February, they submitted a new consolidation proposal. This time there was no attempt to define any financial plan or corporate structure; the idea was simply to get a general blessing for the specific railroads the Vans would include in their system. The ICC then would presumably include this Van Sweringen system as part of its final consolidation plan; the precise mechanics

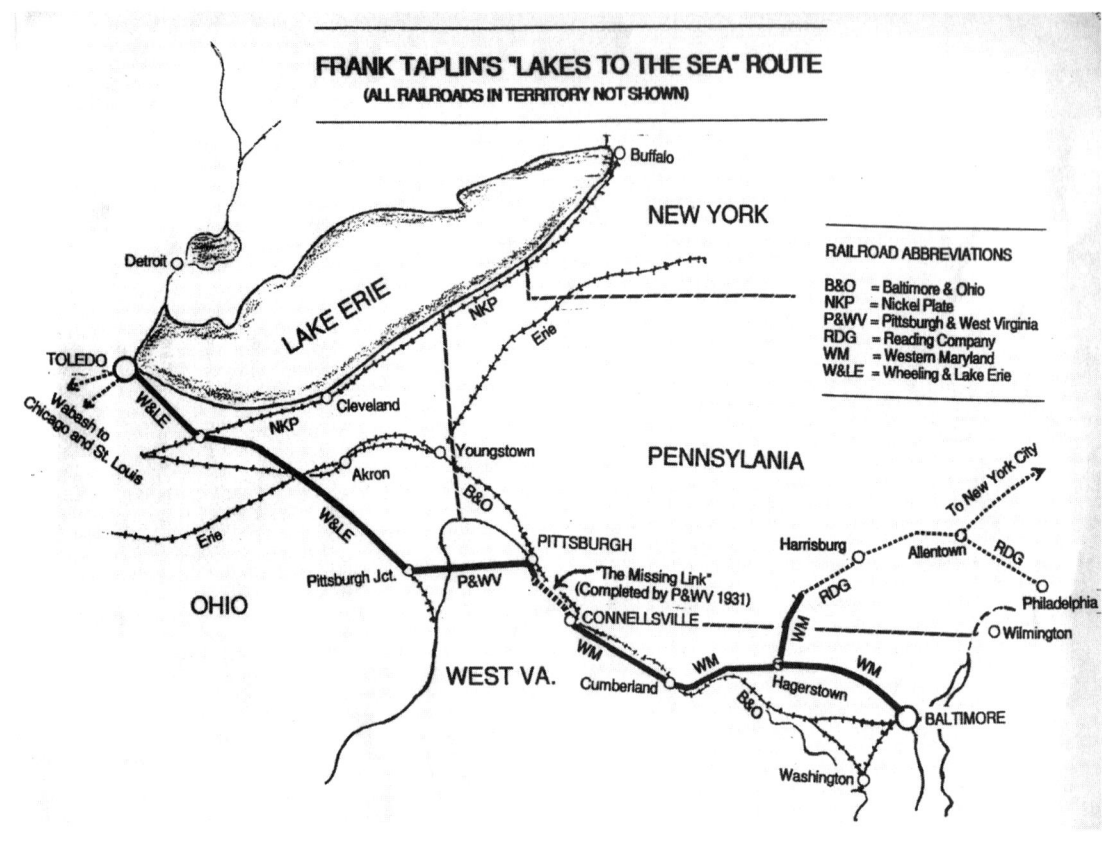

of corporate merger would follow afterward. Included, of course, were all the lines they already controlled—the C&O, the C&O's Hocking Valley subsidiary, the Pere Marquette, the Nickel Plate, the Erie, and the Wheeling & Lake Erie. In addition, they proposed taking the Lackawanna, the Chicago & Eastern Illinois, and several smaller lines that were to be allocated under the consolidation program. Nothing was said about the Missouri Pacific; that campaign was only just getting under way and was technically a secret anyway.[12]

Hard on the heels of the Vans came two contenders for the Wheeling & Lake Erie, the only railroad in their sphere that seemed to be contested. It was also vulnerable. The Wheeling still sat in its regulatory limbo: The Vans held the majority of the stock, but they could not manage the railroad, and the ICC's Clayton Act decision made its ultimate disposition uncertain. Much depended on whether the Commission would include a fifth eastern system in its final plan; if it did, the Wheeling seemed certain to be a key component.

Frank Taplin was the first to show up in Washington. He

was far from finished fighting the Van Sweringens and had every hope of stringing together his combination of the Wheeling & Lake Erie, his Pittsburgh & West Virginia, and the Western Maryland from the great lakes to the Atlantic, informally known as his "lakes to the sea" plan. (His Connellsville extension was now well underway to bridge the gap between the Pittsburgh & West Virginia and the Western Maryland.) In early February, he made his own application to absorb the Wheeling and the Western Maryland and continued to pick up Wheeling stock.

William H. Williams of the Wabash (with Atterbury offstage but definitely present) also joined the fray. Williams went to the ICC in June with his plan for a fifth eastern system, built on remnants of the old Loree plan. He would acquire the Lehigh Valley (which was also now in the Pennsylvania fold) plus the same Toledo-to-Baltimore route made up of the Wheeling, the Pittsburgh & West Virginia, and the Western Maryland. Both Williams and Taplin also pushed the ICC to order the B&O to divest itself of the control of the Western Maryland it had bought in 1927.

Other proposals came from the B&O and Loree, who by then had moved off into a different sphere. Only the New York Central stayed mostly aloof from the feeding frenzy. Ever cautious and conservative, Pat Crowley was the opposite of Atterbury and confined himself to buying an 8 percent interest in the Lackawanna, using the proceeds from the sale of the Central's Wheeling & Lake Erie stock to the Vans. As the ICC was sorting out the various competing applications, General Atterbury's new Pennroad was paying no attention and buying railroad stocks on a major scale. Among other things, it picked up Henry Ford's Detroit, Toledo & Ironton (a secondary but strategic north-south line running from Detroit into southern Ohio) and made heavy investments in New England. So far, however, it had stayed out of the Van Sweringens' path.[13]

Even so, Atterbury always had his eye on the "lakes to the sea" route with a combination of opportunism and apprehension. In the hands of, say, the New York Central or the Van Sweringens—or some unknown hostile power—the route was a potential threat to his company. On the other hand, it would make a nice addition to the Pennsylvania, especially as a more direct freight route between the Midwest and the Baltimore-Washington area. So as Taplin and Williams were carrying their own banners into the ICC, he continued off-and-on private negotiations with Taplin to buy the Pittsburgh & West Virginia.

A deal was finally struck in September. Pennroad agreed to pay $170 a share, nearly $38 million in total, for the Taplin group's 72 percent interest in the P&WV but left Taplin as chairman and president. Persistent ungentlemanliness had served Taplin well: He and his group received close to the $200-a-share price Atterbury had spurned as exorbitant three years earlier, a fully satisfying profit for their original investment of $52 a share. And Taplin had sealed the sale in September—a month before October 1929. Furthermore, he still ran the railroad and was also free to push his "lakes to the sea" campaign and to continue harassing the Van Sweringens. Atterbury had little to lose, since he controlled the Wabash directly and the P&WV indirectly. In November, Pennroad also offered to buy the Western Maryland as part of the Wabash's fifth system.[14]

As promised, the ICC at long last released its "final" consolidation plan on December 9th, 1929, proposing twenty-one systems nationwide. As the Vans probably expected, the news was good and bad, but mostly good. On the plus side, the Commission finally officially recognized the Van Sweringens as the operators of a fourth eastern system and legitimized most of what they had acquired—specifically, the C&O, the Hocking Valley, the Nickel Plate, the Pere Marquette, and the Erie. They were also assigned the Lackawanna, U.S. Steel's Bessemer & Lake Erie (which connected Lake Erie at Conneaut, Ohio, with the Pittsburgh area), and a mass of smaller lines. But they were denied the Wheeling & Lake Erie, which was hardly surprising considering the Clayton Act problem and the railroad's vital place in some fifth system. The Chicago & Eastern Illinois, which at the time was not officially in the Van Sweringen fold, went to the Chicago & North Western. The ICC likewise ignored the Vans' incursion into the Missouri Pacific, also still in process, and set that railroad up as the center of its own system. As part of its Missouri Pacific system, however, it thoughtfully included the Denver & Rio Grande Western, the Denver & Salt Lake, and the Western Pacific—raising the possibility that perhaps the Van Sweringens might soon reach San Francisco.[15]

And to the dismay of the brothers and their allies, the ICC proposed a fifth system primarily based on the Loree, Williams, and Taplin schemes. It was to include the Lehigh Valley, the Wabash, and the "lakes to the sea" route consisting of the Wheeling & Lake Erie, the Pittsburgh & West Virginia, and the Western Maryland. The Norfolk & Western was included to give the system both coal traffic and financial strength, although it had no direct connection with any of the other lines and few traffic flows in common; they were all to be linked in Ohio through a half-ownership of the Detroit, Toledo & Ironton. And for reasons that seemed to defy transportation logic, the Commission also threw in the Seaboard Air Line Railway, a system that covered the Southeast from Richmond to Florida. In all, the ICC's fifth system seemed merely a thrown-together collection of leftovers with little unity, financial strength, or traffic-generating ability—"drunks holding each other up," as the Vans' William Wenneman remarked. An outraged O. P. viewed the plan as the obvious result of Atterbury's machinations.[16]

The fifth system's incoherence was only one problem. How it was to be translated into reality was a huge question mark, since its key components already had been snatched by other railroads. The Pennsylvania now controlled most of the lines, either directly or through Pennroad—it had the Lehigh Valley, the Wabash, Pittsburgh & West Virginia, the Detroit, Toledo & Ironton, and the Norfolk & Western. The B&O had the Western Maryland, and the Vans held the Wheeling & Lake Erie. Because the Commission had no power to force consolidations, it was not clear how it would inspire the corporate self-sacrifices necessary to put the new system together.

Undoubtedly the ICC hoped to clean up the situation through its role as antitrust policeman. Already it had cited the Vans and their allies for the Wheeling & Lake Erie takeover, but so far to little avail. During 1929, it also duly filed Clayton Act suits against the Pennsylvania for its Lehigh Valley and Wabash holdings and against the B&O for its control of the Western Maryland. Ultimately, the ICC rendered negative judgments against these purchases, but in the end neither railroad was dislodged.[17]

In any event, the "final" plan proved to be anything but final. In addition to the thorny problems of railroad ownership, objections and counterproposals came from everywhere —railroads, states, communities, and numerous other groups. The process promised to churn on, and there were political hints that possibly the ICC would be given stronger powers to enforce whatever "final final" plan it devised. But in the meantime it had at least put its official blessing on the Van Sweringens' basic eastern system. That gave them hope that they could now begin their own consolidation process at last.

Sixteen

The Summit III: Consummation in Cleveland—and a Jolt

While their railroad empire was sluggishly but surely coming together in 1929, the brothers' physical creations in Cleveland were simultaneously taking mature form—albeit also with a few irritating bits of untidiness to clean up.

The Union Terminal construction project was proving every bit as difficult as the pessimists had predicted. While the Cleveland Union Terminals Company itself only owned three and a half miles of line—just what was needed to connect with the existing rail routes—virtually every inch was a major undertaking. The eastern approach required a long cut averaging forty feet deep and wide enough to accommodate six or more tracks, plus extensive hillside construction. At the western end was a 3,450-foot-long heavy steel and concrete viaduct that was built to carry four tracks 100 feet above the Cuyahoga River—high enough to clear the large lake freighters which constantly moved up and down the river with their iron ore, petroleum, and aggregates. This was followed by more cuts and street overpasses on the city's West Side. At the terminal railroad's center was the fiendishly difficult job of fitting the station, tracks, platforms, and yards into the multi-layered, multi-purpose building and roadway complex—much of it on sloping ground. In addition, the terminal company and the railroads had to electrify seventeen miles of line (to be operated by twenty-two new electric locomotives owned by the CUT) as well as rebuild and relocate over ten miles of approach lines (some in heavily built-up areas), eliminate all existing grade crossings, and build new outlying passenger stations at East Cleveland and Linndale. Chief Engineer Henry Jouett was indeed a busy man.

But it was all now moving along toward a hoped-for completion date of January 1930. On October 23rd, unannounced to the press, the brothers and some railroad officials rode what was reported as the first passenger train into the new station—a two-car test train hauled by a plebeian New York Central steam switcher. The Terminal Tower was effectively complete and occupied. Behind the Tower, the Medical Arts and the Builders Exchange Buildings both opened in 1929, although neither was formally completed until the next year. The third of the three-building grouping, the Midland Bank Building, was underway. Yet two large strings of the terminal development remained embarrassingly untied.[1]

One was the entire complex of traction facilities, both within the Union Terminal and beyond. The terminal was to be the focus of an extensive urban rapid transit system as well as the terminal for Cleveland's six electric interurban railways. To that end, it incorporated elaborate traction facilities separate from the steam railroad station, which included two separate large concourses, stairways, and platforms to accommodate six tracks. (Space was provided for an additional four tracks, too.) The terminal's eastern approach was built to accommodate four main-line rapid transit tracks as well as a grade-separated junction with a future subway spur under Huron Road. The subway eventually would reach Euclid Avenue to serve the extensive commercial district east of the Square.

In addition to the terminal itself, extensive work was already underway on the first line of the new rapid transit system, the route between Coit Road in East Cleveland and Lakewood on the city's West Side. The terminal's massive western approach viaduct over the Cuyahoga valley included provision for two rapid transit tracks and overhead wire supports; west of there a connecting line was graded to carry the route to the Nickel Plate's right-of-way, which it would follow to Lakewood. (The prescient Vans had seen to it that

In this mid-October 1930 view looking east toward Cedar Glen on Cleveland's East Side, the Vans' East Side rapid transit line is nearing completion. Grading and bridges are finished, support structures for the overhead electric catenary wires are in place, and track work is beginning. In the background are (in succession) two Nickel Plate main-line tracks plus a freight siding, two electrified tracks for New York Central passenger trains using the Union Terminal, and two tracks for the Central's Belt Line freight route. All of this was built on what originally was the Nickel Plate's main-line right-of-way.
Cleveland Union Terminal photo, John A. Rehor collection

the Nickel Plate's 1915–1922 West Side grade-crossing elimination project provided space for rapid transit tracks for this line as far as West 110th Street.) On the East Side, a seven-mile rapid transit line was being completed alongside the Nickel Plate–Union Terminals Company line as far as the new East Cleveland railroad station at Superior Avenue. This work, which was done as an adjunct to the rebuilding and partial relocation of the railroad lines, included bridges, stations, and steel structures to carry the overhead electric wires. East of East 55th Street, a complex system of tunnels was built to handle a three-way grade-separated junction for the East Cleveland, Shaker Heights, and future southeastern rapid transit routes. By the end of 1929, basic work on the East Cleveland line was largely complete and track-laying was underway as far as the new East Cleveland railroad station at Superior Avenue. (The section from there to Coit Road had been held up by a lawsuit from the City of East Cleveland, which objected to the planned car-storage yard in a residential area.) In all, the cost of all the various traction-related facilities in the terminal project was estimated at $20 million, paid for mostly by the railroad-owned Cleveland Union Terminals Company and the Nickel Plate.[2]

But in this case, the Vans' vision was both ahead of and behind the reality. To be sure, the Shaker Heights line would enter the terminal over the new rapid transit right-of-way as had always been planned. That, after all, was the Van Sweringens' Book of Genesis. But the interurbans were another story. Three of Cleveland's six interurban companies had expired four years earlier, and the remaining three were in varying stages of terminal illness. Private autos and buses had made the entire interurban industry obsolete with bewildering speed. While there was still hope that high-speed city entries would make the survivors competitive and strong again, none of them could pay the cost.[3]

The prospects were brighter for the planned rapid transit lines, which seemed to have an important place in the large, congested city. But despite the extensive—and expensive—construction work, the details of who would operate them and how they would be integrated with the city's existing transit system had not yet been seriously addressed. For that matter, even the technical details of the operation apparently were not settled. Significantly, although construction of the East Cleveland line was well advanced, neither cars nor electric substation equipment had been ordered.

Indeed, of all the many Van Sweringen enigmas, their rapid transit thinking may be the murkiest. Apparently the $20 million was being spent with no clear operating or management plan and no commitments from anyone. Years before, the brothers had created several of their own transit-related corporations, including the Cleveland Interurban Railroad, which operated the Shaker Heights line, and the Cleveland Traction Terminals Company, which was to lease the Union Terminal's traction facilities. Did they intend for one of these to operate the rapid transit system independently of the local Cleveland Railway's streetcar and bus network? If so, it would have lacked essential feeders and probably defeated its own purposes. Or were they essentially building the facilities on speculation, under the more practical assumption that the Cleveland Railway would operate them as part of its citywide system? If that was so, there is no present evidence that the Cleveland Railway made any efforts in that direction. The Cleveland Railway was going its own way with engineering studies and seemed to take the attitude that the Vans' East Side line was unwelcome competition.

In any event, the brothers resolved their presumed dilemma in their usual fashion: They decided to buy control of the Cleveland Railway and manage it jointly with their own transit companies. As always, it was done through a made-for-the-purpose holding company—but this time with a new financial twist. Rather than buy the controlling stock outright, they devised a scheme to essentially rent the stock at a far cheaper initial outlay. In 1929, the railway's stock sold for about $100 a share. The new Van Sweringen holding company, called Metropolitan Utilities, Inc., would pay Cleveland Railway stockholders $10 a share if they deposited their stock with it under a purchase option arrangement. Metropolitan then would hold and vote the stock and could buy the stock outright at $100 at any time for up to twenty years—if it chose to. In the meantime, the stockholders would be paid a guaranteed 6 percent return on their shares. (The 6 percent figure was essential, since the stockholders already were guaranteed this amount under a 1909 municipal agreement known as the Tayler Grant, which ran until mid-1934.) Said another way, the Van Sweringens would get control for only 10 percent of the stock's value plus the 6 percent annual payment obligation.[4]

Accordingly, Metropolitan Utilities was born at the end of March 1929 as a wholly owned subsidiary of the Vaness Corporation, the brothers' personal holding company. At the same time, Metropolitan took over full ownership of the various Van Sweringen traction companies—the Cleveland Interurban Railroad, the Cleveland & Youngstown Railroad, the Cleveland Traction Terminals Company, and the Traction Stores Company. Thanks to its generous terms, it had gathered 93 percent of the Cleveland Railway's stock by midyear, for which it paid $3.1 million. (In all, Metropolitan's various holdings were valued at $13.6 million.) Unlike such holding companies as Alleghany and the Chesapeake Corporation, Metropolitan Utilities was financed internally through loans from Vaness; it never sold its securities to the public. The brothers officially took control of the Cleveland Railway on April 24, 1930, and the ubiquitous Charles L. Bradley became chairman of its board.[5]

Metropolitan Utilities occupied just a tiny corner of what was now an immensely complex $3 billion railroad and real estate empire, but it had huge implications for Cleveland. For years, the city had shuffled around various rapid transit plans, none of which had gone anywhere. Now there was the means and incentive to put together an integrated system of urban rapid transit and surface lines—something which even the big-league cities of New York, Boston, Philadelphia, and Chicago had only partly accomplished.

The brothers faced a somewhat similar problem in the Terminal Building complex, which they ultimately solved the same way. A key element in the plan was a large, first-class department store to occupy the prime Public Square frontage next to the Terminal Tower building. But as the Terminal

The new Terminal Tower in February 1930, as seen from the less common vantage point of West 6th and Superior Avenue looking east toward the Public Square (at left rear). At left center is the Vans' cleaned-up Hotel Cleveland, its years of suffering through construction finally ended. A glimpse of the west end of the underground railroad terminal can be had in the right foreground; in the right rear is the Medical Arts Building. Generous space for future additions to the complex is abundantly clear.
Cleveland Union Terminal photo, John A. Rehor collection

neared completion, the space for the store remained an extremely visible void. With the Hotel Cleveland on its west flank and empty space on its east, the Terminal Tower looked like a giant one-winged bird. Unhappily, the brothers found no enthusiasm among the local merchants. Most of Cleveland's leading stores, notably Halle Brothers and the Higbee Company, were comfortably settled "uptown" on Euclid Avenue in the area of 13th Street and were disinclined to abandon their large and, they felt, better-located facilities for the expense and uncertainties of moving to the Square. Another large store, the May Company, was already on the Square and obviously saw no benefit whatsoever in relocating.

Failing to find a suitable local retailer, the Vans then tried to lure Chicago's Marshall Field. (The railroad terminal itself had also gone west for support. To operate the station's res-

Consummation in Cleveland—and a Jolt • 193

taurants and retail concessions, Bradley successfully enticed the famous Fred Harvey organization to come to Cleveland, Harvey's first and only venture in the East.) This alarmed the established local stores, who pleaded with O. P. not to bring in outside competition. Left with few acceptable alternatives and time marching on—but at the same time hoping to keep peace in Cleveland—the brothers then decided to buy themselves a local tenant. In July 1929, Vaness purchased the Higbee Company—which ironically had started its life just off the Square in 1860 but had joined the uptown exodus in 1910. To return it to the Square, the Vans paid $7.5 million for full ownership, a price judged far above the store's net worth and earnings record.[6]

If nothing else, the price matched the Van Sweringens' tastes and ambitions. Although it was one of Cleveland's best stores, Higbee's was rather ordinary by New York and Chicago standards and had only a limited number of departments. The Van Sweringen version would move it up to the national top level. The Terminal complex's architects, Graham, Anderson, Probst & White, were commissioned to design what was advertised as the largest department store to be built in the United States in the past twenty years. The thirteen-story building was to cost $10 million and "was intended to be the epitome of modern retail merchandising concepts in an atmosphere that resembled more the private club than the public market." The building included a large restaurant (with several smaller ones planned), a 550-person auditorium for civic and cultural events, and direct access to both the Union Terminal's rapid transit concourse and the Terminal Tower. Work finally began in 1930.[7]

As the new Higbee Company store was being sketched out in 1929, Shaker Square opened for business. The $2 million complex of twelve neo-Georgian buildings was symmetrically wrapped around the four quadrants of the new tree-shaded "common," which was bisected by the rapid transit line. Shoppers at the exclusive retail stores thus could ride to it from their Shaker homes or could stop off on their way in or out of town. Or they could drive to the complex and park right in front of the stores. The low-rise units, some of which included upstairs professional offices, were harmonious but varied to give the illusion of a village rather than a shopping complex.

Shaker Square's showpiece was Stouffer's Shaker Tavern, an elaborate large restaurant in the style of an idealized colonial inn or mansion. The two-story Tavern's main dining room accommodated 200 people and had four small private dining

One of Shaker Square's four quadrants shortly after opening in 1929, with retail stores at ground level and professional offices above. Although the architectural style was consistent, each quadrant was different.
Cleveland Press Collection, Cleveland State University

The Van Sweringen version of an early New England town common with a unique Van Sweringen difference: Through Shaker Square's center runs the suburb's downtown lifeline, the Shaker Heights "Rapid."
Anthony Krisak photo. Richard Krisak collection

rooms; upstairs were eight bedrooms intended for guests of tenants of the newly expanded Moreland Courts apartment complex, which was connected at the restaurant's rear. The Tavern's operator, A. E. Stouffer, had rapidly moved upscale from his beginnings only seven years earlier with a dairy stand downtown in the Arcade. For Stouffer and his sons, it would be the beginning of their own kind of empire.[8]

Out beyond Shaker Heights, the Shaker Country Estates project was taking satisfying form. Work so far consisted pri-

The new overpass at Shaker Boulevard and Warrensville Road is ready for the express roadways which were to stretch east into the Country Estates. Similar bridges were built at Green and Richmond Roads.
Anthony Krisak photo, Richard Krisak collection

marily of building and rebuilding the roadway system that served the area, which included the exorbitantly elaborate extension of Shaker Boulevard and its connecting Gates Mills Boulevard, several lesser new roads such as Brainard Road, and various extensions and improvements to the old farm roads. The local municipalities, the villages of Pepper Pike and Beachwood, were cooperating in laying water mains and sewers along all the new boulevards and other main roads. Initially 214 home sites were laid out, although almost no home construction had begun.[9]

And as an appropriate enhancement for the development, the brothers enticed The Country Club (its full proper name) to move from its rarified quarters near the lake at Bratenahl to a 200-acre site on Lander Road in the Country Estates, financed by cash advances from the Van Sweringens' Cleveland Terminal Building Company. (It would supplement the Pepper Pike Country Club, which had located nearby in 1925.) In 1929, the club broke ground for its $1.2 million facility, centered on a large limestone clubhouse designed in the inevitable Georgian Revival style by the Vans' favorite architect, Philip Small, who also happened to be a club member.[10]

True to the temper of 1929, the brothers also dipped into the hyperactive general stock market to the tune of about $30 million, mostly investing in Cleveland industrial companies such as Otis Steel, the Glidden Paint Company, Midland Steel

Products, and White Motors. They also put $1.5 million into the newly formed Midland Bank, which had been reorganized by their Union Trust friends, the Sherwins and the Bradleys. The bank was to be the prime tenant of one of the three new buildings to be grouped together behind the Terminal Tower.[11]

By August 1929, it was estimated that the brothers' personal holding companies had a net worth of somewhere between $120 million and $160 million. Their own personal net worth was something over $100 million—probably more than any Morgan partner. Furthermore, they had shot up to that exalted height in less than ten years. Within only a few more years the peak promised to be higher still: The Missouri Pacific was still being methodically gathered in and the Chicago & Eastern Illinois was not yet consummated. The Union Terminal complex was just in the process of opening, and more buildings were planned for it. The Shaker Country Estates was moving close to the point where land sales could begin. The prospect of consolidating their eastern railroad system had now improved and perhaps might be imminent—as was the possibility of owning a link to the Pacific Coast. Planning also had started for an Alleghany-like holding company to contain the burgeoning Cleveland real estate ventures and still another company for some new activities. Almost all of this would start or mature during 1930 and 1931.[12]

Admittedly, most of the latest acquisitions had not been the bargains of earlier years; the Missouri Pacific was the most dramatic case in point. But measured against their potential, these purchases were worth it. Besides, it was unlikely that they would ever come cheaper. As Yale economist Irving Fisher famously pronounced, "Stock prices have reached what looks like a permanently high plateau."[13]

Early in September the stock market, which had pumped itself up into a frenzy during the summer, began to lose a little air. It was not much, but the pumping seemed to stop for the moment. The price per share of the largest single component of the Vans' wealth, the Alleghany Corporation, hit a peak of over 56 between September 3rd and 5th but then slowly deflated to about 50. The market dropped more severely on September 10th, and Professor Fisher now hedged his "permanently high plateau" prophesy slightly, saying: "There may be a recession in stock prices but not anything in the nature of a crash." Nothing seemed especially imminent, though; for several weeks the market just gyrated up and down, but more down than up.[14]

But in mid-October, it had started dropping more abruptly. On Thursday, October 24th, there was sudden pandemonium as prices plummeted and sellers discovered that often there were no buyers. Happily, the panic was short lived, as the large New York bankers came quickly to the rescue. The market stabilized and rose again. It was over. Colonel Ayres, the Vans' own chief economist, proudly remarked for the press that no other country could have come through such a bad crash as well.[15]

But it was not over. Monday the 28th was frightful again, and Tuesday the 29th was cataclysmic, a date that lives in economic infamy. This time there was no organized support whatsoever; everyone was trying to cash out in a headlong scramble. The disaster was slightly tempered by a rally at day's end, however, and the next day prices perversely rose. But for two weeks it was mostly a dreary succession of lesser drops. Then at last the toboggan ride ended and the market steadied.

Unperturbed as always, O. P. Van Sweringen continued making acquisitions and planning for new projects. The purchase of the Missouri Pacific and the negotiations for the Chicago & Eastern Illinois were still underway, of course. The day after the crash, O. P. even extended help to his friend (and railroad shipper) Richard O' Hara, whose Bremo Corporation was suddenly in trouble. And viewed with a little perspective, his railroad stocks were not fatally hurt. Nickel Plate dropped from its peak of 192 to 110, C&O from 279 to 160, Pere Marquette from 260 to 140, and Missouri Pacific from 101 to 46. Yes, the immediate losses were all substantial, but in almost every case the 1929 lows were higher than the peak price four years earlier. Even the more vulnerable holding companies were reasonably above water. Alleghany had gone from its high of 56 to 18, but remembering that its original par value was 20 only nine months earlier, this did not seem catastrophic.[16]

And there seemed to be hope. After the fall finally stopped in mid-November, stock prices steadied and began marching upward again. It looked like the carnage was over. Alleghany started back up too, although sluggishly. By the year's end, it was averaging about 24 dollars per share. By January 1930, a genuine and substantial market recovery was underway. True, the brothers were now noting a disturbing drop in their railroad carloadings as industry slowed, indicating the possibility of a recession. But that was not necessarily alarming; after all, the postwar recession of 1921–1922 had been brief and there was no reason too think that this would be different. The august Harvard Economic Society said on December 21st: "A depression seems improbable; [we expect] recovery of business next spring with further improvement in the fall." And, three weeks later, it noted, "There are indications the severest phase of the recession is over." The purging was done, and although they might have to endure a short business dip, the brothers kept moving ahead, as always. There was much to be finished in the next two years.[17]

Seventeen

Completions and Complications: 1930

The year 1930 opened optimistically. Thus far the national economy had refused to pick up, but the stock market had. Between January and March 1930, stock prices recouped almost half the losses of the previous October and November. Alleghany, which was still a bit unstable, had done better by bouncing up to 36 at one point. Surely the economy would not be far behind; President Hoover predicted in March that the worst effect of the crash on unemployment would be over within two months.

It was a good thing. Alleghany needed stable railroad earnings; the Missouri Pacific and the Chicago & Eastern Illinois were just entering its fold and would need to begin producing their share. In Cleveland, the Terminal project was at a critical point—except for the department store, the construction work was largely finished and the office buildings were open for occupancy. Their long-term financing was still unsettled, however, and the department store was yet to be built. (And all that was merely the first phase of a larger complex on the site.) Then there was the Shaker Country Estates, still in its gestation stage, and the uncompleted rapid transit projects.

Confident that the trauma was behind them, the brothers moved on to wrap up the holdovers from the happier days of 1929 and start some new projects. Their New Year's baby was another kind of holding company called the Pittston Company, born January 11th. Pittston was a peculiar sidestep in the Van Sweringens' enterprises. Neither railroad nor real estate, it was a ragtag collection of operating and holding companies concerned primarily with mining and distributing anthracite coal to New York and other northeastern markets. (In 1930, anthracite was still the staple home heating fuel in the East and also had many industrial uses—but already it was in decline.) Conceived by Charles Bradley in his role as the Erie Railroad's board chairman, it apparently came about as a way to segregate the Erie's several Pennsylvania coal-mining subsidiaries from the railroad and give them an added sales and distribution network. The presumed result would be an integrated mine-to-consumer coal-marketing operation.[1]

To that end, Pittston was to lease and operate the Erie's Pennsylvania Coal Company and Hillside Iron and Coal Company properties, plus some others which were later added. To Pittston would be added a variety of companies handling wholesale and retail selling, storage, and delivery services. In the latter part of 1929—shortly before the crash—the Vans paid $13.2 million for control of a company called U.S. Distributing Company. U.S. Distributing was itself a holding company that owned a collection of companies involved in distributing coal, ice, and building materials as well as local trucking and warehousing. Nine other local New York and Boston coal distributors were also brought in at an additional cost of $9.4 million. Pittston emerged as an especially complex operation involving twenty-six separate companies (the total eventually grew to thirty-one).[2]

Pittston's purpose was rather narrow and specialized, but its concept had interesting implications. It could own and sell commodities carried by rail—which railroads themselves could not do under the 1906 Hepburn Act—and it could (and did) operate trucks and warehouses. In other words, Pittston had the potential to be part of a one-stop product marketing operation which integrated production, transportation (by rail or road as appropriate), temporary storage, and both wholesale and retail sales under a single management.

Planned in the autumn glow of 1929, Pittston was to be financed by an issue of $21.5 million in common stock (based on $20 a share), which would be offered first to Erie stockholders. Most likely the Van Sweringens hoped to maneuver the sale so that they would end up with their usual 51 percent stake and outside buyers would take up the difference. Accordingly, they persuaded the Morgan bank to underwrite part of the issue. Now, though, the environment was bleaker; the market may have been rebounding, but nobody rushed to Pittston. As Erie stockholders, the Alleghany and the C&O volunteered to buy $15.3 million in shares during February 1930, a generous gesture which saved some underwriting embarrassment. By May, the various Van Sweringen companies had spent a total of $19.2 million and owned 90 percent of Pittston, surely not what the brothers first intended.[3]

Financing was not Pittston's only problem. Charles Bradley, the company's primary sponsor, apparently was either preoccupied with other matters or simply a slipshod delegator in this case. He left it to Harvey D. Gibson, president of the New York Trust Company and a Pittston director, to handle the details of purchasing the various coal-distribution companies which were to be put under the holding company. Gibson turned out to be too generous a negotiator and employed the previous owners to run them at high salaries—creating an expensive and top-heavy organization which further hindered Pittston's financial outlook. Bradley's handling of the Pittston affair so angered O. P. that a rift opened between the two close associates which never fully healed, despite M. J.'s efforts to make peace between them.[4]

Although it was a subsidiary of the Alleghany Corporation and the C&O, Pittston was put in a sort of organizational no-man's-land, with no direct management by either of the Van Sweringens or others in their immediate ruling circle—or by any railroad officer. (Considering the Hepburn Act and other legal implications, it probably was thought best to give the company as independent a face as possible.)[5] Four of the company's seven directors were Van Sweringen associates of one type or another—Charles Bradley's brother Alva; Paine, Webber & Company's Kenneth Steere; John Murphy (the brothers' personal lawyer); and Otto Miller. Essentially the unwieldy enterprise became the fiefdom of its president, Michael Gallagher, a longtime coal operator and former general manager of Cleveland's powerful M. A. Hanna Company.[6]

Pittston was an unexpectedly expensive experience, but at least that problem was solved for the moment. Of more immediate concern was financing their Cleveland real estate operations—and again the Vans were deeply immersed in a scheme carried over from 1929.

Alleghany's instant success early that year had encouraged the brothers to try the same magic with their Cleveland ventures, which now included the six-building Union Terminal complex, the vastly expanded Shaker development, the rapid transit projects, and the city transit system. Since it was nearing completion, the Union Terminal project particularly needed permanent funding. As they looked at all their current obligations and future plans, they concluded that they should raise $60 million from outside sources through a new super–real estate holding company.

Beginning in early 1929, the brothers broached the idea with their customary New York banking patrons. This time they found a frustrating and annoying apathy; despite the still-booming stock market, their financial friends were clearly wary. The Morgan bank begged off completely and emphatically; it knew railroads, it said, but it never touched real estate. Morgan partner George Whitney suggested the Guaranty Company, a close Morgan ally and a Van Sweringen underwriter. Guaranty was equally unenthusiastic about what it saw as essentially a complex, expensive speculative development with hopeful estimates but no earnings record. In a June 1929 letter to O. P., Guaranty's President Joseph Swan diplomatically praised the bold concept but then loftily sniffed, "I do not feel that the securities which are to be issued will be of quite the character which our particular list of clients would buy enthusiastically. . . . I have no doubt you will find no difficulty in obtaining other bankers of a little less conservative disposition." "For the first time in a decade," one writer later observed, "their business was not good enough for their great friends in New York."[7]

Going downscale was unthinkable, and the Vans—reported by Morgan partner Harold Stanley to be "terribly sore at Guaranty"—pressed to reopen the proposal. While Morgan deftly kept clear itself, it pressured Guaranty to cooperate with the Vans. The bank reluctantly came around, although it took some time; it was not until September 1929 that serious analyses and negotiations began. Then came the October crash, but by December everyone had gathered up their nerves again. President Hoover and his various assemblies of business and labor leaders had concluded that the stomach-churning phase of the readjustment was over and that the wisest course was to ignore it and continue working and investing as before.[8]

Now enmeshed in the scheme but still ambivalent, the Guaranty people pushed O. P. for concessions to make it more saleable. As Pittston had proved already, the market may have been recovering but it was not snatching up new speculative securities. What the size of the issue should be and what specific financial mechanisms should be used were the subjects of arguments into the spring of 1930, and in the end O. P. found himself forced into some unpleasant and potentially perilous compromises. For one, the amount to be raised was cut in half, from $60 million to $30 million, by confining the financing strictly to the Union Terminal development. The Shaker Heights, Shaker Estates, and transit ventures were left to whatever other means the brothers could use. The $30 million would be raised through an issue of notes—the equivalent of debentures, or unsecured bonds—carrying a 6 percent interest rate. The Vans would get all the company's common stock in exchange for their interests in the various properties. All this, everyone hoped, would allow the Vans their usual full control and at the same time assure the buyers of a reasonably secure investment.

But to the bankers that was still not quite enough, and they insisted on something more to give the notes a firmer financial base. They suggested that the Vans contribute $10 million of their own, an idea which violated O. P.'s credo of maximum equity for a minimal cash outlay. The alternative they adopted was a dangerous one for the Vans: To provide the desired financial ballast, the brothers agreed to give the new company 500,000 shares of Alleghany stock, which would be frozen in a segregated account until half the issue of notes had been paid off.

That by itself was not too bad. The brothers still essentially owned the stock and voted it; they were simply restricted in liquidating it. Under normal circumstances, it would be released back to them once the required $15 million of notes had been retired. But there was also a nasty joker: If the total market value of that Alleghany stock fell below one-half the value of the outstanding notes, the brothers would be personally required to make up the difference by feeding in other negotiable securities. (In exchange, they would get an equivalent amount of the new company's stock.) The effect of that was to put the Vans in a kind of double jeopardy. As one writer later put it: "Before [this] contract was made, a decline in the market price of Alleghany merely decreased the Van Sweringen assets; with the new arrangement it increased their debts as well."[9]

The new holding company, christened the Van Sweringen Corporation, was incorporated on April 21, 1930. Its name not only lacked the imagination of Alleghany (which O. P. had named personally) but it was also confusing, since there had long been a Van Sweringen Company which owned and managed most of the suburban properties and continued to do so. Again, it was a marketing expedient: The bankers thought the Van Sweringen name gave the new enterprise better public recognition and an aura of quality.

Thus, with high hopes on the part of the Vans and probably crossed fingers at Guaranty, the Van Sweringen Corporation notes were launched to the public in mid-May. In their zeal to get the issue on the market quickly and attractively, both parties were a bit casual in their prospectus. Such items as the Union Terminal project's earnings record, its leasing success, and its future commitments were not mentioned, nor were certain features which could substantially lessen the company's asset base. The appraised value of the assets themselves—primarily the Terminal Tower, the three other office buildings, and the Hotel Cleveland—suddenly increased by a total of $10 million. Yet-undeveloped building sites, which previously had been carried on the books at no value, miraculously turned out to be worth slightly more than $16 million. (And this despite the advice of one Guaranty consultant, who reported that in Cleveland the brothers were "believed to have over-reached themselves in the real estate field." Furthermore, he noted, "real estate in Cleveland . . . at present . . . is in a depression and the Van Sweringens' realty in a considerable depression.")[10] Even so, it was a hard sell. In the happier days of 1927, the Vans' Chesapeake Corporation had sold out within an hour, but in 1930, it took almost eight months to clear out the Van Sweringen Corporation notes.

Two other financing efforts in the same period were more successful. To wrap up the Missouri Pacific campaign, Alleghany sold another $25 million bond issue in April. Also that month, the Chesapeake & Ohio split its stock four for one and issued $38.3 million in new stock to finance various improvement projects and its absorption of the Hocking Valley Railway, a longtime subsidiary and key component of its route to the Great Lakes at Toledo. In order to maintain their level of stock control, the Vans went to J. P. Morgan for a $32.5 million loan to their Chesapeake Corporation to buy a proportion of the new shares. The Chesapeake Corporation sat a step below Alleghany in the hierarchy and almost exclusively held the Vans' C&O interest. With its income and collateral based on the solid and prosperous C&O, the Chesapeake Corporation was no Van Sweringen Corporation, and the bankers had few qualms about the company. The loan was to run for three months beginning in July 1930, but as it turned out, it needed to be extended—and extended.[11]

But if the Vans' new financial creations were beginning to struggle through some dreary (but surely just temporarily dreary) times, the two brothers could always take solace in their physical accomplishments. And in mid-1930 they could at last celebrate one of the grandest and most hard-won of those accomplishments—and the end of one of the longest-running dramas in their career.

On June 28th, an assembly of 2,500 dignitaries filed into the Cleveland Union Terminal's concourse for its formal dedication luncheon. Appropriately, Newton D. Baker—former mayor, former secretary of war, and, not incidentally, a Van Sweringen lawyer and financial backer—was toastmaster. Baker in turn introduced the speakers—Cleveland Mayor Thomas Marshall, the New York Central's Pat Crowley, the Nickel Plate's Walter Ross, chairman of the U.S. Chamber of Commerce Julius H. Barnes, and the Union Terminal's chief engineer, Henry Jouett. Other railroad presidents and lesser officials mingled in the crowd of local civic leaders, politicians, and businesspeople. The brothers, of course, were nowhere to be found, but they listened to the proceedings on the radio at Daisy Hill. Afterward, most of the dignitaries took a ceremonial inspection trip over the Union Terminal line while admiring crowds surged down the ramps into the station at a rate estimated at 4,000 people an hour. Many lingered until almost midnight.

That made it official; the railroad terminal was finally

Cleveland's red-letter day finally came on June 28, 1930, when notables from the railroad world and the city's civic elite gathered in the new Union Terminal's concourse for the dedication luncheon.
Cleveland Press Collection, Cleveland State University

In virtually every picture ever taken of him, the New York Central's Patrick E. Crowley seems to wear a worried frown. He displays it here as he arrives for the Union Terminal ceremony and is greeted by the Vans' Charles Bradley.
Cleveland Press Collection, Cleveland State University

fully open for business. (Actually, four trains of the New York Central's Big Four subsidiary had been using it since the first of the year.) As the Vans had dreamed over a decade before, the Public Square was now the focus for virtually all of Cleveland's public transportation. Over seventy daily trains of the New York Central and the Big Four (officially the Cleveland, Cincinnati, Chicago & St. Louis Railway), arrived or left the station, carrying Clevelanders to New York, Boston, Chicago, Cincinnati, St. Louis, and much of the country in between. (But the Central's regal *20th Century Limited* disdained Cleveland entirely and passed through town on the lakefront line.) Ten Nickel Plate trains provided a more modest but comfortable service to New York, Chicago, and St. Louis. Inevitably absent was the Pennsylvania Railroad, which stubbornly stayed in the ramshackle Union Depot on the lakefront. (Many of its passengers used its newer station on Euclid Avenue at

Completions and Complications • 207

East 55th Street.) Cleveland's lesser lines—the Erie, the Baltimore & Ohio, and the Wheeling & Lake Erie—also hung back, at least for the time being. Two of them eventually came around: the B&O in 1934 and the Erie in 1949. The Wheeling & Lake Erie never did and instead gave up all service in 1938.

From the outside, Cleveland Union Terminal certainly looked nothing like a typical large metropolitan railroad station. In a radical break from the traditional palace-style architecture of such things, it was emphatically unmonumental and, in fact, invisible. Its principal gesture to the old grand style was its main entrance on the Public Square, which also served as the Terminal Tower's entrance—an impressive portico consisting of five high entrance arches which jutted out

Inside the new underground terminal, passengers embarked and disembarked through this spacious concourse. The view looks toward the Public Square.
Cleveland Union Terminal Collection, Cleveland State University

208 • Invisible Giants

Cafeterias and snack bars fed the Terminal's multitudes, but first-class dining could be had in this opulent setting, designed by the Vans' Philip Small and decorated with oak paneling from Sherwood Forest.
Cleveland Union Terminal Collection, Cleveland State University

from the building itself and opened into a long, rather narrow concourse with a vaulted ceiling soaring 46'8" above the floor. The entrance portico was decorated by allegorical murals by Jules Guerin, who had done similar work in New York's Pennsylvania Station and at the 1915 Panama-Pacific Exposition in San Francisco. The entrance concourse itself served multiple purposes in keeping with the Vans' conception of a unified urban center: It opened into the Terminal Tower elevator lobbies as well as the ramps leading down to the railroad and rapid transit station concourses and the Hotel Cleveland. Soon, too, it would open to the new department store.[12]

Otherwise, the station's facilities were all below street level, reached by long ramps and stairways from the Public Square; above them were the Van Sweringens' various airrights buildings, both present and future. Said differently, the station was part of a large, complex, but single structural organism.

Nevertheless, travelers found spaciousness and opulence inside. The overall feeling of richness was conveyed by floors and walls of varying types of marble, bronze chandeliers,

Completions and Complications • 209

bronze railings and trim on such fixtures as the train announcement board and platform gateways, wood paneling in the three restaurants, and, in the waiting room, an ornamental plaster ceiling and mahogany benches. (A "wonder palace," the *Cleveland Plain Dealer* called it in one headline.) The main railroad concourse rose into a skylight, the only part of the structure which could be seen on the surface level. (But that was at the rear of the complex where it was seldom noticed.)

It was opulent but utilitarian, too. Since the station was to serve two types of transportation—intercity railroad trains and local rapid transit (plus, it was still hoped, some interurbans)—it was laid out to separate the flow of people using each. The large steam railroad concourse was flanked by two smaller traction concourses, each reached by its own pedestrian ramps from the Square. Underground passageways also led from these two concourses to the planned streetcar loops to be built underneath the Public Square.

In keeping with the Vans' vision of the Union Terminal complex as a self-contained city, the station incorporated 175,000 square feet of commercial space for stores, restaurants, and services—all of them chastely set behind marble fronts and large plate-glass windows with elaborate statuary bronze framing. Included was a large drug and variety store, sandwich shops, a tearoom, a bookstore, a toy store, a candy shop, a men's clothing store, a vast 22-chair barber shop, and a large lunchroom. In a personal Van Sweringen touch, the restaurant facilities included a separate formal dining room designed by their favorite architect, Philip Small, and "furnished in the manner of a club lounge." It was paneled in antique English oak with ebony and holly inlay and had an elaborately decorated ceiling and its own separate entrance foyer, checkroom, and bathrooms; it was quickly labeled as Cleveland's most beautiful dining room. The Oak Room, as it was called, was intended as much for downtown businessmen as it was for first-class railroad passengers. All of the commercial concessions were operated by the legendary Fred Harvey organization, and on opening day the waitresses were outfitted in the traditional "Harvey girls" uniforms.

Stairways led from the three concourses to the track area below. Initially the stairways and platforms were built to serve six rapid transit tracks (which could be expanded to ten) and twelve intercity steam tracks; the steam railroad portion was designed to be expanded to the south to accommodate twelve more tracks. (In the meantime, the expansion area was used as a temporary coachyard.) The rapid transit section included two high-level platforms for the planned east-west line then

Midland Bank

Another sample of Van Sweringen splendor was the Midland Bank's main lobby, located in the adjacent Midland Building.
Cleveland Union Terminal Collection, Cleveland State University

under construction, and the other traction platforms and stairways were designed to be adaptable for either low- or high-level facilities as needed. The only immediate tenant of the traction section was the Shaker Heights line; since it was still leasing its rebuilt city streetcars, it used low-level platforms and a turnaround loop. This was to be only temporary until the larger rapid transit system was completed and new equipment was bought. Until then, neither of the two traction concourses would be fully opened.

In an era when steam locomotives hauled virtually all main-line railroad trains, there was no smell of coal smoke in the Union Terminal. The station was the only passenger terminal outside New York City worked entirely by electric power. Seventeen miles of track were strung with 3,000-volt direct-current overhead catenary wire, and all trains through the station were pulled and switched by the twenty-two large, handsome black General Electric locomotives. (The electrification and the locomotive fleet had been designed to be compatible with an eventual full electrification of the New York Central's New York–Chicago main line.) New York Central trains changed engines at Collinwood (East 152nd Street) on the city's East Side and at the suburban station at Linndale on the west; the Nickel Plate picked up and dropped electric power at East 37th Street and West 38th Street.

The Union Terminal project also included a commodious new East Side station at Superior Avenue in East Cleveland, built to serve the city's eastern suburbs and the Heights area. All New York Central and Nickel Plate passenger trains operating east of Cleveland stopped at the East Cleveland station, and it became a busy spot in its own right. An adjacent station was also built for the Vans' East Side rapid transit line, which was almost complete.

For the two railroads which had financed it, the Union Terminal represented the pearl of great price. The railroad portion of the terminal project alone came to $88 million—almost 47 percent more than the original estimate—and $40 million more was spent in rebuilding access lines and building new support facilities. Additionally, $20 million was allocated to rapid transit work, much of which was "temporarily" absorbed by the Union Terminals Company or the Nickel Plate, since only the Shaker Heights line was actually operating. As of the opening date, the Van Sweringens' own company, the Cleveland Terminal Building Company, had spent $31 million for the Terminal Tower and other air-rights buildings. The grand total thus came to $179 million—the equivalent of $1.5 billion in 1990s dollars and almost as much as the Van Sweringens had paid for their entire railroad empire.[13]

Because the dedication ceremony was held for the railroad terminal, it was inevitably almost entirely a railroad show. In fact, the trade magazine *Railway Age* devoted an entire large issue to the project (but failed to mention the Van Sweringen name once). For the two brothers, though—and for the city of Cleveland—the Union Terminal's party commemorated more than just a new railroad terminal. Since the Terminal Tower and other office buildings never had formal openings of their own, this was their celebration, too. The Terminal was now the working foundation of the Van Sweringens' city within a city that not only would give Cleveland a new physical face but would also redirect its commercial growth. Burbled *Business Week* magazine: "When the development is finished, one may work, eat, sleep, go to the theater, watch the stock market, ride taxicabs, see his doctor, all without leaving the Van Sweringen domain." It might have added that weather—especially Cleveland's often cruel winters—never intruded on the domain. But if one did leave it, one had only to go downstairs to reach any point in the country and, in the future, anywhere in the city, too. In the fashionable later term, it was to be a large-scale application of synergy: All enterprises would prosper because the others were there.[14]

The Union Terminal's opening also marked the end of the odd arrangement whereby the Van Sweringen organization managed the railroad-owned Cleveland Union Terminals Com-

Cleveland Union Terminal's single biggest engineering feat was its massive 3,450-foot-long viaduct over the Cuyahoga River valley at the station's west end. In this view looking east (note the Terminal Tower in the rear center), one of the terminal company's twenty-two electric locomotives takes out a westbound New York Central train. Note also the vacant track space on the viaduct's near side, provided for the Vans' planned West Side rapid transit route.
Anthony Krisak photo, Richard Krisak collection

pany. Charles Bradley, who had overseen the project for the Vans, turned over its presidency to the Central's Pat Crowley and received $200,000 for his efforts. Afterward, the terminal company continued to be corporately and operationally separate, but for all practical purposes it was a part of the New York Central system. In the meantime, Bradley hardly lacked for work. He remained chairman of the Erie, and the brothers leaned heavily on him for financial strategy and to manage their Cleveland projects. In addition to heading the Cleveland Terminals Building Company, he took charge of their new Metropolitan Utilities enterprise, becoming chairman of the Cleveland Railway when Metropolitan Utilities assumed control on April 24th. (George McGwinn, his lieutenant in the Union Terminal project, moved in as the Cleveland Railway's vice president and took over the presidency the next year.) As part of the same effort to unite the city's transit enterprises, Bradley also served as president of the Cleveland Interurban Railroad, the Vans' own rapid transit operation.[15]

To help the Vans plan their integrated transit system,

Completions and Complications • 213

George McGwinn persuaded them to hire a noted local consultant with considerable expertise in the field—one Peter Witt. The brothers seldom held grudges, particularly where someone could offer both professional and political help. Neither, apparently, did Witt. He remained on Metropolitan's payroll from March 1930 until 1937, although in the end he produced little of practical use.[16]

An even longer road ended, too. On July 20th, Shaker Heights rapid transit cars began regular service into the terminal. It had taken seventeen years, but the promises were finally kept. Now Heights riders were whisked directly to the Public Square over a completely private high-speed right-of-way that covered the six miles from Shaker Square to the Terminal in only twelve minutes. Rush-hour expresses took only ten minutes, and the system's longest trip—8.8 miles from the Warrensville Road or Lynnfield terminals—was accomplished in twenty-two minutes, including stops at the carefully spaced suburban intersections.[17]

Concurrently the rapid transit line terminated its traditional operating contract with the Cleveland Railway and began running the trains on its own. The Vans' Cleveland Interurban Railroad, which until then had essentially been a company only on paper, became a true transit operator, with its own management, crews, and shop. (Its new shop building in Kingsbury Run valley also opened in 1930.) Fortunately—thanks to the sickly state of the nearby interurban lines—the Cleveland Interurban could draw on a pool of experienced managers, trainmen, and shop workers who found themselves out of work elsewhere. Many of its first employees migrated north to Cleveland from the Northern Ohio Traction & Light Company's recently abandoned lines south of Massillon. One aspect of the operation did not change, however; the leased 1914 Cleveland Railway cars still hummed along as they had since 1920—and as they would for the next twenty-nine years. But to symbolize the new era, some cars had their Cleveland Railway yellow paint replaced by green with a yellow sunburst motif on their front ends—supposedly signifying suburbia's greenery and the dawn of the new day.[18]

And in characteristic fashion, the Vans immediately started reaching toward the new day of their rapid transit system. Taking advantage of their control of the Cleveland Railway, they had the railway company rebuild one of its recently delivered articulated streetcars for high-speed testing on the Shaker line. Fitted with a railroad-style pantograph and motors rewound for a top speed of 65 miles per hour, it was then taken out to Shaker Heights for a special run. The result was both encouraging and embarrassing. Embarking early one summer Sunday morning with the brothers aboard, the souped-up car covered the nine miles to the Union Terminal in twelve minutes—a spectacular terminal-to-terminal average of 45 miles per hour. Reputedly it hit 70 miles per hour on the long downgrade from Shaker Square. But once it got into the Terminal, the car could not negotiate the tight turning loop and had to be backed out. The trials ended there, probably less for technological reasons than for growing financial worries. Plans were drawn, however, to adapt some of these cars for high-level platforms on the projected East Cleveland rapid transit route.[19]

While the Union Terminal was the most dazzling Van Sweringen achievement of the new (and now more sober) decade, the brothers continued to put money into improving their railroads where they could. Taking advantage of what everyone predicted would be a short-lived recession, the Chesapeake & Ohio embarked on a massive multi-year program to rebuild its main line through West Virginia to handle more traffic and to accommodate larger locomotives and cars. Financially strong itself from the steady flow of profitable coal, the C&O found it could negotiate good prices from contractors who were now becoming hungry for work. Beginning in June 1930, thirteen mountain tunnels were enlarged, replaced, or supplemented with new bores; when the project ended six years later, the railroad had a high-capacity plant which was still serving its needs over seventy years later.[20]

The C&O also poured $3.4 million into rebuilding and expanding the Greenbrier, its luxurious West Virginia mountain resort hotel complex. While the Van Sweringens seemed to avoid the Greenbrier themselves, they well appreciated its prestige value and its usefulness in coddling freight customers, fellow railroad executives, and political friends. Planned with the Vans' architect Philip Small in the heady days of 1929, the hotel's capacity was more than doubled, from 250 rooms to 580, new facilities were added, and the outlying "cottages" were renovated. Despite the "recession," work began in 1930 and was completed the next year.[21]

To complement the Greenbrier's new glory, John Bernet also created an innovative luxury train to serve it. The C&O–Pere Marquette affiliation had opened up an entirely new passenger route linking cities in Michigan and Ohio with the Greenbrier at White Sulphur Springs as well as the equally posh Homestead at Virginia Hot Springs. Concurrent with the hotel planning in 1929, Bernet's brilliant public relations assistant, L. C. "Dick" Probert, designed a new train over the route and gave it a name appropriate to its intended clientele —the *Sportsman*. (Probert's everlasting contribution to American advertising iconography, by the way, was the C&O's sleeping cat Chessie, who first "slept like a kitten" in 1933.) The *Sportsman* made its first run on March 31, 1930, and carried not only the plushest of Pullman accommodations but also deluxe "Imperial Salon" coaches which approached the roominess and comfort of parlor cars. Although C&O's tracks came nowhere near Cleveland, the Vans and Bernet made certain their city also would have a link to the resorts, and the Nickel Plate carried a through sleeper to the *Sportsman* at its C&O junction at Fostoria, Ohio.[22]

Conceived in a confident world and born into an uncertain one, the Greenbrier expansion, the *Sportsman* and, above all, the Cleveland Union Terminal symbolized the state of all the varied Van Sweringen ventures in mid-1930. Some were finished, some were underway, some were waiting for the right time to start—but all now seemed to be at some indistinct pivotal point. The entire country was taking a deep breath and waiting to see what was coming next; the stock market was behaving poorly again and the business pickup had yet to pick up. On June 28th, the day of the Union Terminal opening, the resolutely hopeful professors at the Harvard Economic Club proclaimed that "irregular and conflicting movements of business should soon give way to sustained improvement." Others began wondering about the definition of "soon."[23]

Eighteen
Taking Stock: 1930

The "irregular and conflicting movements of business" during the first half of 1930 were beginning to cause some concern in the new Terminal Tower offices. Perversely, however, it was the year in which the Van Sweringens could take the most pride in the physical state of their several empires, if not their immediate financial prospects. Almost everything which had been underway for the past several years was finally complete, or nearly so. So, like 1924, the midyear of 1930 is an appropriate spot to halt the narrative and look at what had been created so far.

By the most common calculation, the Van Sweringens now controlled 29,431 miles of rail line—11 percent of the total U.S. mileage. In the six years since 1924, they had almost tripled the size of their system. (The total mileage figure varied according to one's definition of "control" and could include or exclude such partly owned but not fully controlled lines as the Denver & Rio Grande Western and the Kansas City Southern. But it was no less than 23,000 miles.) However measured, it was by far the largest group of railroads in the country under a single control. There were now seven major railroad companies in the fold: the Chesapeake & Ohio, Nickel Plate, Erie, Pere Marquette, Wheeling & Lake Erie, Missouri Pacific (which included the Texas & Pacific and several others), and Chicago & Eastern Illinois. In a more indistinct category were the Kansas City Southern (in which the Vans had a one-fifth interest and effective control) and the Denver & Rio Grande Western, of which the Missouri Pacific owned half.[1]

Sadly, however, none of the various Van Sweringen railroads were much closer to consolidation than they were in 1924. The only significant step forward was the shared top management of the C&O and the Pere Marquette, and that was only a year old. The ICC's "final" consolidation plan gave some hope for more positive moves soon, but there were still many kinks to work out. One was the Wheeling & Lake Erie, their chronic legal problem child, which was in the awkward position of being theirs but not theirs. The ICC had allowed them to keep ownership of the controlling stock, but that stock had to be voted by independent trustees; there were also no Van Sweringen representatives on the railroad's board. Furthermore, Frank Taplin's Pittsburgh & West Virginia still held on to its minority interest, and, with Pennroad's tacit support, Taplin continued to give the brothers grief wherever he could. As of 1930, the "fifth system" was a live issue that was sanctioned by the ICC, and the Wheeling was an essential part of it.

Merger problems aside, the newly expanded Van Sweringen system made much theoretical sense as a unified network. As with the original eastern system, traffic flows could feed one another well and there was a healthy diversity of commodities and industries. The weaknesses were mostly financial—especially the Missouri Pacific's heavy debt, the Erie's almost equally burdensome financial structure, and the Chicago & Eastern Illinois' underperformance. So far, national prosperity had papered over those problems, but at some point they needed to be addressed. As of mid-1930, however, the major challenge for the Van Sweringens was simply to digest the mass of disparate companies and make them a more coherent whole.

The ICC's final consolidation had given the Vans their original four railroads—the C&O, Nickel Plate, Erie, and Pere Marquette. Assuming that the tortured planning process would end soon, this implied that the Commission would bless a merger or some form of operation as a single unit. In the western territory, the Commission had specified an ex-

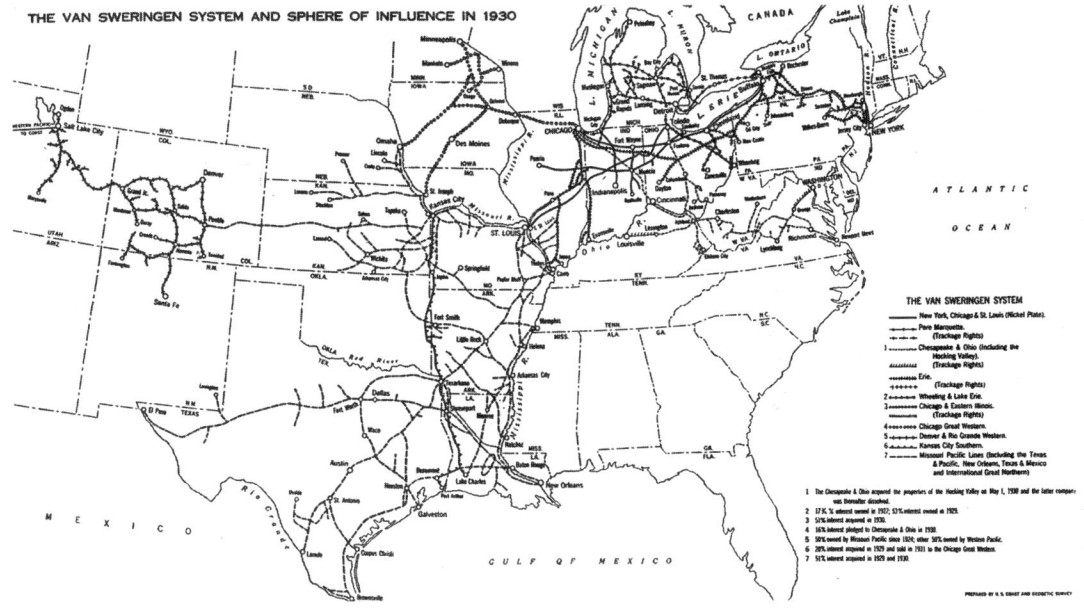

panded Missouri Pacific which included the Rio Grande and the Western Pacific, creating a St. Louis-to-San Francisco line, among other things. That too was encouraging for the Vans, since their MoPac was to be preserved as its own system. At this date, however, the ICC had voiced no opinions about their control, so the green light was a dim one. The odd railroads out were the Wheeling (which was to go to the Wabash-dominated fifth system), the Chicago & Eastern Illinois (which had unaccountably been made part of the Chicago & North Western), and the Kansas City Southern, which was allocated to the Union Pacific. As yet, though, nothing was really final, and the Vans were preparing for further battles, both to legitimize what they already had and to expand their territory. Where to expand? The ICC had put the New England lines in their own regional groupings, and that seemed to be the next direction to go.

The preeminence the two brothers had achieved in the railroad industry was reflected on a small scale—but more visibly—in their dominion over Cleveland. The "City of Van Sweringen," as a *Business Week* headline read, began with a virtually rebuilt city center anchored by the soaring spike of the Terminal Tower, the hotel and other new buildings around it, and the railroad terminal beneath it. From there their own dedicated high-speed transit line skimmed past six miles of Cleveland's huddled masses to deliver its patrons to Shaker

Square, the manicured neo-Georgian gateway to the Van Sweringens' outer domain. This huge realm stretched ten miles eastward through a carefully controlled landscape of homes, schools, churches, country clubs, and rolling greenery. Almost everyone else in the city rode the large yellow streetcars of the Van Sweringen–controlled Cleveland Railway, which were constantly in sight looping around the Public Square and trundling over the 250 route miles of track that reached into all parts of town. (Soon, it was planned, those cars would end their runs underground at the Public Square terminal, where passageways would lead to the Terminal complex.)

The Union Terminal complex itself now included five finished buildings—the Terminal Tower, the original Hotel Cleveland, and the harmonious grouping of the Medical Arts, Builders Exchange, and Midland Bank Buildings. Each of the last three had its special distinctions. The Medical Arts Building, of course, was a prestigious place for doctors and dentists to have their downtown offices. On the tenth floor of the Builders Exchange was the Guildhall, a complex of public and private restaurants with facilities for intimate business luncheons and meetings. Although more oriented to businesspeople and out of the stream of the general public, the Guildhall's facilities were very much in the Van Sweringen mold; they included a main Tudor Room with a faux-timbered ceiling and a smaller Colonial Room. A popular public attraction was a two-story-high exhibit hall on the seventeenth floor, designed for various building industry displays built around "A Home in the Sky," a complete two-story show house demonstrating the latest construction and furnishing techniques. The building also incorporated the 1,700-car Terminal Garage, the primary parking facility for the terminal complex. Inside the entrance to the Midland Building, the last to be completed, was a stairway leading up to the Midland Bank's grand lobby, which was two stories high and had classical columns, elegant chandeliers, an elaborately decorated ceiling, and carved-wood paneling. The bank's headquarters and banking facilities occupied four floors of its namesake building. All three buildings had underground interconnections with each other and with the Union Terminal–Terminal Tower–Hotel Cleveland grouping. A sixth building, the Higbee Company's new thirteen-floor department store, was now finally underway on the Terminal Tower's east flank.[2]

Interestingly, although the Terminal Tower absolutely dominated Cleveland, it was not really the city's largest; the Union Trust Building had at least 40 percent more internal space.

(But with their three-building satellite complex added in, the Vans controlled the most office space in the city.) Inside, the Tower was heavily populated by Van Sweringen enterprises and those of Van Sweringen friends and connections. Their business connections began in the first-floor lobby with a Union Trust branch bank and, upstairs, the Nickel Plate's headquarters offices and the C&O–Pere Marquette corporate and executive offices. Railroaders create their own kind of symbiosis, and at least fifteen other railroads had off-line traffic offices in the building—including, of all things, the Pennsylvania-controlled Wabash and Lehigh Valley and Loree's Delaware & Hudson. The Missouri Pacific was there, of course, plus several large Western railroads such as the Union Pacific, the Santa Fe, and the Northern Pacific. Prophetically, American Airways also had its local office on the tenth floor, neighboring some of the railroads. The lofty crown of the building, which began at the thirty-second floor, was exclusive Van Sweringen domain, including the brothers' real estate companies, their accounting and treasury offices, their top executives and personal staff, the elaborate boardroom serving their multitudinous companies, and their own personal lair. The only exceptions were the 42nd-floor public observation deck and a soda fountain on the floor above. Now two years old, the observation deck was already a major attraction for both Clevelanders and out-of-towners, who claimed they could see over thirty miles on a clear day. At night, a battery of 239 floodlights illuminated the tower's top floors and pinnacle.[3]

The brothers' personal quarters were on the thirty-sixth floor, partway up the Terminal Tower's narrow pinnacle, in what *Fortune* magazine aptly called the "conning tower." Here was a hushed blend of isolation and subdued splendor. Their spacious 20-by-30-foot adjoining offices occupied about one-third of the floor and looked northeast over the Public Square and the lake beyond. A passageway connected the two offices, the doors of which were never closed. Aside from two small combination conference and waiting rooms and space for secretaries, there were only two other equally large offices on the floor—one for Charles Bradley and one for Darwin Barrett, the brothers' chief of staff, personal envoy, and general confidential assistant. Dark oak paneling, low-level lighting, and working marble fireplaces in each office transmitted a hushed, magisterial atmosphere. The paneling had come from one huge tree in England's Sherwood Forest which had recently fallen and had been discovered by the owner of a Cleveland woodworking business. (And thus, to the office workers, the Van Sweringen executive suite was known as "Sherwood Forest.")[4]

In similar quarters immediately below were John Bernet, close friend and associate Benjamin Jenks, and the boardroom for the brothers' multiple corporations. Both floors were reached by a private elevator from the thirty-second floor in addition to the two public elevators. An anonymous but even more palatial adjunct to the Van Sweringen suite lay behind an unmarked door at the far north corner of the Terminal Tower's twelfth floor. There, in a compact area nestled against the Hotel Cleveland, was their private living and dining suite, designed for both their personal use and for regular business luncheons and dinners, meetings, and overnight guests. The three-story suite included three dining and meeting rooms, four upstairs guest bedrooms, and a magnificent two-story library and living room, all of it designed and furnished in the usual Old English–Gothic style by Philip Small. The living room was a smaller version of the vast Ship Room at Daisy Hill, with a large stone Gothic-style fireplace; a vaulted, beamed ceiling; and paneling from the same Sherwood Forest oak (which also was used in the Union Terminal's Oak Room restaurant). The guest rooms, two each on the thirteenth and fourteenth floors, looked down on the Public Square and Union Terminal–Terminal Tower portico; these were designed primarily for out-of-town business guests and were seldom used by the brothers themselves, who preferred to retreat to "the farm" every day at the end of work. In addition to the suite's entrance from the Terminal Tower, its three floors were reached by a private elevator from the Hotel Cleveland, which was also used to bring up meals from the hotel kitchen.

The suite's main dining room, which seated about thirty people and included a fireplace, was the scene of daily "staff and associates" luncheons, where ideas and issues could be discussed informally. O. P. presided at one end of the long table and M. J. at the other. The luncheon regulars included Darwin Barrett, Charles Bradley, Herbert Fitzpatrick, John Bernet, and other railroad presidents; out-of-town Van Sweringen executives and business visitors were also often invited. Adjoining were two smaller dining rooms—one holding twelve people and one for private four-person conferences.[5]

Outside the Terminal Tower and its satellite buildings was vacant space for future additions to the complex. Depending on building sizes and configurations, there was provision for about eight additional buildings around the Union Terminal area and even more potential building sites over the temporary coachyards at the rear. (This area also was to accommodate an expansion of the railroad terminal.) Plans for some of these sites included two more main bank buildings, the Higbee department store (which was underway by then), several commercial buildings, and the city's central post office. The Hotel Cleveland, which was now twelve years old and the senior member of the complex, was to be expanded with an 800-room addition. Possibly there would be a "merchandising mart," along the lines of Chicago's famous institution, and a theater.

Downstairs in the Union Terminal, the marble-walled railroad concourse was reassuringly busy serving its eighty-five trains a day. By the time the terminal opened, some of the old local trains had dropped off the timetables as people drove their new Model A Fords and Chevrolets (or secondhand Model Ts) to nearby places. Some Clevelanders even braved long-distance drives to places such as Buffalo, Toledo, and Detroit, but it was a major effort. Most long-distance travelers took the train, and New York Central or Nickel Plate trains took one almost anywhere—either directly or through connections at the big gateway cities such as Chicago, Cincinnati, and St. Louis. Homebound families of industrial workers from the South, for example, crowded the trains to Cincinnati, where they usually transferred to the Louisville & Nashville—or to Chicago to pick up the Illinois Central. There were some exceptions: To go southeast to, say, Pittsburgh or Youngstown, passengers either took the Pennsylvania from the decrepit old Union Depot or its more pleasant East 55th Street station or the Erie from its grimy little station nestled in the Union Terminal's shadow under the High Level Bridge. Another option was the Baltimore & Ohio, whose trains left from its Canal Road station, close by the Erie and also directly below the Union Terminal. Those going to Philadelphia or Washington also rode the Pennsylvania or the Baltimore & Ohio.

There was a new way to get places, but aside from a few people who were both rich and brave, it was not much of an option. Eleven miles west of the Terminal Tower, the five-year-old municipal airport had just completed its new terminal building, and in 1930 it became the first field in the United States to be lighted for nighttime flying. Eleven airlines were now flying mail services, and three offered passenger service. Pennsylvania Air Lines operated a single round trip between Cleveland, Pittsburgh, and Washington, carrying four to six passengers in its single-engine Fairchilds. (The next year it would graduate to Stinson Trimotors.) The Ford Trimotors of Stout Air Lines flew four trips each way between Cleveland

and Detroit, with connections to Chicago. (Surprisingly, at that time there was no through rail service between Cleveland and Detroit; passengers changed at Toledo.) Finally, American Airways scheduled two round trips to Chicago (one of them continuing to Kansas City) and one to Cincinnati and Louisville. Air travelers to Detroit did not need to trek out to the airport, however; they could go to the lakefront pier at East 9th Street downtown and catch one of Thompson Aeronautical Services' six daily seaplane flights to Detroit—and get an extra thrill in the process.[6]

Also, in the depths of the Union Terminal, the Shaker Heights rapid was doing an excellent business from its new quarters, which were reached through the East Traction Concourse. For the year 1930, it would carry 3 million passengers to and from the suburb—double the 1.5 million of 1924 and more than triple its first full year of business in 1921. Now at last complete—or as complete as any Van Sweringen enterprise ever was—it boasted six miles of first-class grade-separated right-of-way between the Terminal and Shaker Square, where it divided to run down the two wide boulevards. The Moreland branch had been extended a short distance from its Lynnfield Road terminal to Warrensville Center and eventually was to continue toward Chagrin Falls. The Shaker Boulevard line was also extended about half a mile eastward from Courtland Road to Warrensville Center, partly laid in the vast new grade-separated right-of-way which was then being completed to carry it on through the Shaker Country Estates tract and up Gates Mills Boulevard to the edge of the Chagrin River valley.[7]

But despite its high-toned territory and generally high engineering and construction standards, the Shaker rapid still had the marks of a shoestring operation. Indeed, it was a classic example of the brothers' lapses into expediency in order to create a service before completing the more ideal permanent physical form. The modified leased 1914 city streetcars still soldiered on, and all but three stations consisted of simple open wooden shelters with cinder platforms. (Even the new Shaker Square in all its neo-Colonial perfection was served by a most downscale wooden shelter.) All that would pass, though, once the larger rapid transit system was further along and standard designs for new equipment and facilities decided upon.

That time seemed not far away. Much of the East Side leg of the new city rapid transit system was now almost complete. As Shaker Heights rapid riders passed through the elaborate newly built junction at East 55th Street, they could see the

fresh grading of this route and follow it briefly as it swerved away and crossed a heavy girder bridge over the New York Central's freight line. From there, the nearly finished portion of the line followed the Nickel Plate–Cleveland Union Terminal route eastward as far as the terminal company's new East Cleveland station; future work would take it a mile and a half beyond to Coit Road, following the Nickel Plate main line. As noted earlier, all the major work was done; the basic station structures and platform stairways were there, as were the overhead electric catenary support structures, and one track was down most of the way.

In the meantime, the development of Shaker Heights was even more satisfying. Since 1920, the village's population had grown tenfold, from 1,616 pioneering souls to 17,793, and in fact it was now in the process of reincorporating as a city. A large new brick city hall was underway to replace the quarters in the little single-story Van Sweringen Company engineering office building. The community now also had nine public schools, with one more on the way (all of them considered among the best in the region), three private preparatory schools, and five churches. Even so, the original Shaker tract was not yet fully filled out, but this was the Van Sweringen way. As with all their projects, the brothers worked in the longest practical time frames and were never in a rush for quick sales. According to one account, they did not expect the Shaker

In 1930, the Shaker Heights rapid transit line began using the new Union Terminal and multi-car trains carried commuters to and from the new downtown office complex. In this later scene, an outbound train turns onto Moreland Boulevard just east of Shaker Square. Behind is the Moreland Courts apartment complex.
J. Wm. Vigrass photo

Country Estates development to be completed until 1950, a quarter-century from its inception. And there was much still to develop. Counting the Country Estates, the Vans' Shaker tracts now totaled 13,725 acres, of which only about 4,800 had been sold.[8]

Out in the Country Estates territory, the basic work was done on two of the most important new boulevards. The local roadways of the 590-foot-wide Shaker Boulevard extension were complete to its terminal at the large circle at Brainard Road, and grading and overpasses for the express roadways and rapid transit tracks was also finished. From Brainard Road, the new Gates Mills Boulevard now stretched northeast to the Chagrin valley and included a large center area at its outer end to accommodate the rapid transit terminal and car storage yard. Waterlines and fireplugs were installed along the boulevards, and work had started on the residential streets themselves. In August 1930, The Country Club opened its new clubhouse and golf course on Lander Road, giving Shaker Heights and the Country Estates a total of four country clubs.

Golf was not the only Van Sweringen–sponsored amenity in Shaker Heights. The old lakes of the Shaker colony had been preserved, expanded, and landscaped as parkland, as had a tributary stream. Shaker Heights also now boasted a riding club, the Cleveland Tennis Club, and the Shaker Heights Canoe Club—the last to help both residents and outsiders enjoy the charms of the Shaker Lakes.[9]

Admittedly, not everyone was charmed. Many architectural critics deplored Shaker's derivative, traditional architecture and its lack of aesthetic vigor. In these circles, Shaker Heights was damned as insipid and uncreative, a bastion of high-level Babbitry. Henry-Russell Hitchcock, for one, sneered at "the Van Sweringen developments, with their pathetic detached villas, alternately English and Colonial." Perhaps the critics had a point; it is true that stability and creativity have never coexisted particularly well. Cleveland's strivers and its more settled upper classes clearly preferred stability in their Colonial, Tudor, and Chateau strongholds, which subtly but unmistakably bespoke their status. The Terminal Tower's retrogressive style was similarly scorned; few critics or later architectural historians even deigned to mention it. Hitchcock dismissed it as "an obvious bid for publicity"—an ironic criticism considering its unassuming and emphatically anti-publicity creators. But he had unknowingly put his finger on the Van Sweringen paradox.[10]

Inside the Terminal Tower's top floors was another paradox, this one invisible but all powerful. Almost everything the

Secreted away in the Terminal Tower was the Vans' private dining and hospitality suite. Its centerpiece was this ornate living room, shown here after a post–World War II redecoration but still retaining the essential Van Sweringen design.
Chesapeake & Ohio Railway photo, H. H. Harwood, Jr., collection

brothers touched was built in the most solid way and designed with a unique imagination to last for the ages. To complete them in the Van Sweringen manner usually required huge capital investments that would be tied up for years, sometimes decades, before they could pay off. Yet the medium which created it all and held it together was a seemingly hodgepodge assembly of ethereal corporate entities built on the wispiest of underpinnings. It was the tradeoff required to carry out the Van Sweringen credo of undisputed control with the least possible personal outlay.

The basic technique was unchanged since its genesis in 1916: loans, installment payments, and, most of all, holding companies built on the principle of a highly leveraged capital structure. Since then, both the loans and the holding company relationships had multiplied as new acquisitions were added and ever-larger projects begun. By mid-1930, the chart of Van Sweringen corporate relationships was a wondrously tangled labyrinth of some 275 separate companies—beginning at the top with pyramided holding companies and extending down through various operating companies and their sometimes numerous subsidiaries. (The Missouri Pacific alone had eighty subsidiary or affiliated companies, and the Erie had fifty-one.) Connecting them in what sometimes appeared to be no logical pattern was a mass of crisscrossing lines representing ownership and control relationships. Some of these extended from holding companies, some from operating companies, and some from obscure subsidiaries of operating companies. Furthermore, the chart seemed to be constantly in motion, with assets and corporate relationships shifting as legal and financial needs dictated.

Unchanging at the top of it all was the Vaness Company, the brothers' "personal basket." As before, the two Van Sweringens held 80 percent of Vaness's stock, with the remainder divided between longtime intimates Charles Bradley and Joseph Nutt. But there was always a mystery about what, if anything, was above Vaness. The brothers themselves theoretically worked as a partnership, but later evidence revealed that there may never have been any formal partnership document. Apparently whatever business relationship existed between them worked strictly on that intense brotherly bond.[11]

Through Vaness and the General Securities Corporation—a similar private holding company which was dissolved in late 1930—the two brothers controlled all else with amazingly little investment of their own. For example, in 1930 it was calculated that their personal financial stake in the Chesapeake & Ohio was less than 1 percent, and it was only 1.7 percent for the vast Missouri Pacific system. In all, it was estimated that the brothers controlled corporate assets valued at $3 billion through an investment of less than $20 million—and much of that consisted of loans in one form or another.[12]

By this time the Van Sweringen–style multi-layered, leveraged holding company technique was a widely accepted—and often applauded—part of American business. Their structures and operating methods varied, but most were built on the same principle—that prosperity would continue, providing a steadily rising income to support the obligations and provide returns for all. The utilities industry seemed to be the most fertile breeding ground, and the Van Sweringens' most famous peer, Chicago's Samuel Insull, was the most spectacularly successful practitioner. The English-born Insull had built a sprawling midwestern electric utilities empire which also included several interurban railways and Chicago's rapid transit system; like the Vans, he used capital creatively to build, rebuild, and improve his properties. Indeed, the Van Sweringens and Insull were widely viewed as the best of this new breed of businessman.

Even so, something else which never seemed to change was the brothers' personalities and lifestyles. At ages 51 and 49 respectively, they were still relatively young in years but had all the traits of stereotypical old maids. Like many others, an anonymous *Fortune* magazine writer was baffled by these unlikely entrepreneurs: "The aggressive Van Sweringen instincts have somehow sprung out of two gray and retiring bachelors whose private habits are almost prim. They don't

The brothers avoided photographers at all costs, and until they were hauled into congressional investigations in the 1930s, few pictures of them existed in any form. One newspaper photographer caught a serious O. P. and M. J. (right rear) and a cheerful Charles Bradley on a Cleveland street about 1930.
Cleveland Press photo,
H. P. Francis collection

drink or serve drinks. They don't smoke. They have no known vices, large or small. O. P.'s nearest vice is a fondness for sleep; he likes to sleep and is adept at it. . . . When a crisis arises in the Van Sweringen affairs, does O.P. pace the floor? No. Instead he goes home to Daisy Hill, sleeps, sleeps some more, and returns fired with ideas. . . . He is visibly sensitive, shy. It actually hurts him to talk about himself." M. J. most likely did pace the floor, mentally if not physically.[13]

Their press representative Joseph Doherty added: "Neither brother had any instinct for grasping at social happiness. Their own company was all they needed." That was almost true, but not entirely. As times turned tougher, Daisy Jenks would usually call on them to give a little cheer when they returned to Daisy Hill at the end of the day.[14]

Another part of their regular daily routine was a stop on the way home to Daisy Hill to call on their two sisters, who still lived in the Vans' South Park Boulevard mansion in Shaker Heights. The ostensible purpose was to pick up any mail for them which might have gone there, but it was mostly simply to keep contact and a watchful eye. Otherwise, the brothers lived almost entirely separate lives from their three older siblings. Herbert, the eldest brother, also now lived in Shaker Heights with his wife; after his Florida misadventures ended, he was largely supported by a trust fund set up by O. P. and M. J. A series of strokes later forced him to live with his son and his family in Buffalo, where he died in 1942.[15]

And as always, they did little more than work, whether in the Terminal Tower or home at Daisy Hill Farm. (*Business Week* noted that Daisy Hill had "one of the busiest private wires" in the country. Its switchboard controlled eighty lines.) There were few vacations of any length and certainly no trips to Europe or any place remotely exotic. They remained a pair of Cleveland homebodies who went not much of anywhere except for the constant necessary shuttling to New York—usually riding the overnight joint Nickel Plate–Lackawanna passenger train and staying in their always-reserved Suite 1423 at the New York Central–owned Commodore Hotel, next to Grand Central Terminal. (They had no private car of their own, either; when they traveled, they usually made use of a Nickel Plate, C&O, or Erie office car assigned to one of their railroad executives—often Nickel Plate car 27.) Said O. P., "We have no wish—and we see no necessity—for moving to New York and proceeding to open up offices or, in general, to live the life that so many seem to think should go with our present jobs." And although they had now remade Cleveland, they took no active part in the city's life. Nor was there any

O. P. (right) and M. J. in 1933.
Wide World

golf, boating, or other outdoor pastimes of the well-to-do, although the more active M. J. still rode horseback when he could.[16]

They were also toying with one of those classic "what ifs" that so often uselessly tantalize anyone looking back. The brothers already had begun talking between themselves about retiring from business. Most likely the nervous and conservative M. J. initiated the notion, although O. P. was all too aware of his own physical weaknesses. William Wenneman, O. P.'s private secretary at the time, recalled that O. P. told him that they planned to retire when he reached 50, which would be August 24, 1929. But because of their Missouri Pacific campaign, they set the date back to M. J.'s 50th birthday, July 8, 1931. In anticipation, according to Wenneman, they sold half a million Alleghany shares in 1929—then bought them back in 1930. But despite the story's painful "What if?" poignancy, one wonders if O. P. ever would have been able to carry through the idea. Could he have given up his constant drive to build and expand—and if he had, what would he then have done with himself?[17]

Their closest business associates and their personal office staff remained remarkably stable and inbred too—the same tight little group of trusted Clevelanders that had worked with them since earlier days. Joseph Nutt, at 59 the eldest of the inner circle, had become chairman of Union Trust after the senior John Sherwin retired in 1929 and intermittently served as the Republican Party's national treasurer. While never a full-time Van Sweringen associate, he was an essential advisor, financial facilitator, and friendly source of funds. Charles Bradley, now 45, remained at O. P.'s right hand as a manager and financial advisor and was also one of the Midland Bank's principal founders and directors; his star had somewhat dimmed, however, following the Pittston Company fiasco.

Darwin Barrett continued to be O. P.'s most chief personal assistant and regular confidential emissary to the New York bankers; the financially astute 27-year-old William Wenneman served as his personal secretary. Legal work was a lifeblood of Van Sweringen operations, and the brothers relied heavily on Herbert Fitzpatrick as their chief railroad and "outside" lawyer, while John Murphy handled much of their personal and "inside" corporate work. (The bachelor Fitzpatrick maintained his legal residence in Huntington and often stayed at Daisy Hill during the work week.) A newcomer to the management circle was the brothers' principal Missouri Pacific corporate liaison, its secretary and treasurer, William Wyer. The 35-year-old Wyer was a graduate of Yale and M.I.T. who had come to Cleveland from former board chairman William Williams's New York office and became another in the Vans' collection of first-class technical minds.

In keeping with their self-effacing bosses, the office staff continued to live without formal titles except for various legally required positions in the holding companies. M. J.'s role was undefined, but as the pragmatic organizer he had charge of the office staff's work and all of the myriad details that went with it. "Often O. P., after looking at a sketch or plan, would sink back in his chair and say 'well, that's fin-

O. P. (left) with his top personal staff during the Pecora Committee hearings in June 1933. Behind him at left looking typically grim is Darwin Barrett, chief personal assistant and informal Van Sweringen secretary of state; in the center is lawyer John P. Murphy. Frank Ginn, a prominent Cleveland lawyer and Van Sweringen associate from the early days, offers his advice at the right.
Cleveland Press Collection, Cleveland State University

In this apparently composite photo, O. P. confers with his chief railroad lawyer, Herbert Fitzpatrick, in 1933.
Cleveland Press, H. H. Harwood, Jr., collection

ished,' and M. J.'s retort was always the same: 'This is just where I begin.'" And, of course, he took care of all those personal details of his brother's life that O. P. either ignored or was oblivious to.[18]

Indeed, the Van Sweringen success formula was an odd one, but somehow it was spectacularly successful in inspiring confidence and all the support that went with it. The problem, of course, was that now, in mid-1930, the myriad ethereal financial structures supporting their empires were at their most vulnerable point: All of the most costly real estate projects—especially the Union Terminal building complex and Shaker Country Estates—were just coming on line, as the later jargon would have it. Even in the best of times, it would take several years before they could begin to pay off. Integrating the railroads and addressing the financial weaknesses of some of them would also take time. The Van Sweringens anticipated all of that. But to nurse all these enterprises through their growing pains and keep their complex financial structure stable, they also expected that the same healthy income growth of the past would continue. On the other hand, any prolonged downturn in the railroad or real estate business could well destroy it. M. J. may have been a bit nervous, but that was his nature; O. P.'s nature was to be stubbornly optimistic and confident that he could work around any problems.

Nineteen
Sudden Darkness

History is often perverse. At almost the same moment of the Van Sweringens' apotheosis at the Cleveland Union Terminal opening, their juggernaut began to lurch and shudder. As guests at the June 1930 dedication ceremony were admiring the lush commemorative book containing artists' renderings of the new buildings, their sumptuous facilities, and the elaborate decorative touches, the brothers and their bankers and brokers were watching some unsettling behavior in the securities that underlay everything.

The stock market did remarkably well through March, but then paused, lost its momentum, and dropped badly again in June. It was not the violent convulsion of the last October, but it was bad enough, and it got no better afterward. It just kept sliding downward. Nor did the national economy look like it was going to turn and lead the market back up. Heedless of the steady stream of incantation from Washington, New York, and Cambridge, it also continued ceaselessly downward. By the year's end, the national unemployment rate had climbed to almost 9 percent and was heading upward steeply.

Everyone was beginning to suffer, but the Vans were especially vulnerable in numerous ways. To begin with, their two principal businesses—railroads and real estate—were (and still are) especially sensitive to economic fluctuations. Indeed, that was now showing up dramatically as railroad income began dropping sharply and suburban real estate sales dried up. For the full year 1930, gross revenues for the major Van Sweringen railroads were down 13 percent from 1929, while net income dropped a disturbing 37 percent. And in both areas, the brothers had just finished investing vast amounts of money in large-scale new ventures which had yet to pay off—the Union Terminal complex, Shaker Country Estates, and the Missouri Pacific. In short, they were dangerously overextended. That, combined with their financing methods, could be lethal—and quickly.

There were two different deadly financial perils. First, their structure was built on loans and bond indentures, which in turn were secured by collateral consisting mostly of stocks. As the market value of the stocks declined, the value of the collateral ceased to cover the requirements of the loans or the bond indentures. In the case of some of the loans, that meant that more collateral had to be supplied or the amount of the loan reduced by paying off part of it. For some bond indentures, a drop in collateral value brought other unpleasant events into play, such as the trustees taking control and impounding income. The other big danger was the basic operation of the leveraged holding-company system: It promised great profits when income was rising, but when income dropped, it went abruptly into reverse. Income at the top dropped in a geometric ratio, while the fixed-payment requirements of bond interest and preferred-stock dividends remained resolutely unchanged.

Thus, the Vans' outward expansion abruptly stopped—temporarily, they still assumed—and an inward struggle began, a frantic scramble to keep their diaphanous financial structure from disintegrating. Although they had built their careers as adroit financial manipulators, their hearts—especially O. P.'s heart—were in new ventures and in building things. Now the venturing and building stopped and manipulations for survival became everything. They would take many forms, some of them exotic, but they came down to just a few basic strategies—extend the due dates of obligations, obtain more loans, renegotiate troublesome indentures, and move cash around from those subsidiaries that had it to those that needed it.

There were plenty of specific potential trouble spots, but

the first alarms came in two places—the newborn Van Sweringen Corporation and their old broker, Paine, Webber & Company. The first and loudest was the Van Sweringen Corporation and Cleveland real estate in general. Practically the moment it was born, this newest offspring proved to be a most demanding child. Hoping to make its $30 million issue of notes more secure and saleable, the brothers had agreed to the treacherous segregated-assets provisions which obligated them to keep about $15 million worth of Alleghany stock in a sequestered account as a form of collateral. Should the price of that stock drop, something had to be done to restore the total value to $15 million. There were several methods of restoring it, none of which was very appealing: The brothers could pump in more Alleghany shares, or some other securities of equal value or cash, for that matter. Still another way was to try to prop up Alleghany's stock price by buying it in the market—or to simply pray that the price would rise on its own. The last course looked more and more hopeless.

When the Van Sweringen Corporation was launched in May, the brothers duly deposited 500,000 Alleghany shares, which they somewhat artificially valued at $30 a share—thus providing the required $15 million. (Actually it was selling in the market for about $26 at the time.) Afterward, the price of the Alleghany stock in the segregated-assets account promptly started plunging and hit $19\tfrac{3}{4}$ in mid-June. There followed some gyrations up and down, but by October 1st, it was at 18. As a result, the brothers now found themselves spending millions in a futile effort to keep up the price of Alleghany stock and to pump more into the account.

And by late 1930, that cash was sorely needed. The second problem appeared simultaneously: During their acquisition and construction projects, the brothers' Vaness and Alleghany Corporations routinely had large running debts to their stockbrokers, Paine, Webber & Company. In April 1930, Vaness's outstanding balance stood at $46.7 million. Up to that point, this had caused no particular alarm; it had been a regular element in Van Sweringen operations for years. Paine, Webber had a firm margin policy, however—the value of the collateral behind these loans must be 25 percent higher than the amount of the loans. By the end of May, the loan balance Vaness owed had been slimmed down to about $35 million, but with the stock market misbehaving again, the collateral value was slipping. Self-protection strategy called for a further partial liquidation of the debt to avoid a forced liquidation in the market. Self-protection was not all that was at stake either; the size of the Van Sweringen debts also jeopardized the broker and, by extension, whatever was left of confidence in the financial markets.

So large amounts of cash were now needed on two fronts—the Van Sweringen Corporation's segregated-assets account and the Paine, Webber loan account. Where to find the money? There was only one practical source: The brothers had raised $30 million from the Van Sweringen Corporation note issue and another $10 million from a mortgage on the three-building group next to the Terminal Tower—$40 million in total—which was intended to give the Union Terminal complex a stable financial foundation. Instead, it now had to be used to prop up the teetering structure.

As might be expected, the mechanics of doing so were complicated, but in effect the $40 million in cash was channeled into the Terminal Building Company, the Van Sweringen Corporation's chief operating subsidiary, and then disbursed in various ways to resolve the problems. To settle the problem with the Paine, Webber account, the Building Company bought some securities from Vaness; the Paine, Webber loan account was then reshuffled and partly liquidated, at first by reducing the total debt to about $17 million by the end of September. But at that point, the value of their collateral had sunk to only $19.9 million—about $2.3 million short of the broker's requirement. This required still another purchase and stock shuffle.[1]

In the meantime the Van Sweringen Corporation's now-voracious segregated-assets account was also eating up cash as the Building Company fruitlessly bought Alleghany stock in the open market to shore up its price and to plug the account. In this case, the Van Sweringen Corporation was in the particularly paradoxical position of spending much of its patrimony solely to protect itself from itself.[2]

That strategy only held back the water temporarily and drained virtually the entire $40 million in the process—all the cash the brothers had available. Still the market was sliding down, and in late October, as if to celebrate a one-year anniversary, it plunged again. This time the Van Sweringen stocks suffered even more than most; on October 22nd, the bellwether Alleghany hit an all-time low of $10\frac{1}{4}$, putting the segregated assets account $5.8 million under water with no resources to pull it out.

At the time, the brothers were scrambling from meeting to meeting. On Tuesday the 21st, O. P., M. J., Barrett, and Wenneman were in New York huddling with bankers. That evening, O. P. embarked alone for what Wenneman called "a very hush-hush" trip to Washington—presumably for a

Wednesday morning meeting with President Hoover. From there he was scheduled to go directly to Boston to join John Bernet and lawyer W. H. Boyd; incredibly, they were to meet with the New England governors to discuss an extension of the Van Sweringen system into the region via the Boston & Maine. In the meantime, M. J. and the two assistants remained in New York to meet with the Morgan people.

(Considering his circumstances over the past several months, O. P.'s New England quest seems quixotic indeed, but it had its own perverse logic. Oblivious to the rapidly crumbling economy, the railroad-consolidation fracas was still going on, with several large pieces of the ICC's 1929 plan hotly disputed. One was New England, which the Commission had left with its own independent rail system. But through its Pennroad Corporation, the Pennsylvania Railroad was acquiring a heavy stake in both the Boston & Maine and the New Haven, southern New England's only two railroad systems aside from the New York Central's Boston & Albany link. The Van Sweringen system was thus potentially without any friendly entry to the territory, which still was a reasonably healthy manufacturing center and coal consumer.)

But Alleghany's nosedive on the 22nd jolted the bankers, who concluded that the situation of the Van Sweringen Corporation was now hopeless and that by all rights the brothers were finished. They needed an urgent meeting quickly to decide what to do next. M. J., who was still in New York with Barrett and Wenneman, would say and do nothing without his absent brother, who had then left Washington on his train to Boston. Wenneman and a badly shaken Barrett went to Pennsylvania Station to pull O. P. off the train when it came though in the late afternoon; O. P. and M. J. then went by themselves to an impromptu private gathering late that night at the home of Morgan partner Thomas Lamont. Attending along with the brothers were Arthur Anderson, another Morgan partner, and Guaranty Trust's two top officers, W. C. Potter and Joseph Swan.[3]

Three large problems had to be solved immediately: the Vans' large debts to Paine, Webber (Alleghany stock was selling below the margin again), the ever-deepening pit of the Van Sweringen Corporation's segregated-assets account, and the Van Sweringen Corporation's need for cash, in which the most immediate concern was money to make interest payments on its notes. In all, the group estimated that $40 million would be required.

By this time, Morgan and its New York allies were having many meetings of this sort, but this was one of the most serious crises for everyone in the room and many outside it. For their part, the Morgan and Guaranty banks found themselves in a disagreeable quandary. Not only had they been the Vans' financial backbone for many years, but just a few months earlier they had underwritten large securities issues for Alleghany and the Van Sweringen Corporation. In short, their reputations were at stake. Then there was Paine, Webber's financial stability to worry about. As of late October, the brothers owed the broker about $19.5 million—and Paine, Webber in turn owed the banks substantial amounts on its own debts. It was not in any immediate danger itself, but with the markets plummeting, no chances were to be taken.

Beyond all that were wider and deeper issues. Whatever the shortcomings of their financial methods, the brothers were now national economic powers, controlling the largest single segment of the country's transportation system. (And President Hoover was hoping that a successful resolution of the railroad-consolidation program—of which the Vans were a key part—would help restore confidence and begin a recovery.) Further, the Van Sweringen name had become a synonym for solidity and integrity. News of their collapse might well send the fragile financial markets into worse convulsions than they had already been through. Liquidating the Vans' assets at distress-sale prices in an already severely depressed market would be counterproductive anyway; nobody would recover anything close to what they were owed.

One Van Sweringen story has it that back in 1916, O. P. had said that he thought owing and owning were both equally effective in ensuring one's position in the world. If one owed enough, his creditors would not dare risk toppling him. If the story is true, he was once again a visionary ahead of his time—a time which had now come.[1]

Somehow the Vans had to get $40 million to tide them over. Yet there was clearly no way now that it could be raised through any type of public-securities offering; it would have to come from the bankers themselves in the form of a loan. But by the standards of the time, the amount was huge and the assets which would be behind it were suddenly dubious. Nevertheless, the Morgan partners decided that it had to be done, both for their own selfish good and for the good of the country. (Perhaps some of them fondly recalled old Pierpont Morgan personally stopping the 1907 panic in the same manner.)

The amount finally settled upon was $39.5 million at 6 percent interest, to be borne primarily by Morgan and Guaranty with the balance spread among four other New York banks. (Interestingly, George Baker, Jr., personally took on the portion assigned to his First National Bank, feeling that it "was not appropriate" for the bank itself. His father, it will be recalled, was an early Van Sweringen supporter, particularly on the Erie venture.) Given the size of the loan and the dubious quality of the Vans' securities, virtually every Van Sweringen corporate holding would be required as collateral—including most securities which were already pledged to several Cleveland banks.

That decided, O. P. went on to his Boston meeting the next day, Thursday the 23rd, and returned to New York Friday to work out more details. In the process, his blend of bullishness, bull-headedness, and outright defiance emerged again; he dumbfounded the bankers by asking for an additional $5 million unsecured loan to use as working capital to save his empire. As M. J. told it to Wenneman afterward, the bankers balked, at which point O. P. "pulled his chair over to a window in [Thomas] Lamont's office, propped his feet on the sill, and with his back turned to Lamont, George Whitney, Harold Stanley, Arthur Anderson, and several Morgan lawyers, ignored all their arguments. After a while they capitulated and told my brother they would agree."[5]

That night, he returned to Cleveland and spent Saturday with Union Trust President Wilbur Baldwin to negotiate a way of subordinating his $17 million Cleveland bank debts to the New York loan by making them personal Van Sweringen debts secured by Vaness stock. This cleared the way to allow the New York banks to give Vaness part of their loan.[6]

The $39.5 million loan from New York bankers was completed October 30th and was to run for four and a half years, to May 1, 1935—enough time, it was thought, "to cover the whole depression . . . and let them out of the woods," as Thomas Lamont later testified.[7]

Using part of the loan proceeds, the problem of the segregated-assets account was solved by substituting solid government securities for the disgraced Alleghany stock, which was pulled out and added to the loan collateral. Paine, Webber & Company was paid, and it in turn paid some of its debts to the same banks which had put together the $39.5 million Van Sweringen loan—giving those banks some of their money back instantly. There was also enough left for the Van Sweringen Corporation to pay interest on its notes for a while and for the Vans to pay their interest on the loan.

Predictably, the price was steep. As already noted, the brothers were forced to pledge virtually everything they owned —their entire stake in Alleghany and all its railroads, the Van

Sweringen Corporation with its downtown real estate, the Pittston Company, the Cleveland Railway, and a bundle of miscellaneous industrial stocks. And, having cleaned out all the securities, good and bad, the bankers also asked for the brothers' own personal guaranty—themselves, in other words. The idea apparently was that if the brothers ever accumulated a new fortune in some other business, they would still be responsible for this debt. It was also tactfully suggested that the banks be given representation on the various Van Sweringen boards of directors, but this violated O. P.'s most sacred precepts and was just as politely refused. He did agree, however, to give them veto power over any policy decisions.[8]

However things were worded, the reality was clear: The New York banks now controlled virtually the entire Van Sweringen empire. In the short span of a few months, the brothers had gone from masters of the railroad industry and the heroes of Cleveland to what amounted to indentured servants. Actually the banks were kind, and the illusion of complete Van Sweringen management was maintained. The bankers not only left the brothers in charge but deferred to them in matters of tactics and protocol. With one exception, they stayed away from Cleveland and out of the day-to-day operations. Their reasons probably were less humanitarian than pragmatic. The brothers had created a peculiarly individualistic structure whose size and complexities defied easy understanding, not to mention management. It was in the banks' own best interests to let the Vans run it in their way, while hoping that the stock market and the economy would rise soon and resolve all the problems.

The situation inevitably created tensions in the relationship, however. O. P. was proud and stubborn and still viewed the unfolding debacle as a temporary setback which would soon be righted. He resented any visible indications that he was not still in control and resisted any efforts to tamper with any part of his creations. Over the next several years, numerous financial negotiations were necessary as various parts of the empire ran into trouble; in all of them, he insisted that Van Sweringen control of the companies not be compromised and that the basic structure remain intact. Despite his reduced status, he somehow succeeded, one more testament to that mysterious persuasive power.

Actually, the $39.5 million loan was now merely the Vans' largest personal debt. They also owed four Cleveland banks a total of $17.1 million—including over $7 million to Joseph Nutt's Union Trust—and had pledged their own assets for those, too. (Most of the Cleveland loans covered the suburban real estate and the transit enterprises.) Another $2.1 million was added to the big New York loan in early 1931, the first installment of the extra $5 million that O. P. had insisted upon. (He never drew the balance.) Thus their personal liability totaled $58.7 million in loans or guarantees. In addition, the Alleghany and Chesapeake Corporations had large loans and some other nasty problems of their own.[9]

As this was playing out, the physical works slowly froze. Work on the East Side rapid transit ceased in September 1930, only a few months short of completion, leaving rail, ties, and overhead wire stockpiled at the Shaker line's Kingsbury Run yards. Since the Union Terminal's two traction concourses were built to serve this line and its various planned extensions, they remained largely deserted. The Shaker Heights line used three stairways and two platforms; the entrances to the remaining thirteen stairways and four platforms (including two full high-level platforms) were locked or temporarily sealed. Most of the smaller stores in the Union Terminal concourses were closed or consolidated as it became clear that the buyers would not come soon. The entire West Traction Concourse eventually was largely closed off and its vacant shop space partly taken over for the Cleveland Union Terminals Company's engineering office.[10]

By the end of 1931, national unemployment had reached 16 percent and was still climbing. The economy was in a frightening dive, and fewer people now called the situation merely a "recession." Whatever its label, it hit Shaker Heights early and hard. New land sales suddenly stopped, many homeowners could not meet their mortgage payments and property taxes, and the city itself suffered for funds. At the end of the 1930–1931 school year, one-fourth of the school system's teachers were not rehired, and salaries of the survivors were cut by 25 percent—and paid in scrip. One resident recalled: "We had a program called 'A man a block.' The idea was to give work to those neighbors out of work. The neighbors got together, and one man who was out of work did odd jobs around the neighbors' homes for money." In some cases, the banks holding mortgages on now-vacant Shaker homes leased them to the rapid transit trainmen for the interest costs in order to keep them maintained and occupied. Just being readied for the market, the vast new Shaker Country Estates never had a chance.[11]

The Union Terminal complex had the misfortune of adding an enormous amount of new downtown office space at just the time demand began to die. Fortunately for the Vans, they controlled enough companies and had enough business connections that the various buildings did better than might be expected, but they were far from fully occupied. As Cleveland's new prestige address, the Terminal Tower was relatively well filled, although an extensive space occupied by the local chamber of commerce earned no rent. The three-building Prospect Avenue cluster was less fortunate, particularly the Builders Exchange Building, which was less than half occupied. Equally problematic was the Hotel Cleveland, which had suffered low occupancy through the disruptive years of the Union Terminal construction and now faced the deepening Depression's baneful influence on business travel.

To aid the cause, some other Van Sweringen companies were conscripted to help fill the Prospect Avenue group. In 1931, the Erie Railroad, which until then had stayed aloof in its traditional Hudson Terminal headquarters in lower Manhattan, picked up and relocated to the Midland Bank Building. The Cleveland Railway somewhat reluctantly moved into the Midland from the Hanna Building in the same year.

In what was probably the last grand Van Sweringen gesture, the new Higbee Company store opened on September 8, 1931—the finest department store that Cleveland had ever seen. Despite the economic gloom, everyone in town turned out to see it. Local historian James Toman later wrote that: "By the time the store closed that evening checkers at the doors had tallied a staggering 359,079 patrons." (Unfortunately, most were there to look at the new marvel rather than buy.) Afterward it did as well as any store could under the circumstances, but for the next several years its cost and the times were against it. Beyond the Higbee store, all thoughts of further building on the many open Union Terminal sites vanished. The single exception was a new central post office located over the Terminal tracks on Prospect Avenue, which was finally begun in February 1932. As a federally owned building, however, this was not really a Van Sweringen development and only made use of the Terminal air rights.[12]

With downtown real estate stagnant, the Vans and their banking partners were forced to perform more emergency surgery on the repository of all this property, the Van Sweringen Corporation. The big 1930 New York bank loan had taken care of the segregated-assets account problem, but they now faced the larger question of the company's viability. Its only source of income was the Cleveland Terminals Building Company, which was not enough to pay the interest on its $30 million note issue and its portion of the New York bank loan. In fact, as of July 1931, the Vans were no longer able even to pay the interest on the $39.5 million 1930 loan, which was then only nine months old. Logically enough, the bankers balked at making more loans merely to pay themselves the interest, but, also reluctant to foreclose, they decided simply to let it accrue as part of the loan itself. By the end of September 1931, the Van Sweringen Corporation reported a $1.6 million deficit and an almost bare treasury. Its share of the loan proceeds was now used up. It was increasingly clear to the embarrassed Guaranty Trust bankers that the holding company had been a mistake from the beginning.[13]

On the other hand, it was now part of the collateral held by the New York banks, and the bankers, if not the brothers themselves, worried intensely about how to reduce its obligations short of bankruptcy—which also was not ruled out. The worrying actually started in the spring of 1931, and during the summer various plans and counterplans were argued over. At one low point in June, it looked like the Morgan and Guaranty banks would help no more, and O. P. seriously considered abandoning his old backers to try Kuhn, Loeb & Company. In the end, though, Morgan reluctantly stuck to them and continued to try to work out a new plan. In September, much to O. P.'s dismay, the bankers paid a rare visit to Cleveland to look over the situation personally. At almost the same time, there was yet another bad break in the securities markets, pushing the price of the Van Sweringen Corporation notes from the original price of $1,000 to a new low of $400. (They had been recently trading at about $500.) By October, the price was down to about $350.[14]

The staggering price depreciation provided the opportunity to resolve the problem by buying up the notes and eliminating the obligation to pay interest on them. In late October, the Vans and their bankers worked out an offer which the distressed noteholders could hardly refuse: All notes could be redeemed for $500 cash plus twenty shares of Van Sweringen Corporation stock. (The stock sweetener was meant to appeal to any noteholders who might still have faith that the Van Sweringen Corporation would eventually recover and prosper.) The offer was immensely successful. Using the proceeds and interest from the government securities in the segregated-assets account and a Union Trust loan, the Vans were able to buy all but $1.2 million of the original $30 million issue. This took the pressure off the Van Sweringen Corporation—for the time being, at least—and, of course, also wiped out the noxious segregated-assets account.[15]

Two years later, *Fortune* magazine praised the maneuver as the "Smartest Deal in Depression History." It may well have been, but it was possible only because of the precipitous drop in value of notes which were practically brand new. Thus, the noteholders understandably were less admiring than *Fortune*; they reluctantly accepted the offer because it was the best they could hope for under the circumstances. Nevertheless, some securities dealers came back with comments like "the general reaction of customers is that they have been gypped"; "rotten deal, but the best you can get"; "[the] keynote is disgust." Nonetheless, it was the fairest and most equitable solution to what was a technically tangled quandary. The brothers proved to be just as creative and canny going downhill as up, although their halos had vaporized.[16]

By this time, however, the Van Sweringen Corporation was the lesser of the brothers' nightmares. At the same time that their misbegotten real estate holding company was being rescued, the heart of their empire—Alleghany Corporation, with all the railroads—was moving headlong into disaster.

Twenty
The Rails Roll Downgrade

Critical as the Van Sweringen Corporation's woes were, they were really just an unpleasant and expensive sideshow in the view of the New York bankers, who now had a lien on the brothers and their empires. The heart of the Van Sweringens' world was their railroads, and in one form or another all the railroads were controlled through the Alleghany Corporation. Alleghany's health was their major concern, and by 1931 that looked none too good either.

If real estate is especially sensitive to business conditions, railroading is equally so. Thanks to the capital which the brothers provided for rebuilding and upgrading, and to Bernet's management, the Van Sweringen railroads were still surviving reasonably well. In fact, several of them were outperforming their larger peers in the business. At the end of 1930, all but one were still in the black. (The exception was the Chicago & Eastern Illinois, which celebrated its first year under Van Sweringen control with a record $7.5 million deficit.) Now indisputably the Van Sweringen strongman, the Chesapeake

& Ohio suffered only a modest traffic decline and earned a respectable $34 million. But the overall picture was unsettling. The newly and dearly acquired Missouri Pacific did worse than the average, helped along by a severe summer drought in its agricultural territory. The MoPac's revenues dropped 16 percent, but its net income was down almost by half. The Erie's gross income slid the same 16 percent, and its net income was off an even more alarming 59 percent. Reflecting the auto industry's sudden doldrums, the Pere Marquette saw its net income plummet by 73 percent.[1]

While discouraging, such performances did not necessarily imply disaster, at least not yet. But like most railroads, the Vans' companies carried heavy debt loads and were leveraged on their own. Still, thus far all but the wayward Chicago & Eastern Illinois were still covering interest payments on their debt and had a reasonable amount of cash. But for the Van Sweringen structure, this was not enough; the critical criterion was their ability to keep paying dividends at the same level as before. Alleghany depended entirely on those dividends to pay its regular bond interest; without them, it would be forced into default and probable bankruptcy. The Vans made certain that their railroads kept up their regular dividends through 1930 and into the following year—but with earnings still heading down toward the red line, that could not continue long. If it did, the railroads would quickly drain their cash and risk their own bankruptcies. The Nickel Plate, for example, was forced to pay out over $2 million in dividends during 1931 but ended the year with a $210,000 deficit; the Missouri Pacific and its subsidiaries paid almost $10 million. Soon enough the brothers had to bow to reality. One by one during 1931, their various railroads ceased their dividends until only the Chesapeake & Ohio was left. Fortunately, the coal-hauler could keep paying, and it became the brothers' rather grubby angel.[2]

As the dividends dried up, the leverage principle went into reverse with a vengeance. The C&O gave some solace, but thanks to the Vans' multilayered holding company structure, it was not enough to sustain Alleghany. The C&O's stock was held by an Alleghany subsidiary, the Chesapeake Corporation, which was another public holding company with its own fixed financial obligations. The C&O's payout went there first, and what was left filtered up to Alleghany. That was ominous enough, but Alleghany had another problem peculiar to itself. In financing its 1929–1930 acquisition binge, it had sold three separate bond issues which together originally totaled $85 million. In designing the indentures of these three bond issues, the New York bankers protected themselves and their bond-buying clients by inserting clauses similar in effect to the Van Sweringen Corporation's now-infamous segregated-assets account. Their basic aim was to maintain a prescribed value behind the bonds. In this case, it took the form of an indenture requirement that the combined value of cash and the various securities pledged as collateral for the bonds must amount to at least 150 percent of the face value of the outstanding bonds. The securities underlying the bonds were those of railroads (particularly the Missouri Pacific) or holding companies—specifically, the fairly solid Chesapeake Corporation, the inglorious Pittston Company, and the more dubious Terminal Shares, Inc.[3]

This meant that if the Alleghany Corporation had $85 million in bonds outstanding, its cash and those pledged securities had to be worth at least $127.5 million on the market. If they were not, the bond trustee—Guaranty Trust—could impound the company's income and assume voting control. The bank was not necessarily required to exercise this control; if it chose, it could leave the Van Sweringens in charge—but under its sufferance and supervision. (Such a situation was not considered a default in the usual sense, and the bank could exercise these powers only as long as the ratio was below 150 percent.) As of early 1931, this was not yet a problem, but the signs were grim.

With Alleghany threatened, it quickly became necessary to lighten its capital load and bolster its cash. To do so, the brothers slipped back over to the dark side. Their first maneuver made what was originally an unsavory action even more so. It will be remembered that in 1929 Alleghany had paid a princely $20 million to the meatpackers Armour and Swift & Company for their various switching railroads in Missouri and real estate companies—what amounted to corporate bribery for Nickel Plate meat traffic. The properties had been put into a holding company called Terminal Shares, Inc., and the original purchase was largely financed by an issue of notes. In late December 1930, Alleghany unloaded its Terminal Shares investment onto the Missouri Pacific, obligating the railroad to pay installments of $1.6 million a year to amortize the notes. The unhappy railroad followed orders, and by early 1933 it had paid out $3.2 million, at which point it was forced to stop.[4]

By August 1931, Alleghany had worked its bonded debt down to $77.9 million from the original $85 million, but the value of the underlying securities had sunk to $99.6 million—$17.2 million below the 150 percent minimum. In September,

Guaranty impounded the income of all three bond issues and nominally took control—although it elected to keep its hands off and let the brothers continue to manage the company. Since Alleghany was still solvent otherwise and the bank was anxious to keep the Vans as viable as possible, little really changed. But in addition to a lien on almost everything the brothers owned, the New York bankers now also could directly manage Alleghany any time they chose.[5]

As this was happening, the Vans continued their struggle to lighten Alleghany's obligations, and their next stratagem matched the Missouri Pacific–Terminal Shares deal in marginal morality. Back in 1930, at the same time they were desperately trying to shore up Vaness and their Van Sweringen Corporation, they were helping to bail out their Chicago traffic-manager friends in the Bremo Corporation. The Bremo group had bought control of the Chicago Great Western Railroad in October 1929, just in time to get caught by the crash with large brokerage loans outstanding and collapsing collateral. The Vans obligingly came to the rescue, loaning the failing holding company nearly $4 million, which was channeled through the C&O's Virginia Transportation Corporation subsidiary. In exchange, Bremo gave a promissory note which effectively represented a lien on its control of the Great Western.

Things got no better, of course. The Bremo group did its best to milk cash out of its victim by declaring unearned dividends, but by 1931, it was having problems merely paying the interest on the Van Sweringen loans. At this point, the brothers hardly wanted to foreclose and inherit another ailing railroad, but they did need a favor. With Alleghany's own cash bind now worsening, they decided to ask their friends at Bremo to take the Kansas City Southern off their hands.

By then, the Vans had second thoughts about their one-fifth interest in the KCS, which they had bought in mid-1929 for $10.1 million. It had been rather casually acquired in the first place, and the brothers' hope of folding the railroad into the Missouri Pacific system had dimmed when the ICC grouped the KCS with the Union Pacific in its final system plan. Lacking full control, they had little leverage to convince the Commission otherwise, and there were some antitrust and other legal difficulties anyway. Considering their cash needs, they could afford to sacrifice it—provided they could find a willing buyer with the kind of cash needed. Alleghany had bought its Kansas City Southern stock at the peak of the market, paying an average of $96 a share; in 1930, KCS stock sank to a low of $34, and by the fall of 1931 it was averaging about $15 with a low of $7. Obviously the Vans stood to take a severe loss, but their Bremo friends could soften it.

And soften it they did, by agreeing that the Chicago Great Western would take on Alleghany's KCS stock for $3.1 million, or $30 a share. Already drained of most of its cash, the anemic Great Western could scarcely afford this kind of burden. There were also multiple legal uncertainties, not the least of which was that same pesky Missouri law prohibiting railroad acquisitions without permission from the state's Public Service Commission. The Vans had resolved the problem swiftly in the Missouri Pacific's case but ignored it when they bought the Kansas City Southern stock—thus their ownership technically was not even legal. Furthermore, the Vans protected themselves with an option clause which assured them, in the words of the Great Western's historian, "that in case the purchase should turn sour, the entire loss would fall on the hapless Great Western. But if a profit should occur within two years Alleghany could claim half of it." In the meantime, the KCS stock would be out of hostile hands and, if the circumstances happened to work out, the Vans probably could repurchase it without Bremo's objection. Helpless, the Great Western signed the agreement on October 5, 1931.[6]

By the end of 1931, Alleghany's outlook was even darker. Gross revenues of all Van Sweringen railroads together were down 30 percent from their 1929 levels and were 17 percent less than the past year; net income was only one-quarter of the 1929 figure and had dropped 56 percent in one year. The Missouri Pacific was still in the black, but barely so; it eked out only a $1.4 million profit on $95.3 million revenues, while two of its major subsidiaries—the International–Great Northern and the Gulf Coast Lines—posted deficits. The Nickel Plate, the Pere Marquette, the Erie, and, of course, the Chicago & Eastern Illinois were also now in the red by varying amounts. Only the C&O was producing anything resembling a substantial net income, thanks partly to its inherent efficiency but mostly to the happy coincidence that its nonunion Pocahontas region coalfields were rapidly displacing the more costly and depleted traditional Western Pennsylvania mines. (And, indeed, it could even afford to introduce a fine new passenger train. In April 1932, Bernet and L. C. Probert inaugurated the *George Washington,* which was advertised as the country's "first long-distance air-conditioned sleeping-car train.")[7]

By then few people were riding in new air-conditioned sleeping cars. But there was one type of railroad cargo which was growing spectacularly—unemployed transients were hopping freight trains to anywhere, usually anywhere west. The Missouri Pacific was a particular beneficiary of this traffic; the railroad counted some 13,745 migrants in 1929 and 186,028 in 1931. And those were just the ones who got counted and presumably caught.[8]

Heedless of the railroads' rapidly disintegrating financial position, the Interstate Commerce Commission's consolidation program limped onward, having taken on a life of its own which seemed to defy happenings in the outside world. The "final" 1929 ICC plan still had not resolved disagreements, particularly among the eastern railroads—and most particularly over the Commission's proposed fifth eastern system. The Van Sweringens, the Pennsylvania, and the Baltimore & Ohio all now controlled pieces of the fifth system, while Frank Taplin and the Wabash's William H. Williams continued to agitate for it—undoubtedly with license from the Pennsylvania's General Atterbury. Already, however, cooler financial heads—not the least of which was the Wabash's banker, Kuhn, Loeb & Company—were questioning the economic viability of the fifth system. For the Vans, the Wheeling & Lake Erie remained the perennial bone of contention and Frank Taplin remained a relentless harasser. The brothers also had what were clearly becoming quixotic hopes to enter New England by controlling the Boston & Maine, the Maine Central, and the Bangor & Aroostook.

In the meantime, the hapless Herbert Hoover was becoming desperate for some dramatic development that would raise business optimism. Encouraged by Professor Ripley, the architect of the ICC's consolidation plan, the president pressured the railroads to settle their differences and present a unified proposal which could lead to some concrete action. After some complex negotiations and arm-twisting (particularly the arm of General Atterbury), the Pennsylvania, the New York Central, the B&O, and the Van Sweringens made peace with one another, and on October 1, 1931, they jointly applied to the ICC asking it to modify its 1929 final plan. In essence, the four railroads simply agreed that the fifth system idea should be scrapped and—with a few exceptions—each of them could keep the railroads they had already acquired.

Happy that the four major eastern systems finally seemed to be together on something, the ICC acquiesced to their petition and in July 1932 redrew its consolidation map for the territory. It eliminated the fifth system irritant entirely and divided up its components largely as the four railroads had asked. The Vans got most of what they wanted: the Wheeling

& Lake Erie, the western part of the Pittsburgh & West Virginia, and the Chicago & Eastern Illinois—plus the Lehigh Valley. The Pennsylvania took the Wabash and Norfolk & Western, and the B&O took the Western Maryland. The eastern section of the Pittsburgh & West Virginia was to be jointly owned by all four lines. New England, though, was still left to itself. Joseph Eastman threw up his hands and complained that the 1929 ICC plan had been "slaughtered" and that everyone should start all over again. But he was also a realist and stated what was becoming obvious: Whatever the plan, nobody (except perhaps the government) now had the money to effectuate it.[9]

Certainly the Van Sweringens did not. As of late 1931, they were facing two kinds of corporate death threats. First, all of their railroads but the C&O and the Wheeling & Lake Erie were reaching a point where they would not be able to meet debt maturities or bond interest obligations, meaning bankruptcy and probable loss of control. And even if they were not reaching that point, the brothers' instrument of control—the Alleghany Corporation—was itself in serious jeopardy.

To take Alleghany first: It was now effectively a protectorate of Guaranty Trust, its income was impounded, and its financial hands were tied. As of the fall of 1931, its income was shrinking anyway as the various railroads ceased paying dividends. The most recent of its three bond issues—the so-called "Alleghany 5s of 1950"—were not even earning their interest-payment requirements.[10] Yet at the time, Alleghany also owed Paine, Webber & Company $11.7 million. Dumping its Kansas City Southern stock onto the Chicago Great Western helped lighten the debt, but by the end of the year the loan's collateral—consisting mostly of Missouri Pacific securities—was worth less than the amount owed. By January 1932, the nervous broker had had enough and was finally forced to demand payment.[11]

Some collateral could be liquidated without compromising Alleghany's control of the railroads, and by doing so, the Paine, Webber debt was further whittled down to $5.7 million by late January—but that was the irreducible minimum. To avoid its own bankruptcy, Alleghany had to raise additional cash by selling more of the Paine, Webber collateral. That, though, put its control in danger—the gravest of Van Sweringen sins. Thus the only reasonable solution was to sell some of Alleghany's railroad securities to another Van Sweringen company, and the only clear candidate was the Chesapeake & Ohio.

So in February, the C&O bought Erie, Nickel Plate, and Pere Marquette stock from Alleghany for a total of $5.6 million—$1.9 million above their market value at the time, but by a peculiar coincidence almost the same amount as Alleghany owed to Paine, Webber. This in turn created more complications. The C&O's treasury lacked the full purchase amount, but its credit was sound, so it issued two-year notes to Paine, Webber totaling $3.9 million. (The two-year limit was specifically designed to bypass the ICC, which had jurisdiction over longer-term financing.) Then there was the inevitable problem of the C&O directly acquiring railroad stocks without the ICC's permission and possibly in violation of the Clayton Act. That was solved by the old smokescreen the Vans had used for the Chicago & Eastern Illinois purchase: Rather than buying the stock outright, the C&O actually bought an option on it. Alleghany continued to hold it and vote it. And the C&O did not disclose the exact nature of its payment in its accounting, identifying it merely as a "special deposit."[12]

The Van Sweringens' dark arts had temporarily waved disaster away from Alleghany; at the same time, Herbert Hoover belatedly rushed in to help keep the railroads themselves afloat. Caught in his conservative ideology of self-reliance, the president thus far had been loath to involve the federal government in relief programs, but by the fall of 1931, he was facing what was now a full-blown international economic crisis. In the United States, banks were closing, basic industries were withering and cutting wages, and the entire railroad industry was heading toward collapse. Late in the year, the administration finally pushed through the act creating the Reconstruction Finance Corporation (RFC) to provide large-scale loans to financial institutions, railroads, and industry. Hoover signed it in January 1932 and picked the millionaire financier Eugene Meyer to organize and head the agency.

As O. P. Van Sweringen later testified, "We were on the doorstep waiting for them to open." Joseph Nutt, their close associate and a power in the Republican Party, helped assure a welcome when the door did open. O. P. brought along Colonel Ayres, who made the presentation while the restless and forceful Meyer strode around, periodically hitting the conference table for emphasis. At one point Meyer interrupted Ayres to inject a bit of black comedy: "My associates and I started to buy control of the Missouri Pacific in 1929. But you had started first and had too big a lead, so we dropped out. Jesus!" he shouted, giving the table an extra hard thump. "Suppose we had been successful!"[13]

By the end of February, the Missouri Pacific, Erie, Nickel Plate, and Chicago & Eastern Illinois were all receiving RFC loans. The Pere Marquette joined the line of supplicants in July, and by the year's end the Van Sweringen railroads as a group had drawn out $57.7 million. Adding in the affiliated Denver & Rio Grande Western, the total came to $64.1 million. The Nickel Plate was the most immediately needy, taking $18.2 million during the year to avoid imminent bankruptcy. Among other things, it faced an October maturity date for $20 million in unsecured notes that had been used to acquire Alleghany's Wheeling & Lake Erie stock in 1929. The Missouri Pacific was close behind with $17.1 million. In the process of applying for the various loans, there were some selective lapses in corporate memory to help assure the RFC that these were deserving cases. The Missouri Pacific neglected to mention that it had committed itself to the malodorous $19 million Terminal Shares purchase and had already paid out $3.2 million. And lest anyone doubt that it was bereft of financial support, the C&EI overlooked the fact that it was really owned by the wealthy C&O—but since the ICC supposedly was unaware of that too, it was best left unsaid anyway.[14]

It was another hairbreadth rescue, but even as the RFC's doors opened in early 1932, things were spiraling downward so furiously that the agency could do only so much, which was not enough.

Twenty-one
A New World

The only joy that 1932 offered the brothers was that there were no new life-or-death crises. It was not much solace. Resourceful as they were—and they were amazingly so—all they could do was buy time with the hope that business would pick up before the time ran out. Unpaid interest was now being added to the large New York bank loan of late 1930 as well as a $32.5 million loan also made in 1930 to the Chesapeake Corporation. (The latter was necessary to retain the holding company's control of the C&O when the railroad issued new stock to finance its improvement program and the absorption of its Hocking Valley subsidiary.) Everything was pledged in one form or another, and anxious bankers watched and regulated every financial move. Unpaid property taxes and assessments for new roads and utilities were beginning to accumulate on the Cleveland real estate, particularly the huge, largely undeveloped Shaker Country Estates tract. (And every day the Vans were reminded of that as they drove through the vacant miles on their way to and from Daisy Hill. It was a constantly humbling sight.)[1]

There were now even problems meeting expenses for the Van Sweringens' personal staff. The brothers' own income still came primarily from whatever stock dividends they could still get; while they had also drawn some salaries from their various railroad chairmanships, they had given them up by the end of 1929 to head off criticisms from minority stockholders. Vaness had traditionally paid their own office force, drawing from the dividend income from the companies below it. But with those dividends now drying up, the Vans were forced to go directly to their railroads, real estate companies, and lower-level holding companies, most of which were still generating cash, if not profits. Beginning in 1930, all the Van Sweringen companies were assessed proportionate shares to cover Vaness's office expenses under the theory that they were receiving management services. These companies were still generating cash, if not profits.[2]

And under pressure from the New York bankers, the Vans also had reluctantly cut staff wages twice since 1930—another personal humiliation, since they had always prided themselves on their generosity to employees. As the office head, Darwin Barrett cut his own $75,000 salary by one-third and most of the others by 20 percent, sparing only Wenneman, who had been due for an increase. In the past, M. J. had helped pay the expenses of friends and employees who had fallen on hard times, keeping their names in a "little black book" he carried with him; he still tried to do so, but at reduced rates.[3]

Yet there was no pickup in sight. Quite the opposite. The depression—almost everyone now called it by its proper name—was deepening rapidly. And what seemed all the more terrifying was that nobody knew why. In hindsight at least, the stock-market crash was readily explainable; values were well overinflated and due for some grounding. But at the time of the crash, the economy itself looked strong and should not have been greatly affected. There just seemed to be no reason for this relentless slide. Nonetheless, it was happening. By the end of 1932, unemployment had reached an unprecedented 23.6 percent; iron and steel production plummeted to less than one-quarter of the 1929 level, and automobile production was slightly worse than that. On February 1, 1932, the railroad industry followed what most other businesses already had done and cut wages by 10 percent across the board. Out on the Van Sweringen system, rows of cold steam locomotives and surplus freight cars filled the yard tracks at places such as Hornell, New York; Conneaut, Ohio; Grand Rapids, Michigan; Huntington, West Virginia; North Little Rock, Arkansas; and Kansas City, Missouri, as they waited out the dark years. Many would never roll again.

It was, in fact, the most catastrophic year in American railroading, and the Van Sweringen system suffered as grievously as the rest. When 1932 ended, their railroads reported a total revenue drop of 22 percent below the miserable previous year and 45 percent less than 1929. And where their system (excluding the Denver & Rio Grande Western and the Kansas City Southern) had netted $86 million in 1929, it was $4.4 million in the red in 1932. Were it not for the C&O's saving graces, the total deficit would have been $28 million.

Some individual performances were far worse. As before, the Missouri Pacific was turning into the champion loser. Its stock, which the Vans had bought at prices of up to $101 a share, had skittered to a low of $1.50 per share. Total revenues for the MoPac and its subsidiaries were half those of 1929, and its system deficit was a frightening $14 million. Even the always-worrisome Erie performed better, showing only a $3.1 million deficit—better even than the far smaller Chicago & Eastern Illinois. With its heavy debt handed down from pre–Van Sweringen days, the Missouri Pacific was in extremely perilous shape, and the Chicago & Eastern Illinois was virtually a lost cause. As always, the C&O was the only bright spot, and it remained quite bright. Despite the prostrate economy, the railroad churned out a respectable $26.7 million net income in 1931 and $23.5 million in the nadir year of 1932. Its traditional regular dividend could be maintained and its credit was comparatively sound.

For whatever comfort it was, the Vans were far from alone in their misery; indeed, they were in the best of company. The price of New York Central common stock plunged from a peak of $256\frac{1}{2}$ in 1929 to $8\frac{3}{4}$ during 1932, and the company finished the year with an $18.3 million deficit. The fall of the almighty Pennsylvania Railroad was only slightly less dizzying. It kept in the black, but General Atterbury watched in dismay as its stock went from 110 to $6\frac{1}{2}$ in those three years. To maintain its unbroken record, the Pennsylvania kept up its dividend payments but cut them from 8 percent in 1930 to 1 percent in 1932. The Baltimore & Ohio also ran a deficit in 1932 and wavered on the brink of bankruptcy; it was kept solvent mostly through Reconstruction Finance Corporation loans.

Nor were the Vans the only victims of their own misjudgments. Egg fairly dripped from General Atterbury's face. His shrewd strategic acquisitions in the last great years of the consolidation wars suddenly became flapping albatrosses. The Wabash went bankrupt in 1931, and the Lehigh Valley came perilously close to doing so after running deficits beginning that year. It survived only through two hasty RFC loans but remained a financial weakling as its anthracite markets gradually dried up. Pennroad's Pittsburgh & West Virginia stock, bought at 170, sold for as low as 6 in 1932. (Fortunately Pennroad had no bonded indebtedness to worry about, only unhappy stockholders.) At the B&O, Dan Willard's dream of a low-grade freight shortcut across northern Pennsylvania died, leaving him with the Buffalo, Rochester & Pittsburgh and the Buffalo & Susquehanna as mere feeder lines, but costly ones. Worse was Willard's ill-advised $25 million purchase of the Chicago & Alton in late 1930. But nothing quite matched the Van Sweringens' rapidly developing disaster with the Missouri Pacific.

And to rub in the salt, the "losers" in the 1920s consolidation scramble—particularly Leonor Loree and Frank Taplin—turned out to be the winners, having sold out at the top of the market. (Taplin later boasted that he had seen the trouble coming.) So had the always-shrewd Rockefellers in unloading the Wheeling & Lake Erie and the Western Maryland, as well as the fortunate owners of the Buffalo, Rochester & Pittsburgh and the Buffalo & Susquehanna. Pat Crowley's comparative passivity was also at least partly vindicated by sparing the New York Central even worse ignominy. (The 67-year-old Crowley had bowed out a year earlier, replaced by new blood in the form of Frederick E. Williamson from the Burlington.)[4]

While the railroad industry was falling apart, Cleveland's banking system began developing cracks. O. P. might have recognized an ominous symptom when Joseph Nutt approached him in the fall of 1931 to ask a favor: Union Trust had been suffering heavy withdrawals during that summer and was facing a September 30th statement of financial condition required by Ohio's superintendent of banks. To help brighten the bank's decidedly dim picture, Nutt asked O. P. to have the Van Sweringen Corporation make a bookkeeping entry transferring to Union Trust the $10 million in solid government securities which the Van Sweringen Corporation was holding to stabilize its baneful segregated-assets account. Nutt's plan was simply to move the $10 million to a Union Trust account just long enough qualify for the financial statement; nine days later, it was to be transferred back to the Van Sweringen Corporation. Innocently or not—it was never certain how much he knew—O. P. agreed, and the deed was done.[5]

By 1932, the new Midland Bank was in serious trouble, having barely moved into its palatial quarters in the Vans' Midland Building. To save it from state liquidation, the city's strongest bank, Cleveland Trust, agreed to take it over, giving it a secure haven, but at the price of vacating its Midland Building offices and banking rooms. Seventeen years would pass before the grand lobby was again occupied.[6]

Union Trust's growing problems soon claimed Joseph Nutt himself, who resigned his chairmanship in 1932, forced out by uneasy directors. (Publicly, though, he claimed that he left primarily to spare the bank any possible political repercussions from his role as treasurer of Herbert Hoover's reelection campaign.) Nutt had long been one of the closest in the Van Sweringens' inner circle and a Vaness stockholder and director; under him, Union Trust had been the brothers' principal local financial backer. Now, thanks in part to its large and shakily secured Van Sweringen loans, the powerful Union Trust was heading the way of the Midland Bank, but with no rescuer.[7]

Nutt's political judgment was no better than his lending sagacity. The rest of the country knew something had to change, and even if nobody was really sure what Franklin D. Roosevelt would do (nor was he entirely sure himself), the voters emphatically repudiated the doomed Hoover in November. The new president proceeded to change many things, but already the environment was irrevocably changing by itself—and moving swiftly away from the world of the Van Sweringens and their friends.

But the Van Sweringens had much more immediately pressing problems by early 1933, particularly the dismal railroad situation. In early February, on the eve of his 65th birthday, John Bernet returned to the roots of the Vans' railroad empire, taking over the Nickel Plate presidency from the retiring Walter Ross. This time though, he also remained in charge of the C&O and the Pere Marquette, so that the heaviest responsibility for reviving the Vans' eastern system now fell on his aging shoulders. The Nickel Plate was now facing bankruptcy, thanks in large part to the $20 million note issue which had fallen due in October 1932 and which was now technically in default—although negotiations were under way for an extension.

Characteristically, Bernet charged in vigorously, spending as much money as he could scratch up to modernize the railroad. (Despite the wreckage around him, O. P. remained resolutely bullish and willing to support whatever could be practically done.) Following his successes in applying efficient, high-horsepower steam locomotive designs to the Erie and the C&O, Bernet charged his Advisory Mechanical Committee to come up with something similar for the Nickel Plate. The result was a fast-freight adaptation of the C&O T-1 2-10-4

John Bernet's magnificent Berkshires remained the backbone of the Nickel Plate's fast freight service until 1958, well into the diesel era. Nearing the end of its long and highly productive life, No. 735 shows off its muscle west of Bellevue, Ohio.
John A. Rehor photo, H. H. Harwood, Jr., collection

built three years before—a classic 2-8-4 Berkshire design so successful that it was holding its own against diesels twenty-five years later. At the same time, he ordered new switch engines, high-capacity locomotive tenders (to boost train speed by eliminating fuel and water stops), and 1,200 new higher-capacity steel freight cars. To help pay for it all, he repeated his Erie technique and purged the Nickel Plate roster of 119 obsolescent locomotives (one-third of the Nickel Plate's roster) and 7,154 freight cars. Bridges were also strengthened for the larger locomotives, which began arriving in the fall of 1934.[8]

But the unhappy Missouri Pacific was a different story; its sharply reduced revenues were no match for the enormous debt legacy dating from the George Gould and Kuhn, Loeb eras (and which the Vans themselves modestly enhanced). It was only matter of time before MoPac would have to declare bankruptcy, and the time came quickly. The brothers managed to hold off until Section 77 of the Federal Bankruptcy Act was passed in early 1933 to ease railroad reorganizations. Among other things, the new provision gave the Vans at least an outside chance of preserving some of their equity—and possibly even their control—by putting the railroad into a trusteeship supervised by the ICC rather than a receivership, which normally would sell the property for the bondholders and creditors.

They then succumbed. On March 31, 1933, the superlatively costly Missouri Pacific became the first railroad to declare bankruptcy and file for reorganization under Section 77. The Chicago & Eastern Illinois followed several weeks later. Well over half of their railroad empire was now lost to them, although they could hold out some hope that with better times—which were sure to come soon—they could reassert their interests.[9]

When Franklin D. Roosevelt took office in March 1933, he faced a desperate national railroad situation. By then total rail revenues were half their 1929 level, net income had vaporized into a $139.2 million net deficit, and employment had been cut by 41.5 percent. Obligations to pay the interest on debt, on the other hand, had actually risen in the same period, thanks partly to those last exuberant acquisition and construction binges of the sunny late 1920s which were now being completed in much bleaker weather—Cleveland Union Terminal being an outstanding example. Since debt and other fixed costs were always proportionately high in the railroad business, the low traffic volume threatened to bring mass insolvencies. Already over 42,000 route miles were in some form of bankruptcy or receivership—about 17 percent of national total—and a large majority of the surviving railroads were not covering their fixed charges. By the end of 1932, the Reconstruction Finance Corporation had pumped $337.2 million into various railroads in the hope of keeping them afloat, and in cases such as the Missouri Pacific and its affiliates (which ultimately got $31.9 million), the money simply went into a sinkhole.[10]

The Depression's devastation was not the only problem. Perceptive analysts noticed that something else was happening to the railroads, too—something that even good times might not cure. Coincident with the Depression came the first real flowering of intercity motor trucking and the end of the railroads' virtual monopoly on overland freight hauling. The trend had begun earlier, but primitive roads and equally primitive technology had held motor operations to relatively short runs and light loads. By the early 1930s, however, trucking was growing up quickly—substantially aided, ironically, by the Depression itself. Large-scale publicly financed highway projects were in full swing by 1928, especially in the Midwest at the heart of the Van Sweringen system, and they continued through the depression as public works projects. Furthermore, trucking fitted the lean times; goods were being shipped in small lots and on short orders to keep down inventory costs. And it offered income to unemployed workers (many of them railroaders) willing to risk a little money to buy a secondhand truck or two. With fast, personal, door-to-door service, they had little trouble skimming off the cream of the railroads' high-profit merchandise freight.

The damage showed up quickly. In 1930, railroads were still carrying 75 percent of the country's intercity freight business and trucks were carrying only 4 percent. (Most of the rest went by the waterways.) After ten years of steady erosion, the intercity freight business carried by rail would slip to 61 percent while the trucks would take over 10 percent. Trucks were not the sole interlopers, either; aided by federal improvement projects, the inland waterways also increased their share of the freight traffic—and oil pipelines began to proliferate. So even though the depression would end someday, there were clear signs that the railroads would never be the same again.[11]

Thus, governmental rail-consolidation planning efforts continued but with new faces and radical new approaches. All through the 1920s, both the railroads and the government planners had assumed that rail business would continue to expand. That being so, few people worried about the numerous paralleling routes (and, in fact, both the Pennsylvania and the B&O were planning some new ones). Instead, the battles all revolved around how this large pie would be divided up. But now policy planners were worrying about how to deal with an industry that was not only severely shrunken and financially prostrate but might never recover its previous strength. In the oppressive gloom of early 1933, there was even serious talk about government operation, mostly from idealists such as Joseph Eastman and Senator Burton K. Wheeler, a maverick progressive from Montana. But with memories of the World War fiasco, few others—including Franklin Roosevelt —wanted to touch that idea. Short of that, one obvious new goal was to achieve greater operating efficiency by concentrating traffic on fewer lines and eliminating redundancies and other waste. Competition, which ruled 1920s thinking, was now less important than economy.

As a presidential candidate, Roosevelt had made efficiency the keystone of his transportation policy, and once elected he quickly tried to put it into action. Joseph Eastman at last came into his own as a leader in the deliberations and negotiations leading to the Emergency Railroad Transportation Act, signed in June 1933. In part the act was a stopgap effort to reduce costs by coordinating railroad facilities, pooling equipment, and the like—pending some more permanent solution to the problem. A federal coordinator of transportation was to oversee this exercise, and the job inevitably went to Eastman himself. (He also continued as an ICC commissioner.) Another purpose was to make a few permanent regulatory reforms, not the least of which was to put railroad holding companies under the ICC's jurisdiction. This, needless to say, was one of Eastman's particular fixations, first fostered by his frustrations with Van Sweringen financing. Fortunately for the Vans, that provision was not retroactive, so what they had already done was safe from regulatory attack. But for the future, the technique would be useless in bypassing the Commission.[12]

At the same time, Roosevelt informally encouraged a dramatic new railroad consolidation plan. Sponsored by Boston financier Frederick H. Prince, it was a farsighted attempt to radically reduce the competitive waste that had chronically plagued the railroads. (Prince, incidentally, had been one of the several villains in the Pere Marquette's early history and had been the Vans' first contact when they went after the railroad in 1921.)

To put his plan together, Prince picked 34-year-old John W. Barriger, III, an MIT graduate who had worked both in railroad-operating jobs on the Pennsylvania and as a financial analyst for Kuhn, Loeb & Company—and whose railroad knowledge was next to bottomless. Barriger virtually discarded the concept of competition except over broad areas and came up with only seven regional systems instead of the ICC's twenty-one. He pared down the eastern region to just two systems—one dominated by the New York Central and the other by the Pennsylvania. Significantly, every one of the eastern Van Sweringen roads, including the C&EI, were to be folded into the New York Central—very likely what A. H. Smith had been thinking ten years earlier (Barriger was also a dedicated student of railroad history). The actual consolidation program was to be financed by the federal government.[13]

But in the end, Eastman could accomplish little as coordinator, and both the Prince plan and the ICC's 1932 final consolidation plan vanished into oblivion. The Prince plan was too extreme for its time; the investment bankers liked it, but it was anathema to the railroad managers, their unions, and freight shippers fearful of monopoly. General public support turned out to be too tepid to push it further against that opposition. As for the ICC's scheme, it was now philosophically obsolete and, in any event, financially impossible to implement. Thus the thirteen-year consolidation effort ended after consuming enormous amounts of executive and bureaucratic time and many millions of dollars—much of it misspent—with none of the original hopes realized. Large-scale railroad mergers would have to wait another three decades, and then they would follow wholly different alignments. Ultimately they would gravitate to something very close to the Prince plan that had been dismissed as too revolutionary in 1933.

By then, everything was unraveling. Not only was railroading close to collapse when Roosevelt took office, but much of the banking system was already in the throes of collapsing. Most of the Cleveland banks managed to stay open during the panic of late February, although the Union Trust and the Guardian Trust were closed by the end of the month. On March 5th, the day after his inauguration, Roosevelt declared a national bank holiday, and all Cleveland banks closed. By March 13th, three—the Cleveland Trust, the Central National Bank, and the National City Bank—were allowed to reopen, but the Union Trust and the Guardian Trust Company were not; they began the long process of liquidation. Not coincidentally, both had heavy outstanding Van Sweringen loans—Union Trust about $16 million, including unpaid interest, and Guardian about $4.5 million—most of them secured only by the brothers' own personal guarantee. Since Union Trust had been the Vans' primary local banker (it also had the mortgage on Daisy Hill as well as many private Shaker Heights properties), the brothers were now essentially without credit in their hometown. Ironically, later analysis seemed to indicate that Union Trust was really solvent enough to have reopened, and some of its partisans claimed that Roosevelt had revenged himself on Joseph Nutt for his role in helping Hoover's campaign. But it never did, and its assets were eventually taken over by the newly organized Union Bank of Commerce. The Guardian Trust had some special problems of its own, including devious real estate dealings by its subsidiaries and officers, and its president went to jail.[14]

And as if all the frantic financial first-aid efforts were not enough, the Van Sweringens had to face a world that had turned inside out. Inevitably, the personal suffering created by the depression brought bitterness and hostility. The hosannas of the 1920s were replaced by catcalls and worse—public investigations, litigation, criminal actions, and general humiliation. The last of those cut deepest for people of O. P. and M. J.'s extreme sensitivities. Not only had their personal image crumbled away, but they now stood as betrayers instead of benefactors.

Scorched security holders were just one burden on their consciences and maybe the lesser one. After all, presumably these people knew the risks and made their investments with eyes wide open. At the least, they were responsible for their own actions. Furthermore, they were scattered around the country and thus tended to be more abstract than real. Ruined bank depositors in Cleveland were something else. They were innocent, human, and close by. Their savings had vaporized or were frozen when their banks went under—partly because of heavy, incautious, and incestuous Van Sweringen loans. Large and diverse as it was, Cleveland had its small-town aspects, where names were familiar and attached to real people, and the Van Sweringen name was the best known—exalted for its solidity, probity, and spectacular works. Now their vision was reinterpreted as a case of obsessive megalomania and greed. "The story of Cleveland is the story of a small group of acquisitive men gone mad," hyperventilated liberal journalist John Flynn in the national *Harper's Monthly Magazine*.[15]

The rhetoric may have been overheated, but it reflected a popular feeling. Raymond Cragin, a competitive local real estate operator, visited a Guaranty Trust representative in July 1933 and delivered the opinion that "the Van Sweringens reached the zenith of their popularity in Cleveland the day the Union Terminal was opened. Up to that time they had public backing in anything they wanted to do, but since that date their popularity has steadily declined, reaching its lowest point in the last week when the Ohio Senate's investigation of the affairs of the closed banks, the Guardian Trust Company and the Union Trust Company, revealed to the public that the Van Sweringens had tremendous loans at these institutions on which interest was not being paid. The thing that probably made the small depositor . . . most bitter was the knowledge that the Van Sweringens were still living in the most palatial establishment in Cleveland, Daisy Hill Farm, had a large mortgage on it and had not paid any interest on the mortgage in some time."[16]

All of that was true enough, but most people did not know —nor, probably, did they care—that the brothers had suffered just as devastating losses as everyone else—more, most likely. Their income was now largely limited to the dividends from their Cleveland Railway stock, which the bankers had allowed them to continue drawing, plus occasional personal loans. (At one point, the bankers quietly but fruitlessly discussed among themselves the possibility of moving the brothers into a "modest flat" somewhere.) Furthermore, rather than running from their debts or sheltering their assets, they had pledged everything they had on the future of their businesses. Whatever their misjudgments and ethical lapses, they believed wholly in owner-management and in the owners' responsibilities to their companies, and they stuck with them. (In contrast, Sam Insull, their fellow business hero of the 1920s, fled the country; he later returned to face several fraud trials and finally to die legally exonerated but disgraced and penniless.)[17]

The business press was more polite and merely relegated them to nonpersonhood. As *Fortune* magazine noted in early 1934, "The Van Sweringen brothers . . . are usually described in the past tense, as though they had ceased to exist." To their bankers and brokers, the name Van Sweringen now represented an embarrassment, a probable sunk cost instead of an opportunity for profit.[18]

Nationally, there was a political scramble to expose the villains and deeds which allegedly had caused the crash and the Depression. Reformers set to work even before the 1932 election. In April of that year, the Senate Committee on Banking and Currency launched what became a landmark investigation of Wall Street's loose-jointed operations during the ebullient late 1920s, which led directly to a string of stricter laws regulating banking, securities dealing, and holding companies. It began by looking narrowly at stock-market manipulations, but by early 1933 had expanded into banking and holding-company practices. By then, too, the inexorable and aggressive Ferdinand Pecora had become its chief counsel, and although its chairman was actually Senator Duncan U. Fletcher, it was known by all as the Pecora Committee. Pecora had a fertile field with much to reap and proceeded to produce a series of sensational revelations through the year.

The Van Sweringens' turn before Pecora came in early June 1933. They got particular attention, of course, as examples of the evils of the holding-company system and for their role in the collapse of Cleveland's Union Trust and Guardian banks. Pecora also revealed their help to Joseph Nutt in artificially inflating the assets of Nutt's Union Trust Company by $10 million for its 1931 audit by Ohio's superintendent of banks—causing more local ill will and political repercussions.[19]

Ultimately, the brothers came off mostly just as secondary sinners supporting the chief villains in Pecora's crusade—

Putting the best face on things, O. P. Van Sweringen (left) and chief counsel Ferdinand Pecora smile at one another during the June 1933 hearings.
Cleveland Press Collection, Cleveland State University

Looking certainly sadder and possibly wiser, banker and Van Sweringen partner Joseph Nutt may be contemplating the events of 1929.
Cleveland Press Collection, Cleveland State University

those being the Morgan bank; Kuhn, Loeb & Company; Dillon, Read & Co.; and the rest of the New York financial axis. But for the first time, the closely kept details of the Van Sweringens' methods began to emerge in public. In the past, some details had been divulged during ICC hearings, but these

A New World • 267

were more limited and got little public circulation. Now every new revelation was national front-page news.

Pecora was merely the herald of the hostile new political world. Following up on the Union Trust revelations, in April 1934, O. P. was indicted for his role in the $10 million window-dressing scandal, along with Joseph Nutt and Union Trust's president, Wilbur Baldwin. Already bitter and humiliated over Union Trust's fate and his own situation, Nutt was beside himself for exposing his friend O. P. to such persecution. His tears and repeated apologies, noted an unsympathetic William Wenneman, "became embarrassing to us all." Nutt never did fully recover.[20]

By claiming that he was merely trying to do a friend a favor and that he had never asked the reason, O. P. was able to dodge prosecution for the deal. Ultimately, the charges against Nutt and Baldwin were also dropped. But for the Van Sweringens, it remained a festering issue in Cleveland along with a relentlessly multiplying number of others elsewhere.

Twenty-two

The Cruelest Year

Concurrent with Pecora's persecutions in mid-1933, two of the brothers' less savory emergency maneuvers literally backfired. With the Missouri Pacific's bankruptcy, the $20 million Terminal Shares purchase contract came quickly to light, and the Reconstruction Finance Corporation, having by now put $23.8 million into the Missouri Pacific and the Texas & Pacific, took an extremely dim view of the obligation. On May 22, 1933, it filed a motion with the court overseeing the railroad's reorganization to void the contract and recover the $3.2 million Missouri Pacific already had paid Alleghany, rather properly claiming that the price was unreasonable and the properties unnecessary. The matter was left to a court-appointed special master to study and recommend some action to the court, a process that dragged it out for several years and subsequently brought on more trouble.[1]

At almost the same time that the Terminal Shares sins were exposed, the Kansas City Southern–Chicago Great Western sale blew up. It will be recalled that during Alleghany's last crisis in 1931, the Vans had tried to lighten its Paine, Webber & Company broker debts by peddling its Kansas City Southern interest to the struggling Great Western at the inflated price of $3.1 million. This in turn was a tradeoff for $4 million in sub rosa loans the Vans had made (via the C&O) to the Great Western's parent, the Bremo Corporation, which Bremo could not pay. In good times, the Great Western–KCS pairing might have made theoretical sense, creating a single route between the Twin Cities and the Gulf of Mexico. But the times were surely not good, and the weakling Great Western probably was not the company that could have carried it off anyway. By 1933, it was heading toward bankruptcy, which had some messy legal implications. And with investigations and exposures of financial malfeasance now daily news items, the three parties—Bremo, the Vans, and Paine, Webber—also doubtless knew they were each in some kind of awkward spot. Through the Vans, Paine, Webber itself was directly involved in Bremo. The Vans' own dealings with Bremo stemmed from their relationships with the large freight shippers in the group—which had implications of rebates or kickbacks for business.

In the end, everyone prudently agreed on a graceful retreat. In July 1933, the Great Western repudiated the purchase; Paine, Webber took back the Kansas City Southern stock; and the Vans wrote off the $4 million Bremo debt. Paine, Webber kept the KCS stock (it never went back to Alleghany) as well as the $300,000 which the Great Western had already paid in. It had been an unhappy experience for everyone, but especially for the poverty-stricken Great Western, which finally succumbed to bankruptcy in early 1935.[2]

Paradoxically, in the midst of the chronic and ever-compounding financial turmoil, the Van Sweringens proceeded to take on yet another business. It would be their last corporate acquisition and was an interesting, if mysteriously clouded, one. At some time during 1933, another holding company called the Standard Carloading Corporation quietly appeared. Standard Carloading was a variation on the Pittston Company theme—a collection of what were basically railroad freight shippers and trucking services.

Standard Carloading was a two-headed creature controlling more-or-less complementary transportation businesses. One head consisted of the National Carloading Corporation, a freight-forwarding company which operated or controlled five other freight forwarders. These were a unique breed of railroad freight shipper which specialized in consolidating small merchandise shipments into full carloads, which they then dispatched under their own names. The other head, U. S.

Truck Lines, Inc., was a holding company controlling a large group of trucking companies operating localized pickup and delivery services or carrying specialized cargoes. One subsidiary, for example, was Anchor Motor Freight, which delivered new automobiles to dealers.

These companies had been created or assembled during the 1931–1933 period and were principally organized by none other than John Bernet's oldest son, William G. Bernet, and the younger Bernet (who was 39 in 1933) managed most of them in one form or another. The master holding company, Standard Carloading, essentially was owned by three Van Sweringen railroads—the C&O, Pere Marquette, and Erie—but in a peculiarly backhanded form. One-third was held by the Lake Erie Coal Company, a Canadian Pere Marquette subsidiary which operated a coal-receiving dock and a lake steamer operating from Eireau, Ontario. The C&O's own holding company, Virginia Transportation, owned another one-third. The final third was allocated to a New Jersey subsidiary of the Erie called the Erie Land and Improvement Company. Like Pittston, Standard Carloading had the potential to be part of a unique one-stop transportation service integrating trucking, shipping, and rail operations under one management, with one bill to the customer, although it never developed as such.[3]

New holes kept opening. The most gaping and threatening was now the Missouri Pacific's bankruptcy and its effect on the Alleghany Corporation. The huge holding company had stumbled into early 1933 intact, held together by the C&O's bailout a year before. Now, though, another crisis loomed. The third of Alleghany's three bond issues—those "5s of 1950"—was heavily backed by various Missouri Pacific securities. Now in trusteeship, the MoPac no longer paid even bond interest and would not do so until the bankruptcy was terminated—which would be years away. With most of the income for this particular Alleghany bond issue now cut off, it was in its own danger of default, which jeopardized the Vans' control of the Missouri Pacific and might even put Alleghany into bankruptcy. (The other two issues were more stably backed by Chesapeake Corporation securities and were in less danger.)

The crisis hit in October 1933 when there was no cash left to pay interest then due on the "5s of 1950." The Morgan bank temporarily plugged the hole with a $550,000 loan and did the same to cover another payment due in April 1934. That allowed time for the Vans and their bankers to come up with some permanent solution, which turned out to be a clever plan to create a new special class of preferred stock which would serve to fund the unpaid interest for five years.

It worked like this: Rather than receive interest for the next five years, the bondholder would turn in his coupons representing that interest; for each year's interest (which would have been $50 per bond) he got one share of the new preferred stock—five shares in place of the five years' interest. The stock was convertible to common and had some voting rights. Since the next interest payment was due in October 1934, the bondholders were supposed to decide whether to accept the offer before September. In effect it was another time-buying device, but ultimately this bond issue depended on the Missouri Pacific's recovery and the hope that the Vans' MoPac equity somehow would be preserved.[4]

The brothers and their staff then launched into an intense selling campaign for the plan, which was modestly successful, but found they had to extend the deadline twice. By late November, they had about three-quarters of the bonds pledged. In the meantime, another new provision had been added to the federal bankruptcy law—Section 77-B—which allowed them to reorganize Alleghany and, in this circumstance, force all remaining bondholders to accept their plan. At the end of 1934, they filed for a voluntary reorganization under the new law to clean up the affair—"a mild case of bankruptcy so that a real failure might be avoided," as one report put it.[5]

Through all these frantic financial hole-patchings, investigations, lawsuits, and general assaults, O. P stubbornly refused to capitulate to anything, and his creative mind never seemed to stop. Nor did he appear any less controlled, stolid, and self-assured. One close associate later recalled: "In the awful days, we sat around waiting for the heavens to crash—we would have word that an action next day in New York or Chicago or St. Louis would doom all our enterprises. No one could see any way out. But next morning there would be O. P. on the long-distance telephone in his office, and by noon he would have worked something out with the creditors that saved the day." Outwardly at least, he impressed his staff with iron nerve and strong faith in what he and the rest of them had done.[6]

But obviously much was going on inside, and the differing personalities of the two brothers made it more than clear. Said Joseph Doherty: "Under his calm surface O. P. was worried but no one could ever detect it. . . . [His] hair had turned grey in the elapsed period since 1930, but there was something in the glance he gave you that set him apart from the ruck. His less sanguine and more conservative brother, Mantis, appeared to be faring not quite as well. The anxiety in his eyes reflected his concern for his older brother who was applying himself unstintingly to his many problems." M. J., nervous and hypertensive to begin with, was now much more so. In fact, Doherty remarked, he seemed to reach "a state of mind bordering on panic."[7]

But snippets of hope were beginning to appear by the dawn of 1934. While unemployment reached an all-time peak of almost 25 percent in 1933, most other measures were perking up. Coal, steel, and auto production began climbing out of the abysmal depths of 1932, and railroad revenues and tonnage followed. To be sure, the figures were extremely modest —1933 national rail-freight revenues were 1.7 percent above those for 1932; by the end of the following year, they were 7.5 percent ahead of 1932's revenues. The heights of 1929 were still far away for everyone, but it was a genuine trend.

Thanks in part to Bernet's efforts on the C&O, the Pere Marquette, and the Nickel Plate—and Charles Denney's efforts on the Erie—several of the Van Sweringen lines showed new hope. The Nickel Plate edged marginally back into the black in 1934, and the Erie and the Pere Marquette both cut their deficits substantially. The little Wheeling & Lake Erie showed surprising strength, having even weathered the worst years with meager profits. And the C&O did well enough that the Vans felt they could safely increase its dividend in late 1933 to help hold the Chesapeake and Alleghany Corporations together. As usual, the Missouri Pacific and its subsidiaries were another story. Their 1933 revenues were generally below even the awful 1932 figures, but they did pick up in 1934. The system deficit, however, remained stubbornly intractable; it climbed from $14.3 million in 1932 to $16.6 million in 1933, leveled slightly to $16.3 million in 1934, then resumed its upward march to $18.5 million in 1935. All that the unfortunate railroad lacked was a plague of locusts, but it hardly needed that since it now had something worse—the Dust Bowl, whose black windstorms regularly ravaged its agricultural territory during much of 1934 and 1935.

Downtown Cleveland real estate continued to be mostly grim, but it also offered glimmers of brighter days. The Terminal Tower's space was about 77 percent occupied, but only 67 percent of it was actually generating rent. The Midland Bank Building was now shorn of the Midland Bank but otherwise was reasonably comfortably filled at over 70 percent—thanks in part to the Erie and the Cleveland Railway; the Builders Exchange and Medical Arts were poorer performers at 49 and 61 percent, respectively. The Hotel Cleveland was faring ex-

By 1935, M. J. was clearly showing the strains of the struggle to survive.
Cleveland Press,
H. H. Harwood, Jr., collection

tremely poorly, averaging 41 percent occupancy during 1934. With its Shaker Heights rapid transit connection and Public Square streetcar terminal location, the Higbee Company store was proving popular but was heavily burdened by the costs of acquiring and building it and was thus far unprofitable. Cheeriest of all, one more piece of the original Union Terminal plan was put in place in September 1934 when the new central post office opened. Unlike the other buildings, however, it had no direct underground connections to the main complex, but it was at least adjacent to everything and helped fill out O. P.'s ultimate plan.[8]

The Cleveland Railway remained in the black and faithfully continued to pay its required 6 percent return, which held Metropolitan Utilities together and, with the banks' sufferance, allowed the brothers some income for their living expenses. But it too had suffered income losses, and the Van Sweringen management was accused of plundering a special maintenance-and-renewal fund for the dividend money.

Metropolitan also made an odd purchase in 1934 which seemed to indicate that the aborted East Side rapid transit line might soon come to life, although not in its originally planned form. That year, the Cleveland Interurban Railroad—Metropolitan's subsidiary which operated the Shaker Heights rapid transit—picked up ten lightweight interurban electric cars secondhand from the recently deceased Kentucky Traction & Terminal Company in Lexington. Although capable of a top speed of only 40 miles per hour, the cars were apparently intended as a cheap and expedient means of putting the East Side route into business; when times were better, they would be replaced by heavier and faster new equipment. The 12-year-old veterans duly arrived at the rapid transit line's Kingsbury Run yard, where they sat awaiting the call to duty. It never came in their lifetimes.[9]

Soon afterward, the Metropolitan structure began to crack. Three Cleveland banks held notes of the Cleveland Interurban totaling about $4 million. Two of the banks—Union Trust and Guardian Trust—had closed and were either in reorganization or liquidation. (The third was the solvent Cleveland Trust, which had inherited the Cleveland Interurban Railroad debt from the Midland Bank.) Together the three banks decided to protect their collateral by taking control of the Cleveland Interurban, and in 1935 it was effectively taken away from Metropolitan's management and put under banker direction. It was only a minor chunk taken out of the brothers' empire, but it was an enormous sentimental and symbolic loss. The Shaker Heights rapid transit line had been both the foundation of their suburb and their entry point to the railroad business—and it was still very much what made Shaker such a special community.[10]

But that was only the least consequential event in what turned out to be the cruelest year for the two Van Sweringens. By the time 1935 ended, there would be almost nothing recognizable left from what had been.

The first disaster was precisely predictable. For almost five years, the succession of time-buying maneuvers had set several clocks to ticking. On May 1st, time ran out. The $39.5 million New York bank loan of October 1930—now swelled to $51.2 million by an add-on loan and accumulated unpaid interest —fell due, and the bankers finally concluded they had reached the end of the road. At stake were all of the Van Sweringen empires; virtually every business entity the brothers owned or controlled had been pledged as collateral for the loan: Alleghany (with all the railroads and railroad holding companies), the Van Sweringen Corporation and subsidiaries (essentially the entire Union Terminal complex except for the railroad station and post office), the Higbee Company, the Van Sweringen Company (Shaker Heights and beyond), and the Pittston Company, plus various lesser and unrelated holdings.[11]

The bankers realistically recognized that the brothers' businesses were not going to recover soon, and they no longer could afford to continue pumping in money. And since their own incomes were now improving, the timing was advantageous for them to take what they knew would be some large tax losses. At the same time they were gracious (and practical) enough to abstain from an immediate foreclosure. They really were not anxious to inherit all those properties themselves; it would be politically untenable, if nothing else. But they did intend to sell all the collateral; the only questions were when and how. It was not entirely a straightforward case, however. For one thing, the Vans also owed a total of about $22 million to the defunct Cleveland banks, and some of the same collateral was involved in both sets of loans. When they made the big loan back in October 1930, the New York banks effectively had taken priority rights on it, but the Cleveland banks still had a claim. Then there was the brothers' own personal guarantee which had been tacked onto both the New York and Cleveland debts.

Because of that personal guarantee, the bankers knew it was in their best interests to try to cooperate with the Vans and give them a chance to keep control of their properties if they could. By doing so, there was at least a chance that they could recover some day and thus be able to pay off the remainder of the debts. So the brothers still had a chance of staying in business if they could raise enough money to buy out the collateral and satisfy everyone.

The crisis had been well anticipated and there were intermittent efforts to work something out before the May 1st deadline, but the date came and went with no resolution. The usual complex alternative financing plans were kicked back and forth between New York and Cleveland while O. P. desperately looked for new money somewhere. He had few options; New York was now closed to him, as were the Cleveland banks. Complicating his quest was his long-rooted refusal to give up his traditional personal control of his businesses, even though this was actually an illusion at the time. Some individual Cleveland investors gave tentative commitments, but these turned out to be frustratingly fleeting.

In the midst of this came a brutal, unanticipated shock: John Bernet, now 67 and in ill health, but still trying to be everywhere and do everything, suffered a collapse and ten days later died of an arterial blockage on July 5th. The Vans, the B&O's Daniel Willard, railroad and industrial executives, and his own large family filled St. Agnes Church at 80th and Euclid for a mass attended by five Catholic bishops. Afterward, the genuinely bereft brothers wrote a testimonial which spoke as much to the end of an era as the loss of a man: "We have lost our friend, the business world has lost one of its outstanding figures, and the railroad industry lost a genius. Mr. Bernet's association with us had covered a period of twenty years, during which we came to know his sound philosophy, his innate kindness for everyone, his robust sense of humor, his rugged honesty, and his genius for operating railroads. . . . He never ceased to be a plain man. . . . He was one of our first citizens."

Charles Denney, the Erie's president, had seemed to be Bernet's heir apparent, but the brothers had been less impressed with him and surprised everyone by promoting William J. Harahan back to his old job. Harahan, whom Bernet had displaced as C&O president six years earlier, moved up from Richmond to Cleveland to head the C&O, Nickel Plate, and Pere Marquette; Denney was left where he was on the Erie. At age 67 and in poor health himself, Harahan did his best to fill in, helped by Bernet protégés such as Gus Ayres on the Nickel Plate and Robert Bowman on the Pere Marquette. (Almost coincidentally too, stomach cancer had forced archenemy W. W. Atterbury to resign the Pennsylvania's presidency in April, and he died five months later.)[12]

Bernet was the first to succumb, but the emotional and

physical strains were clearly showing elsewhere in the Terminal Tower offices. In another blow, Darwin Barrett, their right-hand man, was forced to take a sick leave. Barrett had come down with tuberculosis and already had been intermittently away at sanatoriums; he was absent, for example, at the initial presentation to the RFC in early 1933, leaving the burden to O. P. and Colonel Ayres. With Barrett gone, O. P. had to lean more heavily on Herbert Fitzpatrick and William Wenneman. Charles Bradley also was now ailing. M. J. was in an especially worrisome state; he looked increasingly haggard and had also been forced to take extensive time off to rest. Joseph Doherty observed: "Worry over the severe ordeals to which O. P. had been subjected, and the loss of fortune, and the anticipation of other untoward events to come, had completely unnerved him."[13]

Besides the unceasing office crises, M. J. had some female complications to deal with—one negative, the other happily positive. As Daisy Hill's senior manager, he found himself increasingly battling Daisy Jenks. Now approaching her mid-50s, she was undergoing her own physical and emotional stresses and was becoming irritable and demanding. More happily, though, he had become interested in Mary Snow, the attractive blond widow of Ralph Snow, a lawyer and Shaker Heights landowner. M. J. kept the relationship as secret as possible, taking her to discreet places without O. P.'s knowledge.[14]

In the meantime, the sword was rapidly descending. The New York bankers had decided to have a public auction of all the securities in their collateral and could not wait much longer than September, since they needed to have their tax losses by the end of the year. O. P. kept doggedly at it and finally hit his jackpot in August. He called on George A. Tomlinson, one of his Terminal Tower tenants who was a wealthy Great Lakes shipping operator and an occasional business associate. (O. P. had put him on the boards of the Missouri Pacific and the Cleveland Railway, among other things.) The burly 66-year-old Tomlinson was reaching the end of a fascinatingly checkered career which included an early stint as a cowboy (reputedly captured and tortured by Ute Indians), work in Buffalo Bill shows, a turn as a newspaper reporter and editor, some time as a Great Lakes steamship agent, and, finally, ownership of one of the largest freighter fleets on the lakes.[15]

Tomlinson had no desire to take on the Van Sweringen empire and was reluctant to invest much himself, but he did want to help. He suggested a seemingly unlikely angel, George

The "two Georges" who saved the railroad empire: George Ball (left) of Muncie, Indiana, and O. P.'s Cleveland friend George Tomlinson, shown in November 1936.
Cleveland Press Collection, Cleveland State University

A. Ball of Muncie, Indiana. Like Tomlinson, the 72-year-old Ball had already made his own fortune—in his case from manufacturing Ball Brothers Mason canning jars—and was at the point in life where he was not looking for new business adventures. But there was some mutuality among Tomlinson, Ball, and the two brothers. Ball and Tomlinson had a distant family relationship through Tomlinson's wife, and they were close friends; Ball in turn was a large Nickel Plate freight customer, and the Vans had him put on the Nickel Plate's board in 1932.

Tomlinson and his wife were about to leave Cleveland for a long vacation in Colorado to escape Ohio's hay-fever season, and it was decided that the four of them would drive to Muncie to see Ball; the Tomlinsons would then continue on west. So on Sunday, August 11th, O. P., M. J., and Mr. and Mrs. Tomlinson bundled into the Vans' Buick and, with M. J. driving, set off early in the morning. (The departure followed some dawn-hour uncertainty and argument about who would drive, with Daisy Jenks warning M. J. about taxing himself, M. J. insisting, and the Vans' single surviving chauffeur standing by.) Arriving in mid-afternoon, O. P. then did his persuasive best with the wispy, aging Ball, concluding, quite accurately, that he had run out of options and was at the end of his own road.[16]

Ball was noncommittal but at least encouraging; more negotiations quickly followed, while at the same time the New

York bankers calculated what they would take for the Van Sweringen collateral. In the process they broke the securities up into four large parcels—one of which included Alleghany and the railroad portion of the empire, one of which included all the Cleveland downtown and suburban real estate, and two others that included mostly miscellaneous industrial stocks which the Vans had bought at the height of the boom. Everyone agreed to let the last two groups go to outside bidders, since they were superfluous to the brothers' primary businesses. The first two were the keys to the empires, and it appeared that they could be had together for about $3 million.

Ball soon acquiesced, largely as a philanthropic gesture and, it was said, because he disliked eastern bankers and was inclined to rescue a fellow midwesterner from their clutches. The new foursome—the two brothers, Tomlinson, and Ball—set about putting together a new holding company which, they hoped, would successfully bid on Alleghany and the real estate companies. What emerged was a clever new variation on an old theme. A new holding company, pointedly called the Midamerica Corporation, came to life on September 28th with $2 million in common and preferred stock, but this time none went to the brothers. Ball took two-thirds and Tomlinson the remainder, theoretically leaving the Vans with no equity and no power. But since the purpose was to keep them in control of their businesses, an option was added: Over the next ten years, the brothers could buy 55 percent of the voting common stock from Ball and Tomlinson at their cost plus interest. In the meantime, they would continue to manage everything. (The ten-year period was picked to allow the brothers time to work off their considerable remaining debts, a reasonable assumption since business was beginning to recover.)[17]

The auction was set for 3:30 P.M. September 30th at Adrian Muller & Company's austere and dreary salesroom in downtown Manhattan—which, appropriately enough, faced the cemetery of St. Paul's Chapel. The room was filled with both the financially mighty and the idly curious. Flanking O. P. were Ball and Colonel Ayres, who would do the bidding for Midamerica. As one newspaper reporter wrote, "Although Mr. Van Sweringen's plump, pale face betrayed no emotion, his beady, dark brown eyes traveled upward to the ceiling and downward again to his fingertips with a regular, nervous motion."[18]

Although O. P. seemingly had engineered another potential coup, it was no sure thing. There were other individuals and groups who had been closely following the Van Sweringens' affairs and who were especially interested in Alleghany—which the stock market valued as almost worthless and thus could be had absurdly cheap. One was none other than the old Boston pirate Frederick H. Prince, and the equally aging Leonor Loree was always a wild card. (Loree was 77 by then, but still defiantly unretired.) An astute stockbroker named Robert R. Young, who was backed by several General Motors executives, also had marked Alleghany as an intriguing opportunity. His partner, Frank Kolbe, showed up at the auction as an observer.

But despite the considerable anticipation, speculation, and tension, the auction turned out to be a stuffy charade. The bankers, represented by Morgan partner George Whitney and the lawyer F. A. O. Schwarz, put in their minimum bids for each lot; for the two key Van Sweringen lots, Colonel Ayres merely raised them by a token amount, the bankers declined to go further, and Midamerica got them. (Hallgarten & Company, a securities dealer, picked up the two odd lots of industrial stocks.) For a total cost of $3.1 million, Midamerica now had the entire Van Sweringen empire—valued at $3 billion at its peak. And the brothers were still in business.

Visibly relieved, O. P. was quoted afterward as saying: "I'm sorry it had to be done this way. I'd rather have paid the bills." He meant it. Daisy Jenks later wrote: "Only we who knew them best in the last years knew their all-consuming desire to make up every dollar of loss caused through depression and bank failures."[19]

Nonetheless it was another triumph—possibly O. P.'s greatest, considering the stakes. Not only were the brothers effectively back in control, they could also receive a salary from Midamerica to keep themselves whole. It was the fitting culmination of an astonishing five-year fight for survival, at which *Fortune* magazine could only marvel: "It is probably not too much to say that the Van Sweringen control today is the most ingenious and resourceful example of corporate patching, plugging, gluing, taping, and general self-preservation that can be found in the annals of U. S. industry." O. P. himself was back to expansive thinking: "Going back on the train O. P. was full of plans for the future. . . . He wanted to expand Midamerica by getting added capital to buy in Alleghany senior securities," reported Wenneman. And with the economic outlook improving, there was the opportunity to begin working off the debts which had been such a burden on their consciences.[20]

But the cruelest year had not ended yet.

Twenty-three
The Last Train

M. J. was not at the auction. His chronic high blood pressure had steadily worsened over the past several years, and by September he was thoroughly exhausted. That spring he had been forced to drop his office duties and rest at Daisy Hill, although he then returned for light duty—but in uncertain shape. He had made it to New York but sequestered himself with Wenneman in the Savoy Plaza while O. P. endured the stress of the auction. That night he returned to Cleveland by himself; O. P., now optimistic about his business prospects but worried about his brother, stayed over to work out Midamerica financing details with Manufacturers Trust.[1]

The two then treated themselves to an auto trip to O. P.'s birthplace at Wooster, Ohio, and on to Kentucky, piloted by their single surviving chauffeur. M. J. was still not well and was regularly taking digitalis, but he seemed to improve on the trip. Still, he was not up to the office work; without M. J., and with Darwin Barrett also hors de combat, O. P. and the beleaguered staff did their best to struggle through the complexities of Midamerica's creation, the auction, and its aftermath.

On October 17th, M. J. announced to the Daisy Hill staff that he was "going to the hospital for a little physical checkup" and would be back in a few days. Somewhat cryptically he added "When I get back there are going to be some radical changes." Puzzled insiders at the estate speculated that might mean marriage to Mary Snow.[2]

Although nobody showed alarm, M. J. did not return "in a few days." There were varying reports that he was resting, that he had intestinal flu, and that the flu and his high blood pressure had damaged his kidneys. By early December, it was clear that there was something very serious, and O. P. brought in two heart specialists in succession, each of which delivered the same prognosis: Bluntly put, M. J. was slowly dying and nothing could be done. He began to slip in and out of consciousness. Joseph Doherty remembered: "O. P. would visit him every morning on the way to work and every evening on the way to Daisy Hill. There were days when he remained away from the office, and sat at his brother's bedside through the wee hours of the night."[3]

The phone call came to Daisy Hill at five in the morning on Thursday, December 12th. Ben and Daisy Jenks drove O. P. down to University Hospital, where M. J. was still conscious, but the two brothers said nothing for those last ninety minutes. M. J. died at 7:10, aged 54.[4]

O. P. left at 7:30 for Daisy Hill again. That evening, H. Horton Hampton, a close friend from the early Union Terminal project days and now a Nickel Plate vice president, called to offer condolences. Doherty reported: "He sat beside O. P. in the shadowy 'ship room', neither of them uttering a word. For what seemed like an hour the silence was unbroken, except for the occasional sputter of coals in the fireplace. O. P. gave the appearance of a man who was seeing grinning gargoyle faces in the gloom of the chamber. His usually well-combed hair was . . . tossed and tousled. . . . Finally, Hampton placed a hand on O. P.'s shoulder. O. P. turned around and glanced at him for the first time. And then he spoke: 'I have faced many serious problems. I have always been able to find the solution. But now I don't know what to do, or how to do it, or where to go from here.'"[5]

Over 400 people crowded into Daisy Hill's Ship Room for the funeral the following Saturday afternoon, although O. P. and other immediate family members were upstairs. The Reverend Charles H. Myers, an early minister at Shaker Heights's original community church, Plymouth Congregational, came over from Detroit to conduct the service. M. J.'s twelve pallbearers included Charles and Alva Bradley, Walter Ross's son

George Ross, architect Philip Small, Horton Hampton, John Murphy, and John Sherwin, Jr. When his estate was settled, it was valued at $3,067.85 (aside from insurance), almost half of which was represented by seven saddle horses.[6]

Afterward, O. P. regularly lit the lamps in M. J.'s office every morning and turned them off when he left. The Jenkses moved into Roundwood Manor with him and persuaded him to use a bedroom close to them so that they could keep an eye on him. Always conscious of O. P.'s delicate health, Daisy Jenks became more protective than ever, watching him and nagging him to take care of himself.[7]

For several weeks he acted "anesthetized and functioning in a vacuum," but then gradually came back to life and went to work. There was more than enough to get his teeth back into—so much, in fact, that it seemed impossibly overwhelming to any ordinary businessman. In addition, he now had to deal with that inner void; always basically a lonely person, he was now much more so. Duane Brown, the Jenkses' butler and a part-time housekeeper at Roundwood Manor, remembered: "He would just sit in a chair by the hour in one of the big rooms. You'd find him there late at night. . . . I'd bring him a glass of milk and crackers, help him get undressed, and tuck him into his bed."[8]

O. P. was also without his strongest railroad executive, John Bernet, and his chief assistant Darwin Barrett was also clearly failing. But at least his personal position was the strongest it had been in five years, since the New York banking group had relinquished its hold on all the Van Sweringen businesses. Midamerica had taken Vaness's place as the peak holding company, controlling the railroad system through the Alleghany Corporation and the Cleveland suburban and downtown real estate companies through separate tendrils; O. P. was president of Midamerica under the agreement with Ball and Tomlinson, who were quite happy to leave everything in his hands. (Vaness itself continued life as a personal Van Sweringen company; it had heavy debts but few assets.)

On the other hand, although the New York banks had sold out, they had not left the scene. Most of the old debts were still there, and O. P. not only had to work with the New York banks to resolve them but also faced a stickier situation with the debts he owed to the liquidating Cleveland banks. Most of these had been loaned for his Cleveland properties, which themselves were heading toward bankruptcy. And for the time being, Guaranty Trust still technically controlled Alleghany, since the market value of the bond collateral had been below the 150 percent minimum. At the same time, it was restricting Alleghany's income, one of O. P.'s principal sources. Alleghany itself was still undergoing its "mild case of bankruptcy" under Section 77-B, primarily to work out problems paying the interest on the "5s of 1950" bond issue.

Happily, one of those problems resolved itself in February 1936, when the value of the collateral on two Alleghany bond issues climbed over the 150 percent mark and Guaranty Trust released its grip on them. O. P. now had undisputed control over all the railroads but the Missouri Pacific and the Chicago & Eastern Illinois and the free use of Alleghany's income. The Alleghany reorganization also went relatively smoothly, and it emerged from bankruptcy in September—although the long-term outlook for the Missouri Pacific securities behind the vulnerable bond issue was not so much murky as opaque.[9]

The Missouri Pacific, which had been the source of such hope in 1929, had now become a legal nightmare. The principal problem was that in characteristic style O. P. was not willing to see his control wiped out or significantly reduced as the railroad reorganized—which traditionally was almost a matter of course in such cases. To preserve his stock equity, he had first put together a reorganization plan in early 1935 which would call on the Reconstruction Finance Corporation to put in another $100–$125 million, in effect underwriting the equity in expectation of a strong earnings recovery. The proposal created an internal conflict within the agency between RFC chairman Jesse Jones, who favored the loan, and his chief railroad examiner, John W. Barriger, who did not. A Texas multimillionaire, Jones admired the Vans—O. P., he later said, "owned America's most brilliant mind." He was also anxious to develop his home state, which the MoPac blanketed. Barriger felt that some of the Vans' dealings were dishonest, particularly the business-buying schemes such as Terminal Shares. In the end Barriger, helped by a younger fellow M.I.T. graduate named Alfred Perlman, managed to prove that the Van Sweringen business projections were "an air castle." The idea died in a political tangle when the new chairman of the Senate Committee on Interstate Commerce, Burton K. Wheeler, was pulled into it.[10]

O. P. did not give up, and he put together another craftily constructed plan, which *Fortune* magazine characterized as having "no flavor of compromise about it . . . an aggressive proposition extremely favorable to the stockholders." Essentially it would reduce the old debt marginally, make much of the old fixed-interest obligations contingent on income, and keep most of the equity. That, of course, was anathema to the large bondholders, who favored the traditional method of substantially reducing the debt, converting it to their own equity, and ultimately putting control in their hands. As the largest single creditor, the RFC was caught in the middle.[11]

As it developed, the Missouri Pacific reorganization became a lawyer's Valhalla, spawning litigation which was destined to stretch out over twenty-three years (and more), outliving most of the original parties and, in some cases, their successors. In the process it also produced efforts by the RFC to "dig up dirt," as Barriger later put it, and the old Terminal Shares affair was one rich source, backing Barriger's convictions about the brothers' dubious dealings with large freight shippers. After a three-year legal struggle, the MoPac's 1929 purchase of the various Missouri switching railroads was finally repudiated by the judge in charge of the bankruptcy, and new litigation started in December 1935 to recover the $3.2 million the MoPac already had paid. The RFC also tried to bring a criminal suit against the railroad's management for failing to mention the purchase commitment when it applied for its loans, but by the time it had completed its investigation of the entire deal, the statute of limitations had run out.[12]

Despite the legal quagmire, O. P. was aggressively optimistic. In fact, his ever-expansive mind began developing a scheme to coordinate the reorganizations of the Missouri Pacific, the Rio Grande, and the Western Pacific—all of which were in bankruptcy by the end of 1935—with the idea of cementing the link to the Pacific. Discussions were held with Arthur Curtiss James and the executives of the three lines but died before any agreements were reached.[13]

And while dealing with new enemies in the Missouri Pacific case, O. P. continued to be harassed by at least one old one—Frank Taplin. By 1936, General Atterbury was gone and so were the Pennsylvania's expansive ambitions, but Taplin still headed the Pittsburgh & West Virginia under Pennroad and still had his sights set on the Wheeling & Lake Erie. Adding to his irritation with the Vans, the profitable Wheeling had been slow to pay off the old dividend arrearage on its prior-lien preferred stock, which at the time was the key to the Vans' control. (They owned almost all of that issue through the Nickel Plate, and as long as the arrears were unpaid they had full voting control of the railroad.) Until the arrears were cleared, the Wheeling could pay nothing on the stock Taplin and his friends owned. In May of 1936, he declared renewed warfare and managed to expand his representation on the Wheeling's board.

The RFC's Jesse Jones finally engineered a compromise which rearranged the Wheeling's capital structure in a way that retained Van Sweringen control but paid off the arrears, gave the Taplin group regular dividend income, and allowed it somewhat greater voting power. That technically ended the long feud and, as a happy by-product, gave the cash-needy Nickel Plate $4 million when the old prior-lien arrears were completely paid. Taplin may or may not have been completely silenced, but unknown to everyone, he was close to the end of his own road.[14]

There was much else to occupy O. P. during that hectic year. The Chicago & Eastern Illinois bankruptcy was also unresolved and the Cleveland situation was a shambles of unpaid debts, unpaid mortgages, and ever-mounting arrears in property taxes. New roads and road improvements and utility lines for the vast and vacant Shaker Country Estates had been largely built by Cuyahoga County and the local municipalities, who were now desperate for assessment money. The Van Sweringen Company and its suburban land subsidiaries succumbed to Section 77-B bankruptcy in February 1936. Downtown, the Higbee Company had already filed under Section 77-B in August 1935; the Van Sweringen Corporation and its Terminal Building Company went down in October 1936, leaving almost nothing of his Cleveland creations still floating. In October, the administrators of the Cleveland banks were looking into the possibility of placing O. P. into personal bankruptcy to try to recover their claims. The Cleveland Railway was still turning out its 6 percent return, and thus Metropolitan Utilities was still viable (but without control of the Shaker Heights rapid transit operation), but its ability to keep paying this was questionable. Furthermore, Metropolitan's commitment to buy out the Cleveland Railway stock it was "renting" looked impossible, considering that its market value was now as much as 40 points lower than Metropolitan's promised purchase price.[15]

The political onslaughts also continued and multiplied. As federal transportation coordinator, old nemesis Joseph Eastman began an inquiry into Vaness Company records, and in November 1935 a routine application by George Tomlinson to become a director of the Missouri Pacific's Fort Worth Belt Railroad triggered an Interstate Commerce Commission investigation of Midamerica's railroad control. More ominously, the politically powerful populist Burton K. Wheeler had ascended to the chairmanship of the Senate's Interstate Commerce Committee in 1935 and was eager to launch his own version of the Pecora Committee investigations. Wheeler was an outspoken advocate of strong business regulation in general and outright government ownership of railroads. Under the guidance of Joseph Eastman and liberal lawyer Max Lowenthal, he organized a large-scale inquiry into railroad financial manipulations during the 1920s with particular emphasis on railroad holding companies—with the Van Sweringen system as his special target. Having already cosponsored the Public Utilities Holding Company Act, Wheeler aimed for something similar for the railroad industry—among other things.

Wheeler's subcommittee started its investigation work in mid-1936; it immediately descended on the Terminal Tower to gather up the most private Van Sweringen files, sparking O. P.'s ire. Hearings were scheduled to begin in December; Max Lowenthal acted as its chief and the senatorial committee itself included a conscientious junior senator named Harry S Truman, who turned out to be one of its more active (and less belligerent) participants. By the time it concluded over a year and a half later, it had amassed a hearing record of twenty-three printed volumes and had minutely examined the Van Sweringen career as never before or since.

On the plus side, the railroads were beginning to recover substantially. All the Van Sweringen eastern lines were in the black except the Chicago & Eastern Illinois, and even its deficit was the lowest in seven years. The Chesapeake & Ohio reported the highest earnings in its history, and thanks partly to its Wheeling & Lake Erie dividend windfall, the Nickel Plate's profit almost exactly equaled the 1929 figure. Charles Denney seemed to have the Erie on the way to recovery, producing a $2.2 million profit for the year, and both the Pere Marquette and the Wheeling & Lake Erie had had their best years since 1929. The Missouri Pacific system remained deep in the red, but its deficit was the smallest since 1932 and was 45 percent less than the previous year.

Shaker Heights land sales were also now reviving somewhat, and as a reflection, ridership on the community's rapid transit line climbed back close to its 1930 level. The line's banker-managers even bought seven "new" cars in 1935 from the defunct Aurora, Elgin & Fox River Electric Company in Illinois, and the next year they extended the Shaker Boulevard line a mile farther east to Green Road. The extension took advantage of the hugely elaborate grading and bridgework originally intended to carry a four-track rapid transit line and express highway into the Shaker Country Estates. The Estates land itself remained mostly barren, but it was an encouraging move to stimulate life in the territory.[16]

Yet that one enormous void remained. Wenneman recalled that "whenever we brought O. P. a good report, he only said 'If only my brother were here. That news would have

Alone, tired, and harassed by investigations—but also determined and defiant: O. P. in June 1936.
Cleveland Press collection, Cleveland State University

made him happy.'" And also: "If I'd listened to my brother and we had quit when he wanted to, he'd still be alive."[17]

Despite the Midamerica coup, O. P. still felt a strong moral obligation to clear his debts, particularly with the New York banks. To anyone with less optimism, the job seemed impossible; Wenneman and John Fackler, O. P.'s real estate lawyer, privately calculated that he would need to earn $15 million a year for the rest of his life to have enough left after taxes to pay off the debts and accumulated interest. Heedless, O. P. continued making progress in negotiating his way out with Morgan and the others. The Cleveland banks were proving to be harder sells—an unpleasant reversal from the easygoing ways of Joseph Nutt and their other friends in the past.[18]

One more of the numerous New York banker meetings was scheduled with George Whitney of Morgan for Monday November 23rd, so a weary O. P., along with Wenneman and lawyer Herbert Fitzpatrick, made ready to leave on the overnight *Nickel Plate Limited* early Sunday evening. William Wyer, the Missouri Pacific's corporate secretary and treasurer, came along to handle some MoPac business in the city. The Nickel Plate's office car 27 was attached to the train's rear end during its 10-minute stop at the Union Terminal. At one minute after six, the blue-uniformed gateman closed the bronze gates to the platform stairway, and amid the usual banging shut of steel train doors, a Union Terminal electric tugged Nickel Plate No. 8 on its way east, passing an inbound Shaker Heights rapid transit car just outside the station. Wenneman and Wyer got on at East Cleveland, while O. P. and Fitzpatrick waited at the little frame depot at Willoughby, the most convenient station to reach from Daisy Hill.

No. 8 reached Buffalo at 10 P.M., where the Lackawanna took over for the rest of the trip to the New York ferry terminal at Hoboken. At 4:05 A.M., the train, now the Lackawanna's *New Yorker*, drifted into the big division-point station at Scranton. During the ten-minute Scranton stop, a switching crew had to hustle to uncouple part of the train, add a diner for the early risers who wanted breakfast before arriving at Hoboken, and put it back together. This night they hustled a bit too much and miscalculated a coupling. A loud crash jolted the three passengers in the C&O office car awake. A hasty inspection showed minor damage to the office car, and the highly embarrassed Lackawanna quickly pulled out one of its own private cars, the *Scranton*, which was held there for charters and special parties. A bit shaken and rumpled but unhurt, O. P., Fitzpatrick, Wyer, and Wenneman were transferred and bedded down once more.

O. P. ended his last ride aboard the Lackawanna's private car Scranton, *which also became his hearse.*
E. A. Seibel photo, H. H. Harwood, Jr., collection

In the meantime, the New York train had left, and the Scranton was put on the rear of the next best train out, the *Merchants Express*. This was a fast schedule designed for eastern Pennsylvania businesspeople and shoppers which left Scranton at 8:30 in the morning and arrived at Hoboken at 11:40. After breakfast, remembered Wenneman, "The four of us talked railroad consolidations and O. P. wanted to see maps and mileages. He looked them up in the Official [Railway] Guide. Tiring of that, he said 'We won't be in 'til noon; I think I'll take a nap.'"

As the train clicked through the New Jersey suburbs nearing Hoboken, Wenneman went back to wake his boss and found him semiconscious and breathing unevenly. Wenneman and Fitzpatrick did what they could to help him while Wyer alerted the train conductor to get a doctor at Hoboken. Dr. Benson O'Grady was waiting when the train arrived and gave O. P. a shot of adrenalin but could do nothing else. O. P. died about 12:10. Six years of intense stress and one bad jolt, and his heart had given out. He was 57, and he had lived only eleven months and ten days beyond his brother. Later, friends found some sort of solace in the thought that he had fittingly died on a railroad train, although ironically neither the car nor the railroad were his.[19]

Back in Cleveland, the headlines were large and black; the

editorials were properly reverent but restrained. For 1936 was no time for a dispassionate evaluation of the Van Sweringens' career, and Cleveland was no place for it anyway. Too many wounds were still open and too many expensive dreams were standing uncompleted and unproductive. And the end itself was too abrupt and incongruous; it was a bewildering anticlimax, and nobody quite knew what to make of it. *Cleveland Press* writer Ben Williamson perhaps best exemplified the bafflement:

> Perhaps time will give us perspective on these brothers and their business genius. Their accomplishments were magnificent in scope. They leave for Cleveland a great physical heritage in Shaker Heights and the terminal buildings.
> They leave no personal riches, no collections of art or literature, no personality by which to be remembered.
> They leave a tangled pattern of bold design. They leave Wall Street and its House of Morgan apparently ready to untangle it.
> They leave a record as the nation's greatest exponents of the holding company method of corporate expansion—on credit.
> That is the success story of Oris Paxton and Mantis James Van Sweringen.[20]

Probably there were none more mystified than the two old men who had come to the East Cleveland station the next morning, November 24th, to meet the Nickel Plate's night train from New York. The Georges, Ball and Tomlinson, stood in the suburban station pondering the writhing nest of serpents which had just landed in their laps. But there was not much they could do about that at the moment. Their immediate job was to be formally present to meet the train, which rolled in at 8:10, paused for a few minutes to exchange passengers, then chuffed on toward downtown Cleveland. As it pulled out, the usual sound of people talking and baggage cart rumblings was broken by the sharp snap of a parting airhose —the last car had been uncoupled and stood still at the platform. O. P. was back home. Fitzpatrick and Wenneman debarked, and the body was removed from the car and taken to a Euclid Avenue funeral home.

The funeral was scheduled for 2:30 P.M. Wednesday the 25th at Daisy Hill. It turned out to be a typical Cleveland late fall day, with gray skies, raw air, and intermittently swirling snow. Over 900 people showed up, so many that amplifiers had to be installed so that everyone could hear. The Reverend Charles Myers had made his second trip from Detroit to Daisy Hill in less than a year to conduct the simple service and deliver the eulogy, with many of the same faces lined up as pallbearers, including the two Bradley brothers, George Ross, George Arnold, and Horton Hampton; new ones included Darwin Barrett, William Wenneman, and the Jenkses's son Davidson Jenks. The eulogy, like M. J.'s, was short and unadorned, but Dr. Myers caught the key to O. P. and, indeed, any creative mind: "For such men, the realization of hopes never comes, for one hope succeeds another and one aspiration grows out of another."[21]

Twenty-four
Epilogue I: New Empires from Old

It was the final irony and the most bizarre: The entire Van Sweringen empire—so carefully wrought, so tightly guarded, so tenaciously preserved, and so highly personal—had fallen by accident to two virtual strangers who wanted no part of it. George Tomlinson was 67 when O. P. died, and George Ball was 74. Both were wealthy enough already, and at their ages they had no desire to expand their business domains, much less to take on the tangles of this particular one.

By the time O. P. died, George Ball was virtually Midamerica's sole owner. Tomlinson sold most of his stock to Ball in December 1935, keeping only a nominal 1.33 percent interest for himself. (The old Midland Bank, by then part of Cleveland Trust but still a Van Sweringen creditor, had bought a 5 percent interest in Midamerica from Tomlinson. In 1937, Ball also bought out this interest, giving Midland a substantial profit and himself almost a 99 percent ownership.) Ball in turn faced a potentially enormous inheritance tax problem. The market value of Midamerica's stocks had risen substantially, and as of April 1937, his theoretical capital gain amounted to $10.1 million. To get his house in order before selling, he set up the George and Frances Ball Foundation in March 1937 and gave it his Midamerica common stock.[1]

In the meantime, the old Van Sweringen managers continued running the companies, albeit with the infighting and power struggles inevitable in any management vacuum. The sedate and stately Sherwood Forest on the Terminal Tower's thirty-sixth floor became an armed camp, and the interoffice warfare continued in one form or another for several turbulent years while the ultimate fate of the Van Sweringen empire was slowly settled.

Herbert Fitzpatrick and Charles Bradley were considered the two senior survivors and immediately became rivals for O. P.'s place as head of Midamerica; lawyer John Murphy was a dark-horse contender. Bradley seemed to take it for granted that he would be chosen, but Ball picked Fitzpatrick, supported by O. P.'s old aides Darwin Barrett and William Wenneman. In another blow to Bradley and Murphy, Fitzpatrick was also named chairman of the Chesapeake & Ohio and the Pere Marquette, the key railroads in the empire. (He also kept his old titles of vice president in charge of law on the C&O, Nickel Plate, and Pere Marquette, but he relinquished his Missouri Pacific position.) Bradley was thus left where he had been as the Erie's board chairman and as overseer of the Cleveland real estate and transit operations—most of which were in bankruptcy. George Tomlinson served as nominal chairman of the Missouri Pacific, although since the system was being run by the court-appointed trustees, his position was mostly ceremonial.[2]

William Harahan continued in Bernet's old position as the senior railroad operating executive, heading the C&O, Nickel Plate, and Pere Marquette; like Bradley, Charles Denney remained mired on the Erie. Harahan's tenure was short, however; he died at age 70 in December 1937, setting off still another struggle. Again Charles Denney, backed by Bradley, seemed the obvious candidate; again he was bypassed for George Brooke, the C&O's operating vice president.

Ball wasted no time in selling Midamerica's properties, although in the Van Sweringen tradition, the job turned out to be complicated and laden with litigation. Several potential buyers showed up quickly. Fellow freebooters Frank Taplin and Frederick Prince tried to get a bid together, but Prince traveled extensively and they soon ran out of time. (Taplin's own time permanently ended in June 1938 when he succumbed to a stroke at age 62.) The most serious buyer was a

One of the many Van Sweringen legacies was a group of modern, financially strong, and competitive railroads. Here a Nickel Plate "Van Sweringen Berkshire" carries on the heritage as it bangs west through Painesville, Ohio, at 60 miles per hour in 1957.
H. H. Harwood, Jr., photo

group headed by stockbroker Robert R. Young and his partner Frank Kolbe and otherwise consisting of Woolworth store heir Allan P. Kirby and four of General Motors' topmost executives—Donaldson Brown, chairman of GM's Finance Committee; John T. Smith, GM vice president and general counsel; GM president Alfred P. Sloan, Jr.; and director Pierre S. DuPont. Kirby was a staunch friend and financial backer of Young; Brown and Smith were the most active of the GM group. In March the Young-Kolbe-GM group offered $5.6 million for 75 percent of Midamerica's Alleghany stock. (Midamerica was to keep most of the various Cleveland real estate companies and dispose of the Cleveland Railway stock itself.)

The planned sale had disturbing implications for the railroad industry and raised some broader questions about business ethics. General Motors was an extremely large railroad freight customer, and it was not clear whether GM would divert as much traffic as it could to the old Van Sweringen railroads at the expense of other lines. Furthermore, since the GM insiders were investing as individuals and not for their company's account, they stood to profit personally for any such diversions. In addition, at this time GM was just embarking on a large-scale program to enter the new diesel-locomotive market and was fighting the inertia of traditional steam-minded railroad managements. The Van Sweringen lines had the potential to provide a large captive market for GM diesels and give it a decisive leverage with the rest of the industry.

The GM executives in the Young buying group prudently took the precaution of asking Senator Wheeler's opinion. The response was violently negative, and they quickly backed away, leaving Young, Kolbe, and Kirby on their own. Van Sweringen stalwarts Fitzpatrick and Bradley also fought the sale, and the Cleveland banks complicated matters further by maintaining that O. P.'s option to buy control of Midamerica remained a part of his estate and should be used to help satisfy the Van Sweringen debts.[3]

The subsequent story is predictably tortuous and has been well told elsewhere. In brief, the Young group took control of Alleghany on May 5, 1937, but it soon turned out that control of the key railroad, the Chesapeake & Ohio, was another matter. An intense struggle ensued between Young and the Morgan and Guaranty Trust banks, which were supported by Van Sweringen loyalists Fitzpatrick, Barrett, and Wenneman; for a time, Bradley and John Murphy backed the Young-Kolbe-Kirby group. Poor old George Ball also later found himself caught in the dogfight and by then doubtless regretted ever having met O. P. Van Sweringen. (He survived the ordeal, though, and lived to almost 93.)

In April 1942, Young (by now without Kolbe, but with Allan Kirby as a silent partner) finally wore down the opposition and won undisputed control of the C&O—and along with it the Nickel Plate and the Pere Marquette. He was also carrying on O. P.'s old crusade to maintain a controlling equity in the Missouri Pacific's unending reorganization battle. As part of the Alleghany pot, Young also inherited the Pittston Company, which was finally shed in 1954. (Pittston continued on as a Virginia-based conglomerate in 2001, having gradually shed all its original businesses.)[4]

The Van Sweringens' new heir was the antithesis of everything Van Sweringen. A short, slight, feisty Texan, Robert R. Young was variously described as brilliant, contentious, litigious, egotistical, messianic, and publicity-hungry. He was a bit of all of those—certainly one of the most colorful and controversial characters to come onto the twentieth-century railroad scene. And where the stolid O. P. was the image of quiet deliberation and serene self-assurance, Young was emotionally volatile; many who dealt with him (including some of his earlier GM backers) considered him unreliable, if not unstable. Certainly he was not to be controlled by anyone. But he also had some progressive ideas and became a master at promoting them.

There were some similarities, too. Like the Van Sweringens, Young was an outsider to the railroad business and got into it only because an interesting opportunity presented itself. And his restless ambition was not essentially different from O. P.'s; neither remained static for long and both constantly moved on to larger conquests. There was also a far more hidden kinship: despite their wildly differing personalities, O. P. Van Sweringen and Robert R. Young were both basically lonely men.

Young's principal skills had been in finance and stock speculation. After a ragged start, he went to work for General Motors in 1922 at age 25 and five years later was an assistant treasurer and a protégé of GM's finance committee chairman, John J. Raskob. In 1929, he joined Raskob in a short-lived private investment company, but unlike his mentor, he foresaw trouble coming, sold short, and made himself a fortune right before the crash. Young and another GM alumnus, Frank Kolbe, then moved on to become independent stockbrokers, working with a small and select group of clients that included some of their old General Motors associates. Beginning in 1932, he had kept his shrewd eyes on Alleghany and bought large blocks of its preferred stock for his firm and his GM friends. He even attempted to get a seat on Alleghany's board, but was rebuffed by Guaranty Trust, which at that time really held the company's reins. In 1935, he met the quiet, retiring, but greatly wealthy Allan Kirby. The two personality opposites meshed well together, and Kirby remained a fiercely loyal partner and financial backer for the rest of Young's life.[5]

Young's experiences after his original Alleghany purchase in 1937 created strong mutual animosities between him and the New York banking establishment; almost needless to say, most of the railroad industry also rejected him as an inexperienced outsider and unwelcome irritant. In return, he made himself into a self-proclaimed reformer of both Wall Street and the "ossified" railroads which, he proclaimed, were Wall Street's servants. His mastery of aggressive advertising and public relations took the C&O, the railroad business, and the country on a wild ride which had both positive and negative effects.

After the end of World War II, Young began moving to consummate the frustrated Van Sweringen dream of merging their eastern railroads into one unit. By this time, it could only be a partial Van Sweringen system, since the C&O had allowed the Erie to go into bankruptcy in 1938. But beginning in 1945, he engineered plans to merge both the Pere Marquette and the Nickel Plate into the C&O.

The Pere Marquette merger was accomplished in 1947, but the Nickel Plate union ran into trouble when a group of preferred stockholders threatened a fight over the terms of the merger. It was the type of problem common in merger negotiations and a relatively minor one at that, but Young elected to drop the entire proposal. In November 1947, the C&O divested itself of its Nickel Plate stock by distributing it to C&O stockholders, thus casting off the original root of the Vans' railroad empire. During 1946 and 1947, Alleghany and the C&O also sold their Wheeling & Lake Erie stock to the Nickel Plate, which leased that line in 1949 and wiped out its identity. So in the end, the old Van Sweringen system split apart, with an independent Nickel Plate–Wheeling & Lake Erie combination going one way and a slightly mismatched Chesapeake & Ohio–Pere Marquette combination going another.[6]

Young never explained why he gave up the Nickel Plate without his usual fight, but the most likely probability is that he had already decided to move in a new direction. By this time, Young had convinced himself that his ideas could breathe new life into what he viewed (partly correctly) as a moribund industry. The prosperous C&O had provided generously for his various crusades and railroad experiments, including innovations in passenger service, advanced technical research (headed by an aeronautical engineer), and sophisticated financial management. But its territory and the nature of its business hardly contained his ambitions. In an ironic reversal of old A. H. Smith's aspirations, he determined to go after the New York Central—which was still vast and powerful but now suffering from the postwar sickliness that was affecting all eastern railroads. In late 1946, Alleghany began secretively buying New York Central stock and by early 1947 was publicly expanding its interest. Before long, Young could announce that the C&O effectively was the Central's largest single stockholder.

Young's initial strategy was to have the C&O take control of the Central and unify their management short of a merger. As expected, his efforts turned into a replay of his struggle with the New York banking establishment over control of the C&O, only this time the battle was more brutal. The first round was fought in 1947 and 1948, and since he was attempting to unite the C&O and the Central, it inevitably hinged on the Interstate Commerce Commission's judgment. The campaign was conducted as much in the newspapers as it was in the ICC's hearing room, but the Central's managers and financial backers managed to defeat him. The second time around, he decided to launch a direct frontal attack with a proxy fight.

Before doing so, he took a bold risk and sold all of Alleghany's C&O interest, hoping to avoid any regulatory problems by leaving himself and Alleghany as free agents with no other railroad attachments. Alleghany's C&O holdings went to his ally and friend, the maverick Cleveland financier Cyrus Eaton, in January 1954, and the last bond between Alleghany and the Van Sweringens' eastern railroad system was broken. Young's gamble succeeded; he captured the Central in 1955 after a bitter, name-calling proxy battle that got national headlines. Like O. P. Van Sweringen's miraculous recovery with Midamerica in 1935, it was his greatest triumph—which then turned equally tragic. On January 25, 1958, he ended his own life with a shotgun blast.[7]

While Young progressively cast off the Vans' eastern railroad empire, he did his best to hang on to the western one. Thanks largely to his doggedness in fighting for Alleghany's equity in the Missouri Pacific, that railroad's reorganization consumed twenty-three years—the longest on record for any major railroad. When it finally emerged from bankruptcy in 1956, Young had won at least a partial victory by creating a peculiar new class of stock which gave Alleghany a vague future opportunity to regain control if the railroad prospered sufficiently. But in 1974, with Young and Allan Kirby both gone, this awkward structure was eliminated; Alleghany received a settlement of cash and stock and relinquished any claims of control—finally ending the Van Sweringens' misbegotten Missouri Pacific venture after forty-five years.[8]

The Missouri Pacific itself went on to fulfill the brothers' predictions of growth and prosperity, but much later than they had ever imagined. Another too-late justification of their vision came in 1976, when the Missouri Pacific finally absorbed the Chicago & Eastern Illinois, giving it the direct line to Chicago that the Vans had intended in 1929. At the end of 1982, the MoPac system succumbed to the new era of megamergers and was absorbed by the Union Pacific.

The other Van Sweringen railroads underwent a diaspora, scattering and eventually recombining into similar mega-systems. The first to leave the fold—involuntarily—was the Erie. Having barely survived the worst of the depression, it was hit hard by the 1937 recession and ran out of cash. Denney desperately tried to get a $6 million RFC loan, but the agency insisted that the parent C&O back the loan. Fitzpatrick and the C&O's board refused (at this time Young had not yet established himself on the C&O). RFC chairman Jesse Jones had some heated words for the C&O, but nobody backed down, and in January 1938 the Erie went into one more bankruptcy. It emerged again in 1941 divorced from any affiliation with the C&O or Alleghany, although it and its successor company remained in the Van Sweringens' Midland Building until the end of their corporate lives. Afterward, the Erie lived modestly until hard times returned and it merged with the also-fallen Lackawanna in 1960. Bankruptcy came again in 1972, the Erie Lackawanna was folded into the government-backed Conrail system in 1976, and subsequently much of the original Erie system was either downgraded to secondary status or abandoned entirely.[9]

The Nickel Plate's fate was happier. With or without Robert R. Young, Bernet's fast, lean railroad regularly embarrassed the New York Central as Nickel Plate Berkshires banged across the flatlands at 70 miles per hour, easily outrunning their nearby competition. But as a new wave of mergers developed in the 1960s, it found a large, stable home for itself with the Norfolk & Western (N&W). In a merger that would have brought joy to General Atterbury, the Pennsylvania-dominated N&W folded in the Nickel Plate, the Wabash, and Taplin's old Pittsburgh & West Virginia in October 1964. Afterward, the historic name was scratched off the frosted glass in the Terminal Tower office doors, replaced by an alien "Norfolk & Western." That too soon disappeared as offices were moved south to the N&W's traditional headquarters in Roanoke, Virginia. (The N&W, always the C&O's chief competitor, lost its Pennsylvania influence four years later and in 1982 was merged into the Norfolk Southern Corporation. In 2001, Norfolk Southern and the C&O's successor, CSX Transportation, were still competitors, the only two large railroad systems left east of the Mississippi.)

More prosperous than ever ("a cross between a bank and a country club," said one envious Erie employee), the C&O not only remained in Cleveland but took over virtually all of the old Van Sweringen space in the Terminal Tower's upper floors, including the executive offices on the thirty-fifth and thirty-sixth floors and the Vans' private dining and living suite on the twelfth floor. During Robert R. Young's reign, it was also his nominal headquarters, although Young was not entranced by dreary Cleveland. The Texas populist based himself in New York's Chrysler Building, with a pied-à-terre in the Waldorf Towers and mansions in Palm Beach and Newport. He did admire the Vans' Terminal Tower amenities, however, and imported the flamboyant interior designer Dorothy Draper to redecorate the private dining and living suite, which he christened the Greenbrier Suite after the C&O's grand resort hotel at White Sulphur Springs. (Young was far more entranced by the Greenbrier itself, which he used regularly and which Dorothy Draper also overhauled.)

Other railroaders were always puzzled by a company with headquarters that were almost 100 miles from its nearest tracks, but the elegant old Van Sweringen facilities and the amenities of Shaker Heights had a strong hold on C&O's officialdom. And when Cyrus Eaton took control in 1954, he made certain that everyone stayed put. (Under Eaton's regime, the Greenbrier Suite sometimes played host to Russian dignitaries as part of the dedicated capitalist's own personal campaign to thaw the Cold War.) Gradually, though, that tradition died, too. In 1963, the Chesapeake & Ohio bought control of the Baltimore & Ohio; afterward, the two companies gradually consolidated their headquarters functions and moved most to Baltimore. But the executive offices steadfastly remained in the Terminal Tower until an even larger merger with the Seaboard System Railroad, an agglomeration of southeastern lines, created CSX Transportation in 1986 with its headquarters in Jacksonville, Florida. (Through all this, the C&O corporate name remained intact until it legally disappeared September 2, 1987.) Perhaps appropriately, the Van Sweringen executive suites on the thirty-fifth and thirty-sixth floors were among the last active offices; Sherwood Forest was finally vacated in 1986. When the last employees packed up and left, the Van Sweringen era had truly ended.[10]

Beyond Alleghany and the railroads, most of the old Van Sweringen Cleveland properties were already in bankruptcy when O. P. died and were enmeshed in the tangle of Cleveland bank liquidations and problems with mortgage and tax arrears. They were subsequently scattered and gradually untangled, and most recovered as strong entities of their own. The leisurely course of history finally validated the brothers' visionary planning.

Metropolitan Utilities disappeared quickly. By the time of O. P.'s death, the Cleveland Railway's original franchise within the city had expired and the city government was becoming increasingly uncomfortable with the Van Sweringen control agreement. There had been strong political undercurrents in Cleveland for public ownership since the Tom Johnson days, and that sentiment was now building. In November 1935, Mayor Harold Burton appointed Edward Schweid as city traction commissioner and charged him with investigating the transit company's financial situation. Schweid reported that it was not earning the required 6 percent return, at which point Burton threatened a city takeover if it were not turned back to the stockholders. The dividend was cut to $1\frac{1}{2}$ percent at the end of 1936 and suspended after April 1937.

By this time, O. P. was gone and Ball was anxious to throw back this political hot potato. Charles Bradley, who was personally under some attack for his chairman's salary, resigned in May 1937, and on October 8th the Metropolitan Utilities representatives all left the board, ending the old Van Sweringen control. After over six years in a sort of political purgatory, and operating without a city franchise, the Cleveland Railway finally was bought by the city in April 1942, becoming the Cleveland Transit System.[11]

The Shaker Heights rapid transit line followed a somewhat similar path. To protect their loan collateral, the consortium of Cleveland banks (two of them defunct by that point) took the Cleveland Interurban Railroad away from Metropolitan Utilities in 1935. The banks became anxious to liquidate the line but were also sensitive to its sacred status in Shaker Heights (where some of the bank administrators lived). The suburb's government was determined to preserve the community's unique lifeline, and after difficult negotiations, the banks capitulated and sold the operation to the City of Shaker Heights in 1944 for its scrap value, $1.3 million. Meticulously maintained, the line remained the community's pride and joy until it became part of the Greater Cleveland Regional Transit Authority in 1975. Afterward it was rebuilt, reequipped, and integrated with the area's bus and other rapid transit lines—another long-deferred Van Sweringen dream.[12]

In the meantime, the stillborn Van Sweringen east-west rapid transit route was finally completed. After a quarter-century of plans, talk, and false starts, the Cleveland Transit System opened the East Side line to Windermere in East Cleveland in March 1955, making extensive use of the grading and structures built by the Vans (and inherited by the Nickel Plate). At the same time, the Union Terminal's never-opened west traction concourse, which had been boarded off for twenty-five years, was rehabilitated and opened. The West Side extension opened five months later, again taking advantage of Van Sweringen planning and construction that dated as far back as 1916—although the western portion of its route was changed to follow the former Lake Shore & Michigan Southern main line rather than the Nickel Plate to Lakewood. It was subsequently extended in stages to the airport.[13]

But as the Union Terminal's rapid transit facilities were at last coming to life, the railroad station itself was dying. Like its magnificent contemporaries in Cincinnati and Buffalo, Cleveland Union Terminal had the misfortune of being born too late. By the time its doors opened, rail passenger patronage had peaked and was beginning to decline. The depression accelerated the trend, and except for a brief Indian summer in World War II, train riders steadily melted away. Thanks to its strategic location at the nexus of several New York Central main lines and the addition of the Baltimore & Ohio and the Erie as tenants, the Terminal continued to be relatively busy through the 1950s, but afterward its trains disappeared quickly. When the government-sponsored Amtrak was created in 1971, it ended all remaining intercity passenger service through Cleveland. Amtrak later returned to the Terminal briefly but then rerouted its few trains over the original lakefront line, served by an appropriately modest new station near the site of the long-deceased Union Depot.

Incongruously, the last train operation from the grandiose station was a weekday Erie Lackawanna commuter run to Youngstown, which finally expired in 1977. After years in a humiliating limbo (which included use for indoor tennis courts and an Elvis Presley memorial celebration), the Union Terminal was reborn as a creatively designed multilevel shopping gallery in the new Tower City complex. Symbolic of what has happened to intercity travel, long-distance passengers still use the Union Terminal—but only to reach the airport on the rapid transit.

Although also born at the wrong time, the large Higbee Company department store had a happier fate, thanks to its unmatched location and Van Sweringen–designed facilities. Thwarted elsewhere in the Vans' old corporate world, Charles Bradley and John Murphy bought the Higbee stock from the George and Frances Ball Foundation in May 1937, and after a tangle with Robert R. Young over ownership, took it out of bankruptcy and made it a huge success. After Bradley's death in 1943, Murphy headed the store and bought the building from Metropolitan Life in 1949. He became honorary chairman in 1968 and died the following year at 82.[14]

The brothers' personal crown jewel, Daisy Hill, had a mixed but mostly appropriate afterlife. As with the Vans' suburban properties, the legal situation took some time to unravel. The property itself had been put in the names of the Jenks family, but there were loans and mortgages held by Union Trust and The Society for Savings and, of course, unpaid property taxes. Union Trust's liquidator finally arranged for New York's Parke-Bernet Galleries to auction the mansion's furnishings, art, and artifacts in late October 1938.

The four-day event fetched $89,287 for items which, some claimed, originally had been bought for about $1 million. The estate property was subdivided and developed as a highly exclusive private enclave; eventually about sixty homes occupied the 477 acres. As for Roundwood Manor itself, not even Cleveland's most wealthy was willing or able to cope with its fifty-four rooms. The huge house lay vacant until 1946, when it was bought by restaurant owner Gordon Stouffer and its size trimmed to thirty rooms—the form it retained at the turn of the twenty-first century.[15]

For the most part, the assets of the various Van Sweringen real estate companies grew steadily in value—especially the Union Terminal group and Shaker Heights—although in some cases, working out the maze of debts and tax arrears slogged on into the late 1950s. The old Shaker Country Estates tracts proved the most difficult problem, and in some areas the original Van Sweringen deed restrictions were eased to encourage development. (The sumptuous Van Sweringen boulevards with their generous provision for rapid transit and express roadways probably never will be completed as planned.) The Van Sweringen Company itself folded in February 1959.

The Vaness Company, the Vans' onetime summit holding company and "personal basket," became mostly a shell company when Midamerica took over its holdings in 1935, but it remained as the liquidating agent for the brothers' bank creditors. The old debts were finally resolved by 1951, and in October of that year it too dissolved.[16]

Inevitably the Van Sweringen inner circle faded slowly away. Plagued with health problems, both Darwin Barrett and Charles Bradley died in 1943, Barrett at 51 and Bradley at 58. Barrett was made a C&O vice president in 1938 and held the title until he died, but his tuberculosis forced him to move to Colorado for the last year of his life. A more robust Joseph Nutt survived to 74, succumbing in December 1945 and bitter to the end. Ben Jenks followed in 1951 at age 81, after which his wife Daisy moved to Arizona to be near her two children. Philip Small, the Vans' favorite architect, lost everything when the brothers' work stopped and left Cleveland for California—but later returned, successfully resumed practice, and finally died there in 1963 at 73. George Tomlinson died January 25, 1942, the day before his 73rd birthday, but, as already noted, George Ball lived on to October 22, 1955, two weeks short of his 93rd. Lawyer Herbert Fitzpatrick resigned his C&O chairmanship in 1940 and retired to his beloved Huntington. But he remained a company director—as well as a living legend in that part of West Virginia—until his death at

90 in 1962. Another strong survivor, Daisy Jenks, died in Arizona in March 1967. She was 86.[17]

By the early 1970s, virtually all the close friends and associates were gone, and the Van Sweringen companies either had disappeared or had shed all the brothers' original businesses and moved in other directions. But the buildings, the communities, and the railroads were all intact and mostly strong and thriving—largely thanks to the money and management skills which either built them up or created them in the first place. In addition, a certain spectral aura remained in Cleveland which was difficult to define but, if one were sensitive, gave the strong sense that the brothers themselves were still very much present.

Twenty-five
Epilogue II: The Ghosts

Cleveland, 1951:

The Van Sweringens had been gone only fifteen years, but somehow it seemed much longer. Even at this date, O. P. and M. J. Van Sweringen were oddly disembodied beings—names without people attached. They had no face or form. There was no clear picture of them as personalities, no record of anything memorable they said, little sense even of what they looked like. Of course, most Clevelanders recognized the names, some not so fondly—and most knew that they built the Terminal Tower, the Union Terminal, and Shaker Heights and its rapid transit line. But if the name was in people's minds, it was nowhere visible. "They were the builders of modern Cleveland," said local writer George Condon, but there was no Van Sweringen Building, Boulevard, Park, Library, School, Hall, Memorial, Foundation, or anything else. Yes, there were some stories, but they also had a detached, mythical aura about them. And yes, some of their old associates were still around, but they preferred to talk about other things. The Van Sweringen brothers had, in brief, already entered a sort of twilight world and were fading quickly even from memory.

On the other hand, a sense of their presence was inescapable. It was not just the obviously solid structures such as the Terminal Tower and other Terminal Group buildings, the revered and well-patronized Shaker rapid, and the perennially distinguished Shaker Heights. There was another Van Sweringen presence that was just as visible but not so noticeable to most people: the ghosts of their unfulfilled visions. To those who recognized them, these had the same ethereal aura as the brothers' own images.

Green Road, near the eastern border of the City of Shaker Heights, marked the entryway to an eerie, surreal landscape. To its west were the well-settled older sections of Shaker Heights; to the east was to have been the Van Sweringens' ne plus ultra, the six rolling miles of onetime farmlands which were to be the Shaker Country Estates, linked to Shaker Heights and Cleveland by a network of boulevards and rapid transit lines. All the trappings of that super-community were there: the vastly broad boulevards, the traffic circles, the rapid transit rights-of-way, the heavy concrete overpasses, even the fireplugs neatly spaced every few hundred feet. But there was no life. The bridges spanned nothing; weeds grew where there were to be express roadways and rapid transit tracks. At Brainard Road were the beginnings of a boulevard and rapid transit grading to Chagrin Falls; at Lander Road and Gates Mills Boulevard was the beginning of a highway–rapid transit underpass that would never be completed. Residential streets curved off the boulevards and abruptly ended in clumps of bushes.

This was the desolate scene along outer Shaker Boulevard at Richmond Road in 1951. The Richmond Road overpass was to have spanned a pair of express roadways and two rapid transit tracks—with room for two more. Surrounding were to have been the large tracts and mansions of the Shaker Country Estates.
H. H. Harwood, Jr., photo

At the far eastern end of the spectral Shaker Country Estates was Daisy Hill, or what remained of it. The wooded 477-acre estate still kept some of the same feeling that it had when it was a single estate, although it was now dotted with discreetly designed and unobtrusively located homes; some of the old bridle paths and estate driveways were now private roads. Roundwood Manor, the Van Sweringen mansion, still stood, but only about half as grand, shorn of part of its wings and reduced from fifty-four rooms to about thirty. Nearby, the large old Jenks house, originally adapted from two original farmhouses, looked much as it did when the brothers paid their regular visits.[1]

Ghosts of the mechanical kind inhabited Shaker Heights. The community itself—which had by 1951 been a full-fledged city for twenty years—kept to all the original Van Sweringen standards and was very alive and healthy in its traditionally understated way. But while the bustling rapid transit line was fully as strong as the city which now owned it, its equipment and facilities spoke of unfulfilled plans. Although many of its cars were new or secondhand since the Van Sweringen era, the same modified 1914 city streetcars regularly whined back and forth—intended as temporary expediencies when the line opened in 1920, to be replaced by custom-built rapid transit cars once the east-west and the Shaker lines were integrated. Similarly, the simple little wood shelters and cinder platforms awaited more elaborate masonry stations and platforms which never appeared.

Less visible, except to perceptive railroad passengers, was the almost-complete East Side rapid transit line which hugged the south side of the joint Nickel Plate–Cleveland Union Terminal railroad route to the East Cleveland station. Grading, heavy bridges, and viaducts were all in place; heavy steel towers for the overhead wires marched regularly alongside the Nickel Plate tracks. At major cross streets such as Mayfield Road, Euclid Avenue, and Superior Avenue, empty shells of stations looked out at the streets, while inside, stairways led up to nonexistent platforms and gaped vacantly at the sky. By 1951, the single track which had been laid in 1930 was gone, replaced by profuse weeds.

At East 55th Street, where the Shaker Heights rapid was to join both the East Side line and the interurban to Akron, the complex separated junction with its tunnel underpasses stood mostly completed, and the Shaker cars dove through tunnels that seemed to have no purpose. Following the double-track Shaker line from here into the Union Terminal, observant riders could see clear evidence of what was to have been a

Silent and useless for over twenty years, the nearly complete Van Sweringen East Side rapid transit line patiently awaits a few finishing touches. Hidden in the underbrush behind the gaunt catenary-support tower are platform stairways for the intended Cedar Glen station. Soon after this 1951 photo, the savior finally arrived.
H. H. Harwood, Jr., photo

four-track rapid transit right-of-way, including an elaborate four-track bridge over the Nickel Plate–Union Terminal tracks near East 37th Street. (By then, the Erie was using part of the vacant extra track space for its single-track connection to the Terminal.)

The Union Terminal itself was haunted everywhere. At the eastern end was an elaborate separated rapid transit entrance for four tracks which included a separated subway junction and subway portals aimed to run under Huron Road to East 9th Street. The Shaker rapid terminal was a busy lighted pair of platforms with darkness on each side of it. To its east were stairways to what was to be the terminal area for the interurbans; to its west were two high-level platforms and stairways for the east-west rapid transit line and its planned branches. All were deserted.

Upstairs the two large traction concourses flanking the main railroad concourse were a strange mixture of semi-life and no life. Because of the Shaker line's entrance and several stores, the east concourse was partly viable, but numerous bronze-trimmed stairway entrances were closed or blocked off. Aside from an exit from the Shaker terminal, the west traction concourse was blocked off with wooden barriers, and the elaborate storefronts were either vacant or used by Cleveland Union Terminals Company engineering offices. A bizarre sight in the west concourse was a synchronized station clock in the dark behind the wooden barrier, faithfully but pointlessly keeping exact time for nonexistent rapid transit riders. From both the east and west traction concourses, passageways led toward the never-built underground Public Square streetcar terminal.

At the Terminal's west end, the massively heavy Cuyahoga viaduct curved over the river valley. It carried two electrified railroad tracks, but there was a wide, vacant strip on its north side for two additional rapid transit tracks. Grading and other provision for the West Side rapid line extended along the Nickel Plate right-of-way as far as West 110th Street.

A walk around the outside of the Union Terminal revealed many more "might-have-beens." At the Terminal's rear was a graded ramp to the Cuyahoga valley level, intended as the Pennsylvania Railroad's future access—in case it ever relented. It never did, of course. Also at the back side of the Terminal were footings for the planned future commercial buildings, and up at the street level behind the Terminal Tower were several large vacant areas meant for buildings. The eastern face of the Guildhall Building (originally the Builders Exchange) and the western wing of the Terminal Tower were unadorned, virtually blank brick walls—which were clearly temporary pending the never-built office buildings which would adjoin them.

Upstairs in the Terminal Tower, the Van Sweringen spirits had more solid form. The building itself still held the title of tallest west of Manhattan and seemed to be visible from everywhere in the city. The brothers' own private executive offices and boardroom on the thirty-fifth and thirty-sixth "conning tower" floors (and their private elevator) were now the Chesapeake & Ohio's executive suite and kept much of the same expensively paneled decor—although with efforts to brighten the more somber Van Sweringen tones. And downstairs, the Vans' private dining and living suite on the Terminal Tower's twelfth floor was still very much alive but just as anonymous from the outside. Also now occupied by the C&O and named the Greenbrier Suite, it continued its original function as a facility for company executives and guests, and, as in Van Sweringen days, on each workday the top company officers trooped in for the president's staff luncheons. During Robert R. Young's regime, interior designer Dorothy Draper had done her best to brighten the place with bold colors and new fixtures, but the Van Sweringens' darker and perhaps stuffier Old English atmosphere was difficult to dislodge and showed through everywhere.

The Van Sweringen spirit could be spotted elsewhere, if

one knew what they were looking at—usually in Cleveland's more refined spots. For example, there was the rich Old English paneling and aristocratic ambience of the Oak Room restaurant in the Union Terminal—or the early American and English furnishings and decor of The Country Club in Pepper Pike, one of the few physical expressions of the Country Estates dream. Or that grand onetime lobby of the Midland Bank in the Midland Building, which in 1951 had been given a second life by the Central National Bank.

And then there were their graves in Lake View Cemetery on Cleveland's East Side. Appropriately, the wooded hillside of Lake View slopes down to a multi-track railroad right-of-way, which in 1951 carried the tracks of the New York Central, the Cleveland Union Terminals Company, and the Nickel Plate—plus the uncompleted East Side rapid transit. There all together below them were the symbols of their beginnings, their apogee, and their final failure.

But there was something else to ponder there too: the final expression of the Van Sweringen enigma. For Lake View is the ultimate home of Cleveland's rich and powerful—among them John D. Rockefeller, James A. Garfield, John Hay, Mark Hanna, and Newton D. Baker—with monuments and other memorials to match. Not so for the Van Sweringens. They lie together in what is to all appearances a single grave, which is light years in spirit from such grandiose gestures as the Terminal Tower, the Country Estates, or Daisy Hill—not to mention that 30,000-mile railroad system stretching from the Atlantic to Salt Lake City. For O. P. and M. J. there is only a simple slab, lying flat and almost flush with the ground, practically invisible, with the two names, their dates, and one other word: "Brothers." Nothing more.

Cleveland Union Terminal nocturne.
Richard J. Cook photo,
Allen County Historical Society collection

Notes

Introduction

1. Harlan Hatcher quote from his *The Western Reserve: The New Connecticut in Ohio* (New York: Bobbs-Merrill, 1949), 318.

2. George E. Condon, *Cleveland: The Best Kept Secret* (Garden City, N.Y.: Doubleday, 1967), 183.

1. Oasis in a Gritty City

1. Raymond F. Blosser, "Untitled Biography of the Van Sweringens of Cleveland," second-draft typescript with corrections and annotations by William H. Wenneman, William Wyer, the author, and others, 1946, located at Western Reserve Historical Society, Cleveland, Ohio, 12–13. Hereafter referred to as "Blosser ms."; handwritten comments by William H. Wenneman are so noted. Also, Joseph Doherty, "Smooth Is the Road" *Tracks,* May 1956, 55. *Tracks* was the employee magazine of the Chesapeake & Ohio Railway; Doherty's piece is a serialized history of the C&O. Doherty worked for the Van Sweringens as their public relations representative during the 1920s and 1930s; he later worked for the C&O.

2. Taylor Hampton, "Cleveland's Fabulous Vans: Boyhood of Two Shy Brothers," *Cleveland News,* August 2, 1955; Ian Haberman, *The Van Sweringens of Cleveland* (Cleveland, Ohio: Western Reserve Historical Society, 1979), 6; Blosser ms., 24.

3. Blosser ms., 11–12; telephone interview with J. Paxton Van Sweringen, July 19, 2001; Hampton, "Cleveland's Fabulous Vans: Boyhood of Two Shy Brothers."

4. Joseph F. Doherty, "Smooth Is the Road," *Tracks,* November 1955, 54.

5. Ibid., 47; Doherty, "Smooth Is the Road," *Tracks,* July 1956, 55–56; Blosser ms., 52–53; Virginia Taylor Hampton, "The Fabulous Van Sweringens: Empire Building," typescript ms., 1965, Western Reserve Historical Society, Cleveland, Ohio, 183.

6. Taylor Hampton, "Cleveland's Fabulous Vans: Lured by Shaker's Farms," *Cleveland News,* August 3, 1955, 8; Blosser ms., 4.

7. See Doherty, "Smooth Is the Road," *Tracks,* February–March 1956, 52; and August 1956, 52–54.

8. Doherty, "Smooth Is the Road," *Tracks,* December 1955, 48; William Ganson Rose, *Cleveland: The Making of a City* (Cleveland, Ohio: World Publishing Co., 1950), 647–649.

9. Blosser ms., 24.

10. See Rose, *Cleveland: The Making of a City,* 1069; James A. Toman, *The Shaker Heights Rapid Transit* (Glendale, Calif.: Interurban Press, 1990), 11; Eric Johannessen, *Cleveland Architecture, 1876–1976* (Cleveland, Ohio: Western Reserve Historical Society, 1979), 101.

11. Quoted by Doherty in "Smooth Is the Road," *Tracks,* December 1955, 49. See also *System* magazine, December 1919, 1090.

12. See Wallace Cathcart, "Shaker Colony," in *Shaker Heights Then and Now,* edited by Arthur H. Beduhn (Shaker Heights, Ohio: Shaker Heights Board of Education, 1938), 2–20.

13. Rose, *Cleveland: The Making of a City,* 568, 733.

14. Haberman, *The Van Sweringens of Cleveland,* 9; Blosser ms., 26, 30.

2. The Ideal Suburb

1. U.S. Congress, Senate Committee on Interstate Commerce, *The Van Sweringen Corporate System: A Study in Holding Company Financing,* 77th Congress, 1st Session, Report No. 714 (Washington, D.C.: Government Printing Office, 1941), 8. (This four-volume report, with transcriptions of numerous original documents, was the product of an investigation by a Senate committee headed by Senator Burton K. Wheeler of Montana which began in 1936. It is hereafter referred to here as the Wheeler Report.) Also, Blosser ms., 31.

2. Doherty, "Smooth Is the Road," *Tracks,* December 1955, 49.

3. Blosser ms., 40; James A. Toman, *The Shaker Heights Rapid Transit* (Glendale, Calif.: Interurban Press, 1990), 11; James A. Toman and Blaine S. Hays, *Horse Trails to Regional Rails: The Story of Public Transit in Greater Cleveland* (Kent, Ohio: Kent State University Press, 1996), 45, 64; O. P. Van Sweringen testimony before the Interstate Commerce Commission in the Cleveland Passenger Terminal Case (1920); reproduced in Harry Christiansen, *Northern Ohio's Interurbans and Rapid Transit Railways* (Cleveland, Ohio: Transit Data, 1965), 105.

4. Wheeler Report, 8; Taylor Hampton, "Cleveland's Fabulous Vans: Lured by Shaker's Farms," *Cleveland News,* August 3, 1955, 8.

5. For an account of Johnson and his reign, see George E. Condon, *Cleveland: The Best Kept Secret* (Garden City, N.Y.: Doubleday, 1967), 152–176.

6. Quoted by Doherty, "Smooth Is the Road," *Tracks,* December 1955, 51.

7. Blosser ms., 35–36.

8. Ibid., 151.

9. For a history of the Roland Park development, see James F. Waesche, *Crowning the Gravelly Hill: A History of the Roland Park-Guilford-Homeland District* (Baltimore, Md.: Maclay Associates, 1987). For details on the Roland Park streetcar operation, see Michael Farrell, *The History of Baltimore Streetcars* (Sykesville, Md.: Greenberg Publishing Co., 1992), 69, 237–239.

10. Ian Haberman, *The Van Sweringens of Cleveland* (Cleveland, Ohio: Western Reserve Historical Society, 1979), 12; F. A. Pease Engineering Co., map: "Shaker Heights Parkway Frontages and Subdivision of South Side, Cleveland Heights Village, July 1909," *Cleveland Press,* November 25, 1936.

11. David G. Molyneaux and Sue Sackman, eds., *75 Years: An Infor-*

mal History of Shaker Heights (Shaker Heights, Ohio: Shaker Heights Public Library, 1987), 24–25.

12. Joseph G. Blake, "The Van Sweringen Developments in Cleveland" (Senior thesis, University of Notre Dame, 1968), 28–29. In collection of Western Reserve Historical Society, Cleveland, Ohio.

13. O. P. Van Sweringen testimony to Interstate Commerce Commission, Cleveland Passenger Terminal Case (1920), in *Northern Ohio's Interurbans and Rapid Transit Railways,* 105.

14. Brian J. Cudahy, *Cash, Tokens and Transfers: A History of Mass Transit in North America* (New York: Fordham University Press, 1990), 84, 117; Toman and Hays, *Horse Trails to Regional Rails,* 77–78. Toman and Hays also cover Cleveland's seemingly constant later subway plans, none of which materialized.

15. Jim Toman and Dan Cook, *Terminal Tower Complex, 1930–1980* (Cleveland, Ohio: Cleveland Landmarks Press, 1980), 63; William Ganson Rose, *Cleveland: The Making of a City* (Cleveland, Ohio: World Publishing Co., 1950), 712.

16. Wheeler Report, 9.

17. *Electric Railway Journal,* November 4, 1911, 1006.

18. *Sandusky* [Ohio] *Register,* March 31, 1911. See also *Electric Railway Journal,* April 8, 1911.

19. Toman, *The Shaker Heights Rapid Transit,* 12.

20. Ibid., 17; Wheeler Report, 11.

21. Louise D. Jenks, *O. P. and M. J.,* privately printed, probably Cleveland, Ohio, ca. 1940. Copies are in the collections of the Cleveland Public Library and the Western Reserve Historical Society.

3. Mr. Smith Sells a Farm

1. Blosser ms., 43–44.

2. S. O. M. was the road's formal name—short for Solon, Orange, and Mayfield, three townships through which it passed.

3. Blosser ms., 49, based on interview with Mrs. Chapman.

4. Edward Hungerford, *Men and Iron: A History of the New York Central* (New York: Thomas Y. Crowell Co., 1938), 409; *Biographical Directory of Railway Officials in America: 1922 Edition* (New York: Simmons Boardman Publishing Co., 1922), 577.

5. O. P. Van Sweringen testimony before the ICC, Cleveland Passenger Terminal Case (1920), reproduced in Harry Christiansen, *Northern Ohio's Interurbans and Rapid Transit Railways* (Cleveland, Ohio: Transit Data, 1965), 105; Blosser ms., 49.

6. *Traveler's Official Railway Guide,* June 1868 (New York: J. W. Pratt & Co., 1868; reprint, National Railway Pub. Co., 1968); *Official Guide of the Railways,* June 1916 (New York: National Railway Pub. Co., 1916).

7. Wheeler Report, 179–180.

8. William Ganson Rose, *Cleveland: The Making of a City* (Cleveland, Ohio: World Publishing Co., 1950), 559, 591, 629–630, 700, 705, 743; Jim Toman and Dan Cook, *Terminal Tower Complex, 1930–1980* (Cleveland, Ohio: Cleveland Landmarks Press, 1980), 6; Ian Haberman, *The Van Sweringens of Cleveland* (Cleveland, Ohio: Western Reserve Historical Society, 1979), 32–34; Walter C. Leedy, Jr., "Cleveland's Terminal Tower—The Van Sweringens' Afterthought," *The Gamut,* no. 8 (Winter 1983). *The Gamut* is a publication of Cleveland State University.

9. O. P. Van Sweringen testimony before the ICC, Cleveland Passenger Terminal Case (1920), in *Northern Ohio's Interurbans and Rapid Transit Railways,* 105.

10. Wheeler Report, 10–12, 181–196.

11. Haberman, *The Van Sweringens of Cleveland,* 23–24.

12. O. P. Van Sweringen testimony before the ICC, Cleveland Passenger Terminal Case (1920), in *Northern Ohio's Interurbans and Rapid Transit Railways,* 105; Wheeler Report, 11.

13. Toman and Cook, *Terminal Tower Complex,* 45; Rose, *Cleveland: The Making of a City,* 734, 767; Eric Johannessen, *Cleveland Architecture, 1876–1976* (Cleveland, Ohio: Western Reserve Historical Society, 1979), 134.

4. Mr. Smith Sells a Railroad

1. One legend about the name of the Nickel Plate has it that William H. Vanderbilt said "I wouldn't buy that damned railroad if it were nickel-plated." Another is that it came from a corruption of the company's initials, "NYCL." But most historians give the credit to the Norwalk, Ohio, *Chronicle,* which reportedly referred to the line during its construction as "the great New York and St. Louis nickel-plated railroad." At the time, Norwalk had hoped the railroad would build through the town and locate its shops there. See John A. Rehor, *The Nickel Plate Story* (Milwaukee, Wis.: Kalmbach Publishing Co., 1965), 19.

2. For the early history of the Nickel Plate, see Rehor, *The Nickel Plate Story,* 17–40. For profile of W. H. Caniff, see page 52, and Taylor Hampton, *The Nickel Plate Road: The History of a Great Railroad* (Cleveland, Ohio: World Publishing Co., 1947), 212–213.

3. Rehor, *The Nickel Plate Story,* 59.

4. Wheeler Report, 18.

5. Ibid., 18, 212; O. P. Van Sweringen testimony before the ICC, Cleveland Passenger Terminal Case (1920); reproduced in Harry Christiansen, *Northern Ohio's Interurbans and Rapid Transit Railways* (Cleveland, Ohio: Transit Data, 1965), 105.

6. Wheeler Report, 19–20.

7. Ibid., 20–21, 216–218; Blosser ms., 65 and Wenneman note, 65.

8. Rehor, *The Nickel Plate Story,* 67–68; *Biographical Directory of Railroad Officials in America* (New York: Simmons-Boardman Pub. Co., 1922), 48.

9. *Railway Age,* July 21, 1916, 91.

10. Morgan created Northern Securities in late 1901 as a way to end the warfare between rival railroad titans E. H. Harriman and James J. Hill. His new holding company was to control all of the then-existing routes between Chicago and the Pacific Northwest. But to Morgan's dismay, Theodore Roosevelt condemned it as the arch-symbol of the evils of monopoly and filed suit to have it dissolved. The case—finally decided in Roosevelt's favor by the Supreme Court in 1904—became the landmark event in Roosevelt's trust-busting crusade and marked the beginning of the new era of strict antitrust legislation and enforcement.

11. For a history and analysis of the holding company, see James C. Bonbright and Gardiner C. Means, *The Holding Company: Its Public Significance and Its Regulation* (New York: McGraw-Hill Book Co., 1932).

12. Wheeler Report, 22–23, 223–236.

13. Ibid., 24.

14. Ibid., 23; William Ganson Rose, *Cleveland: The Making of a City* (Cleveland, Ohio: World Publishing Co., 1950), 351, 451, 795–796.

5. Shaping Solid Forms

1. John A. Rehor, *The Nickel Plate Story* (Milwaukee, Wis.: Kalmbach Publishing Co., 1965), 68–69; *Who's Who in Railroading,* 1930 edition (New York: Simmons-Boardman Publishing Co., 1930), 18, 131.

2. Rehor, *The Nickel Plate Story,* 68–70.

3. Ibid., 62, 79.

4. John F. Stover, *American Railroads* (Chicago, Ill.: University of Chicago Press, 1961; reprint, 1976), 187–190.

5. Wheeler Report, 25–28, 238–241.

6. Rehor, *The Nickel Plate Story,* 70–71, 74–75.

7. In 1951, South Moreland was renamed Van Aken Boulevard, honoring Shaker's longtime mayor (and Van Sweringen associate) William J. Van Aken.

8. Physical description of the Shaker Heights rapid transit line based on material in *Electric Railway Journal* 56, no. 6 (1920): 200; and James A. Toman, *The Shaker Heights Rapid Transit* (Glendale, Calif.: Interurban Press, 1990), 19–22. See also Harry Christiansen, *Northern Ohio's Interurbans and Rapid Transit Railways* (Cleveland, Ohio: Transit Data, 1965), 113.

9. Jim Toman and Dan Cook, *Terminal Tower Complex, 1930–1980* (Cleveland, Ohio: Cleveland Landmarks Press, 1980), 63; William Ganson Rose, *Cleveland: The Making of a City* (Cleveland, Ohio: World Publishing Co., 1950), 767.

10. O. P. Van Sweringen testimony before the ICC, Cleveland Passenger Terminal Case (1920), reproduced in Harry Christiansen, *Northern Ohio's Interurbans and Rapid Transit Railways* (Cleveland, Ohio: Transit Data, 1965), 105.

11. *The Book of the Royal Blue,* December 1898, 13. *Book of the Royal Blue* was a promotional magazine published by the Baltimore & Ohio Railroad.

12. O. P. Van Sweringen testimony before the ICC, Cleveland Passenger Terminal Case (1920), in *Northern Ohio's Interurbans and Rapid Transit Railways,* 105; Walter C. Leedy, Jr., "Cleveland's Terminal Tower— The Van Sweringens' Afterthought," *The Gamut,* no. 8 (Winter 1983).

6. A Difficult Birth at the Public Square

1. Walter C. Leedy, Jr., "Cleveland's Terminal Tower—The Van Sweringens' Afterthought," *Gamut,* no. 8 (Winter 1983); Wheeler Report, 31–32, 36.

2. "Obituary: Peter Witt," *Cleveland Plain Dealer,* October 21, 1948; James A. Toman and Blaine S. Hays, *Horse Trails to Regional Rails: The Story of Public Transit in Greater Cleveland* (Kent, Ohio: Kent State University Press, 1996), 85–92.

3. Reproduced in Wheeler Report, 252–253.

4. Ibid., 33; Leedy, "Cleveland's Terminal Tower—The Van Sweringens' Afterthought"; Blosser ms., 86.

5. See Wheeler Report, 248–251.

6. See ibid., 35–44, and exhibits, 277–279, for a detailed account of the financing negotiations.

7. The financial arrangements between the railroads and the Van Sweringens are summarized in the Interstate Commerce Commission's initial decision in Finance Docket No. 1237, The Cleveland Passenger Terminal Case, dated August 12, 1921, reproduced in *The Cleveland Union Terminals Company, Legislation of the City of Cleveland and Documents Pertaining Thereto and Applications and Orders of the Interstate Commerce Commission . . . in Connection with the Union Passenger Terminal . . .* (Cleveland, Ohio, 1930), 286–300, and in Commissioner Joseph Eastman's dissent in the rehearing decision of December 6, 1921, 317–328; Blosser ms., 96.

8. Ian Haberman, *The Van Sweringens of Cleveland* (Cleveland, Ohio: Western Reserve Historical Society, 1979), 43–45; Report and Order of the Commission Dated December 6, 1921, in ICC Finance Docket No. 1237, reproduced in *Legislation of the City of Cleveland*, 312–328.

9. Wheeler Report, 48–54.

7. The Beginnings of an Empire

1. For a detailed analysis of the railroad consolidation features of the Transportation Act of 1920 and the results, see William N. Leonard, *Railroad Consolidation under the Transportation Act of 1920* (New York: Columbia University Press, 1946).

2. Comparative earnings and traffic statistics based on data from *Poor's Manual of Railroads, 1917* (New York: Poor's Manual Co., 1917) and *Moody's Railroad Manual, 1925* (New York: Moody's Investor Services, 1925).

3. Joseph F. Doherty, "Smooth Is the Road," *Tracks*, July 1956, 53.

4. For a detailed history of the Clover Leaf, see John A. Rehor, *The Nickel Plate Story* (Milwaukee, Wis.: Kalmbach Publishing Co., 1965), 119–169.

5. For a detailed history of the LE&W, see Rehor, *The Nickel Plate Story*, 85–117.

6. For details on the financial aspects of the Lake Erie & Western and Clover Leaf acquisitions, see the Wheeler Report, 71–82.

7. Ibid., 65–70, 428–439.

8. Ibid., 74–75, 80–81.

9. See *Operation of Lines and Issue of Capital Stock by the New York, Chicago & St. Louis Railroad Company,* 79 ICC 581, summarized in Wheeler Report, 86–89.

10. Wheeler Report, 91–100.

11. Ibid., 100.

8. To the South, East, and North

1. Wheeler Report, 60–61, 304–307.

2. By now in this narrative it should be plain that in this era the names of many railroads had character. The Pere Marquette's was in honor of the famous Jesuit explorer Father Jacques Marquette, who died in 1675 on the shore of Lake Michigan at Ludington—originally called Pere Marquette—where one of the railroad's predecessors established a terminal.

3. Wheeler Report, 77, 132–133.

4. Ibid., 102.

5. Charles W. Turner, *Chessie's Road* (Richmond, Va.: Garrett & Massie, 1956), 143, 163. This book was republished in significantly expanded form by the Chesapeake & Ohio Railway Historical Society in

1986, with additional chapters by Thomas W. Dixon, Jr., and Eugene Huddleston. Unless noted otherwise, subsequent references are to the original edition.

6. Wheeler Report, 102–106, 365–377.

7. For a discussion of the financing details of the C&O purchase, see ibid., 108–112, 378–382.

8. Interstate Commerce Commission Finance Docket 2732, *Interlocking Directors, New York, Chicago & St. Louis Railroad and Chesapeake & Ohio*; 76 ICC 549; Wheeler Report, 112–113.

9. Wheeler Report, 139.

10. Ibid., 118.

11. Ibid., 118–119.

12. Ibid., 123–129.

13. For a detailed history of the Pere Marquette through 1915, see Paul W. Ivey, *The Pere Marquette Railroad Company* (Lansing, Mich.: Michigan Historical Commission, 1919; reprint, Grand Rapids, Mich.: Black Letter Press, 1970).

14. Wheeler Report, 134–136.

9. Taking Stock: 1924

1. See William Ganson Rose, *Cleveland: The Making of a City* (Cleveland, Ohio: World Publishing Co., 1950), 712, 783, 788, 804, 806, 814, 825.

2. James A. Toman, *The Shaker Heights Rapid Transit* (Glendale, Calif.: Interurban Press, 1990), 46.

3. Ibid., 38.

4. *Huntington* (W.Va.) *Herald-Dispatch,* July 6, 1962.

5. Doherty, "Smooth Is the Road," *Tracks,* July 1956, 54.

6. Biographical information on Darwin S. Barrett from *Cleveland Press,* February 8, 1943.

7. Blosser ms., 151; telephone interview with J. Paxon Van Sweringen, July 19, 2001.

8. Doherty, "Smooth Is the Road," *Tracks,* May 1956, 56–57.

9. Wenneman notation on Blosser ms., 202; and Blosser ms., 4.

10. Doherty, "Smooth Is the Road," *Tracks,* July 1956, 56.

11. Ibid.

12. Doherty, "Smooth Is the Road," *Tracks,* May 1956, 58.

13. Doherty, "Smooth Is the Road," *Tracks,* July 1956, 55; Blosser ms., 95.

14. Doherty, "Smooth Is the Road," *Tracks,* August 1956, 54.

15. Blosser ms., 47–48.

16. Daisy Hill description based on Virginia Taylor Hampton, "The Fabulous Van Sweringens: Empire Building," typescript ms., 1965, Western Reserve Historical Society, Cleveland, Ohio, 188–194; Taylor Hampton, "Cleveland's Fabulous Vans: Their Wonderful Daisy Hill," *Cleveland News,* August 12, 1955, 11; Grace Goulder, "The Story of Daisy Hill," serialized in the *Cleveland Plain Dealer Sunday Magazine,* September 25, October 2, October 9, and October 16, 1966; Blosser ms., 141–150, 202.

17. James M. Wood, "An Eye for Detail," *Cleveland Magazine,* August 1983; Hampton, "Cleveland's Fabulous Vans: Their Wonderful Daisy Hill," 11.

18. Blosser ms., 19.

19. Eric Johannessen, *Cleveland Architecture, 1876–1976* (Cleveland, Ohio: Western Reserve Historical Society, 1979), 133.

10. Some Shadows Fleet By

1. *Railway Age,* March 15, 1924, 751; letter from G. A. Harwood to H. H. Harwood (Sr.), March 13, 1924. In author's possession.
2. Wenneman notation on Blosser ms., 118.
3. For details of Vaness's debts at this time, see the Wheeler Report, 166.
4. For the best brief biographies of Atterbury, Rea, and Willard, see Kenneth L. Bryant, Jr., ed., *Railroads in the Age of Regulation, 1900–1980* (New York: Facts on File, 1988), 16–21 (Atterbury), 359–363 (Rea), and 478–487 (Willard).
5. William M. Leonard, *Railroad Consolidation under the Transportation Act of 1920* (New York: Columbia University Press, 1946), 136–140; George H. Burgess and Miles C. Kennedy, *Centennial History of the Pennsylvania Railroad Company* (Philadelphia: Pennsylvania Railroad, 1949), 579–580.
6. John A. Rehor, *The Nickel Plate Story* (Milwaukee, Wis.: Kalmbach Publishing Co., 1965), 177.
7. Ibid., 176.
8. For a reproduction of the original fully detailed description of the financial plan, see the Wheeler Report, 411–426.
9. Ibid., 146–149.
10. Ibid., 149; Rehor, *The Nickel Plate Story,* 176; Charles W. Turner, *Chessie's Road* (Richmond, Va.: Garrett & Massie, 1956), 191–192.
11. Interstate Commerce Commission Finance Docket 4671, Nickel Plate Unification Case, 2580, quoted in Wheeler Report, 155.
12. O. P. Van Sweringen memo of meeting September 18, 1925, reproduced in Wheeler Report, 440–441.
13. Wheeler Report, 99–100; Rehor, *The Nickel Plate Story,* 178.
14. Wheeler Report, 160–164; Wenneman notation on Blosser ms., 138.
15. Wenneman notation on Blosser ms., 139.

11. Building, Rebuilding, and Juggling

1. For specific details of the interim loans and selected documents, see the Wheeler Report, 456–459, 597–606.
2. Ibid., 462–464.
3. For details, see ibid., 459–470 and 485–487; and Decision of the Interstate Commerce Commission in Finance Docket No. 6114, *Proposed Control of Erie Railroad Co. and Pere Marquette Railway Co. by the Chesapeake & Ohio Railway Co.,* May 8, 1928, sheets 8–10.
4. Wheeler Report, 471–479.
5. Ibid., 472–473.
6. Wood, Struthers & Co. report, "The Erie Railroad Co.—Its Prospects Under Van Sweringen Management," December 1927; *Railway Age,* October 22, 1927, 768; Edward Hungerford, *Men of Erie* (New York: Random House, 1946), 235–244.
7. John A. Rehor, *The Nickel Plate Story* (Milwaukee, Wis.: Kalmbach Publishing Co., 1965), 228–232; Frederick Westing, *Erie Power* (Medina, Ohio: Alvin F. Staufer, 1970), 166–171; Wood, Struthers & Co. report, "The Erie Railroad Co.—Its Prospects under Van Sweringen Management."
8. Decision of the Interstate Commerce Commission in Finance Docket No. 6114, *Proposed Control of Erie Railroad Co. and Pere Mar-*

quette Railway Co. by the Chesapeake & Ohio Railway Co., May 8, 1928, sheets 18–28, 21, and 36; Wheeler Report, 489–495.

9. William H. Wenneman, "My Three Careers in Forty Years," ms., 1978, Western Reserve Historical Society, Cleveland, Ohio, 8.

10. Eric Johannessen, *Cleveland Architecture, 1876–1976* (Cleveland, Ohio: Western Reserve Historical Society, 1979), 180–182.

11. Walter C. Leedy, Jr., "Cleveland's Terminal Tower—The Van Sweringens' Afterthought," *The Gamut*, no. 8 (Winter 1983); Jim Toman and Dan Cook, *Terminal Tower Complex, 1930–1980* (Cleveland, Ohio: Cleveland Landmarks Press, 1980), 15–16.

12. Toman and Cook, *Terminal Tower Complex*, 55–62; William Ganson Rose, *Cleveland: The Making of a City* (Cleveland, Ohio: World Publishing Co., 1950), 802.

13. Wheeler Report, 590.

14. George E. Condon, *Cleveland: The Best Kept Secret* (Garden City, N.Y.: Doubleday, 1967), 191.

15. Taylor Hampton, "Cleveland's Fabulous Vans: They Remodel Downtown," *Cleveland News*, August 5, 1955, 12; Blosser ms., 179.

16. Description of the Shaker Country Estates planning based on The F. A. Pease Company map, "Suggested Platting Plan for the Van Sweringen Company's 'Shaker Country Estates' and Adjacent Territory—1926," in collection of the Cleveland Public Library; news release dated February 27, 1927, in Joseph Doherty papers, Western Reserve Historical Society, Cleveland, Ohio; letter to the author from Harry Christiansen, February 14, 1965; William K. Hellmuth, *The Van Sweringen Developments of Shaker Heights*, 7, unpublished ms. at Western Reserve Historical Society, Cleveland, Ohio. See also Jeffrey Morris, *Beechwood: The Book* (Beachwood, Ohio: Jeffrey Morris, 1997), Chapter 2.

17. Johannessen, *Cleveland Architecture, 1876–1976*, 171–174.

18. News release dated May 20, 1928, in Joseph Doherty papers, Western Reserve Historical Society, Cleveland, Ohio; Johannessen, *Cleveland Architecture, 1876–1976*, 173–174; James A. Toman, *The Shaker Heights Rapid Transit* (Glendale, Calif.: Interurban Press, 1990), 30–33.

12. Consolidation Anarchy I

1. For a detailed account of the various Gould machinations affecting the W&LE and the building of what became the Pittsburgh & West Virginia, see John A. Rehor, *The Nickel Plate Story* (Milwaukee, Wis.: Kalmbach Publishing Co., 1965), 297–301, 317–320, 324–328, 332–334, and 339; see also Howard V. Worley, Jr., and William N. Poellot, Jr., *The Pittsburgh & West Virginia Railway: The Story of the High and Dry* (Halifax, Pa.: Withers Publishing, 1989), 35–78. For a biography of George Gould, see Maury Klein, "George J. Gould," in *Railroads in the Age of Regulation, 1900–1980*, edited by Kenneth L. Bryant, Jr. (New York: Facts on File, 1988), 167–171.

2. For a brief biography of L. F. Loree, see Herbert H. Harwood, Jr., "Leonor F. Loree," in *Railroads in the Age of Regulation, 1900–1980*, 259–267.

3. William Moedinger, Jr., "Blueprint Railroad," *Trains*, June 1943, 26–34.

4. Moedinger, "Blueprint Railroad," 26; William M. Leonard, *Railroad Consolidation under the Transportation Act of 1920* (New York: Columbia University Press, 1946), 147.

5. For a brief biography of Atterbury, see Michael Bezilla, "W. W.

Atterbury," in Bryant, ed., *Railroads in the Age of Regulation, 1900–1980*, 16–21; see also Blosser ms., 119–120.

6. U.S. Senate Committee on Interstate Commerce, *Railroad Consolidation in the Eastern Region: Investigation of Railroads, Holding Companies, and Affiliated Companies*, 76th Congress, 3rd Session, Report No. 1182 (Washington, D.C.: Government Printing Office, 1941), 1232. (Hereafter identified as *Railroad Consolidation in the Eastern Region*.)

7. Interview with John W. Barriger, III, April 5, 1964.

8. *Railroad Consolidation in the Eastern Region*, 1997–1998; Leonard, *Railroad Consolidation under the Transportation Act of 1920*, 147–148.

9. *Railroad Consolidation in the Eastern Region*, 2027;. Leonard, *Railroad Consolidation under the Transportation Act of 1920*, 148–149; Blosser ms., 173.

10. *Railroad Consolidation in the Eastern Region*, 2034; Leonard, *Railroad Consolidation under the Transportation Act of 1920*, 149.

11. See Mary Jane Matz, *The Many Lives of Otto Kahn* (New York: Macmillan Co., 1963), 49–51. Readers should be warned, however, that the author misstates the meeting date as 1923 and, probably as a result, misidentifies the Pennsylvania president as Samuel Rea. The story is repeated with variations in detail and accuracy in John Kobler's *Otto the Magnificent* (New York: Charles Scribner's Sons, 1988), 3–5, and in Stephen Birmingham's *"Our Crowd": The Great Jewish Families of New York* (New York: Harper & Row, 1967), 310–311.

12. Leonard, *Railroad Consolidation under the Transportation Act of 1920*, 150.

13. Rehor, *The Nickel Plate Story*, 350. For a history of the W&LE, see ibid., 282–355.

14. Wheeler Report, 499–502.

15. Ibid., 502–503.

13. Consolidation Anarchy II

1. *Railroad Consolidation in the Eastern Region*, 1981; Howard V. Worley, Jr., and William N. Poellot, Jr., *The Pittsburgh & West Virginia Railway: The Story of the High and Dry* (Halifax, Pa.: Withers Publishing, 1989), 116, 128.

2. Wheeler Report, 502–506.

3. *Railroad Consolidation in the Eastern Region*, 1986–1994; Wheeler Report, 506–507; William N. Leonard, *Railroad Consolidation under the Transportation Act of 1920* (New York: Columbia University Press, 1946), 145.

4. Wheeler Report, 507; John A. Rehor, *The Nickel Plate Story* (Milwaukee, Wis.: Kalmbach Publishing Co., 1965), 336.

5. Wheeler Report, 507–508; Leonard, *Railroad Consolidation under the Transportation Act of 1920*, 145–146.

6. *Railroad Consolidation in the Eastern Region*, 1988; Leonard, *Railroad Consolidation under the Transportation Act of 1920*, 145–146. For details on the construction of the new line, see Worley and Poellot, *Pittsburgh & West Virginia Railway*, 120–121, 127, 131–135.

7. Rehor, *The Nickel Plate Story*, 198–199.

8. For a detailed history and physical description of the Buffalo, Rochester & Pittsburgh, see Paul Pietrak, *Buffalo, Rochester & Pittsburgh Railway* (North Boston, N.Y.: Paul Pietrak, 1979).

9. For a more detailed discussion of the Baltimore & Ohio's involvement in this plan, see Herbert H. Harwood, Jr., "Nothing at the End of the Rainbow: The B&O's Adventures in Western Pennsylvania," *Railroad History,* no. 129 (Autumn 1973): 56–70.

10. Wheeler Report, 513–515.

11. Ibid., 515–517, 720–721.

12. Ibid., 517–518.

13. Wenneman notation on Blosser ms., 177.

14. Worley and Poellot, *Pittsburgh & West Virginia Railway,* 123; the $53 million debt estimate is from the Wheeler Report, 531.

15. Wheeler Report, 519–521.

16. Ibid., 511; Rehor, *The Nickel Plate Story,* 350.

14. The Summit I

1. Quoted in William N. Leonard, *Railroad Consolidation under the Transportation Act of 1920* (New York: Columbia University Press, 1946), 150.

2. Wheeler Report, 535–536.

3. Performance and stock price data from listing for these railroads in *Poor's Railroads, Banks and Insurance Section, 1927 Edition* (New York: Poor's Publishing Company, 1927) and *Poor's Railroads, Banks and Insurance Section, 1930 Edition* (New York: Poor's Publishing Company,1930).

4. Wheeler Report, 537–538.

5. Ibid., 538, 540–549.

6. Ibid., 556.

7. Ibid., 519–521.

8. Ibid., 560.

9. At this writing, there is no comprehensive history of the Missouri Pacific. The background data used here came from the Wheeler Report, 557–559; and *Poor's Railroads, Banks and Insurance Section, 1930 Edition,* 762ff.

10. Wheeler Report, 559.

11. John A. Rehor, *The Nickel Plate Story* (Milwaukee, Wis.: Kalmbach Publishing Co., 1965), 220–221.

12. Interview with John W. Barriger, III, April 5, 1964; stock price data from listings for these railroads in *Poor's Railroads, Banks and Insurance Section, 1927 Edition* and *Poor's Railroads, Banks and Insurance Section, 1930 Edition.*

13. Blosser ms., 199 with Wenneman notation; *Poor's Railroads, Banks and Insurance Section, 1930 Edition,* 769, 775.

14. Wheeler Report, 561–562, 569–574; "Bachelors of Railroading," *Fortune,* March 1934, 163; Alleghany Corporation Annual Report, December 31, 1931.

15. Wheeler Report, 562; Blosser ms., 212.

16. Wheeler Report, 562; Wenneman notation on Blosser ms., 212.

17. Wheeler Report, 562–564; Blosser ms., 215.

18. Wheeler Report, 559–560; Wenneman notation on Blosser ms., 191.

19. *Business Week,* May 28, 1930, 15.

20. Interview with John W. Barriger, III, April 5, 1964.

21. Blosser ms., 180; William H. Wenneman, "My Three Careers in Forty Years," ms., 1978, Western Reserve Historical Society, Cleveland,

Ohio, 8. In "Bachelors of Railroading," *Fortune* gives the date of the Terminal Tower move as June 1, 1929, which apparently is an error (March 1934, 166).

15. The Summit II

1. Wheeler Report, 566–567.

2. At this writing, there is no comprehensive history of the Chicago & Eastern Illinois. For a summary history, see George H. Drury, *Historical Guide to North American Railroads* (Milwaukee, Wis.: Kalmbach Publishing Co., 1985), 64–67.

3. *Poor's Railroads, Banks and Insurance Section, 1930 Edition* (New York: Poor's Publishing Co., 1930), 47ff.; Wheeler Report, 907–908.

4. Wheeler Report, 908–910.

5. Wheeler Report, 1110–1111; Blosser ms., 180; Taylor Hampton, "Cleveland's Fabulous Vans: Missouri Pacific: The Vans' 'First Big Mistake,'" *Cleveland News*, August 16, 1955, 13.

6. H. Roger Grant, *The Corn Belt Route: A History of the Chicago Great Western Railroad Company* (DeKalb: Northern Illinois University Press, 1984), 110–114; Wheeler Report, 505.

7. See *Railway Age*, May 24, 1929.

8. The "2-10-4 type" refers to locomotive wheel arrangement and is a rough indication of size, power, and type of service.

9. Philip Shuster, Eugene L. Huddleston, and Alvin F. Staufer, *C&O Power* (Medina, Ohio: Alvin F. Staufer, 1965), 125; John A. Rehor, *The Nickel Plate Story* (Milwaukee, Wis.: Kalmbach Publishing Co., 1965), 232–233.

10. Virginia Taylor Hampton, "The Fabulous Van Sweringens: Empire Building," typescript ms., 1965, Western Reserve Historical Society, Cleveland, Ohio, 165; William Ganson Rose, *Cleveland: The Making of a City* (Cleveland, Ohio: World Publishing Co., 1950), 863; John A. Rehor, *The Nickel Plate Story* (Milwaukee, Wis.: Kalmbach Publishing Co., 1965), 189.

11. Wheeler Report, 582; George H. Burgess and Miles C. Kennedy, *Centennial History of the Pennsylvania Railroad Company* (Philadelphia: Pennsylvania Railroad, 1949), 639–640.

12. Wheeler Report, 580.

13. See *Railroad Consolidation in the Eastern Region*, 2125–2148, summarized in Wheeler Report, 580–581; William N. Leonard, *Railroad Consolidation under the Transportation Act of 1920* (New York: Columbia University Press, 1946), 154.

14. Howard V. Worley, Jr., and William N. Poellot, Jr., *The Pittsburgh & West Virginia Railway: The Story of the High and Dry* (Halifax, Pa.: Withers Publishing, 1989), 128; Wheeler Report, 582; Burgess and Kennedy, *Centennial History of the Pennsylvania Railroad*, 641–642; Roger Cook and Karl Zimmerman, *The Western Maryland Railway: Fireballs and Black Diamonds* (San Diego, Calif.: Howell-North Books, 1981), 51.

15. Interstate Commerce Commission Final System Plan, as reproduced in *Poor's Railroad Volume, 1931 Edition* (New York: Poor's Publishing Co., 1931), 1873ff.; Wheeler Report, 582–583.

16. William N. Leonard, *Railroad Consolidation under the Transportation Act of 1920* (New York: Columbia University Press, 1946), 158–159; Wenneman notation on Blosser ms., 209.

17. Burgess and Kennedy, *Centennial History of the Pennsylvania Railroad*, 637.

16. The Summit III

1. For a detailed description of the Cleveland Union Terminal engineering and construction work, see *Railway Age,* June 28, 1930, 1555–1556 and 1574–1580. Date of first train from William Ganson Rose, *Cleveland: The Making of a City* (Cleveland, Ohio: World Publishing Co., 1950), 867.

2. James A. Toman, *The Shaker Heights Rapid Transit* (Glendale, Calif.: Interurban Press, 1990), 42, 48, and 56; cost estimate from *Railway Age,* June 28, 1930, 1554.

3. The rural Cleveland & Eastern and Cleveland & Chagrin Falls expired in 1925, as did the Cleveland, Painesville & Eastern in 1926. The Cleveland Southwestern system followed in 1931 and the Northern Ohio Power & Light's Akron line in 1932. The last, the threadbare Lake Shore Electric, was abandoned in 1938.

4. Wheeler Report, 589. For a description of the Cleveland Railway's so-called Tayler Grant franchise of 1909, see James A. Toman and Blaine S. Hays, *Horse Trails to Regional Rails: The Story of Public Transit in Greater Cleveland* (Kent, Ohio: Kent State University Press, 1996), 76.

5. Wheeler Report, 588–590, 849–853; Toman and Hays, *Horse Trails to Regional Rails,* 152.

6. Wheeler Report, 588, 912; Blosser ms., 185 and Wenneman notation.

7. Jim Toman and Dan Cook, *Terminal Tower Complex, 1930–1980* (Cleveland, Ohio: Cleveland Landmarks Press, 1980), 64–68.

8. Rose, *Cleveland: The Making of a City,* 813.

9. News release dated September 1929 and other items in Joseph Doherty papers, Western Reserve Historical Society.

10. *The Country Club: Its First 75 Years, 1889 to 1964* (Pepper Pike, Ohio: The Country Club, 1964), 21–23.

11. Wheeler Report, 590–591; Rose, *Cleveland: The Making of a City,* 802.

12. Wheeler Report, 593.

13. Quoted in John Kenneth Galbraith, *The Great Crash: 1929* (Boston, Mass.: Houghton Mifflin, 1955), 75.

14. Galbraith, *The Great Crash,* 91; Wheeler Report, 594–595.

15. Ayres quote from Galbraith, *The Great Crash,* 110.

16. Wheeler Report, 505; stock prices taken from *Poor's Railroad Volume, 1931 Edition* (New York: Poor's Publishing Co., 1931), 971 (C&O), 991 (Erie), 1023 (Nickel Plate), 1038 (Missouri Pacific), and 1101 (Pere Marquette).

17. Harvard Economic Society quotes from Galbraith, *The Great Crash,* 140–141, 150.

17. Completions and Complications

1. See William H. Wenneman, "My Three Careers in Forty Years," ms., 1978, Western Reserve Historical Society, Cleveland, Ohio, 11.

2. Wheeler Report, 861–862, 868, 993. See also *Railway Age,* January 25, 1930, 316.

3. Wheeler Report, 863–865.

4. Wenneman, "My Three Careers in Forty Years," ms., 11–12. See also Wheeler Report, 862–863.

5. The Hepburn Act of 1906 reinforced the act that created the Interstate Commerce Commission by, among other things, prohibiting any railroad from carrying commodities that it produced, owned, or had an interest in.

6. Wheeler Report, 862–865.
7. Ibid., 873–874.
8. Ibid., 877–878.
9. For full analysis of the Van Sweringen Corporation financial agreement, see ibid., 883–889.
10. Ibid., 882, 889–898.
11. Charles W. Turner, *Chessie's Road* (Richmond, Va.: Garrett & Massie, 1956), 205; Wheeler Report, 1117.
12. *Railway Age,* June 28, 1930, 1557.
13. For extensive detail on the Cleveland Union Terminal facilities, see the full issue of *Railway Age,* June 28, 1930, and the official dedication brochure, *Cleveland Union Station: A Description of the New Passenger Facilities and Surrounding Improvements* (Cleveland, Ohio: Cleveland Union Terminals Company and Cleveland Terminals Building Company, 1930). Available at Cleveland Union Terminal collection, Cleveland State University. See also *Business Week,* May 28, 1930, 16; *Cleveland Plain Dealer,* June 29, 1930; and William Ganson Rose, *Cleveland: The Making of a City* (Cleveland, Ohio: World Publishing Co., 1950), 885–886.
14. "City of Van Sweringen," *Business Week,* October 26, 1929.
15. Walter C. Leedy, Jr., "Cleveland's Terminal Tower—The Van Sweringens' Afterthought" *The Gamut,* no. 8 (Winter 1983); James A. Toman and Blaine S. Hays, *Horse Trails to Regional Rails: The Story of Public Transit in Greater Cleveland* (Kent, Ohio: Kent State University Press, 1996), 152–153; James A. Toman, *The Shaker Heights Rapid Transit* (Glendale, Calif.: Interurban Press, 1990), 56.
16. "Obituary: Peter Witt," *Cleveland Plain Dealer,* October 21, 1948; Wenneman notation on Blosser ms., 210.
17. Toman, *The Shaker Heights Rapid Transit,* 48; Cleveland Interurban Railroad, Timetable No. 1, July 20, 1930.
18. Ibid., 48.
19. Ibid., 59; Harry Christiansen, *Northern Ohio's Interurbans and Rapid Transit Railways* (Cleveland, Ohio: Transit Data, 1965), 117; letter to the author from Harry Christiansen, February 11, 1965.
20. Thomas W. Dixon, Jr., *Chesapeake & Ohio Alleghany Subdivision* (Alderson, W.Va.: Chesapeake & Ohio Historical Society, 1985), 70–77; Charles W. Turner, *Chessie's Road* (Richmond, Va.: Garrett & Massie, 1956), 211.
21. William Olcott, *Greenbrier Heritage* (White Sulphur Springs, W.Va.: privately published by the Greenbrier Hotel, ca. 1965), 56.
22. *Rail* [Chesapeake & Ohio employee magazine], March 1937, 4–5; Charles W. Turner, *Chessie's Road,* 2nd edition, with additions by Thomas W. Dixon, Jr., and Eugene L. Huddleston (Alderson, W.Va.: Chesapeake & Ohio Historical Society, 1986), 273–274, 235–237.
23. Quotation from John Kenneth Galbraith, *The Great Crash: 1929* (Boston, Mass.: Houghton Mifflin, 1955), 150.

18. Taking Stock: 1930

1. James C. Bonbright and Gardiner C. Means, *The Holding Company: Its Public Significance and Its Regulation* (New York: McGraw-Hill Book Co., 1932), 253.
2. Jim Toman and Dan Cook, *Terminal Tower Complex, 1930–1980* (Cleveland, Ohio: Cleveland Landmarks Press, 1980), 58–59; Cleveland Union Terminals Company, *Cleveland Union Station: A Description of the New Passenger Facilities and Surrounding Improvements* (Cleveland,

Ohio: Cleveland Union Terminals Company and Cleveland Terminals Building Company, 1930); William Ganson Rose, *Cleveland: The Making of a City* (Cleveland, Ohio: World Publishing Co., 1950), 862, 864.

3. Occupancy data partly from *Official Guide of the Railways* (New York: National Railway Pub. Co.), issues for February 1930, July 1933; *Official Aviation Guide: August 1930* (Chicago, Ill.: Official Aviation Guide Co., 1930); and interview with J. J. Anzalone, April 1, 1964.

4. William H. Wenneman, "My Three Careers in Forty Years," ms., 1978, Western Reserve Historical Society, Cleveland, Ohio, 8; "Bachelors of Railroading," *Fortune,* March 1934, 61.

5. Ibid., 14–15.

6. James A. Toman and Blaine S. Hays, *Horse Trails to Regional Rails: The Story of Public Transit in Greater Cleveland* (Kent, Ohio: Kent State University Press, 1996), 149; *Official Aviation Guide: August 1930,* tables 14, 27, 29A, 38, 44.

7. James A. Toman, *The Shaker Heights Rapid Transit* (Glendale, Calif.: Interurban Press, 1990), 45, 138.

8. David G. Molyneaux and Sue Sackman, eds., *75 Years: An Informal History of Shaker Heights* (Shaker Heights, Ohio: Shaker Heights Public Library, 1987), 26, 39–41, 43–44; Beduhn, ed., *Shaker Heights: Then and Now* (Shaker Heights, Ohio: Shaker Heights Board of Education, 1938), 23, 27–28.

9. Molyneaux and Sackman, *75 Years,* 26, 59.

10. Henry-Russell Hitchcock, Jr., "Traffic and Building Art: New York and Cleveland Contrasted," *Architectural Record,* June 1930, 557.

11. See Wheeler Report, 8n.

12. For a detailed ownership chart, see Bonbright and Means, *The Holding Company,* 261.

13. "Bachelors of Railroading," 168.

14. Joseph Doherty, "The Irascible Years," unpublished chapter of "Smooth Is the Road," ca. 1958. In former Chesapeake & Ohio Railway files; copy in author's possession.

15. Interview with J. Paxton Van Sweringen, quoted in Molyneaux and Sackman, *75 Years,* 27; telephone interview with J. Paxton Van Sweringen, July 19, 2001.

16. *Business Week,* March 19, 1930, 36.

17. Wenneman notation on Blosser ms., 191.

18. Virginia Taylor Hampton, "The Fabulous Van Sweringens: Empire Building" typescript ms., 1965, Western Reserve Historical Society, Cleveland, Ohio, 187–188.

19. Sudden Darkness

1. Wheeler Report, 914–916, 924–929.

2. For details of these transactions, see ibid., 914–930.

3. Ibid., 931–932; typed insert by William Wenneman included in Blosser ms. The dates and details of the Van Sweringens' activities during the October 21–25 period are taken from the Wenneman description and differ in some respects from those in the Wheeler Report, which apparently came from a secondhand report based on O. P.'s later recollections. Since Wenneman was there and had vivid memories, I have assumed that his account is more accurate.

4. Wheeler Report, 930.

5. William H. Wenneman, "My Three Careers in Forty Years," ms., 1978, Western Reserve Historical Society, Cleveland, Ohio, 12.

6. Ibid.
7. See the Wheeler Report, 938–942.
8. Ibid., 937–939.
9. Ibid., 955, 959.
10. James A. Toman, *The Shaker Heights Rapid Transit* (Glendale, Calif.: Interurban Press, 1990), 56.
11. David G. Molyneaux and Sue Sackman, eds., *75 Years: An Informal History of Shaker Heights* (Shaker Heights, Ohio: Shaker Heights Public Library, 1987), 40; interview with Doris Whistlar Alburn, quoted in ibid., 50.
12. Jim Toman and Dan Cook, *Terminal Tower Complex, 1930–1980* (Cleveland, Ohio: Cleveland Landmarks Press, 1980), 65.
13. Wheeler Report, 960–961, 1143.
14. For a discussion of the various negotiations and plans, see ibid., 960–978; Wenneman notation on Blosser ms., 241.
15. Wheeler Report, 978–983.
16. Ibid., 984; "Bachelors of Railroading," *Fortune,* March 1934, 182.

20. The Rails Roll Downgrade

1. Based on comparative income figures as reported in *Poor's Railroad Volume: 1931 Edition* (New York: Poor's Publishing Co., 1931).
2. The Nickel Plate and Pere Marquette continued paying dividends on their common stock through mid-1931, although both railroads posted deficits for that year. The Missouri Pacific had never paid dividends on its common stock in recent years, but it continued paying its dividends on preferred stock until October 1931. The C&O kept paying regularly, disbursing a total of $3.7 million in each quarter through July 1930 and then $4.8 million each quarter through 1933. Dividend data from *Poor's Railroad Volume, 1933 Edition* (New York: Poor's Publishing Co., 1933), 705 (C&O), 736 (Erie), 775 (Nickel Plate), 786 (Pere Marquette), 796 (W&LE), and 812 (Missouri Pacific). See also John A. Rehor, *The Nickel Plate Story* (Milwaukee, Wis.: Kalmbach Publishing Co., 1965), 221–222; and the Wheeler Report, 1111.
3. Wheeler Report, 1066–1067. For details of the securities underlying the three Alleghany bond issues, see 1067.
4. See *Poor's Railroad Volume, 1935 Edition* (New York: Poor's Publishing Co., 1935), 919; and the Wheeler Report, 1110–1111, 1233.
5. Wheeler Report, 1067–1068.
6. The sordid Bremo–Van Sweringen–Kansas City Southern story is summarized by H. Roger Grant in *The Corn Belt Route: A History of the Chicago Great Western Railroad Company* (DeKalb: Northern Illinois University Press, 1984), 114–115. See also the Wheeler Report, 1072–1073.
7. Financial statistics from *Poor's Railroad Volume, 1932 Edition* (New York: Poor's Publishing Co., 1932); references to *George Washington* in Charles W. Turner, *Chessie's Road,* rev. ed., new chapters by Thomas W. Dixon, Jr., and Eugene Huddleston (Richmond, Va.: Garrett & Massie, 1956), 162, 274–276. Actually, the Baltimore & Ohio's *Columbian,* introduced in May 1931, was the first all-air-conditioned train, but it was a short-run day train—thus the C&O's qualified claim.
8. Frederick Lewis Allen, *Since Yesterday* (New York: Harper & Brothers, 1940), 60.
9. See the Wheeler Report, 1129–1137; and William N. Leonard,

Railroad Consolidation under the Transportation Act of 1920 (New York: Columbia University Press, 1946), 199–205. For full details of the ICC's 1932 modifications to the 1929 plan, see 185 ICC 403 (1932) or *Poor's Railroad Volume, 1934 Edition* (New York: Poor's Publishing Co., 1934), 1–39.

    10. "5s of 1950" was Wall Street shorthand for "5% bonds maturing in 1950."

    11. Wheeler Report, 1073.

    12. Ibid., 1079–1092.

    13. Wenneman notation on Blosser ms., 246.

    14. Wheeler Report, 1101–1102; Rehor, *The Nickel Plate Story*, 224.

21. A New World

    1. Wheeler Report, 1117–1118.

    2. Blosser ms., 231 and Wenneman notation.

    3. Wheeler Report, 1145; William H. Wenneman, "My Three Careers in Forty Years, ms., 1978, Western Reserve Historical Society, Cleveland, Ohio, 11; Joseph F. Doherty, "The Irascible Years," unpublished chapter of "Smooth Is the Road," ca. 1956.

    4. Statistics from *Poor's Railroad Volume, 1933 Edition* (New York: Poor's Publishing Co., 1933).

    5. U.S. Senate, Committee on Banking and Currency, *Stock Exchange Practices: Report Pursuant to Senate Resolution 84 (72nd Congress) . . . and Senate Resolutions 56 and 97 (73rd Congress)*, 73rd Congress, Report 1455 (Washington, DC: Government Printing Office, 1934), 307–308 (hereafter referred to as the Pecora Committee Report); Blosser ms., 267.

    6. Blosser ms., 249.

    7. Ibid.; "Joseph Nutt, Financier, Is Dead at 74," *Cleveland News*, December 18, 1945, 1A.

    8. John A. Rehor, *The Nickel Plate Story* (Milwaukee, Wis.: Kalmbach Publishing Co., 1965), 233.

    9. Wheeler Report, 1105.

    10. Statistics quoted in Earl Latham, *The Politics of Railroad Coordination: 1933–1936* (Cambridge, Mass.: Harvard University Press, 1959), 8, 27; Wheeler Report, 1201–1202.

    11. Market share statistics from Eastern Railroad Presidents Conference, *Yearbook of Railroad Information: 1956 Edition* (New York: Eastern Railroad Presidents Conference, 1956), 4.

    12. For a detailed discussion of the background and creation of the Emergency Railroad Transportation Act of 1933, see Latham, *Politics of Railroad Coordination*, 8–83.

    13. See Latham, *Politics of Railroad Coordination*, 37–39; details of Prince plan from *Poor's Railroad Volume, 1934 Edition* (New York: Poor's Publishing Co., 1934), 39–48; Wheeler Report, 1138–1139.

    14. For an extensive discussion of the Guardian Trust and Union Trust problems, see the Pecora Committee Report, 302–319; William Ganson Rose, *Cleveland: The Making of a City* (Cleveland, Ohio: World Publishing Co., 1950), 905–906; Wheeler Report, 1148–1149; John T. Flynn, "The Betrayal of Cleveland," *Harper's Monthly Magazine*, January 1934, 147.

    15. Flynn, "The Betrayal of Cleveland," 142.

    16. Quoted in memorandum from Hamilton Wilson, Second Vice President, Guaranty Trust, to Alfred Shriver, Vice President, Guaranty Trust, August 1, 1933, reproduced in Wheeler Report, 1271.

17. Blosser ms., 231; Wheeler Report, 1146–1147.
18. "Bachelors of Railroading," *Fortune,* March 1934, 59.
19. See Pecora Committee Report, 307–308, 314, 318–319, 364–381.
20. Wenneman, "My Three Careers in Forty Years," ms., 13.

22. The Cruelest Year

1. Wheeler Report, 1115, 1232–1233; *Poor's Railroad Volume, 1935 Edition* (New York: Poor's Publishing Co., 1935), 919.
2. H. Roger Grant, *The Corn Belt Route: A History of the Chicago Great Western Railroad Company* (DeKalb: Northern Illinois University Press, 1984), 116; Wheeler Report, 1073n.
3. See *Business Week,* July 9, 1930, 9; *New York Times,* November 11, 1931, 34; ownership data from Midamerica Corp. organization chart as of June 30, 1936, Exhibit No. 5, 216, Wheeler Committee hearings record.
4. See Wheeler Report, 1113, 1217–1219.
5. Ibid., 1115.
6. Quoted by Taylor Hampton in "Cleveland's Fabulous Vans: Death Ends the Dreams," *Cleveland News,* August 19, 1955, 9. The source is unidentified but may be either lawyer John P. Murphy or Mrs. Hampton's husband, H. Horton Hampton.
7. Joseph F. Doherty, "The Irascible Years," unpublished chapter of "Smooth Is the Road," ca. 1956.
8. Wheeler Report, 1275; Jim Toman and Dan Cook, *The Terminal Tower Complex, 1930–1980* (Cleveland, Ohio: Cleveland Landmarks Press, 1980), 71–72.
9. James A. Toman, *The Shaker Heights Rapid Transit* (Glendale, Calif.: Interurban Press, 1990), 56.
10. Ibid., 60.
11. Wheeler Report, 1156, 1169n, 1281.
12. Blosser ms., 274 with Wenneman notation; William H. Wenneman, "My Three Careers in Forty Years," ms., 1978, Western Reserve Historical Society, Cleveland, Ohio, 10.
13. Doherty, "The Irascible Years"; Wenneman, "My Three Careers in Forty Years," 13–14.
14. Blosser ms., 261, with Wenneman notation.
15. *Chesapeake & Ohio Lines Magazine,* February 1942, 15.
16. Taylor Hampton, "Cleveland's Fabulous Vans: Rescued by the 2 Georges," *Cleveland News,* August 18, 1955, 18; Wheeler Report, 1161–1183; Blosser ms., 278.
17. Wheeler Report, 1165–1166.
18. *New York Herald Tribune,* October 1, 1935, quoted in Wheeler Report, 1168.
19. O. P. quote from *New York Herald Tribune,* October 1, 1935, quoted in Wheeler Report, 1169; Louise D. Jenks, *O. P. and M. J.,* privately printed, probably Cleveland, Ohio, ca. 1940. Copies are in the collections of the Cleveland Public Library and the Western Reserve Historical Society.
20. "The Current State of Mr. Van Sweringen," *Fortune,* December 1936, 110; Wenneman notation on Blosser ms., 284.

23. The Last Train

1. Blosser ms., 282.
2. Ibid., 285.

3. Taylor Hampton, "Cleveland's Fabulous Vans: Death Ends the Dreams," *Cleveland News,* August 19, 1955, 9; Doherty, "Shadows Fall," unpublished chapter of "Smooth Is the Road," written for *Tracks,* ca. 1956; Blosser ms., 285.

4. *Cleveland News,* December 12, 1935; *Business Week,* December 21, 1935, 26.

5. Doherty, "Shadows Fall."

6. Hampton, "Cleveland's Fabulous Vans: Death Ends the Dreams," 9.

7. Doherty, "Shadows Fall"; Blosser ms., 288.

8. Quoted in Grace Goulder, "Daisy Hill: The Derailment," *Cleveland Plain Dealer Sunday Magazine,* October 16, 1966, 63.

9. Wheeler Report, 1116, 1172.

10. Interview with John W. Barriger, III, April 5, 1964.

11. "The Current State of Mr. Van Sweringen," *Fortune,* December 1936, 182, 184.

12. Interview with John W, Barriger, III, April 5, 1964; Wheeler Report, 1102, 1171; *Poor's Railroad Volume, 1937 Edition* (New York: Poor's Publishing Co., 1937), 1449.

13. Blosser ms., 289, based on information from William Wyer.

14. "The Current State of Mr. Van Sweringen," 189–190.

15. Wheeler Report, 1171, 1309; "Cleveland to the Rescue," *Business Week,* September 21, 1935, 9.

16. James A. Toman, *The Shaker Heights Rapid Transit* (Glendale, Calif.: Interurban Press, 1990), 61, 138.

17. Wenneman notation on Blosser ms., 289.

18. Wheeler Report, 1171–1172; William H. Wenneman, "My Three Careers in Forty Years," ms., 1978, Western Reserve Historical Society, Cleveland, Ohio, 15.

19. Details of O. P.'s last trip in this and previous paragraphs from *Railway Age,* November 28, 1936, 793; *New York Times,* November 24, 1936; *Cleveland Plain Dealer,* November 24, 1936; Wenneman, "My Three Careers in Forty Years" ms., 15; Blosser ms., 295, with Wenneman notation.

20. *Cleveland Press,* November 26, 1936.

21. *Cleveland News,* November 24, 1936; Hampton, "Cleveland's Fabulous Vans: Death Ends the Dreams," *Cleveland News,* August 19, 1955, 9.

24. Epilogue I

1. Wheeler Report, 1173–1174.

2. William H. Wenneman, "My Three Careers in Forty Years" ms., 1978, Western Reserve Historical Society, Cleveland, Ohio, 16; *Chesapeake & Ohio Lines Magazine,* March 1940, 4; *Rail,* January 1937, 3, and April 1937, 21.

3. Interview with John W. Barriger, III, April 5, 1964; memorandum from John W. Barriger, III, to Jesse H. Jones, April 2, 1937.

4. For details of Robert R. Young's battles for control of Alleghany and the Chesapeake & Ohio, see Joseph Borkin, *Robert R. Young: Populist of Wall Street* (New York: Harper & Row, Publishers, 1969), 40–62.

5. Ibid., 37–40.

6. See ibid., 68–69, 69n; John A. Rehor, *The Nickel Plate Story* (Milwaukee, Wis.: Kalmbach Publishing Co., 1965), 279–280, 355.

7. For full details of the two fights for the control of the New York Central, see Borkin, *Robert R. Young,* 97–209.

8. For a detailed account of the late stages of the Missouri Pacific reorganization, see H. Craig Miner, *The Rebirth of the Missouri Pacific, 1956–1983* (College Station: Texas A&M University Press, 1983), particularly 6–17 and 135–154.

9. For an account of the Erie's post–Van Sweringen career, see H. Roger Grant, *Erie Lackawanna: Death of an American Railroad, 1938–1992* (Stanford, Calif.: Stanford University Press, 1994).

10. "Chessie Workers Pack Up for Last Ride," *Cleveland Plain Dealer*, June 28, 1986. For a profile of Cyrus Eaton during this period, see George E. Condon, *Cleveland: The Best Kept Secret* (Garden City, N.Y.: Doubleday & Company, 1967), 294–315.

11. William Ganson Rose, *Cleveland: The Making of a City* (Cleveland, Ohio: World Publishing Co., 1950), 924; *Moody's Public Utilities*, 1937, 1951, 1952 (New York: Moody's Investor Services, 1937, 1951, 1952); James A. Toman and Blaine S. Hays, *Horse Trails to Regional Rails: The Story of Public Transit in Greater Cleveland* (Kent, Ohio: Kent State University Press, 1996), 172, 184–185; Cleveland Railway Company Annual Report, 1937. The Toman and Hays book gives the best summary of the events leading to the sale of the Cleveland Railway, but readers are cautioned that there is a confusion of dates on page 172; in most instances, the date "1935" should be "1937" on that page.

12. James A. Toman, *The Shaker Heights Rapid Transit* (Glendale, Calif.: Interurban Press, 1990), 65, 99.

13. See Toman and Hays, *Horse Trails to Regional Rails*, 253–256.

14. See obituaries for Bradley in the *Cleveland Press*, December 19, 1943, and Murphy in the *Cleveland Plain Dealer*, July 16, 1969.

15. Grace Goulder, "The Story of Daisy Hill," *Cleveland Plain Dealer Sunday Magazine*, September 25, 1966; Taylor Hampton, "Cleveland's Fabulous Vans: Properties Paid Out," *Cleveland News,* August 22, 1955, 6.

16. *New York Times*, October 30, 1951; *Newsweek,* November 12, 1951.

17. Obituaries: D. L. Barrett, Jr., *Cleveland Plain Dealer,* February 8, 1943; C. L. Bradley, *Cleveland Press,* December 19, 1943; Herbert Fitzpatrick, *Huntington* (W. Va.) *Herald-Dispatch,* July 6–7, 1962; Benjamin L. Jenks, *Cleveland Press,* March 12, 1951; Louise Jenks, *Cleveland Press,* March 7, 1967; Joseph Nutt, *Cleveland News,* December 18, 1945.

25. Epilogue II

1. For an extensive description of Daisy Hill as it existed in the mid-1960s, see Grace Goulder's four-part series "Daisy Hill" in the *Cleveland Plain Dealer Sunday Magazine,* September 25 and October 2, 9, and 16, 1966. Most other details in this chapter are based on the author's experiences.

Sources and Acknowledgments

Any Van Sweringen biographer faces a daunting job. If nothing else, this work attests to the brothers' absolute fixation on both personal and business privacy. Their associates and office staff were specifically chosen to be close-mouthed, and their public relations people were steeped in the philosophy that the best publicity is no publicity. When public statements were necessary, reporters and writers seldom got much more than carefully crafted quotes designed to achieve a specific purpose and mention nothing else. Thus, numerous semi-truths and a few pure fabrications helped create an enduring and confusing Van Swerigen mythology.

Furthermore, they left no journals or diaries and, beyond formal business communications, no personal letters of consequence. Without wives and children, they also left no family records or intimate memories. Indeed, few people in their home city of Cleveland could claim to know them. As just noted, their closest associates and employees were circumspect in the extreme during the brothers' lifetimes, and most remained so after their deaths—partly out of admiration for them and probably partly because of sensitivity to the many attacks which came during the last years. As a result, the Van Swerigen story has heavy doses of speculation, hearsay, and legend.

Fortunately for posterity—although it was traumatic at the time—the New Deal's zeal to root out the alleged business villains deemed responsible for the crash and the depression had some positive benefits. Several congressional committees looked into the Van Sweringens' operations, most particularly a wide-ranging Senate investigation begun in 1936 by Burton K. Wheeler's Committee on Interstate Commerce (which included Senator Harry S Truman and his future vice president, Alben W. Barkley). This effort delved as deeply as possible into the Van Sweringens' entire business career, concentrating primarily on their railroad and railroad-related ventures, which most directly interested the committee. At the same time, this committee also investigated the general railroad consolidation power struggles of the 1920s and early 1930s, in which the Van Sweringens played a major part.

The result was a thorough, detailed, and extensively documented report, backed up by many volumes of testimony and numerous original documents. Without the Wheeler Committee's work, it would be impossible to tell the Van Sweringen story. It must be viewed with some caution, however, since it was obviously adversarial and also came too late to have more than nominal input from O. P. Van Sweringen himself, who died shortly before the formal hearings began. By then, too, M. J. was gone, as were John Bernet, A. H. Smith, and several other key people in the Van Sweringen careers. But with that caveat, the Wheeler Committee records and report inevitably form the backbone of this work—as they have all other Van Sweringen studies, published and unpublished.

Aside from the rather sparse published works, two extensive Van Sweringen biographies exist in manuscript form. The most detailed and interesting was done by Raymond F. Blosser in the mid-1940s. Between 1935 and 1944 Blosser was, successively, staff write and head of the Associated Press's Cleveland bureau; he subsequently headed the press relations departments of the Central Railroad of New Jersey and the New York Central. Although his work is, sadly, undocumented, he apparently was able to interview numerous people who had been associated with the Van Sweringens in one form or another. In 1946, he completed a second draft, which was later reviewed and annotated by William H. Wenneman and other close Van Sweringen associates. Wenneman began work in the Van Sweringen offices in 1918, served as O. P. Van Sweringen's private secretary during the 1930s, and subsequently became vice president of finance of the Nickel Plate; his commentary on the Blosser draft corrects many points and adds a considerable amount of personal insight from this period. The Blosser material is currently in the collection of the Western Reserve Historical Society in Cleveland.

The second work, by Virginia Taylor Hampton (who wrote under the name of Taylor Hampton), is essentially an expanded version of a biography published in serialized form in the *Cleveland News* in 1955. Although the manuscript is dated 1965, it is undoubtedly a later version of the manuscript upon which the *Cleveland News* articles were based. Mrs. Hampton was the wife of H. Horton Hampton, a close friend and real estate associate of the brothers and later a Nickel Plate executive. Thus, while the core of her work is based on the Wheeler Report, she was able to add some insights and stories obtained from interviews with the brothers' friends. Like the Blosser work, this manuscript is in the Western Reserve Historical Society collection.

Beyond these, and as might be imagined, reliable insights on the brothers' personalities and working methods are particularly difficult to come by. For the most part, the brothers' close associates left no memoirs and few recorded interviews. But besides his invaluable notations on the Blosser manuscript, William Wenneman produced his own memoirs in 1978 in typescript form, titled "My Three Careers in Forty Years," which is also at the Western Reserve Historical Society. While much of this work covers the time after the Van Sweringens' deaths, it includes some excellent firsthand material on the brothers and their operations. (It is also extremely valuable for anyone interested in Robert R. Young.)

Joseph Doherty, the brothers' public relations representative from 1921 to their deaths, included some revealing personal observations in his history of the Chesapeake & Ohio titled "Smooth Is the Road." Like the Blosser and Hampton works, this was originally intended as a book which was never published. Most of the material did appear, however, in lengthy serialized form in the C&O employee magazine *Tracks* during the 1950s. (The series was never completed, although the manuscript exists.) Doherty also left his Van Sweringen–related papers to the Western Reserve Historical Society, including some manuscript drafts and numerous public relations materials and news releases.

Finally, Louise "Daisy" Jenks produced a short, sentimentalized reminiscence titled *O. P. and M. J.*, privately printed for her children and friends about 1940. Copies are in several Cleveland institutions, including the Cleveland Public Library and the Western Reserve Historical Society.

Besides these sources, the author owes an enormous debt to the late John W. Barriger, III, who was president and executive of several railroads, was the chief railroad examiner for the Reconstruction Finance Corporation during much of the 1930s, and was active in railroading since 1918. Mr. Barriger knew and dealt with the Van Sweringens in several of his roles from the late 1920s until they died. His knowledge of railroad history and operations was bottomless, and he had total recall of events that had happened as many as forty years earlier. One of the high points of my life was a full day spent in Pittsburgh in 1964 being educated by him.

Special thanks go to William C. Barrow, special collections librarian at Cleveland State University, who is the caretaker of the Cleveland Press photo collection and the Cleveland Union Terminal collection. Cleveland State University's CUT collection consists of a comprehensive record of the construction of this project, including photographs, correspondence, engineering drawings, and various publications. Without his help in providing illustrations, this work would be mostly just a mass of dead type.

Also helping with information, reminiscences, illustrations, and other needs were Gerald Adams; Joseph J. Anzalone; John J. Bernet, II; Harry Christiansen; John B. Corns; Milton B. Dolinger; H. P. Francis; William Idsardi; LeRoy O. King, Jr.; Richard Krisak; Robert S. Korach; Professor Walter C. Leedy; Willis A. McCaleb; James Mischke; John A. Rehor; Drew Rolik; Janet Coe Sanborn; James A. Toman; J. Paxton Van Sweringen; J. William Vigrass; and Frank A. Wrabel.

Special thanks to Bobbi Diehl of Indiana University Press; Drew Rolik; Professors K. Austin Kerr, George W. Hilton, and George M. Smerk; Dr. John J. Grabowski of the Western Reserve Historical Society; Richard T. Wallis; and Robert S. Korach and Kate Babbitt for struggling through drafts of the text, suggesting improvements, correcting embarrassing errors, and generally helping to make sense out of an enormously complicated tangle.

Some of the tangle inevitably remains, as do some errors and other lapses for which I am entirely to blame. But my gratitude to all who have been so generous.

HERBERT H. HARWOOD, JR.

Index

Page numbers in italics refer to illustrations.

"accounting," 90–91, 177, 252–53
Adrian Iselin & Co., 157
Advisory Mechanical Committee (AMC), 181
air rights, 62, 63, 68, 70
Akers, Matthew L., 87, 90
Albright, John J., 13
Alfred, Frank H., 102, 180
Alleghany Corp.: bonds, 163–64, 170, 205, 247–49, 283–84; bonds (5s of 1950), 252, 271–72; crises, 246–50, 252–53, 269–70, 271–72; functions of, 159–60, 162–65, 179, 202; reorganizations, 283–84, 293–98; stocks, 163, 164, 170, 197–98, 200, 236, 237
Amtrak, 302
Anchor Motor Freight, 271
Anderson, Arthur, 238, 240
Anderson, Henry W., 122–23, 129
Andrews, Horace, 12
antitrust cases, 154, 160, 179, 187, 286
architects, 34–35, 140, 196, 226
architectural designs: downtown, 69, 133, 134, 208–210, 208, 209, 211, 220–23; interiors, 111, 208, 209, 211, 227; suburbs, 18, 25, 110, 111, 137, 139–40, 195
Arnold, George, 291
Atterbury, William Wallace, 117, 145–48, 146, 182–83, 185–86, 276
Aurora, Elgin & Fox River Electric Co., 287
Ayres, A. R. "Gus," 49, 276
Ayres, Leonard P., 198, 279; MoPac and, 168–69, 170–71, 253

Baker, George F., 92, 95–96, 102, 127
Baker, George F., Jr., 240
Baker, Newton D., 14, 32, 68, 105, 129, 164, 206
Baldwin, Lewis W., 167, 168, 172
Baldwin, Wilbur, 240, 268
Ball, George A., 277–79, 278, 292–93, 295, 303; Ball Foundation, 293, 302
Baltimore & Ohio RR, 56, 117–19, 208, 300; and BR&P, 155–60
bankers: actions of, 238–41, 244, 249, 271–72, 274–76, 279; Cleveland, 47, 295; New York, influence of, 92, 95, 98–99, 203–204. See also names of bankers
Bankruptcy Act, federal, 260–61, 272
banks: casualties, 258–59, 264; investigations of, 266–68. See also names of banks
Barnes, Julius H., 206
Barrett, Darwin S., Jr., 164, 171, 221, 232, 237, 293, 303; personal, 106, 256, 277, 303
Barriger, John W., 169–70, 263, 284, 285
Bernet, John J., 43, 130; Bremo Corp. and, 180; C&O improvements, 180–81; consolidation roles, 117, 120; Erie RR overhaul by, 130–32; fringe benefits to, 164, 222; new trains, 215–16, 250; Nickel Plate, 43–44, 46, 76, 77, 259–60; personal history, 43–44, 106, 271, 276
Bernstein, Alex, 34

Bessemer & Lake Erie, 186
Big Four Route, 63, 207
Black, W. G., 181
bonds: bankers' clauses, 204, 236, 247–48; issues of, 70, 90, 128, 130, 163–64, 204–205
Boston & Maine RR, 238
Bouton, Edward H., 15–17
Bowman, Robert J., 130, 180, 276
Bradley, Alva, 14, 135, 171, 202, 282, 291
Bradley, Charles L., 139, 207, 229; banking roles of, 47, 105, 135; beginnings, 14, 34; Cleveland Ry., 192, 213; corporate roles of, 136, 213, 232; Erie RR, 181, 213; O. P. and, 202, 277; personal, 164, 221, 293, 301, 302, 303; Pittston Co., 201, 202; Vaness roles, 81, 106
Bradley, Morris, 14
Bremo Corp., 179–80, 249–50, 270
Brice, Calvin, 79
Brooke, George, 293
Brown, Donaldson, 294
Brown, Duane, 283
Bryan, John Stewart, 127
Buffalo & Susquehanna RR, 160
Buffalo, Rochester & Pittsburgh Ry. (BR&P), 142, 144–45, 155–60, 156, 165
Burnham, Daniel H., 34, 59
Burton, Harold, 300–301
business methods, Van Sweringen: "accounting," 90–91, 177, 252–53; dubious, 81, 179–80, 248–50, 258, 269–70; purchasing agents, 27, 87; with stocks, 121, 159–60, 165, 192; trusteeships,

337

independent, 160. *See also* holding companies
businesses, Van Sweringen: achievements in, *54, 138,* 206–12, 217–20, 224–28; assets, 127–28; competition in, 103, 142–45, 171–72, 182–87 (*see also* Johnson, Tom L.); debts in, 127, 159, 241–42, 275; financial struggles of, 235–41; goals of, 9, 104–105, 125–26, 134–35, 136–38, 140; innovations by, xi, 131–32, 181, *182,* 215–16; loans to, 42–43, 51, 127; profits, 84, 164–65; risks in, 170, 204, 235–37, 247–50; secrecy in, 91–92, 108, 157–58, 170; staff, 106–107, 108, 112, 231–33, *232, 233;* WWI and, 50–51. *See also* holding companies, Van Sweringen

Calhoun, Patrick, 9
Campbell, J. B., 70
Caniff, William H. "Paddy," 38, 43
Cassatt, A. J., 143, 144
Cedar Glen, *190, 308*
Central National Bank, 310
Chadwick, Cassie, 8
Chapman, Harry and Caroline, 28
Chase Bank, 65
Chesapeake & Ohio Ry. (C&O), *86, 88, 182;* beginnings, 85–89; finances, 163–64, 247, 250, 257, 287; holding companies use of, 202, 253; improvements to, 130, 215; kitten image, 216; later years, 295, 298, 299–300; management, 102, 129–30, 293; mergers, 127, 132, 177, 180–81, 205; stocks, 89–91, 129, 132, 164, 198, 205, 328n2; subsidiaries of, 128, 129, 249, 271; Vans' takeover of, 89–91
Chesapeake Corp., 128, 205
Chicago & Alton RR, 78, 258
Chicago & Eastern Illinois (C&EI), *176, 178;* beginnings, 175–78, 246; ICC and, 184, 186, 252; later years, 261, 298
Chicago Great Western RR, 180, 249–50, 270
Citizens Saving and Loan Co., 47, 51
Clayton Antitrust Act, 40, 154, 160, 187
Cleveland & Chagrin Falls Ry., 104, 138
Cleveland & Youngstown RR (C&Y), 21–22, 33–35, 192.

See also rapid transit, Shaker Heights line
Cleveland, Cincinnati, Chicago & St. Louis Ry., 63, 207
Cleveland Electric Railway, 12, 19. *See also* Cleveland Railway
Cleveland Interurban RR (CIRR), 24–25, 53, 192, 213, 214, 274, 301. *See also* rapid transit, Shaker Heights line
Cleveland, Ohio, ii, *7, 159, 193, 208, 209, 311;* cemeteries, 310; Euclid Heights, 15, 16, 18; Heights, 8–10 (*see also* Shaker Heights suburb); history (1900–1919), 1–2, 5–7, 29–32, 63–64; Marshall Building, 27, 105; mass transit, *see* rapid transit; parks, 10, 226; railroad stations, 29, *30,* 65, *159,* 223 (*see also* Cleveland Union Terminal); railroads in, 29–30, 59, 207–208; real estate, *see* real estate, Van Sweringen; real estate markets in, 5–10, 136, 205, 242–43. *See also* East Cleveland
Cleveland Press, 290
Cleveland Railway, 55, *225;* dividends of, 301; finances, 274, 300–301; Stanley, J., 19, 24; Vans and, 53, 190–91, 213, 214, 220, 243
Cleveland Short Line RR (NYCRR), 32–33
Cleveland Terminal Building Co., 196, 286; functions of, 68, 212, 237
Cleveland Traction Terminals Co., 67, 191–92
Cleveland Transit System, 301
Cleveland Trust Co., 169, 258–59
Cleveland Union Station (proposed), 32, 62, 63
Cleveland Union Terminal, *206, 213, 311;* construction of, 70, 134–36, 188–89; infrastructure of, 210–11, *213,* 308–309; later years, 301–302; planning of, 55–65; political battles, 63–64, 68–70; railroads' use of, 64–65, 207–208, 223, 242. *See also* Union Terminal complex
Cleveland Union Terminals Co. (CUT), 61, 65–70 passim, 126, 136, 212–13; bonds, 65–66, 70; ownership of, 66; stocks, 70
Clover Leaf Route, 78, 80–81, *81*

coal, railroad ties to: anthracite, 92, 94, 143, 201–202; bituminous, 85, 148, 155, 175; Taplin route, 151; Vans' route, 101
Colston, William A., 106
Condon, George, 305
Conrail, 299
The Country Club, 196, 226, 310
Cragin, Raymond, 265
Crowley, Patrick E.: career of, 115, 206, *207,* 258; DL&W and, 185; as negotiator, 117, 119, 152, 158
CSX Transportation, 299, 300
Curtis, Jennie (Sweringen), 3–4
Cutler, Bertram, 150
Cuyahoga County, 286

Daisy Hill Estate, *110, 111,* 112; early years, 27–28, 109–12, 230; later years, 264, 265, 302–303, 307
Delaware & Hudson Co., 143, 144, 145, 147
Delaware, Lackawanna & Western RR (DL&W), 40, 91–92, 184, 185, *289,* 299
Denney, Charles E., 49, 130, 181, 293, 298
Denver & Rio Grande Western RR, 166–67, 254
Detroit & Toledo Shore Line, 78
Detroit, Toledo & Ironton RR, 185, 187
Doherty, Joseph, 109, 230, 272–73, 277, 282
Draper, Dorothy, 299–300, 309
Duncan, William McKinley, 160
Dupont, Pierre S., 294

East Cleveland, 190, 211–12. *See also* rapid transit, East Side line
Eastman, Joseph B., 262–63; ICC and, 83, 123, 252; inquiries by, 286–87; opposition of, 69–70, 91, 132, 153, 162
Eaton, Cyrus, 298, 300
economy, U.S. *See* Great Depression
Emergency Railroad Transportation Act, 263
Erie RR, *93, 131;* bankruptcy, 298–99; bonds, 130; finances, 163–64, 247, 257–58, 287; improvements to, 130–32; management, 181, 243, 293; stocks, 95–96, 164; subsidiaries of, 201, 228, 271; terminals used by, 208; Vans' aquisition of, 91, 93–96
Esch, John J., 83
Esch-Cummins Act. *See* Transportation Act (1920)

338 • Index

Euclid Heights Realty Co., 12

F. A. Pease Engineering Co., 17, 52
Fackler, John, 288
Fairleigh, David W., 87
Fairmount Boulevard, 11–12
First National Bank of New York, 92, 96, 240
Fisher, Irving, 197
Fisher, Lawrence, 164
Fitzpatrick, Herbert, 106, 129–30, 232, *233*, 277, 288–89, 293, 303–304
Fletcher, Duncan U., 266
Flynn, John, 265
Ford, Henry, 185
foreclosure auction, 279–80
Forest City House, *7*, 21, 22, 34
Fort Worth Belt Railway, 179, 286

Gallagher, Michael, 202
General Motors (GM), 164, 211, 294–95
General Securities Corp., 128–29, 228
George, Henry, 13
George Washington train, 250
Gibson, Harvey D., 202
Ginn, Frank, 47, 105, 129–30, 232
Glenville Syndicate, 34
Gould, George, 142–43, 152, 167
Gould, Jay, 142
Graham, Anderson, Probst & White, 34–35; plans by, 61, 70, 134, 194
Graham, Burnham & Co., 34–35
Grand Trunk Western RR, 78
Gratwick, W. H. "Harry," Jr., 10, 11, 13
Gratwick, William Henry, Sr., 10
Great Depression: business casualties, 235–37, 242–43, 260–61, 286 (*see also* Alleghany Corp., crises; bankers, actions of; Van Sweringen Corp.); business ethics and, 248–50, 258, 269–70; foreclosures, 277–80; personal casualties, 255–56, 264–68, 272–73, 276–77; railroad industry, 246–47, 250, 253–54, 256–61; real estate and, 242–43; stock markets in, 197–99, 234; trucking in, 261–62. *See also* banks, casualties
Great Western RR, 180
Greenbrier Hotel, 101, 215, 300
"Greenbrier Suite," 222, *227*, 300, 309
Gregory, Thomas, 41
Guaranty Trust Co., 84, 203; C&EI, 177; C&O, 90–91; financial crises, 238–39,
244, 248–49; Midamerica, 283–84, 295
Guardian Savings & Trust, 43, 44, 45, 264
Guerin, Jules, 209
Guildhall restaurants, 220

Halle, Salmon, 19
Hallgarten & Co., 280
Hampton, H. Horton, 282, 283, 291
Hanna Co. *See* M. A. Hanna Co.
Harahan, William J., 102, 180, 276, 293
Harriman, E. H., 144
Harris, Albert H., 65, 80, 115, 150
Harris, Alfred, 140
Harvey, Fred, 193–94, 210
Harwood, George A., 114, *115*
Hatcher, Harlan, ix–x
Hayden, Stone, 91
Hayden, Warren, 47, 81; and Miller, 34
Hepburn Act, 201, 325n5(2)
Herrick, Myron T., 14, 23
Herrick, Parmely, 14, 34
Higbee Co., *ii*, 21, 194, 243, 286, 302
Hill, Jim, 172
Hillside Iron and Coal Co., 201
Hitchcock, Henry-Russell, 226
Hocking Valley Ry., 184, 205
holding companies: as business method, 228–29, 235; history of, 44–45, 266–68, 316n10(2); laws for, 263; loopholes for, 77; Pennsylvania RR, 147, 183, 185–86
holding companies, Van Sweringen, 227–28; financial crises, 236–37, 240–41, 247–50; freight forwarding, 270; functions of, 90–91, 128, 177, 253; inquiries, legal, 266, *267*, 286–87; mining, 201–202; net worth, 197; numbers of, 127–29, 228; railroads, 45, 81, 121, 128, 179–80, 192; real estate, 10, 25, 61, 67, 68, 204; super, *see* Alleghany Corp.; Vaness Co.; trucking, 201–202, 271. *See also* chart; *names of companies*
"Home in the Sky," 220
Hoopes, Edward, 114
Hoover, Herbert, 237–38, 253
Hotel Cleveland, *ii*, 34–35, 55, *193*; Great Depression and, 243, 273–74
Hubbard, Thomas, 80
Huntington family, 89–90, 91

Insull, Samuel, 228–29, 266
Interstate Commerce Commission (ICC): consolidation plans, 116–26 passim, 182, 183–87, 218–19, 251–52, 263–64; functions of, 66, 74–75, 76–77, 263; laws, 260–61, 263; mergers and, 82–83, 129–30, 132; Taplin feud, 153–54, 160; Union Terminal and, 68–70; Vans' rail system, 251–52. *See also* Eastman, Joseph B.
interurbans, 6, 104–105, 138; future provisions for, 52, 189, 274, 308–309; industry declines, 191, 325n3(1)
investigations, U.S., 266–68, 285, 286–87
investors: celebrities, 164; reactions of, 164, 245; syndicates, 25, 34

J. P. Morgan & Co.: Alleghany and, 162, 164; CUT bonds, 70; financial crises, 238–40, 244; loans from, 91, 127, 205, 271; Pittston and, 202; Vans' introductions, 42, 65; Young, Robert R. and, 295. *See also* Morgan, J. P.; *names of partners*
James, Arthur Curtiss, 172, 285
Jenks, Benjamin L., 14, 19, 222, 303; roles of, 17, 25–26, 27–28
Jenks, Davidson, 291
Jenks, Louise "Daisy," 277, 303, 304; recollections of, 26, 280; roles of, 112–13, 230, 278, 283
Johnson, Tom L., 13, 31–32, 64
Jones, Jesse, 284, 285–86, 299
Jouett, Henry D., 70, 134, 189, 206
Joyce, Patrick H., 179–80

Kahn, Otto, 146, 147–48
Kansas City Southern Ry. (KCS), 174–75, 249–50, 269–70
Kemp, George S., 129
Kentucky Traction & Terminal Co., 274
Kessler, George E., 16
Kirby, Allan P., 294, 295, 296
Kirby, Josiah, 139–40
Kolbe, Frank, 280, 294, 295, 296
Kuhn, Loeb & Co., 146, 147, 167, 244. *See also* Barriger, John W.

Lake Erie & Western (LE&W), 78–80, *79*, *81*
Lake Erie Coal Co., 271
Lake Shore & Michigan Southern Ry. (LS&MS), 37–38, 39–40, 301. *See also* New York Central RR (NYCRR)

Lake View Cemetery, 310
Lakewood, Ohio, 7–8
Lamont, Thomas W., 42, 238, 240
Lancaster, John L., 172
lawyers, *232, 233*. *See also names of lawyers*
Lehigh Valley RR (LV): control of, 145, 146–47; Great Depression and, 257–58; ICC plans, 186–87, 252; prosperity of, 91–93; stocks, 145
Lindbergh, Charles A., 164
locomotives, Van Sweringen: aquisitions, *39, 79, 88, 94, 98, 168, 213,* 294–95; Berkshires, 131–32, *131,* 259–60, *260,* 294, 299; C&O T-1, 181, *182*
Long Lake Co., 25
Loree, Leonor F., 143–48 passim, *144,* 258, 280; Loree Southwestern Lines, 175
Louisville & Nashville Ry., 175
Lowenthal, Max, 287

M. A. Hanna Co., 202
McAdoo, William Gibbs, 51, 63
McGwinn, George, 136, 213, 214
mansions, *25, 110, 111,* 112
Manufacturer's Trust, 281
Marshall Building, 27, 105
Marshall, Thomas, 206
Metropolitan Life, 302
Metropolitan Utilities, Inc., 191–92, 213–14, 274, 286, 300–301
Meyer, Eugene, 253
Midamerica Corp., 279, 280, 283; stocks, 292–93
Midland Bank, 135, 197, 258–59, 292
Midland Corp., 135
Miller, Otto, 47, 81, 202
Missouri Pacific RR, *166, 168;* bankruptcy, 260–61, 271; early years, 165–69; finances, 247, 250, 257, 287; later years, 293, 298; reorganization, 284–85; stocks, 170, 198, 257; Terminal Shares and, 179, 248; Vans' control of, 168–71, 228, 254, 261. *See also* Williams, William. H.
Missouri Public Service Commission, 170–71
Moreland Courts, 139–40, 195, *225*
Morgan, J. P., 79, 88, 93, 239, 316n10(2). *See also* J. P. Morgan & Co.
Murphy, John P., 105, 170, 202, *232;* later years, 283, 293, 302

Myers, Rev. Charles H., 282, 290–91

National Carloading Corp., 270
New York Central RR (NYCRR): BR&P and, 155–58; C&O and, 87–88; Cleveland and, 29–34, 35, 207; DL&W purchase, 185; electric plans, 211; LE&W sale, 80; Nickel Plate sale, 41–43; Pennsy and, 117–18, 143–47; W&LE and, 150–55, 159; Young, Robert R. and, 297–98. *See also* Crowley, Patrick E.; Lake Shore & Michigan Southern Ry. (LS&MS); Smith, Alfred H.
New York, Chicago & St. Louis RR. *See* Nickel Plate Road
New York, Chicago & St. Louis Ry., 121, 122
Newlands, Francis G., 73
Nickel Plate Road, *38, 39,* 48–50, *260, 294;* in Cleveland, 22, 36–37, *54,* 136, 207; dividends, 328n2; early years, 38–39, 41–43, 45; finances, 51, 77, 90, 163–64, 247, 286, 287; improvements, 182, 259–60; later years, 254, 297, 299; management, 49, 106, 130; merger (1922), 81–84, *82;* name, 37; *Sportsman* and, 216; stocks, 45, 82, 164, 198; subsidiaries of, 128, 129; Vans' purchase of, 41–43
Nickel Plate Securities Corp., 45, 80–81, 90–91, 121; stocks, 45, 48
Noonan, William T., 157
Norfolk & Western (N&W), 252, 299; Pennsy and, 88, 118, 186–87
Norfolk Southern Corp., 299
North Union, 9
Nutt, Joseph R., 164, 231–32, 253, 267, 303; early history, 14, 34, *47,* 105, 106; Union Trust, 47, 81, 231, 258–59, 266–68

Oak Room dining room, *209,* 210, 310
O'Grady, Benson, 289
O'Hara, Richard, 179–80, 198
Olmsted Brothers, 16
O'Neal, Charles, 178

Paine, Webber & Co.: Bremo and, 180, 270; C&EI and, 177, 178; loans from, 91, 157, 236–37, 239; Vans' debts to, 252–53
Painesville, Ohio, *294*

Pecora, Ferdinand, 266, *267*
Pennroad Corp., 183, 185–86
Pennsylvania Coal Co., 201
Pennsylvania Co., 44, 147
Pennsylvania RR: C&O T-1, 181; competition of, 40, 88, 117–19, 143–48, 182–83, 185; terminals, 31, 65
Pere Marquette Corp., 128–29
Pere Marquette Ry. (PM), 96, *98;* C&EI and, 177; control by C&O, 132, 180–81, 297; early years, 86, 97–98; finances, 163–64, 247, 287; later years, 293, 297; name history 318n8(2); Standard Carloading and, 271; stocks, 98–99, 164, 198, 328n2; Vans' acquisition, 96–99
Perlman, Alfred, 284
Pershing, John J., 164
Pittsburgh & West Virginia Ry., 143, 148, 151–52; Connellsville, 154, 160; ICC plans for, 186–87, 252; sale of (1929), 185–86; stocks, 186, 258
Pittston Co., 201–202, 295
Potter, W. C., 238
press coverage: *Business Week,* 212, 219, 230; *Cleveland Press,* 289–90; *Fortune,* 221, 229–30, 244, 266, 280, 284; *Harper's,* 265; *Railway Age,* 44, 114, 212
Prince, F. H., 86, 97, 263–64, 280, 293
Probert, L. C. "Dick," 215–16, 250
Public Square, Cleveland, *7,* 21, 22. *See also* Union Terminal complex

railroad business: consolidation of, *see* Interstate Commerce Commission; feuds in, *see* Taplin, Frank E.; laws affecting, 74–75, 76–77, 201, 263; "triple alliance," 117–19, 145, 150
railroads, Van Sweringen: aquisitions, BR&P, 155; C&EI, 177–78; CIRR, 24–25; C&O, 87–91; Clover Leaf, 80; dividend payments, 247, 328n2; Erie, 95–96; finances, 163–64, 235, 250, 252, 273, 287; formations, C&Y, 21–22; improvements to, 130–32, 181–82, 215; LE&W, 80; management, 51, 276, 293; MoPac, 169–70; Nickel Plate, 41–43; PM, 98–99; routes of, 100–102, *101,* 217–19, *219;* sale of (1937), 294–95; traction companies,

340 • Index

192; W&LE, 159–60. *See also names of railroads*
Railway Age, 44, 114, 212
Rand McNally maps, 77–78
rapid transit: city system plans, 104; East Side line, 189–91, *190*, 215, 224–25, 242, 274, 307–308, *308*; terminal for, 189, 211–12, 301; West Side line, 49–50, 104, *213*, 301. *See also* Cleveland Interurban RR (CIRR)
rapid transit, Shaker Heights line, 54–55, *195, 196, 225*; beginnings, 19–22, *23*, 24–26; cars, 53–54, 287; construction, 52–55; extensions, 137–38, *195*, 214–15, 224; later years, 301, 307; NYCRR, joint line with, 33–35; ridership, 224
Raskob, John J., 164, 296
Rea, Samuel, 40, 117, 118, 145, 146
Reading Co., 119
real estate, Van Sweringen, viii, 103; early years, 3, 7–10; holding companies for, 10, 25, 61, 67, 68, 204; Kingsbury Run property, 20–21, 22; later years, 286; purchasing of, 21, 27–28, 136; timeframe for development of, x, 225–26. *See also* Daisy Hill Estate; Hotel Cleveland; Shaker Country Estates; Shaker Heights suburb; Shaker Square; Union Terminal complex
Reconstruction Finance Corp. (RFC), 253–54, 261, 269, 284–85, 298–99
Rehor, John, 122
Ringle, O. C., 10
Ripley, William Z., 75, 76, 85, 90, 92, 123
Rockefeller family, 148, 150
Rockefeller, John D., Jr., 150
Rockefeller, John D., Sr., 10, 143
Roland Park, Baltimore, 15–17
Roosevelt, Franklin D., 262–63, 264, 316n10(2)
Roosevelt, Iselin and Emlen, 157
Ross, George, 283, 291
Ross, Walter L., *83*, 206, 259, 282–83; Clover Leaf sale, 80, 81; Nickel Plate and, 130, 180–81
Roundwood Manor. *See* Daisy Hill Estate
Rowley, Charles Bacon "Carl," 113, 140
Ryan, Thomas Fortune, 177

Schwarz, F. A. O., 280

Schweid, Edward, 300–301
Scott, Frederick W., 122, 123, 129
Scott, George Cole, 122, 123, 127, 129
Scranton private car, 288, *289*
Seaboard Air Line Railway, 187
Seaboard System Railroad, 300
Searles, Edward F., 80
Sedgewick Land Co., 13
Shaker Boulevard, *23*, 24, *137, 306*
Shaker Boulevard line. *See* streetcars
Shaker Country Estates, 136–39, *137, 138*, 195–96, 225–26, 242, *306*
Shaker Heights Country Club, 25
Shaker Heights Land Co., 10, 27–28
Shaker Heights suburb, *25, 138*; deed covenants, 15–16, 18; development of, 9–19, 23, 25, 52–53, 139, 225–26; in Great Depression, 242; incorporation of, 23; land appraisals, 103; land use history, 9–10; Lee Road, 18, 23, *24*; mass transit, *see* rapid transit, Shaker Heights line; population of, 54, 225
Shaker Heights Syndicate, 25
Shaker Lakes line, 12
Shaker Square, 139–40, 194–95, *195, 225*
Shakers, 9–10, 18
Sherwin, John, Jr., 135
Sherwin, John, Sr., 47, 105, 123, 135, 231; MoPac position of, 171
Sherwood Forest paneling, *209*, 221–22
Shriver, George M., 150, 157–58
Sloan, Alfred P., Jr., 164, 294
Small, Philip L., *25*, 113, 140, 196, 303; Oak Room, *209*, 210. *See also* Daisy Hill Estate; Greenbrier Hotel
Smith, Alfred H., *28, 115*; banking connections, 65–66; Clayton Act and, 40–41; consolidation strategies of, 75–76; death of, 114; early years, 28–29; influence of, 79–80, 85, 95; Nickel Plate sale by, 41–42; O. P. and, 28–29, 41; terminal plans and, 32–35, 57–61, 64; USRA, 51, 53
Smith, John T., 294
Snow, Mary, 277, 282
Society for Savings, 302
Special Investment Corp., 128, 129
Sportsman train, 215–16
Stage, Charles W., 5, 13–14, 64, 105

Standard Carloading Corp., 270–71
Stanley, Harold, 203, 240
Stanley, John J., 19, 24. *See also* Cleveland Railway
Statler Hotel, 21
Steere, Kenneth D., 178, 180, 202
stockholder protests, 121–22, 129, 297–98
stocks: brokers of, 91, 157, 280 (*see also names of stock brokers*); markets, 197–99, 234; speculators in, *see* Young, Robert R.
stocks, railroad: conversions of, 120–22, 191–92; dividend payments, 48, 247, 301, 328n2; share prices (1925–1932), 163–64, 257–58; swaps of, 159–60; Van's holdings (1927), 127, *128*
Stouffer, A. E., 195
Stouffer, Gordon, 303
Stouffer's Shaker Tavern, 194–95
streetcars, 6, *7*, 9, 53, *54*, 307. *See also* rapid transit
Swan, Joseph, 203, 238
Sweringen. *See individual Van Sweringens*

Taft, Frederick L., 3, 8
Taplin, Charles, 151
Taplin, Frank E., 151–55, *152*, 184–86, 258, 285–86, 293. *See also* Pittsburgh & West Virginia Ry.
Tayler Grant (municipal franchise), 192
Terminal Shares, Inc., 179, 248, 269, 285
Terminal Tower, *ii, 159, 193*, 220–22; construction of, 134–35; occupancy, 243, 273; suites in, 172–73, 221–22, *227*, 309. *See also* Union Terminal complex
Texas & Pacific Ry., *166*
Toledo, St. Louis & Western, 78, 80–81, *81*
Toman, James, 243
Tomlinson, George A., 171, 277, *278, 279*, 286, 292, 293, 303
Traction Stores Co., 192
Transportation Act (1920), 66, 74–75, 76–77; mergers and, 82–83
trucking industry, 201, 261–62, 270–71
Truman, Harry S, 287

Underwood, Frederick, 102, 130
Union Commerce National Bank, 47
Union Depot, Cleveland, 29–30, *30*, 65, 207

Index • 341

Union Pacific RR, 298
Union Terminal. *See* Cleveland Union Terminal
Union Terminal complex, *133, 159, 193, 208, 209,* 220–23; Builders Exchange Building, *133,* 189, 220, 243, 273; earliest concepts of, 22–23, 69; expansion provisions, 222–23; finances, 65–68, 69–70, 205, 212; Medical Arts Building, 189, 273; Midland Building, *211,* 220, 273, 299, 310; occupants of, 192–94, 210, 242–43; openings, 189, 212, 243, 274. *See also* Higbee Co.; Hotel Cleveland; Terminal Tower
Union Trust Co., 105, 241, 264, 302–303. *See also* Baldwin, Wilbur; Nutt, Joseph R.
U.S. Distributing Co., 201
U.S. Railroad Administration (USRA), 51
U.S. Senate Committee on Banking and Currency, 266
U.S. Steel Corp., 186
U.S. Truck Lines, Inc., 270–71

Van Sweringen brothers, *50, 173, 229, 231;* appearance of, 105; assets, personal, *25,* 109, 112, 135, 196–97 (*see also* Daisy Hill Estate; Vaness Co.); associates of, 34, 47, 105–106, 222; bonds between, 107, 108, 112, 228, 233, 282, 287–88, 310; donations by, 23, *25,* 139; early life, 2–8; income, personal, 256, 265–66, 274; mansions, *25, 110;* name history, 2–3, 8, 107; overview of, vii–xii; personal life of, 109, *111,* 112–13, 229–31; publicity avoidance by, 206, 229; reputation of, 100, 163, 239, 265–66, 305; staff, personal, 282–83, 290–91 (*see also* Jenks, Benjamin; Jenks, Louise "Daisy"). *See also* businesses, Van Sweringen; railroads, Van Sweringen; real estate, Van Sweringen
Van Sweringen, Carrie and Edith, 4, 25, 109, 230
Van Sweringen Co., 18, 23, *24, 25*–26; later years, 286, 303
Van Sweringen Corp., 204–205, 236–37, 240–41, 243–45, 286; banking favors, 258
Van Sweringen, Gerrett, 3
Van Sweringen, Herbert, 4, 14–15, 107, 230
Van Sweringen, James Tower, 2, 3–4
Van Sweringen, M. J., *2, 50, 173, 273,* 283; death of, 281–83, 310; "little black book," 256; personal life of, 277; personal traits of, 4, 5, 63, 230, 272–73; roles of, 232–33, 237–38. *See also* Van Sweringen brothers
Van Sweringen, O. P., *50, 173, 231, 233,* 287; ambitiousness of, 280, 284–85, 296; confidence of, 20, 240, 241, 272; death of, 289, 290–91, 310; personal traits of, 4–5, 26, 41, 107–109, 229–30, 239; politicians and, 237–38; remarks by, 122, 162, 253, 280; salesmanship of, 14, 28, 241; Smith, A. H. and, 28–29, 33–34, 41, 76, 85; temper of, 158, 187. *See also* Van Sweringen brothers
Vanderbilt, William H., 37–38, 39–40
Vanderbilt, William K., Jr., 51
Vaness Co., 80–81; debts of, 116, 236; functions of, 80–81, 106, 128–29, 228; later years, 256, 303; purchases by, 90–91, 96, 157, 194
Virginia Transportation Corp., 128, 129, 249, 271
Virginian Ry., 119

Wabash Pittsburgh Terminal Ry., 142–43
Wabash RR, 142, 144–45, 147, 169, 185, 257; ICC plans for, 186–87, 252
Wenneman, William H., 187, 277; career, 77, 107, 158, 232, 237–38, 293; recollections of, 107, 124, 172, 231, 240, 280, 287–89
West Coast, route plans, 186
Western Co., 81
Western Maryland RR, 143, 150, 186–87, 252
Western Pacific RR, 142, 167, 171
Wheeler, Burton K., 262, 284, 286–87, 295
Wheeling & Lake Erie (W&LE), *149, 159;* ICC plans for, 186–87, 251–52; later years, 208, 287, 297; ownership history, 142, 143, 148–50; stocks, 148, 150, 152–53, 285–86; Vans' stock swap, 159–60, 165. *See also* Taplin, Frank E.
Whitney, George, 164, 203, 240, 280, 288
Wilgus, William J., 63
Willard, Daniel, 117–19, 123, *157,* 160, 258
Williams, William H., 144, 185; LV and, 145, 147; MoPac and, 144, 167, 170–71
Williamson, Ben, 290
Williamson Building, 7, 14, 27
Williamson, Frederick E., 258
Wilson, Woodrow, 50–51
Witt, Peter, 63–64, 68–69, *68,* 214
Wyer, William, 232, 288–89

Young, Robert R., 280, 294, 295–98, 299–300, 302; Higbee Co. and, 302

HERBERT H. HARWOOD, JR., has had concurrent careers as a railroad historian, writer, photographer, and working railroader. He received a B.A. in history from Princeton University and an M.B.A. from Columbia University. For thirty years, he filled various management positions at the Chesapeake & Ohio and Baltimore & Ohio Railroads and their successor, CSX Transportation. He has written eleven books and numerous articles on railroad and electric-railway history and has contributed photos to various other books and articles on those topics.